First World War
and Army of Occupation
War Diary
France, Belgium and Germany

6 DIVISION
Divisional Troops
12 Field Company Royal Engineers,
38 Field Company Royal Engineers
and 459 Field Company Royal Engineers
4 August 1914 - 1 September 1919

WO95/1599

The Naval & Military Press Ltd
www.nmarchive.com
Published in association with The National Archives

Published by

The Naval & Military Press Ltd

Unit 10 Ridgewood Industrial Park,

Uckfield, East Sussex,

TN22 5QE England

Tel: +44 (0) 1825 749494

www.naval-military-press.com

www.nmarchive.com

This diary has been reprinted in facsimile from the original. Any imperfections are inevitably reproduced and the quality may fall short of modern type and cartographic standards.

Contents

Document type	Place/Title	Date From	Date To
Heading	WO95/1599/1		
Heading	6th Division Divl. Engnrs.12th Field Coy R.E. Aug 1914-1919 Apr		
Heading	6th Divisional Engineers 12th Field Company R.E. August & September 1914 Dec 1918		
War Diary	Mom Park	04/08/1914	12/08/1914
War Diary	Mom Park	13/08/1914	16/08/1914
War Diary	Mom Park	17/08/1914	19/08/1914
War Diary	Queenstown	21/08/1914	21/08/1914
War Diary	Liverpool	22/08/1914	25/08/1914
War Diary	Cambridge	06/09/1914	08/09/1914
War Diary	St Nazaire	11/09/1914	11/09/1914
War Diary	Marles	12/09/1914	12/09/1914
War Diary	Crecy	13/09/1914	13/09/1914
War Diary	Jouarre	14/09/1914	14/09/1914
War Diary	Saacy	14/09/1914	15/09/1914
War Diary	Rocourt	16/09/1914	16/09/1914
War Diary	Buzancy	16/09/1914	16/09/1914
War Diary	Mesmin Bivouac		
War Diary	Mesmin Bivouac	18/09/1914	19/09/1914
War Diary	Septmonts	20/09/1914	23/09/1914
War Diary	Bazoches	23/09/1914	23/09/1914
War Diary	Vailly	24/09/1914	29/09/1914
Heading	6th Divisional Engineers 12th Field Company R.E. October 1914		
War Diary	Vailly	30/09/1914	03/10/1914
War Diary	Serches	04/10/1914	06/10/1914
War Diary	Nanteuil	07/10/1914	07/10/1914
War Diary	Vouty	08/10/1914	08/10/1914
War Diary	Fresnoy	09/10/1914	09/10/1914
War Diary	Longueil & Marie	10/10/1914	10/10/1914
War Diary	Arques	11/10/1914	13/10/1914
War Diary	Merris	14/10/1914	14/10/1914
War Diary	Outter Steene	15/10/1914	15/10/1914
War Diary	Bac St Maur	16/10/1914	17/10/1914
War Diary	Lavesee	18/10/1914	22/10/1914
War Diary	Touquet	22/10/1914	24/10/1914
War Diary	Fleur Baix	24/10/1914	24/10/1914
War Diary	Fleur Baix And Touquet	25/10/1914	28/10/1914
War Diary	Fleurbaix	29/10/1914	30/10/1914
War Diary	Rue Du Bois	30/10/1914	30/10/1914
War Diary	Fleur Baix	31/10/1914	01/11/1914
Heading	6th Divisional Engineers 12th Field Company R.E. November 1914		
Miscellaneous	For commencement of November 1st see October War Diary		
War Diary	Fleur Baix	01/11/1914	29/11/1914
Heading	6th Divisional Engineers 12th Field Company R.E. December 1914		
War Diary		30/11/1914	31/12/1914

Heading	6th Div R.E. No. 12th Field Coy Jan-Dec 1915		
Heading	8/Yorks Rt. Jan-Oct 1916		
Heading	6th Division 12th Field Coy R.E. Vol. VI. 1-31.1.15 121/4262		
War Diary		01/01/1915	31/01/1915
Heading	6th Division 12th Field Coy. R.E. Vol VII. 1-28.2.15 121/4505		
War Diary		01/02/1915	11/02/1915
War Diary	Armentieres	11/02/1915	28/02/1915
Heading	6th Division 12th Field Company R.E. Vol VIII. 1-29.3.15 121/4779		
War Diary	Armentieres	01/03/1915	29/03/1915
Heading	6th Division 12th Field Coy. R.E. Vol IX. 30. 3-30.4.15 121/5195		
War Diary	Armentieres	30/03/1915	30/04/1915
Heading	6th Division 12th Field Coy. R.E. Vol X. 1-31.5.15		
War Diary	Armentieres	01/05/1915	31/05/1915
Heading	6th Division 12th Field Coy. R.E. Vol XI. 1-30.6.15		
War Diary	Ypres	01/06/1915	30/06/1915
Heading	6th Division 12th Field Coy. R.E. Vol XII. July-15		
Heading	War Diary of 12th (Fd) Co. R.E. From 1.7.15 To 31.7.15		
War Diary	Ypres	01/07/1915	31/07/1915
Heading	6th Division 12th Field Coy. R.E. Vol XIII. From 1-31.8.15		
Heading	War Diary of 12th (Fd) Co. R.E. From 1.8.15 To 31.8.15		
War Diary	Ypres	01/08/1915	31/08/1915
War Diary	6th Division 12th Field Coy. R.E. Vol XIV Sep 1-15		
Heading	War Diary of 12th (Fd) Co R.E. From 1.9.15 To 30.9.15		
War Diary	Ypres Dist	01/09/1915	30/09/1915
Heading	6th Division 12th Field Coy. R.E. Vol XV Oct 15		
Heading	War Diary of 12th (Fd) Co R.E. From. 1.10.15 To 31.10.15		
War Diary	Ypres District	01/10/1915	31/10/1915
Heading	6th Division War Diary of 12th Field Coy. R.E. From 1.11.15 To 30.11.15		
War Diary	Ypres District	01/11/1915	30/11/1915
Heading	6th Division War Diary 12th Field Coy. R.E. Vol XVII From 1-12-15 To 31.12.15		
War Diary	Ypres District	01/12/1915	31/12/1915
Heading	6th Division R.E. No 12th Field Coy. R.E. Jan-Dec 1916		
Heading	12/DLI Jan-Oct 1916		
Heading	War Diary of 12th Field Coy. R.E. 6th Div. Jan Vol XVIII From 1.1.16 To 31.1.16		
War Diary	Ypres District	01/01/1916	31/01/1916
Heading	War Diary 12th Field Coy. R.E. Vol XIX From 1.2.16 To 29.2.16		
War Diary	Ypres District	01/02/1916	28/02/1916
Heading	War Diary of 6th Division 12th Field Coy. R.E. Vol XX From 1.3.16 To 31.3.16		
War Diary	Ypres District	01/03/1916	31/03/1916
Heading	War Diary 12th (Fd) Co R.E. Vol XXI From. 1-4-16 To 30-4-16		

War Diary	Calais And Herzeele	01/04/1916	16/04/1916
War Diary	Ypres District	17/04/1916	30/04/1916
Heading	War Diary Of 12th (Fd) Coy R.E. Vol 22 From 1-5-16 To 31-5-16		
War Diary	Ypres District	01/05/1916	31/05/1916
Heading	War Diary Of 12th (Fd) Co R.E. Vol 23 From 1-6-16 To 30-6-16		
War Diary	Ypres District	01/06/1916	15/06/1916
War Diary	Herzeele	16/06/1916	17/06/1916
War Diary	Volkeringhove	18/06/1916	30/06/1916
Heading	War Diary Of 12th (Fd) Co R.E. Vol 24 From 1-7-16 To 31-7-16		
War Diary	Volkeringhove & Herzeele	01/07/1916	01/07/1916
War Diary	Herzeele & Ypres	02/07/1916	02/07/1916
War Diary	West Of Ypres	02/07/1916	08/07/1916
War Diary	W Of Pheringhe	09/07/1916	15/07/1916
War Diary	Ypres	16/07/1916	30/07/1916
Miscellaneous	6th Divisional Engineers 12th Field Company R.E. August 1916		
War Diary	Ypres District	01/08/1916	02/08/1916
War Diary	Beauval	03/08/1916	03/08/1916
War Diary	Arqueves	04/08/1916	05/08/1916
War Diary	Engelbelmer	06/08/1916	13/08/1916
War Diary	South Of Envelbelmer On Road To Martinsart	14/08/1916	25/08/1916
War Diary	Bertrancourt	26/08/1916	26/08/1916
War Diary	Amplier	27/08/1916	27/08/1916
War Diary	Gezaincourt	28/08/1916	28/08/1916
War Diary	Vignacourt	29/08/1916	31/08/1916
Heading	6th Divisional Engineers 12th Field Company R.E. September 1916		
Heading	War Diary of 12th (Fd) Co R.E. Vol 26 From 1-9-16 To 30-9-16 Vol 26		
War Diary	Vignacourt	01/09/1916	05/09/1916
War Diary	Ranneville	06/09/1916	06/09/1916
War Diary	Sailly-Le-Sec	07/09/1916	10/09/1916
War Diary	Sandpits	11/09/1916	11/09/1916
War Diary	Citadel	12/09/1916	13/09/1916
War Diary	Montauban	14/09/1916	16/09/1916
War Diary	Montauban	17/09/1916	18/09/1916
War Diary	Meaulte	19/09/1916	20/09/1916
War Diary	Trones Wood	21/09/1916	23/09/1916
War Diary	Guillemont	24/09/1916	30/09/1916
Heading	War Diary Of 12th (Fd) Co R.E. Vol 27 From 1-10-16 To 31-10-16 Vol 27		
War Diary	Mericourt	01/10/1916	06/10/1916
War Diary	Citadel	07/10/1916	07/10/1916
War Diary	Longueval	08/10/1916	18/10/1916
War Diary	Citadel	19/10/1916	20/10/1916
War Diary	Mericourt	21/10/1916	31/10/1916
Heading	War Diary Of 12th (Fd) Co R.E. Vol 28 From 1-11-16 To 30-11-16 Vol 28		
War Diary	Marles-Les-Mines	01/11/1916	06/11/1916
War Diary	Mazingarbe	07/11/1916	28/11/1916
War Diary	Beuvry	29/11/1916	30/11/1916
Heading	War Diary of 12th (Fd) Co R.E. Vol 29 From 1-12-16 To 31-12-16		

War Diary	H.Q. of Coy. Beuvry Advanced section HQ Cambrin word in Cambrin sector	01/12/1916	31/12/1916
Heading	6th Division 12th Field Coy R.E. January To December 1917		
Heading	War Diary January 1917 Vol 30 12th Fd Co R.E.		
War Diary	HQ at Beuvry Advanced Sections (2) at Cambrian work in cambrin sector	01/01/1917	31/01/1917
War Diary	HQ at Beuvry Advanced Sections (2) at Cambrian work in cambrin sector	01/02/1917	28/02/1917
Heading	War Diary Of 12th Co. R.E. Vol 32 March 1917		
War Diary	Bethune To Les Brebis And Trenches	01/03/1917	01/03/1917
War Diary	Les Brebis and Trenches (Loos)	08/03/1917	31/03/1917
Heading	War Diary 12th Fd Co RE Vol 33 April 1917		
War Diary	Les Brebis And Trenches (Loos)	01/04/1917	30/04/1917
Heading	War Diary 12th Field Co RE May 1917		
War Diary	Les Brebis And Trenches (Loos)	02/05/1917	31/05/1917
Heading	War Diary 12th Fd Co RE Vol 35 June 1917		
War Diary	Les Brebis And Trenches (Loos)	01/06/1917	28/06/1917
Heading	War Diary Of 12th Company RE Vol 36 July 1917		
War Diary	Les Brebis And Trenches (Loos)	01/07/1917	13/07/1917
War Diary	La Bourse	14/07/1917	21/07/1917
War Diary	Guestreville	22/07/1917	29/07/1917
War Diary	Les Brebis And Trenches (Loos)	01/07/1917	14/07/1917
War Diary	La Bourse	14/07/1917	22/07/1917
War Diary	Guestreville	22/07/1917	31/07/1917
Heading	War Diary of 12th Co RE Vol 36 From 1-8-17 To 31-8-17		
War Diary	Guestreville	01/08/1917	23/08/1917
War Diary	Les Brebis	24/08/1917	25/08/1917
War Diary	Les Brebis And Trenches	26/08/1917	31/08/1917
War Diary	Guestreville	01/08/1917	23/08/1917
War Diary	Les Brebis And Trenches	23/08/1917	31/08/1917
War Diary	Les Brebis	01/09/1917	30/09/1917
War Diary	Les Brebis	01/10/1917	22/10/1917
War Diary	Equedeques	23/10/1917	28/10/1917
War Diary	Majhicourt	29/10/1917	29/10/1917
War Diary	Rullecourt	30/10/1917	31/10/1917
War Diary	Fins	01/11/1917	17/11/1917
War Diary	Queenscross	18/11/1917	19/11/1917
War Diary	Ribecourt	20/11/1917	30/11/1917
War Diary	Ribecourt	01/12/1917	05/12/1917
War Diary	Mole Trench K3669.7	05/12/1917	10/12/1917
War Diary	Etricourt	11/12/1917	11/12/1917
War Diary	Hendecourt	12/12/1917	25/12/1917
War Diary	Baphuite	25/12/1917	31/12/1917
Heading	6th Divisional Engineers. War Diary 12th Field Company R.E. March 1918		
War Diary	C29C0.5 (Sheet 57c)	01/03/1918	22/03/1918
War Diary	Achiet-Le-Grand	22/03/1918	24/03/1918
War Diary	Mondicourt	25/03/1918	25/03/1918
War Diary	Elverdinghe	26/03/1918	26/03/1918
War Diary	St Jan-Ter-Biezen & Eecke	27/03/1918	30/03/1918
Heading	6th Divisional Engineers 12th Field Company R.E. April 1918		
War Diary	Eecke (Ref Sheet 27) Sapper Camp Iqa5.9. (Sheet 28)	01/04/1918	21/04/1918
War Diary	I 9a5.9. (Sheet 28)	21/04/1918	28/04/1918

War Diary	G10c9.3 (Sheet 28)	28/04/1918	30/04/1918
War Diary	G10d1.9 (Sheet 28)	04/04/1918	27/04/1918
War Diary	G10d1.9 (Sheet 28)	01/04/1918	07/04/1918
War Diary	L9d.0.1 Sheet 27	08/04/1918	29/04/1918
War Diary	G.10.d.9.2	01/07/1918	31/07/1918
War Diary	28/G.21.b.3.3	01/08/1918	20/08/1918
War Diary	27/Lis C 49	21/08/1918	31/08/1918
War Diary	Moulle Bonnay	01/10/1918	11/10/1918
War Diary	Vaux Sur Somme	12/08/1918	12/08/1918
War Diary	Tertry	13/08/1918	29/08/1918
War Diary	Bellinglise	04/10/1918	04/10/1918
War Diary	Magny-la-Fosse	06/10/1918	08/10/1918
War Diary	Mont Brehain	09/10/1918	10/10/1918
War Diary	Bohain	11/10/1918	18/10/1918
War Diary	St Souplet	20/10/1918	31/10/1918
War Diary	Fresnoy Le Grand	01/11/1918	07/11/1918
War Diary	Catillon	08/11/1918	10/11/1918
War Diary	Autreppe	11/11/1918	12/11/1918
War Diary	Avesnes	13/11/1918	13/11/1918
War Diary	Felleries	14/11/1918	23/11/1918
War Diary	St Aubin	24/11/1918	29/11/1918
War Diary	St Aubin	01/12/1918	01/12/1918
War Diary	Ermiton-Sur Biert	02/12/1918	23/12/1918
War Diary	Erp	24/12/1918	31/12/1918
War Diary	Borr	04/01/1919	25/02/1919
Heading	War Diary of 12th Field Coy R.E. From April 1st 1919 To April 30th 1919		
War Diary	Lechenich	01/04/1919	02/04/1919
War Diary	Bruhl	03/04/1919	30/04/1919
War Diary	Bapaume	01/01/1919	19/01/1919
War Diary	Labucquiere	20/01/1919	22/01/1919
War Diary	Beugny	23/01/1919	31/01/1919
War Diary	Beugny	01/01/1919	10/01/1919
War Diary	C29.C.0.4 (Sheet 57c.n.w)	11/01/1919	28/01/1919
Heading	WO95/1599/2		
Heading	6th Division 38th Fld Coy R.E. Aug 1914-Mar 1915		
Heading	6th Divisional Engineers 38th Field Company R.E. August 1914 Mar 1915		
War Diary	Cork	05/08/1914	17/08/1914
War Diary	Conemara	18/08/1914	18/08/1914
War Diary	Liverpool	19/08/1914	19/08/1914
War Diary	Cambridge	20/08/1914	31/08/1914
Heading	6th Divisional Engineers 38th Field Company R.E. September 1914		
War Diary	Cambridge	01/09/1914	07/09/1914
War Diary	S.S. Archimedes	09/09/1914	09/09/1914
War Diary	St Nazaire	10/09/1914	10/09/1914
War Diary	In Train	11/09/1914	11/09/1914
War Diary	Merles	12/09/1914	12/09/1914
War Diary	Framoutiers	13/09/1914	13/09/1914
War Diary	Biercy	14/09/1914	14/09/1914
War Diary	Bezdet	15/09/1914	15/09/1914
War Diary	Villemontoire	16/09/1914	16/09/1914
War Diary	Villeblain	17/09/1914	18/09/1914
War Diary	Paars	19/09/1914	20/09/1914
War Diary	Bourg	21/09/1914	30/09/1914

Heading	6th Divisional Engineers 38th Field Company R.E. October 1914		
War Diary	Bourg	01/10/1914	01/10/1914
War Diary	Dhuisy	02/10/1914	05/10/1914
War Diary	Coutremain	06/10/1914	06/10/1914
War Diary	Largny	07/10/1914	07/10/1914
War Diary	La Breviere (Compeigne Forest)	08/10/1914	08/10/1914
War Diary	Compiegne	09/10/1914	09/10/1914
War Diary	Arques	11/10/1914	11/10/1914
War Diary	Hazebruck	12/10/1914	12/10/1914
War Diary	Vieux-Berquin	13/10/1914	13/10/1914
War Diary	Les Trois Fermes	14/10/1914	14/10/1914
War Diary	Sailly	15/10/1914	16/10/1914
War Diary	Fleurbaix	17/10/1914	17/10/1914
War Diary	Rue-Du-Bois	18/10/1914	18/10/1914
War Diary	Le Quesne	19/10/1914	19/10/1914
War Diary	Grende Flamengerie	20/10/1914	20/10/1914
War Diary	Bois Grenier	21/10/1914	27/10/1914
War Diary	Fleurbaix	28/10/1914	31/10/1914
Heading	6th Divisional Engineers 38th Field Company R.E. November 1914		
War Diary	Fleur Baix	01/11/1914	11/11/1914
War Diary	Rue Du Quesnoy	12/11/1914	16/11/1914
War Diary	Armentieres	17/11/1914	30/11/1914
Heading	6th Divisional Engineers 38th Field Company R.E. December 1914		
War Diary	Armentieres	01/12/1914	31/12/1914
Heading	War Diary 6th Division 38th Field Company R.E. From 1st January 1915 To 31st January 1915 Volume VI 1-31.1.15		
War Diary	Armentieres	01/01/1915	31/01/1915
War Diary	War Diary of 6th Division 38th (Field) Company R.E. From 1st February 1915 To 28th February 1915 Vol VII		
War Diary	Armentieres	01/02/1915	28/02/1915
Heading	6th Division War Diary of 38th (Field) Company R.E. From 1st March 1915 To 31st March 1915 Volume VIII		
War Diary	Armentieres	01/03/1915	31/03/1915
Miscellaneous			
Heading	WO95/1599/3		
Heading	6th Division Divl Engineers 459 Field Co R.E. Formerly 2/2nd W.R. Fld Coy R.E. Oct 1915-Dec 1916		
Heading	War Diary 2/2 W.R. Field Co R.E. From Oct 8-1915 To October 31-1915 Vol 1		
War Diary	York	08/10/1915	08/10/1915
War Diary	Southampton	09/10/1915	09/10/1915
War Diary	Lahayre	10/10/1915	11/10/1915
War Diary	Godewaersvelde	12/10/1915	12/10/1915
War Diary	Vlamertinghe	13/10/1915	13/10/1915
War Diary	H8a5.9.Sh.28N.W.	13/10/1915	13/10/1915
War Diary	Ypres	14/10/1915	31/10/1915
Heading	War Diary of 2/2 W.R. Field Co. R.E. (T) From November 1st 1915 To November 30-1915 Vol II		
War Diary	Vlamertinghe	01/11/1915	01/11/1915
War Diary	H8.A5.9.28N.W.	01/11/1915	01/11/1915
War Diary	Ypres	02/11/1915	24/11/1915

War Diary	Vlamertinghe	25/11/1915	30/11/1915
Heading	War Diary of 2/2 W.R. Field Co. R.E. (T) From December 1st 1915 To:- December 31st 1915		
War Diary	Vlamertinghe H8a.5.9.SH 28 N. W Ypres	01/12/1915	22/12/1915
War Diary	Vlamertinghe	23/12/1915	31/12/1915
Heading	War Diary of 2/2 W. R. Field Co. R.E. (T) From:- January 1st 1916 To January 31st 1916 Vol IV		
War Diary	Vlamertinghe H8 a 5.9.28 N. W Ypres	01/01/1916	24/01/1916
War Diary	Vlamertinghe	25/01/1916	31/01/1916
Heading	War Diary of 2/2 W. R. Field Co. R.E. (T) From:- February 1st 1916 To:- February 29th 1916 Vol V		
War Diary	Vlamertinghe H83a.5.9 SH 28 N.W. & Ypres	01/02/1916	25/02/1916
War Diary	Vlamertinghe	26/02/1916	29/02/1916
Heading	2/2 W.R. Field Co. R.E. (T) From:- March 1st 1916 To:- March 31st 1916 Vol VI		
War Diary	Vlamertinghe H8.a.5.9. & Ypres	01/03/1916	15/03/1916
War Diary	Houtkerque	16/03/1916	16/03/1916
War Diary	Nord	17/03/1916	17/03/1916
War Diary	Ledringhem	18/03/1916	18/03/1916
War Diary	Nord	19/03/1916	25/03/1916
War Diary	Ledringhem	26/03/1916	26/03/1916
War Diary	Herzeele	27/03/1916	31/03/1916
Heading	War Diary Of 2/2 W.R. Field Co. R.E. (T) From:- April 1 1916 To:- April 30th 1916		
War Diary	Herzeele	01/04/1916	01/04/1916
War Diary	Nord	02/04/1916	05/04/1916
War Diary	Calais	06/04/1916	12/04/1916
War Diary	Zutkerque	13/04/1916	13/04/1916
War Diary	Bollezeele	14/04/1916	14/04/1916
War Diary	Houtkerque	15/04/1916	16/04/1916
War Diary	Elverdinghe A18.b8.8 & Canal Bank	17/04/1916	23/04/1916
War Diary	Elverdinghe & Canal Bank	24/04/1916	30/04/1916
Heading	War Diary Of 2/2 W.R. Field Co. R.E. (T) From:- May 1 1916 To:- May 31st 1916 Vol VIII		
War Diary	Elverdinghe & Canal Bank	01/05/1916	06/05/1916
War Diary	Peselhoek A15 b.6.6 & Canal Bank	07/05/1916	30/05/1916
Heading	War Diary Of 2/2 W.R. Field Co. R.E. (T) From:- June 1 1916 To:- June 30th 1916		
War Diary	Peselhoek & Canal Bank	01/06/1916	15/06/1916
War Diary	Burgomaster Farm Brielen & Watou K12	16/06/1916	22/06/1916
War Diary	Burgomaster Farm	23/06/1916	30/06/1916
Heading	War Diary Of 2/2 W.R. Field Co. R.E. (T) 6th Division From:- July 1st 1916 To July 31st 1916 Volume 10		
War Diary	Belgium Sheet 28. N. W. L8	01/07/1916	01/07/1916
War Diary	Herzeele Nord	02/07/1916	02/07/1916
War Diary	Volckerinckhove Nord	03/07/1916	14/07/1916
War Diary	Houtqerke	15/07/1916	15/07/1916
War Diary	Vlamertinghe	16/07/1916	16/07/1916
War Diary	Belgium	17/07/1916	17/07/1916
War Diary	Sheet 28 N. W	18/07/1916	18/07/1916
War Diary	H8a 5.9 & Ypres	19/07/1916	19/07/1916
War Diary	Belgium	20/07/1916	20/07/1916
War Diary	Sheet 28 N. W	21/07/1916	21/07/1916
War Diary	Vlamertinghe	22/07/1916	22/07/1916
War Diary	H8a.5.9 & Ypres	23/07/1916	29/07/1916
War Diary	Wormhoudt	30/07/1916	31/07/1916

Heading	6th Divisional Engineers 2/2 West Riding Field Company R.E. August 1916		
War Diary	Wormhoudt	01/08/1916	03/08/1916
War Diary	Amplier (Somme)	03/08/1916	03/08/1916
War Diary	Acheux (Somme)	04/08/1916	04/08/1916
War Diary	Englebelmer	05/08/1916	26/08/1916
War Diary	Louvencourt	27/08/1916	27/08/1916
War Diary	Beauval	28/08/1916	28/08/1916
War Diary	Flesselles	29/08/1916	31/08/1916
Heading	6th Divisional Engineers 2/2 West Riding Field Company R.E. September 1916		
War Diary	Somme	01/09/1916	01/09/1916
War Diary	Flesselles	01/09/1916	05/09/1916
War Diary	Allonville	06/09/1916	06/09/1916
War Diary	Mericourt D'abbe	07/09/1916	07/09/1916
War Diary	Maulte	08/09/1916	10/09/1916
War Diary	Carnoy & Briqueterie-area A.4.b.8.5	11/09/1916	13/09/1916
War Diary	S.30.b.2.4	14/09/1916	16/09/1916
War Diary	Briqueterie A4.b8.5	17/09/1916	18/09/1916
War Diary	Ville-Sur-Ancre	19/09/1916	21/09/1916
War Diary	Citadel-Area Camp	22/09/1916	23/09/1916
War Diary	A8a.A7d	24/09/1916	24/09/1916
War Diary	Trones Wood S29.d5.5	25/09/1916	25/09/1916
War Diary	S.30.A9.5 (Guillemont)	26/09/1916	30/09/1916
Miscellaneous	War Diary of 2/2nd. West Riding Field Coy. R.E. (T.F) From:- October 1st 1916 To:- October 31st 1916 (Volume) XIII		
War Diary	Sandpit Area Meavlte	01/10/1916	06/10/1916
War Diary	Carnoy	07/10/1916	07/10/1916
War Diary	Montauban	08/10/1916	08/10/1916
War Diary	T.19.a.1.3	09/10/1916	18/10/1916
War Diary	Carnoy	19/10/1916	19/10/1916
War Diary	Sandpit-Area Meaulte Corbie	20/10/1916	23/10/1916
War Diary	Corbie Ailly & Doubelainville	24/10/1916	28/10/1916
War Diary	Pont Remy	29/10/1916	29/10/1916
War Diary	Fouquires	30/10/1916	31/10/1916
Heading	War Diary Of 2/2nd. West Riding Field Coy. R.E. (T) From:- November 1st 1916 To November 30th 1916		
War Diary	Fouquieres Pas-De-Calais and Verquin	01/11/1916	05/11/1916
War Diary	Noyelles	06/11/1916	25/11/1916
War Diary	Noyelles & Lepreol	25/11/1916	26/11/1916
War Diary	Le Preol	27/11/1916	30/11/1916
Heading	War Diary of 2/2nd. West Riding Field Coy. R.E. (T) From:- December 1st 1916 To December 31st 1916		
War Diary	Le Preol Pas-De-Calais	01/12/1916	19/12/1916
War Diary	Noeux-Les-Mines	20/12/1916	26/12/1916
War Diary	Noyelles	27/12/1916	31/12/1916
Heading	6th Division 459th (W.R.) Field Coy R.Es. January To December 1917		
Heading	War Diary Of 459th 2/2nd (W. R.) Field Coy R. E (T) From:- January 1st 1917 To:- January 31st 1917 (Vol XVI)		
War Diary	Noyelles L.11.c.9.1 (Sheet 38.b.NE.)	01/01/1917	31/01/1917
Heading	War Diary Of 459th (West Riding) Field Coy. R. E From:- February 1st 1917 To:- February 28th 1917 Vol XVII		

War Diary	Noyelles L.11.0.9.1	01/02/1917	01/02/1917
War Diary	Sheet 38b H E	02/02/1917	16/02/1917
War Diary	Noyelles & Beuvry	17/02/1917	17/02/1917
War Diary	L.11.c.9.1-386NE	18/02/1917	26/02/1917
War Diary	Philosophe	27/02/1917	28/02/1917
Heading	War Diary of 459th (West Riding) Field Coy. R.E. From March 1st 1917 To March 31st 1917 Volume XVIII		
War Diary	Philosophe G.196.8.7.G.17e.9 1/2 1. & Noyelles LH.d4.5	01/03/1917	31/03/1917
Heading	War Diary Of 459th (West Riding) Field Coy. R.E. From April 1.1917 To April 30.1917 Volume XIX		
War Diary	Philosophe & Advanced Headqtrs Lone Trench	01/04/1917	03/04/1917
War Diary	Junction Keep	04/04/1917	30/04/1917
Heading	War Diary Of 459th (West Riding) Field Co. R.E. From May 1st-1917 To May 31st-1917 Volume XX		
War Diary	Philosophe Adv & Hdgrs At Junction Keep	01/05/1917	31/05/1917
War Diary	War Diary of 459th (West Riding) Field Coy. R.E. From June 1st 1917 To June 30th 1917 Volume (XXI)		
War Diary	Noyelles & Adv Hdqrs Junction Keep	01/06/1917	30/06/1917
Heading	War Diary of 459th (West Riding) Field Coy. R.E. From July 1st 1917 To July 31st 1917 (Volume XXII)		
War Diary	Noyelles & Advd Head 2nd Junction Keep	01/07/1917	31/07/1917
Heading	War Diary of 459th (West Riding) Field Co. R.E. From August 1st 1917 to August 31st 1917 Volume XXIII		
War Diary	Lues treville 36.B.SE.v.Bc.37	01/08/1917	25/08/1917
War Diary	Les Brebis 36.B.NE.L 3.5	25/08/1917	31/08/1917
War Diary	War Diary of 459th (West Riding) Field Coy. R.E. From September 1st 1917 to September 30th 1917 Volume XXIV		
War Diary	Les Brebis 36.B.NE.L 3.5	01/09/1917	30/09/1917
Heading	War Diary of 459th (West Riding) Field Co. Royal Engineer From October 1st 1917 to October 31st 1917 Volume XXV		
War Diary	Les Brebis 36.B.NE.L.3.5	01/10/1917	31/10/1917
War Diary		01/11/1917	30/11/1917
Heading	War Diary of 459th (West Riding) Field Co. R E From Dec 1st 1917 to Dec 31st 1917 Vol. XXVII		
War Diary	Dis Sections 57c. NE L.31.c.0.4 Mto Sec. Metz	01/12/1917	17/12/1917
War Diary	Bailleulmont	18/12/1917	31/12/1917
War Diary	Bailleulmont	01/01/1918	31/01/1918
Heading	War Diary of 459th (West Riding) Field Co. Royal Engineers From January 1st 1918 To January 31st 1918 (Volume XXVIII)		
Heading	War Diary Of 459th (West Riding) Field Coy. RE From Feb 1st 1918 To Feb 28-1918 Vol. XXIX		
War Diary	Beugny	01/02/1918	11/02/1918
War Diary	Beugnatre	12/02/1918	28/02/1918
War Diary	6th Divisional Engineers. War Diary 459th (West Riding) Field Company R.E. March 1918		
Heading	War Diary of 459th (West Riding) Field Company Royal Engineers From March 1st 1918 To March 31st 1918 Volume XXX		
War Diary	Favreuil	01/03/1918	21/03/1918
War Diary	Log East Camp	22/03/1918	26/03/1918
War Diary	Winnezeele Area	27/03/1918	31/03/1918

Heading	6th Divisional Engineers 459th (West Riding) Field Company RE April 1918		
War Diary	Winnezeele Area	01/04/1918	02/04/1918
War Diary	Sapper Camp 1.3c.0.8	03/04/1918	16/04/1918
War Diary	Domino Camp G.Sc.08	17/04/1918	30/04/1918
War Diary	Sheet 28 N W G 11a 7.7	01/05/1918	31/05/1918
War Diary	War Diary of 459th (West Riding) Field Company Royal Engineers From June 1st 1918 To June 30th 1918 (Volume XXXIII)		
War Diary	Sheet 28 N W G 11a.77	01/06/1918	06/06/1918
War Diary	Sheet 27 L 16b.3.6	07/06/1918	30/06/1918
War Diary	Sheet 27 L 16b.3.6 Sheet 28 N W G. 10.c.7.1	01/07/1918	31/07/1918
Heading	War Diary of 459th (West Riding) Field Company Royal Engineers From July 1st 1918 To July 31st 1918 Volume XXXIV		
War Diary	Sheet 28 N W G 27a. 4.7	01/07/1918	31/07/1918
Heading	War Diary of 459th (West Riding) Field Company Royal Engineers From August 1st 1918 To August 31st 1918 (Volume XXXV)		
Heading	War Diary of 459th (West Riding) Field Company Royal Engineers From August 1st 1918 To Sept 1st 1918 To Sept 30th 1918 (Volume XXXVI)		
War Diary	Ribemont Sur L'ancre	01/09/1918	11/09/1918
War Diary	Daours	12/09/1918	13/09/1918
War Diary	Trefcon	14/09/1918	30/09/1918
Heading	War Diary of 459th (West Riding) Field Company Royal Engineers From October 1st 1918 To October 31st 1918 (Volume XXXVII)		
War Diary	Vraignes	01/10/1918	03/10/1918
War Diary	Magny La Fosse	04/10/1918	08/10/1918
War Diary	Ramicourt	09/10/1918	09/10/1918
War Diary	Bohain	10/10/1918	19/10/1918
War Diary	St Souplet	20/10/1918	31/10/1918
War Diary	Fresnoy	01/11/1918	05/11/1918
War Diary	Bohain	06/11/1918	06/11/1918
War Diary	Catillon	07/11/1918	09/11/1918
War Diary	Prieches	10/11/1918	11/11/1918
War Diary	Avesnes	12/11/1918	18/11/1918
War Diary	Sars Poteries	19/11/1918	19/11/1918
War Diary	Leugnies	20/11/1918	20/11/1918
War Diary	L'Ecrevisse	21/11/1918	21/11/1918
War Diary	Beurieux	22/11/1918	22/11/1918
War Diary	Erpion	23/11/1918	23/11/1918
War Diary	St Aubin	24/11/1918	30/11/1918
Heading	War Diary of 459th (West Riding) Field Company Royal Engineers From Nove 1st 1918 To Nove 30th 1918 (Volume XXXVIII)		
Heading	War Diary of 459th (West Riding) Field Company Royal Engineers From Decm 1st 1918 To Decm 31st 1918 Volume No XXXIX		
War Diary	St Aubin	01/12/1918	01/12/1918
War Diary	Ermeton-Sur-Biert	02/12/1918	03/12/1918
War Diary	Evrehailles	04/12/1918	04/12/1918
War Diary	Emptinne	05/12/1918	05/12/1918
War Diary	Havelange	06/12/1918	07/12/1918
War Diary	Terwagne	08/12/1918	08/12/1918

War Diary	Comblain-La-Tour	09/12/1918	10/12/1918
War Diary	Sougne	11/12/1918	11/12/1918
War Diary	Ster	12/12/1918	12/12/1918
War Diary	Malmedy	13/12/1918	13/12/1918
War Diary	Elsenborn	14/12/1918	14/12/1918
War Diary	Montjoie	15/12/1918	15/12/1918
War Diary	Simmerath	16/12/1918	18/12/1918
War Diary	Hasenfeld	19/12/1918	20/12/1918
War Diary	Juntersdorf	21/12/1918	21/12/1918
War Diary	Lechenich	22/12/1918	22/12/1918
War Diary	Meschenich	23/12/1918	31/12/1918
Heading	War Diary of 459th (West Riding) Field Company Royal Engineers From Jan 1st 1919 To Jan 31st 1919 (Volume XC)		
War Diary	Meschenich	01/01/1919	09/01/1919
War Diary	Berzdorf	10/01/1919	31/01/1919
War Diary	Berzdorf	01/02/1919	01/03/1919
War Diary		01/02/1919	28/02/1919
War Diary	Berzdorf	01/03/1919	17/03/1919
War Diary	Durscheven	18/03/1919	31/03/1919
Heading	War Diary of 459th (West Riding) Field Company Royal Engineers From March 1st To March 31/19 (Volume XCII)		
War Diary	Borr	23/03/1919	23/03/1919
War Diary	Lechenich	30/03/1919	30/03/1919
Heading	War Diary of 459th Field Company Royal Engineers From 1st April 1919 To 30th April 1919		
War Diary	Durscheven	01/04/1919	30/04/1919
Heading	War Diary 459th Field Company Royal Engineers From 1/5/19 To 31/5/19		
War Diary	Durscheven (Map Ref. 1. L. 100000 8N. 82.23	01/05/1919	31/05/1919
War Diary	Durscheven	01/06/1919	19/06/1919
War Diary	Stockheim IL k6. 47.4.5	20/06/1919	30/06/1919
Heading	459th Field Company Royal Engineers War Diary From 1-7-19 to 31-7-19		
War Diary	Durscheven Map Ref. L.1. 100.000 8.N.12.23	01/07/1919	31/07/1919
War Diary	War Diary 459 Field Coy. R.E. From 1/8/19 To 31/8/19		
War Diary	Durscheven Map Ref. L.1. 100.000 8N. 17.23	01/08/1919	25/08/1919
War Diary	Durscheven	26/08/1919	01/09/1919
Heading	6 Division Troops 12 Field Coy Royal Engineers. 1914 Aug To 1919 Apr. 38 Field Coy R.E. 1914 Aug To 1915 Mar. 459 (Former Ly 2/2 West Riding) Field Coy R.E. 1915 Marbto 1919 Aug.		
Heading	6 Division Troops. 12 Field Coy Royal Engineers. 1914 Aug To 1919 Apr. 38 Field Coy R.E. 1914 Aug To 1915 Mar. 459 (Former Ly 2/2 West Riding) Field Coy R.E. 1915 Mar to 1919 Aug.		

6TH DIVISION
DIVL. ENGNRS.

12TH FIELD COY R.E.

AUG 1914 - ~~DEC 1918~~ 1919 APR

6th Divisional Engineers

Disembarked ST.NAZAIRE 10.9.14.

12th FIELD COMPANY R. E.

AUGUST & SEPTEMBER 1914.

—

Dec 1918

Instructions regarding War Diaries and Intelligence Summaries are contained in F. S. Regs., Part II. and the Staff Manual respectively. Title pages will be prepared in manuscript.

WAR DIARY or ~~INTELLIGENCE SUMMARY~~ 12" Field Company

(Erase heading not required.)

Army Form C. 2118.

Hour, Date, Place	Summary of Events and Information	Remarks and References to Appendices
1914.		
Moore Park Aug 4 6.45 pm	Received telegram from Commandant Dublin ordering mobilization.	
	Issue orders to CSM, CQMS, Pay Corporal and O/c Horse Collecting Party. One reservist arrives.	
Moore Park Aug. 5.	Issue warrants for families of married N.C.Os and men to return to their homes.	
" 12 noon	Veterinary Inspection. The medical inspection took place before order to mobilize was received. 2nd Lt Jackson, Playfair arrive 8.45 pm	
Aug. 6.	N.Co to Queenstown for Explosives, which arrive in afternoon. Capt Grove reports his arrival at 10.30.	
Aug. 7.	Medals sent to O/c Records. Strength of company 250 and 49 horses. Nose-bags and head-collars freely expended by fractious horses.	
Aug. 8.	Personnel and horses complete except ASC drivers.	
Aug. 9.	Continue marching, fitting harness, and equipment.	
Aug. 10.	Do. Do.	
Aug. 11.	Parade fully mobilized except bicycles and march out of Moore Park. Inoculation against enteric this afternoon. 66 sappers are unwilling to be inoculated as it is voluntary.	
Aug. 12.	Company somewhat hors de combat owing to effects of inoculation	

(9 26 6) W 2[illegible]7—976 100,000 4/12 H W V 9/3298

Instructions regarding War Diaries and Intelligence Summaries are contained in F. S. Regs., Part II. and the Staff Manual respectively. Title pages will be prepared in manuscript.

WAR DIARY 12' Field Company
or
~~INTELLIGENCE~~ SUMMARY
(*Erase heading not required.*)

Army Form C. 2118.

Hour, Date, Place	Summary of Events and Information	Remarks and References to Appendices
9.15 am Aug. 13. Moore Park	Receive wire that 6th Division ordered to England. As several horses kicked owing to paucity of heel-ropes wire to Ordnance for 20. Wire Div Engrs that medical officer Fermoy declines to purchase med. equipment and none received, also that bicycle accessories not yet received	A larger number of heel-ropes, head collars and nosebags are required on mobilization as horses continually breaking and destroying them.
12.15 pm	CRE wires that med. officer says that medicines to field companies have been discontinued.	
12.20	Vet offr comes to see sick horses	
1.0 pm	Accessories for bicycles arrive but no "repair outfits" which are purchased locally. Wire to General and CRE that unit will be complete today	Each bicycle should have a repair outfit issued with it.
11.30 pm	Receive telegram from Div Engrs to be prepared to embark in accordance with Time Table Saturday being reckoned as 4th day.	
8.0 am Aug. 14 Moore Park	Parade fully mobilized and march via BALLYNAHOWN –	
11.30 pm	Receive order not to leave till order comes to do so.	
12.30 pm Aug 15 Moore Park	Div Engrs telegraphs "Base details and first reinforcement will all embark at Queenstown" – telegraph to Div Engrs asking if this means Base details will accompany unit. The reply is in the negative	
Aug 16 Moore Park	Route march.	
11 am	Telephone message from General Cork. "Move of 12' Company RE is suspended until further orders".	

Instructions regarding War Diaries and Intelligence Summaries are contained in F. S. Regs., Part II. and the Staff Manual respectively. Title pages will be prepared in manuscript.

WAR DIARY
or
~~INTELLIGENCE SUMMARY~~
(Erase heading not required.)

12 Field Company

Army Form C. 2118.

Hour, Date, Place	Summary of Events and Information	Remarks and References to Appendices
Moore Park Aug. 17.	Instruction and practice in Field Works	
Moore Park Aug. 18	Instruction and practice in Field Works	
1.35 am Moore Park Aug. 19.	Telegram from Brigade "move Co to Queenstown Wednesday 19th Aug"	
1.30 pm	Leave ~~Fermoy~~ FERMOY	
4.30 pm	Arrive ~~Queens~~ QUEENSTOWN. no ship to take us till 21st, so encamp in Forming Up Place.	
9 am QUEENSTOWN. Aug 21.	Commence embarking on "MAIDAN" at 9 am and finish at 10.30	
4 pm	Leave QUEENSTOWN	
12.30 pm Aug 22. LIVERPOOL	Arrive. Complete disembarkation at 2.30	
6 pm	Leave LIVERPOOL by train	
2 am Aug 23.	Arrive CAMBRIDGE and proceed to camp	
Aug 24	Divisional Route March	
Aug 25.	Group Exercise under G O C XVIth Inf Bde –	
9 pm Sept 6. CAMBRIDGE	Orders received to be prepared to move tomorrow	
2 pm Sept 7. CAMBRIDGE	Orders received to move to ROYSTON and to start at 1 pm. Got away at 2.20 – 20 minutes after receiving the order	
7.0 pm	Arrive ROYSTON and entrain	
2.30 am Sept 8.	arrive SOUTHAMPTON and embark in S.S. OXONIAN – Owing to the small hatches vehicles have to be unloaded and let down the hatchways long-ways	
9.0 am Sept 8	Sail from SOUTHAMPTON	

A F Sargeaunt

(9 26 6) W 257—976 100,000 4/12 H W V 79/3298

Instructions regarding War Diaries and Intelligence Summaries are contained in F. S. Regs., Part II. and the Staff Manual respectively. Title pages will be prepared in manuscript.

WAR DIARY

or

~~INTELLIGENCE SUMMARY~~

(Erase heading not required.)

Army Form C. 2118.

Hour, Date, Place	Summary of Events and Information	Remarks and References to Appendices
Sept 10 -	Arrive St NAZAIRE early	
10 am.	go alongside, disembark and proceed to camp at GRAND MARAIS	
8.30 am Sept 11. St NAZAIRE	at station to entrain, advanced party having arrived at 7.0 am. We are allowed 4 hours to entrain which is much too long and entraining actually takes 1½ hours.	
12.28 pm Sept 11.	Leave St NAZAIRE	
1.30 pm Sept 12 MARLES	Arrive MARLES, and put into siding at 3.15 pm. Leave by march route at 4.45 pm and proceed 6½ m to FERME de BESSY where we billet - pouring with rain	
Sept 13. CRECY	9.0 C 16' I.B informs me he is leaving LACHAPELLE at 10 am but on clearing LACHAPELLE at 9.45 find that there are two Bns in front.	
	March to JOUVARRE - 13 miles. Much delayed by infantry transport continually stopping, and at one hill the R.S & I take 2 hours to take their vehicles up one at a time	
JOUVARRE	1 Section on outposts as Infantry - point out to B.M that it is not usual to use R.E on outposts as Infantry.	
11.25 Sept 14. JOUVARRE	Leave ~~behind~~ at the rear of 16th Inf Bde and march two miles to SAACY - Send the two pontoons to join 38 Co RE under orders from Division. Had to send a sick man from JOUVARRE in a hired cart. The M.O attached to HQrs R.E is hardly ever	

Instructions regarding War Diaries and Intelligence Summaries are contained in F. S. Regs., Part II. and the Staff Manual respectively. Title pages will be prepared in manuscript.

WAR DIARY
or
~~INTELLIGENCE SUMMARY~~
(Erase heading not required.)

Army Form C. 2118.

Hour, Date, Place	Summary of Events and Information	Remarks and References to Appendices
	available for the men in Field Cos and he would appear to be redundant. So far I have had always to get the nearest Battalion M.O to see any sick.	
11 pm Sept. 14. SAACY	Receive Advanced Guard orders for tomorrow march	
7 am Sept 15. SAACY	Leave SAACY and march in MAIN GUARD without incident to point 1½ miles N of CHATEAU THIERRY which we reach at 1.20 and out span in field. Continue march at 6.30 pm and in heavy rain arrive at ROCOURT (8 miles) 11 p.m.	
6 am Sept 16. ROCOURT	Continue march with 16th Inf Bde, at 6 am and reach BUZANCY (13 miles) at noon, where we billet.	
BUZANCY	Move to a bivouac 2 miles due East of BUZANCY - raining hard - During afternoon Capt Grove reconnoitres position along high ground between BILLY and BELLEU.	
~~MESMIN BIVOUAC~~	~~Meet GOC and OC Battalions with Capt Grove and Lt HANNA~~	
MESMIN BIVOUAC	~~at~~ Receive orders at 5 pm to send out officers and carts to collect tools in villages of ROZIERES, SEPTMONTS - NOYANT Lts Turner Jackson and Playfair do this and Lt Turner takes the tools - 140 shovels and 30 picks to the 4th Division at SERCHES - he leaves ECURY with the tools at 8.25 pm The GOC General expresses his pleasure at the good work done in the collection of tools	
Sept. 18	Meet GOC and OC Bns with Capt Grove and Lt Hanna at 6 am. Capt Grove and Lt Hanna accompany the	

(9 26 6) W 257—976 100,000 4/12 H W V 79/3298

Instructions regarding War Diaries and Intelligence Summaries are contained in F. S. Regs., Part II. and the Staff Manual respectively. Title pages will be prepared in manuscript.

WAR DIARY
or
~~INTELLIGENCE~~ SUMMARY
(*Erase heading not required.*)

Army Form C. 2118.

Hour, Date, Place	Summary of Events and Information	Remarks and References to Appendices
	of Bns along the position and afterwards mark the proposed trenches (position of) on an enlarged map. Accompany the Br Gen along the lower slopes of position between VENIZEL and VILLENEUVE	
	During morning Lt. Turner is sent for by CRE to make a map enlargement and orders come from GOC 16 Inf Bde to collect barbed wire. Lts Jackson and Playfair go out to do this but only 330 lb is collected	
Sept 19th 10.30 am	Receive orders to report to 3rd A.C and am told that 12 Fd Co is to remain behind when 6 Div marches today. Report to 3 A.C and receive instructions re 12th Co assisting in the defence of BELLEU - ACY position. Parade company at 1 pm and move to SERMOISE where billets are secured for the men; take the men onto the position and meet Br Gen. Glubb CRE N Div and S.Os from 4th Div and 3rd A.C. Gen Glubb says that no digging is to be done today so men return to billets; O.C. Co. assists in a fuller reconnaissance of the whole position	
Sept 20 SERMOISE	12th Fd Co parades 7.30 am and onto position at 8 - where R W Fusiliers are also allotted for making the defences. The 12 Co dig trenches assist infantry in making overhead cover and lay out trenches, knocking off at 5.30 pm.	

Instructions regarding War Diaries and Intelligence Summaries are contained in F. S. Regs., Part II. and the Staff Manual respectively. Title pages will be prepared in manuscript.

WAR DIARY
or
~~INTELLIGENCE~~ SUMMARY
(Erase heading not required.)

Army Form C. 2118.

Hour, Date, Place	Summary of Events and Information	Remarks and References to Appendices
	Ordered to march to BAZOCHES early on 21st	
7.40 am 21st SEPT MONT	Leave by march route. At 11.25 when on road receive orders to billet MONT NOTREDAME, but on arriving there at 2.30 receive further orders from CRE to proceed to PAARS. When nearly at PAARS we are turned back by G.S.O 6th Div and ordered to return to MONT NOTREDAME to build platform at station for unloading horses. Ride on in advance of company and meet Gen Fowke and Col Dawkins at station and what is required is pointed out. On arrival of company form them into two reliefs, right ½ coy 5 to 6.30 and left ½ coy 6.30 to 7.45 by which time it is too dark to see	
22nd	Continue work on platform which is finished during morning. The platform is 30 yards long and is supported on crib piers of sleepers with wood rails to bridge the gaps between the piers the whole covered with 2" planking. Behind the platform a ramp is made of timber along the whole length so that horses can be led out of trucks across platform and down ramp	

Instructions regarding War Diaries and Intelligence Summaries are contained in F. S. Regs., Part II. and the Staff Manual respectively. Title pages will be prepared in manuscript.

WAR DIARY
or
~~INTELLIGENCE SUMMARY~~
(Erase heading not required.)

1/12' Field Company.

Army Form C. 2118.

Hour, Date, Place	Summary of Events and Information	Remarks and References to Appendices
7.20 am Sept 23.	Leave MONTNOTREDAME and proceed to BAZOCHES under orders of CRE VI Divn, but orders come from G.H.Q. for 12th Fd Co to be temporarily placed under G.O.C. VI Divn. The CRE VI Divn remarks that he has only twice issued orders to the 12' Co and both times the orders have been cancelled	
9 am BAZOCHES	Receive orders to report to HQrs 3' Divn at BRAINE. So set company in motion and ride on to BRAINE. Receive instruction from CRE 3' Divn that 12' Co is to relieve 57th Co at VAILLY. Leave 12' Co in wood 1 mile South of CHASSEMY and go to VAILLY with Adjt 3' Divn to look round by daylight. Germans shell VAILLY periodically and also the pontoon bridge across river. Return to Company at 3.30 pm.	
	Leave all vehicles and horses except 2 single tool carts and water cart in wood 1 mile S of CHASSEMY under 2 Lt PLAYFAIR and march with rest of company at 6.45 to VAILLY. Send one section under 2 Lt Jackson to Town HALL to work with 8' Inf Bde and take	

Instructions regarding War Diaries and Intelligence Summaries are contained in F. S. Regs., Part II. and the Staff Manual respectively. Title pages will be prepared in manuscript.

WAR DIARY or ~~INTELLIGENCE SUMMARY~~ of 12 Field Company

(*Erase heading not required.*)

Army Form C. 2118.

Hour, Date, Place	Summary of Events and Information	Remarks and References to Appendices
	remainder of Company to Sand Pit ½ m S.W of ROUGE MAISON where we all live in burrows so as to be protected from hostile shell fire	
Sept 24. VAILLY	Put up wire entanglement by day in front of R.S.L.I.	
7 pm	parade for night work. digging trenches in connection with LEICESTERSHIRE Regt defences.	
Sept 25	A party on defence of house near ROUGE MAISON - wire entanglement in woods and altering and improving communication trenches to BUFFS	
7 pm	A party making head cover in Leicestershire trenches and other digging tunnel between Buffs and Y. and L.; and making parados against German snipers	
Sept 26	More wire entanglement in Leicestershire woods and on MAISON ROUGE road and improving BUFFS communication	
2 pm	Adjt 3 Div arrives and says that G.O.C. wishes information as to whether Germans are mining	
7 pm	Company parade for night work - viz wire entanglement in front of Leicestershire Regt, head cover, and communication	

(9 26 6) W 257—976 100,000 4/12 H W V 79 3298

Army Form C. 2118.

Instructions regarding War Diaries and Intelligence Summaries are contained in F. S. Regs., Part II. and the Staff Manual respectively. Title pages will be prepared in manuscript.

WAR DIARY or ~~INTELLIGENCE SUMMARY~~ of 12 Field Company

(Erase heading not required.)

Hour, Date, Place	Summary of Events and Information	Remarks and References to Appendices
	trenches for Buffs. When in Buffs trenches receive message	
Sept 26 9.20 pm	at 9.20 pm that G.O.C. wishes entanglement made between K.O.S.B. and Leicestershire trenches; collect 12 men that were working all day and after getting some posts and wire take them to the position and work till 4 am.	
Sept 27. 5.30	Start sapping from K.O.S.B. trench as listening gallery as reported mining. Major Kelsall arrives at 6 pm to investigate alleged mining and we go to the spot together but nothing can be heard. I go again at midnight and at 4 am but can hear nothing.	
27/28	Night work carried out. Look out for Buffs and extending communication trenches, head cover for ~~Buffs~~ Leicestershire and wire entanglement between K.O.S.B. and Leicestershire	
28th 9.45 pm	Heavy rattle of musketry along the line from BUFFS to K.O.S.B. Ceases at 10.4 pm and is nothing serious. Continue various works during the night.	
29th	Continue sapping and during night entanglement ~~and~~ trench works.	

30/9/14

A. T. Sargeaunt major
OC 12 Fd. Co.

(9 26 6) W 257—976 100,000 4/12 H W V 79/3298

6th Divisional Engineers

12th FIELD COMPANY R. E.

OCTOBER 1914.

Instructions regarding War Diaries and Intelligence Summaries are contained in F. S. Regs., Part II. and the Staff Manual respectively. Title pages will be prepared in manuscript.

WAR DIARY
or
~~INTELLIGENCE~~ SUMMARY
(Erase heading not required.)

Army Form C. 2118.

Hour, Date, Place	Summary of Events and Information	Remarks and References to Appendices
Sept 30. VAILLY	Work all through the night digging trenches, erecting obstacles and head cover.	
Oct 1 VAILLY	Continue defence work.	
Oct 2 VAILLY	Under cover of mist erect wire entanglements in front of all KSLI posts on left of line and dig trench to be occupied at night by BUFFS. Preparing for night work when orders are received from 6 Divn to rejoin but G.O.C. XVI I.B. orders the O.C. Coy not to move till he has communicated with the Divn. Orders received at 8 pm that 12 Fd Co may remain at VAILLY for another 24 hours and the order says that 1 ton of barbed wire will arrive at 10 pm. On receipt of this order carry on with work during night, viz barricade near ROUGE MAISON, finishing trench for BUFFS, and head cover for LEICESTERSHIRE Regt. The barbed wire which was said to arrive at 10 pm arrived	
Oct 3 VAILLY	at 3.3 am this morning, and as the entanglements in front of BUFFS are urgently required set the men to work under cover of the morning mist. The mist lifts and Germans are seen on the opposite slopes and before the situation was realized shrapnel fire from 6 guns fell amongst the men	

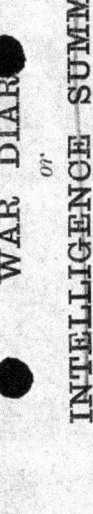

Instructions regarding War Diaries and Intelligence Summaries are contained in F. S. Regs., Part II. and the Staff Manual respectively. Title pages will be prepared in manuscript.

WAR DIARY or ~~INTELLIGENCE SUMMARY~~ 1/12 Field Company

(*Erase heading not required.*)

Army Form C. 2118.

Hour, Date, Place	Summary of Events and Information	Remarks and References to Appendices
	at work, killing one, severely wounding two, and wounding two others. The body of Sapper Byrne is recovered at dusk and he is buried at VAILLY. The 1/12 Fd Co leaves VAILLY at 7.45 pm, joins the vehicles and horses near BRAINE and marches to DHUIZY where they billet - near SERCHES.	
Oct 4. SERCHES	Ride along the proposed retired position with CRA and B.M. 6 Div Artillery	
Oct 5. SERCHES	Receive orders at 2 pm to take up the bridge at MISSY and leave surplus pontoons on river bank; as the section is starting at 5 pm orders are received to bring the spare pontoons to SERCHES, so put wagons of 12 and 31 Cos unloaded. At 5.15 pm receive orders that the bridge is not to be taken up	
Oct 4 SERCHES	3.30 pm receive orders to prepare bridge over VESLE for demolition. Capt Grove and Lt. Turner make reconnaissance; a lattice girder bridge which calculations show to require 10 lbs guncotton. Lt. Turner arranges the charges after dark	
Oct 5. SERCHES	3.30 pm ordered to destroy tonight both bridges over VESLE the charge of 70 lbs on second one having been placed by 31 "Co". After arranging for the demolition, orders are received at 5.30 not to destroy the bridges	

(9 26 6) W 257—976 100,000 1/12 H W V 3298

Instructions regarding War Diaries and Intelligence Summaries are contained in F. S. Regs., Part II. and the Staff Manual respectively. Title pages will be prepared in manuscript.

WAR DIARY or ~~INTELLIGENCE SUMMARY~~ of 12th Field Company.

(Erase heading not required.)

Army Form C. 2118.

Hour, Date, Place	Summary of Events and Information	Remarks and References to Appendices
Oct 6. SERCHES	11.30 am. The Bridge at MISSY is to be taken up tonight after the Lancashire Fusiliers have withdrawn and the charges of guncotton are to be withdrawn from the VESLE bridges. Detail left half company under Capt. Grove for this work and order them parade for 8.30 pm. The bridge contains 5 pontoons and 1 trestle, and 2 vehicles from 2nd B. Train and 3 vehicles from 1st B. Train are to be at cross road immediately south of first S in SERMOISE at 10 pm to take 4 pontoons and 1 trestle, and one pontoon and superstructure are to be taken by 12th Co to replace that which they put into VAILLY BRIDGE and which still stands. Leave OHUIZY at 9 pm and march to NANTEUIL	
Oct 7. NANTEUIL	Left half company arrives 6.30 am having accomplished their mission at MISSY. Leave NANTEUIL at 7.30 pm and march to VOUTY; owing to motor car having gone into a bog on narrow road the leading pontoon is bogged on the opposite side of road and one section has to remain behind to help it out	
Oct 8. VOUTY	Leave VOUTY at 2.30 pm having been ordered to be ready to march at noon and in accordance with 6th Div orders billet at FRAISNOY and receive entraining table in which 12th Fd Co entrains at LONGUEIL St MARIE at 5 am on 10th.	

(9 26 6) W 257—976 100,000 4/12 H W V 79/3298

Instructions regarding War Diaries and Intelligence Summaries are contained in F. S. Regs., Part II. and the Staff Manual respectively. Title pages will be prepared in manuscript.

WAR DIARY or ~~INTELLIGENCE SUMMARY~~ 1/12th Fd. Co

(*Erase heading not required.*)

Army Form C. 2118.

Hour, Date, Place	Summary of Events and Information	Remarks and References to Appendices
Oct 9. FRESNOY.	On visiting 17th Fd Amb. Capt Grove accidentally learns that the entraining table has been revised. No copy of this revised table is received but from O.C. 17th Fd. Amb we learn that 12th Fd Co. is to entrain at ESTREES St DENNIS at 12 noon 10th	
	Leave FRESNOY 1.30 pm and march to LONGUEIL St MARIE where we billet.	
Oct 10 LONGUEIL St MARIE	Leave at 7.50 and arrive at station (ESTREES St DENNIS) 10 am, 2 hours before entraining hour according to orders. On arrival are ordered to entrain at 11 am, and leave at 2.34 pm	
Oct 11. ARQUES	Arrive 8.50 am, and detrain in one hour and await orders. First orders are to find billets in a certain area second orders to billet in conjunction with 17th I.B.	
	Arrive in billet in ARQUES at 2 pm	
11.15 pm	Receive Div orders to march eastward tomorrow as part of A.G. under O.C. 19th I.B.	
Oct 12th 1.30 am	March orders from O.C. 19th I.B.	
	Leave ARQUES at 5.15 am and after various halts reach ½ m short of PRADELLES at 2 pm where we are ordered to billet	

Instructions regarding War Diaries and Intelligence Summaries are contained in F. S. Regs., Part II. and the Staff Manual respectively. Title pages will be prepared in manuscript.

WAR DIARY or ~~INTELLIGENCE SUMMARY~~

1/12th Fd. Co.

(*Erase heading not required.*)

Army Form C. 2118.

Hour, Date, Place	Summary of Events and Information	Remarks and References to Appendices
Oct 13. 9 am	Join column for advance. Column held up, as enemy holding BAILLEUL S.O. Ridge. 12th Fd Co bivouacs in field short of STRAZEELE and officers make reconnaissances during the engagement. When our infantry have cleared MERRIS take the company to that place, and afterwards billet there.	
Oct. 14 MERRIS	Join column for advance at 1.30, but column makes but slow progress and at 7 12th Fd Co is only at OUTTERSTEENE; receive orders to billet at this place.	
Oct 15 OUTTERSTEENE	Leave with 2nd Bde R.F.A. at 1.30 past Les TROIS FERMES to Corner ½ mile W of BLANCHE MAISON where we remain till 8.30 pm when I learn from OC 2 Bde RFA that 12 Fd Co is to follow 17th Inf Bde in an attack on BAC ST MAUR. By mistake no orders are sent to me but acting on orders sent to R.F.A. I send back for bridging wagons and march to STEENWERCK. 11.15 pm report to 6 Div HdQrs and then proceed to CROIX DU BAC and report to HdQrs XVII I.B. Follow 1 Leinster Regt to BAC ST MAUR. Find that swing bridge is open and worked from opposite bank. Reconnaissance reveals no enemy. Get sapper across with rope and pull bridge to allowing infantry to pass over.	

(9 26 6) W 257—976 100,000 4/12 H W V 79/3298

Instructions regarding War Diaries and Intelligence Summaries are contained in F. S. Regs., Part II. and the Staff Manual respectively. Title pages will be prepared in manuscript.

WAR DIARY or ~~INTELLIGENCE~~ SUMMARY

1/12 Field Company

(*Erase heading not required.*)

Army Form C. 2118.

Hour, Date, Place	Summary of Events and Information	Remarks and References to Appendices
Oct 16. 7 am. BAC St MAUR	Endeavour to make reconnaissance to South of river LYS but thick mist prevents me advancing beyond our patrols. At 12 noon go out with Capt Grove and make reconnaissance for defence of bridge at BAC St MAUR – This occupies us till 4 pm. – draw up report on return to billets	
Oct 17.	Leave BAC St MAUR under orders of GOC 17 Inf Bde at 7.30 am marching behind 24 Bty R.F.A via FLEURBAIX. On reaching ~~the~~ Second Q of RUE DE LERREES we are halted owing to infantry being in touch with enemy in front – Do not move till 3 pm when we go into billets at LAVESEE.	
Oct 18 LAVESEE	Infantry advance to attack PREMESQUES – PERANCHIES position. All officers make reconnaissance – personally go as far as S.E end of BASTROUT close behind Leinster trenches. Infantry do not require any R.E. assistance	
Oct. 19. LA VESEE	Send out Lt Turner and Lt Hanna to reconnoitre towards PREMESQUES and HALTE respectively and send all sappers and tool carts to WEZ MARQUART to be in readiness. Nothing can be done before dark, so send out sappers after dusk to strengthen positions at HALTE and PREMESQUES	

Instructions regarding War Diaries and Intelligence Summaries are contained in F. S. Regs., Part II. and the Staff Manual respectively. Title pages will be prepared in manuscript.

WAR DIARY or ~~INTELLIGENCE SUMMARY~~

(*Erase heading not required.*)

of 12 Field Company

Army Form C. 2118.

Hour, Date, Place	Summary of Events and Information	Remarks and References to Appendices
Oct 20.	Battle rages all day. Go during morning to Mt. DE PREMESQUES Return to 17 I.B. HQ at 1 pm and report position of affairs to G.O.C. and ask for Artillery fire to be brought to bear on ground between PREMESQUES and Mt DE PREMESQUES, which is arranged. G.O.C. asks for position at WEZ MACQUART to be strengthened – parade company at 7.30 – select sites for trenches and set men to work. return to billet for tea and continue work after dusk – get into touch with XVIII I.B. to learn their dispositions on right of 17 I.B. line. On returning to WEZ MACQUART receive orders to fall back on line running N and S through E of BOULOGNE – take company back to this line and commence entrenching, but quite impossible to properly site trenches at night on ground that one has not reconnoitred by day. Work till dawn.	
Oct 21	Meet B.M. 17 I.B. at 7.30 at RUE DU BOIS with a view to going along position to see what can be done to further improve and strengthen; but owing to the position being very exposed it is not possible to see all points	

Instructions regarding War Diaries and Intelligence Summaries are contained in F. S. Regs., Part II. and the Staff Manual respectively. Title pages will be prepared in manuscript.

WAR DIARY or ~~INTELLIGENCE SUMMARY~~

(*Erase heading not required.*)

1/12 Field Company

Army Form C. 2118.

Hour, Date, Place	Summary of Events and Information	Remarks and References to Appendices
Sept 21.	Incidentally stop Col. Seely from motoring to WAZ MACQUART which he did not know was now occupied by Germans.	
6 pm	At 6pm send 2 sections of Coy to PORT EGAZE FERME to put up wire entanglement in front of R.B. trenches and 2 sections to RUE DU BOIS to make communication trenches for Leicesters. Both pieces of work were much interrupted by shell and musketry fire. The enemy penetrated behind the R.B. trench where the RE were working, but did not remain there	
Oct 22	Visit the Royal Fusiliers trenches during morning; they asked for entanglements in front of trenches. Receive instructions for 2 Sections to report to 16 I.B. at dusk. Send 2 Sections under Capt Greve to R.7 at 3 pm to prepare materials for entanglement to erect after dusk. Visit 16 I.B. HQ during afternoon to find out what is required and at 4.30 take 2 sections who prepare stakes and pickets under cover. At 6.30 Infantry parties parade for digging new line of trenches to connect with 19 I.B. on right of 16 I.B. whose right is at present S of ~~x in TOUQUET~~ x in BRIDOUX	

Instructions regarding War Diaries and Intelligence Summaries are contained in F. S. Regs., Part II. and the Staff Manual respectively. Title pages will be prepared in manuscript.

Army Form C. 2118.

WAR DIARY ~~or INTELLIGENCE SUMMARY~~ 1/12 Field Company

(*Erase heading not required.*)

Hour, Date, Place	Summary of Events and Information	Remarks and References to Appendices
TOUQUET. Oct 22.	The Infantry are divided into 5 parties to construct 5 lengths of trench and the 2 sections RE are divided into 5 parties to put up entanglement in front of each trench. Start of work is postponed owing to musketry fusillade. but when work is once started it is continued to a finish.	
Oct 23.	At about 8 am the Germans attack 16 I.B. and 2 of the new trenches constructed last night are occupied by them. After various discussions G.O.C. decides to evacuate all the new trenches and to draw the line back whilst I am putting out paper to show positions of proposed trenches a further alteration is decided on which leaves the line between x in BRIDOUX and e in BOUTILLERIE far from satisfactory. Germans penetrate R.I.[illegible] line during day and at 5.30 G.O.C. tells me that they have penetrated at another place so as we have no barbed wire (not having arrived as [illegible] anticipated) I suggest that I should bring the 1/2 Fd Co to man some of the trenches. G.O.C. agrees	

(9 26 6) W 257—976 100,000 4/12 H W V 79/3298

Instructions regarding War Diaries and Intelligence Summaries are contained in F. S. Regs., Part II. and the Staff Manual respectively. Title pages will be prepared in manuscript.

WAR DIARY or ~~INTELLIGENCE SUMMARY~~ of 12 Field Company

(*Erase heading not required.*)

Army Form C. 2118.

Hour, Date, Place	Summary of Events and Information	Remarks and References to Appendices
Oct 23	Bring ~~the~~ company to TOUQUET and occupy some of the back trenches but the night is a quiet one	
Oct 24	Return to LAVESEE at 6.30 am and personally visit CRE at FLEURBAIX who says that we are to move to CROIX MARECHAL. Parade 8.20, collect some barbed wire from 38 Fd Co at BOIS GRENIER and reach cross roads at S of CROIX MARECHAL where message from VI Div for officer to go to them at once so go myself and am told that 16 Inf Bde require obstructions in ditches which run into their position. Send Lt Hammond and 2 Lt Jackson with 12 men and tool cart to see what can be done. Remainder of company move ½ mile N.W. of S in CROIX MARECHAL and bivouac as farms in CROIX MARECHAL are being shelled	
FLEURBAIX	Move into billets in FLEURBAIX into house occupied by VI Div Engineers till this morning, the VI Div HQ having moved rearwards as 2 shells had been dropped into FLEURBAIX. 2 Sections report to 16 Inf Bde for work at TOUQUET this evening.	

Instructions regarding War Diaries and Intelligence Summaries are contained in F. S. Regs., Part II. and the Staff Manual respectively. Title pages will be prepared in manuscript.

WAR DIARY or ~~INTELLIGENCE SUMMARY~~

1/12 Field Company.

(*Erase heading not required.*)

Army Form C. 2118.

Hour, Date, Place	Summary of Events and Information	Remarks and References to Appendices
Oct 25 FLEURBAIX and TOUQUET.	9 am Receive instructions to take Company for work under 16 I.B in front of (E. of) TOUQUET. The Company is employed during the day in erecting wire entanglement in front of fire trenches, digging new trenches, erecting barricade on road. Continue work during greater part of night in pouring rain. Return to billets 4 am 26th.	
Oct. 26th	Visit 16 I.B and 17 I.B to see what work is required tonight and visit ground -	
5 pm	Company parade - 3 Sections to 16 I.B to put up shelters near fire trenches and to continue wire entanglement northwards in front of the Buffs trenches and 1 Section to 17 I.B. to make posts on second line in deep ditch and to make communication trench thereto	
Oct 27th	Work during night of 27/28 with 16th I.B. putting up splinter proof look outs and entanglements - a disturbed night owing to frequent firing	
Oct 28.	Morning to CROIX DU BAC to see CRE and afternoon to 16 I.B re work - Parade as usual at 5 pm and continue shelters and entanglement.	

(9 26 6) W 257—976 100,000 4/12 H W V 79/3298

Instructions regarding War Diaries and Intelligence Summaries are contained in F. S. Regs., Part II. and the Staff Manual respectively. Title pages will be prepared in manuscript.

WAR DIARY ~~or~~ ~~INTELLIGENCE~~ SUMMARY

(*Erase heading not required.*)

of 12 Field Company

Army Form C. 2118.

Hour, Date, Place	Summary of Events and Information	Remarks and References to Appendices
FLEURBAIX. Oct 29.	Visit 18 I.B. re work and in evening one section to put up wire entanglement in front of N. Staffordshire at RUE DU BOIS and one section complete entanglement along the front of 16th I.B.	
Oct 30.	Morning to SAILLY to see how horses are (as our three bridging wagons are there under Bridging Train – Later to 18 I.B. where I meet CRE discuss tonight work – visit 18 I.B. trenches to ask what is wanted	
RUE DU BOIS	Evening make entanglement in front of D.L.I. Trenches at RUE DU BOIS	
	A.B. Sargeaunt Major RE OC 12 F. Co.	

(9 26 6) W 257—976 100,000 4/12 H W V 79/3298

Army Form C. 2118.

Instructions regarding War Diaries and Intelligence Summaries are contained in F. S. Regs., Part II. and the Staff Manual respectively. Title pages will be prepared in manuscript.

WAR DIARY ~~or~~ ~~INTELLIGENCE SUMMARY~~ 1/12th Field Company

(*Erase heading not required.*)

Hour, Date, Place	Summary of Events and Information	Remarks and References to Appendices
Oct 31. 9 am FLEURBAIX	Orders for 2 sections to 17th and 18th Brigades for defence of second line. See Brigadiers and set men to work preparing "sets" of barbed wire entanglement. Sections go out at 6 pm to erect entanglements. At 6.30 orders received for 2 sections to go to 16 Bde. Reply that all 4 sections out with 17 and 18 Bde. Asked to withdraw 1 section from 17 Bde and send to 16 Bde. As I am with 18 Bde and easier to withdraw one section from there, do so at 10 pm and send to 16 Bde where the Brigadier requires a gap to be completed with entanglement. In erecting entanglement it is found best to prepare everything before taking it on the ground. A set consists of 16 long pickets, 32 small pickets to which the stay wires are already fastened and wire in small coils to put 7 strands, viz 3 on uprights and 2 ~~along~~ each line of stays; this makes 75 yards of entanglement.	
Nov. 1.	1 section ordered to SAILLY in connection with approaches to bridges. 1 section to each 16 and 18 Bde. See Brigadiers about work but on return to billet at noon find that the orders for these latter 2 sections are cancelled and that the 3 sections are to be employed in entangling the front	

6th Divisional Engineers

12th FIELD COMPANY R. E.

NOVEMBER 1914.

For commencement of November 1st see October War Diary

Instructions regarding War Diaries and Intelligence Summaries are contained in F. S. Regs., Part II. and the Staff Manual respectively. Title pages will be prepared in manuscript.

WAR DIARY ~~or~~ ~~INTELLIGENCE SUMMARY~~ of 12th Field Company

(Erase heading not required.)

Army Form C. 2118.

Hour, Date, Place	Summary of Events and Information	Remarks and References to Appendices
Nov 1.	of a retired position (which passes east of FLEURBAIX and west of ARMENTIERES east of ERQUINGHAM). All men are employed in getting material ready and after 6 pm they erect 2000 yards of entanglement. In this line gaps of 20 yards are left in the ~~apron~~ fence and a low wire entanglement substituted over these lengths, the idea being that the enemy may make for these gaps which are always in front of a length of fire trench.	
Nov. 2. FLEURBAIX	The entanglement of the line from FLEURBAIX to the river LYS (north of ERQUINGHAM) is completed today. It is decided that the Field Companies shall take over the work on the retired line so far as the 6 Division is concerned relieving the 20 Co for work further in rear. This line is being prepared by R.E., Infantry working parties and civilian labour. A large farm in front of line near ERQUINGHAM will have to be demolished if the back line is occupied and it is estimated that 1100 lbs of guncotton will be required for this purpose	

(9 26 6) W 257—976 100,000 4/12 H W V 79/3298

Instructions regarding War Diaries and Intelligence Summaries are contained in F. S. Regs., Part II. and the Staff Manual respectively. Title pages will be prepared in manuscript.

WAR DIARY or ~~INTELLIGENCE~~ SUMMARY 1/12th Field Company

(*Erase heading not required.*)

Army Form C. 2118.

Hour, Date, Place	Summary of Events and Information	Remarks and References to Appendices
Nov. 3. FLEURBAIX.	O.C. 20 Co. RE reports at 6.30 am that he could not send spades yesterday as arranged so on arrival of civilians at 7 am I have to send them to fetch the spades. Consequently they do not get off to work till 9 am	
7.30 am	Go out to arrange work for N. Staffordshire parties - put them on at 8 am to digging communication trenches and trenches for supports.	
	The 12 Co. constructs shelters, clears foreground etc	
Nov. 4. FLEURBAIX	Continue work with sappers, infantry, and civilians on the retired line. Infantry on communication trenches, civilians on making continuous line of fire trenches, and sappers on shelters etc.	
Nov. 5. FLEURBAIX	Continue work as yesterday. At 2.30 Shrapnel shells burst near our billets, drivers get under cover and on cessation of fire 3 horses are found to be hit one of which dies	
Nov. 6 FLEURBAIX	Continue work as yesterday. Move billets to farm on RUE DELPAS ½ m South of E in ERQUINGHAM.	
Nov. 7.	Continue work as yesterday.	
Nov. 8.	Continue work on retired line.	

(9 26 6) W 257—976 100,000 4/12 H W V 79/3298

Instructions regarding War Diaries and Intelligence Summaries are contained in F. S. Regs., Part II. and the Staff Manual respectively. Title pages will be prepared in manuscript.

WAR DIARY ~~or~~ 1/12 Field Company

INTELLIGENCE ~~SUMMARY~~

(Erase heading not required.)

Army Form C. 2118.

Hour, Date, Place	Summary of Events and Information	Remarks and References to Appendices
Nov. 9.	Continue work on retired line - Prepare wire entanglements and go out after dusk to put up in front of trenches on line in front of BOIS-GRENIER	
Nov. 10.	Continue work on retired line - prepare wire entanglement and put up after dusk	
Nov. 11.	As yesterday	
Nov. 12.	Civilians employed on retired line - Sappers prepare low wire entanglement by day and erect after dusk. One section to BUFFS TRENCHES after dusk to renew entanglement - One section on roads at CROIX DU BAC. A few men employed in making experimental grenades to fire from rifle. Co paraded as Lord Roberts passes billets.	
Nov. 13.	Personally to MEERUT Division to see experimental mortar. Civilians and Queens Westminsters employed on retired line. One section at CROIX DU BAC - one section preparing wire entanglement for BOIS GRENIER line which is put up at night. 2 sections prepare timber and to 16' I.B. tonight to erect shelters.	

Instructions regarding War Diaries and Intelligence Summaries are contained in F. S. Regs., Part II. and the Staff Manual respectively. Title pages will be prepared in manuscript.

WAR DIARY or ~~INTELLIGENCE~~ SUMMARY

1/12 Field Company

(*Erase heading not required.*)

Army Form C. 2118.

Hour, Date, Place	Summary of Events and Information	Remarks and References to Appendices
Nov. 13.	Lieut Turner with CSM and 6 men and explosives to blow gap in railway 100x in front of our lines near PORT EGALE FERME	
Nov. 14.	Civilians collecting brushwood for fascines. Queens Westminsters have one company digging communication trenches near ERQUINGHAM. Try 2 experimental rifle grenades which fail to explode; only propelled 60 yards. Send to ESTAIRES for timber. RE preparing sets for wire entanglement. See B.G. 16 I.B. re requirements.	
Nov. 15.	Queen Westminsters making fascines. Send to ESTAIRES for more timber for shelters etc.	
Nov. 16.	Finish shelters and entanglement round farm of retired line at ERQUINGHAM - making fascines - civilians cutting brushwood	
Nov. 17.	Civilians cutting brushwood - sappers making fascines - at 2.30 No1 Section to 16 I.B. with 2' fascines for communication trench. Make small trestles for same with longitudinal runners on which to place transverse fascines but this gives too little cover so place fascines on floor of trench. A rifle grenade is satisfactorily fired today; it flew 200 yards and exploded, in plough	

Instructions regarding War Diaries and Intelligence Summaries are contained in F. S. Regs., Part II. and the Staff Manual respectively. Title pages will be prepared in manuscript.

Army Form C. 2118.

WAR DIARY ~~or INTELLIGENCE SUMMARY~~ of 12 Field Company

(Erase heading not required.)

Hour, Date, Place	Summary of Events and Information	Remarks and References to Appendices
Nov 17. (cont.)	Obtain truck at ARMENTIERES Station for 18 I.B. to run to and fro to RUE DU BOIS with rations etc. A message comes during afternoon to say line is broken and truck cannot be taken along line so party under 2Lt Playfair is sent to repair the line, which necessitates putting in two new lengths of rails	
Nov. 18.	Sappers making fascines and to ARMENTIERES to make iron loop hole plates. No 2 Section at dusk to improve communication trench to BUFFS with short transverse fascines on longitudinal planking. Civilians on night digging for 16 I.B.	
Nov. 19.	Collecting brushwood and making fascines. A wooden gun bound with wire is effectively fired. Making iron loop holes at ARMENTIERES. No 1 Section on pontoon bridges over dykes. We were to have put up trip wires in front of 16 I.B. trenches but owing to snow on ground the B.G. thinks it too light for such work	
Nov. 20.	Making and laying fascines in 16 I.B. trenches. Continuing experiments with wooden mortar and rifle grenade	

Instructions regarding War Diaries and Intelligence Summaries are contained in F. S. Regs., Part II. and the Staff Manual respectively. Title pages will be prepared in manuscript.

WAR DIARY
~~or~~
~~INTELLIGENCE SUMMARY~~

(*Erase heading not required.*)

12th Field Company.

Army Form C. 2118.

Hour, Date, Place	Summary of Events and Information	Remarks and References to Appendices
Nov 21 to Nov 24	Continue making and laying fascines. Experiments with wooden mortar and hand grenades. Altering advanced trench near FLAMINGERIE FARM by night. Mining in advanced trench of D.L.I. towards Germans.	
Nov. 25.	Making fascines for 16 and 18 I.B. Laying fascines for 16 I.B. Making up charges to put in advanced trench of Leicestershire Regt in case Germans take it. Mining continued in D.L.I. advanced trench	
Nov. 26.	Have some successful experiments in discharging rifle grenades (which burst on impact) and some bombs from a wooden wire bound mortar; these bombs burst by time fuse. Div. C.R.A. and C.R.E. watch the experiments. A large demand for fascines	
Nov. 27.	Making chevaux de frise of barbed wire to throw over parapet as entanglement. Send section to TOUQUET to fix machine gun shield and improve trenches. With Capt Grove to RUE DU BOIS where galleries are being run towards Germans – right gallery 28', left gallery 43' long German trench 43' distant	

Instructions regarding War Diaries and Intelligence Summaries are contained in F. S. Regs., Part II. and the Staff Manual respectively. Title pages will be prepared in manuscript.

WAR DIARY

or

~~INTELLIGENCE SUMMARY~~

(*Erase heading not required.*)

1/12' Field Company

Army Form C. 2118.

Hour, Date, Place	Summary of Events and Information	Remarks and References to Appendices
Nov. 28 -	Charges placed in advanced trench near FLAMINGERIE FARM to blow up if occupied by enemy. Experiments in cutting barbed wire entanglement by machine gun fire at 3rd G Bde - not a practical method. Make up some grenades in jam tins (illd) but these can be only thrown 20 yards. Continue making, distributing and laying fascines - Railway line in front of RUE DU BOIS blown up this evening by Lt. Turner with a few men.	
Nov. 29.	Making up parapets and forming firing steps for 16 I.B. Enemy have strong wire entanglement in front of their trenches opposite the 16 I.B. Collecting brushwood and making fascines	
	A.T. Sargeaunt — Major RE OC 1/2 F Co 30/11/14	

6th Divisional Engineers

12th FIELD COMPANY R. E.

DECEMBER 1914.

Instructions regarding War Diaries and Intelligence Summaries are contained in F. S. Regs., Part II. and the Staff Manual respectively. Title pages will be prepared in manuscript.

WAR DIARY or ~~INTELLIGENCE SUMMARY~~

1/12 Fd Co.

(*Erase heading not required.*)

Army Form C. 2118.

Hour, Date, Place	Summary of Events and Information	Remarks and References to Appendices
Nov 30.	1 Section constructing bridge over river Lys near BRASSERIE - BAC ST MAUR of trestles to replace pontoon bridge - 5 spans - 1 section to DESPLANQUES FARM to make chevaux de frise of barbed wire - others making fascines - 1 section afternoon to 16 IB for work in fire trenches. Party to RUE DU BOIS for clearing empty houses between the two lines - Making hand barrows and parapets for 16 IB.	
Dec 1st	1 Section making chevaux de frise at RUE DU BOIS 1 section on trestle bridge. 2 sections on fascines.	
Dec 2nd	H.M. The King's visit. Making and cutting up fascines	
Dec 3rd	Mining continues at RUE DU BOIS - Improving fire trenches of 16 IB - Part of these trenches flooded with water, investigate this and conclude that small dam has burst in enemy's lines and so partly filled ditches which cross our lines. Making hand barrows, hand grenades with jam pots, arm racks for trenches, fascines etc. At night take party to make bridges in trenches across the ditches to carry parapets and foot ways.	

Instructions regarding War Diaries and Intelligence Summaries are contained in F. S. Regs., Part II. and the Staff Manual respectively. Title pages will be prepared in manuscript.

WAR DIARY or ~~INTELLIGENCE SUMMARY~~ 1/12 Field Co

(*Erase heading not required.*)

Army Form C. 2118.

Hour, Date, Place	Summary of Events and Information	Remarks and References to Appendices
Dec 4.	2 sections move to farm N.W by N of BOIS GRENIER to be nearer their work and to continue work in trenches. Turning out hundreds of fascines daily and distributing to 16 and 18 I.B. Making arm racks, hand grenades, hand barrows and fascines.	
Dec 5.	2 sections in 16 I.B. trenches, 1 section at DESPLANQUES FARM making chevaux de frize, remainder hand grenades, hand barrows and fascines. Party of civilians at night deepening ditch in front of CULVERT FARM.	
Dec 6.	2 sections in 16 I.B. trenches - 2 sections making fascines hand barrows - hand bombs, arm racks etc. Party in evening to RUE DU BOIS to blow up ruined house near enemy's line but party is fired on and the intention is given up as not worth ~~the~~ candle	
Dec 7.	2 sections 16 I.B. trenches - Remainder making fascines, arm racks, hand bombs etc - Evening party to RUE DU BOIS to fell 10 large trees which interfere with Artillery Fire	
Dec 8.	2 sections 16 I.B. trenches - others making fascines, hand bombs, Marmis hand grenades arm racks etc. As much water	

Instructions regarding War Diaries and Intelligence Summaries are contained in F. S. Regs., Part II. and the Staff Manual respectively. Title pages will be prepared in manuscript.

WAR DIARY ~~or INTELLIGENCE SUMMARY~~ 1/2 Field Company

(*Erase heading not required.*)

Army Form C. 2118.

Hour, Date, Place	Summary of Events and Information	Remarks and References to Appendices
Dec 8	in trenches other 2 sections to CULVERT FARM in evening to deepen ditches. Water flowing back along ditches from Enemys lines through our lines - necessary to make bridges over ditches and make culverts to carry parapets on enemy's side of communication trench	
Dec ~~Oct~~ 9	TO RUE DU BOIS - decision made to give up forward trench. 2 sections 16 I.B. trenches - Remainder making fascines rifle rests for rifle grenade throwing, hand bombs of jam tins, arm racks etc.	
Dec 10.	2 sections in 16 I.B. trenches dealing with water, and improving fire trenches - one section to RUE DU BOIS to improve wet trenches - remainder making fascines, periscopes, arm-racks, stands for firing rifle grenades etc one section at 9 pm to RUE DU BOIS to make new fire trench by sapping, which is to take the place of the forward trench.	
Dec. 11.	2 sections in 16 I.B. trenches - one section at RUE DU BOIS. Remainder making fascines, arm. racks etc	

Instructions regarding War Diaries and Intelligence Summaries are contained in F. S. Regs., Part II. and the Staff Manual respectively. Title pages will be prepared in manuscript.

Army Form C. 2[illegible]18.

WAR DIARY ~~or~~ ~~INTELLIGENCE SUMMARY~~ of 12 Field Company

(*Erase heading not required.*)

Hour, Date, Place	Summary of Events and Information	Remarks and References to Appendices
Dec. 12.	2 Sections 16 I.B. trenches – 1 Section RUE DU BOIS – Remainder making fascines, periscopes arm-racks etc. A large demand daily from units for plain wire, sand bags, fascines and timber. When stationary as we are now a Field Co requires a store-keeper who can purchase and issue materials; last month there were over 70 bills in my imprest account.	
Dec. 13.	Arrangements made for the company to have baths today. Party at work sapping new trench RUE DU BOIS.	
Dec. 14.	2 Sections to 16 I.B. trenches – party at RUE DU BOIS and party with Queens Westminsters – Remainder making fascines, arm-racks, periscopes hand grenades etc.	
Dec. 15.	2 Sections 16 I.B. trenches (billeting BOIS GRENIER) – party with Queens Westminsters (billeting CHAPELLE D'ARMENTIERES) Remainder making fascines, periscopes, arm-racks, and wooden gratings for placing in trenches.	
Dec. 16.	Gallery at RUE DU BOIS fallen in and water in it – suggest this be given up as since it was decided to give up the enemy's trench as the objective it has no practical use	

(9 26 6) W 257—976 100,000 4/12 H W V 79/3298

Instructions regarding War Diaries and Intelligence Summaries are contained in F. S. Regs., Part II. and the Staff Manual respectively. Title pages will be prepared in manuscript.

Army Form C. [illegible]8.

WAR DIARY ~~or~~ ~~INTELLIGENCE SUMMARY~~

1/2 Field Company

(*Erase heading not required.*)

Hour, Date, Place	Summary of Events and Information	Remarks and References to Appendices
Dec 16.	2 Sections 16 I.B. trenches dealing with water and improving fire trenches - party with Queens Westminsters, Remainder making fascines, wooden gratings for trenches, arm racks etc.	
Dec 17.	2 Sections 16 I.B. trenches making bridges over ditches, improving parapets etc - party with R. Fusiliers - Remainder making fascines, hand grenades, arm racks etc.	
Dec. 18.	2 Sections 16 I.B. trenches - 1 section R.7. 1 section making fascines, arm racks, periscopes etc	
Dec 19.	2 Sections 16 I.B. - 1 section R.7. 1 section making fascines, hand grenades, arm racks, dug-outs.	
Dec 20.	2 Sections 16 I.B. working in trenches and dealing with water 1 Section R.7. clearing streams and making temporary bridges. 1 Section making dug-outs, hand grenades, arm racks etc	
Dec 21 - Dec 24	2 Sections 16 I.B. - 1 section R.7. 1 Section making trench platforms, dug-outs etc	
Dec 26 - Dec 28	1 Section 16 I.B. trenches - remainder making fascines, hurdles dug-outs hand grenades platform etc 1st London Co take over 16 I.B. and 12 F1 Co take over 17 I.B. line	

Instructions regarding War Diaries and Intelligence Summaries are contained in F. S. Regs., Part II. and the Staff Manual respectively. Title pages will be prepared in manuscript.

WAR DIARY ~~or~~ ~~INTELLIGENCE SUMMARY~~ of 12th Field Company

(*Erase heading not required.*)

Army Form C. 2118.

Hour, Date, Place	Summary of Events and Information	Remarks and References to Appendices
Dec 29 - 30.	Preparing materials for breastwork which is to be put up behind existing trenches owing to water continually rising in trenches - Also making platforms, dug outs grenades etc - Put up 100' of hurdles and dug outs behind left Bn of 17th I.B. - Infantry finding carrying party and diggers. Party clearing stream behind right and centre Bns	
Dec 31.	Continue preparing materials for breastwork - dug outs grenades, platforms - etc.	

31/12/14

A. G. Sargeaunt
Major RE
OC 12 FD Co

6th Dir

R. E.

No. 12. Field Coy

Jan - Dec 1915.

Index..............................

SUBJECT.

No.	Contents.	Date.
	8/ Yorks Rt July - Oct, 1916	

(63,965). Wt.15,820—176. 2000. 9/21. Gp.164. A.&E.W.

6th Division 121/4262

12th Field Coy RE.

Vol VI. 1 — 31.1.15.

Instructions regarding War Diaries and Intelligence Summaries are contained in F.S. Regs., Part II. and the Staff Manual respectively. Title pages will be prepared in manuscript.

WAR DIARY or INTELLIGENCE SUMMARY.

(Erase heading not required.)

12th Co R.E.

Army Form C. 2118.

Hour, Date, Place	Summary of Events and Information	Remarks and references to Appendices
1915 Jan 1st	Company moved to new billet at ASYLUM of ARMENTIERES, leaving one section behind in old billet to load & send on stores. 2 sections at night to 17th I.B. erecting 100x revetment with shelters for centre battalion. Transfer of stores from old billet proceeded throughout day.	
Jan 2nd	Transfer of stores from late billet & preparation of material for breastworks. One section by night to centre battalion 17th I.B. improving shelters in breastwork	
Jan 3rd	Transfer of stores completed. Section left behind rejoined company after dinners. Preparing material for breastworks. Party at night to left battalion 17th I.B. to demolish ruined house in front of line.	
Jan 4th	Preparing material for breastworks. Erecting 150x revetment with shelters for centre battalion 17th I.B. at night.	
Jan 5th	Preparing materials for breastworks.	
Jan 6th	Erecting revetment for breast-works at RUE DU BOIS, for right battalion of 17th I.B.	

(9 26 6) W 257—976 100,000 4/12 H W V 79/3298

Instructions regarding War Diaries and Intelligence Summaries are contained in F. S. Regs., Part II. and the Staff Manual respectively. Title pages will be prepared in manuscript.

WAR DIARY

~~or~~

~~INTELLIGENCE SUMMARY~~.

(*Erase heading not required.*)

Army Form C. 2118.

Hour, Date, Place	Summary of Events and Information	Remarks and references to Appendices
1915 Jan 7th + 8th	Continued preparation of materials for breastworks + erection of revetment for right battalion of 17th I.B. at RUE DU BOIS.	
Jan 9th	16th Inf: Bde was to have taken over right + centre sections of 17th I.B front i.e from Rly at RUE DU BOIS to LILLE - BOULOGNE road, 17th I.B. relieving the right battalion of the brigade on its left. LEINSTERS reported trenches at RUE DU BOIS untenable on account of water. 16th I.B. obtained permission of Div. H.Q. to postpone taking over this section till next night. 17th I.B. asked for Company to complete breastwork at RUE DU BOIS. 3 sections to that place to erect more revetment + to build sand-bags to raise breastwork already constructed to a height of 4'6".	
Jan 10th	Preparing revetment materials + shelters for dug-outs. Order received from the C.R.E. for company to work for both 16th + 17th I.B's increasing front to be served by company by one battalion. Party at night to RUE DU BOIS erecting shelters behind breastwork.	
Jan 11th	Preparing materials by day. Two sections to rt battalion 17th I.B. at night erecting 60x revetment with shelters (new pattern built into	

(9 26 6) W 257—976 100,000 4/12 H W V 79/3298

Instructions regarding War Diaries and Intelligence Summaries are contained in F. S. Regs., Part II. and the Staff Manual respectively. Title pages will be prepared in manuscript.

WAR DIARY

~~or~~

~~INTELLIGENCE SUMMARY.~~

(Erase heading not required.)

Army Form C. 2118.

Hour, Date, Place	Summary of Events and Information	Remarks and references to Appendices
Jan 11th (contd)	parapet & roofed with corrugated iron.	
Jan 12th	Preparing materials. One section at night to 16th I.B. erecting old pattern shelters behind breastwork at RUE DU BOIS.	
Jan 13th	Preparing materials. One section at night to 16th I.B. erecting 80x revetment with new pattern shelters to join right & left battalions. One section at night to 17th I.B. to put together under cover shelters for breastwork to be built behind left battalion.	
Jan 14th	Preparing materials. One section to 16th I.B at night constructing bridges to carry breastwork across two water-ways at RUE DU BOIS. One section to 17th I.B. at night erecting 60x revetment with shelters.	
Jan 15th	Preparing materials. One section at night to 16th I.B. erecting 50 yards revetment with shelters in support of rt battalion at RUE DU BOIS.	
Jan 16th	Preparing materials for breastworks & trenches.	
Jan 17th	One section to RUE DU BOIS by day to erect shelters in breast=works. One section each to 16th & 17th I.B's at night erecting 60x	

Instructions regarding War Diaries and Intelligence Summaries are contained in F. S. Regs., Part II. and the Staff Manual respectively. Title pages will be prepared in manuscript.

WAR DIARY

~~or~~

~~INTELLIGENCE SUMMARY.~~

(Erase heading not required.)

Army Form C. 2118.

Hour, Date, Place	Summary of Events and Information	Remarks and references to Appendices
Jan 17th (contd)	revetment + shelters for breastworks in each.	
Jan 18th	Section to 17th I.B. at night erecting revetment + shelters for 36x breastwork. Section to 16th I.B. making bridge over stream + felling trees at RUE DU BOIS.	
Jan 19th	36x breastwork for 17th + 80x breastwork for 16th I.B's.	
Jan 20th	Erecting shelters at RUE DU BOIS by day. 36x breastwork for 17th + 100x for 16th I.B's by night.	
Jan 21st	36x breastwork for 17th + 100x for 16th I.B's	
Jan 22nd	36x breastwork each for 16th + 17th I.B's.	
Jan 23rd	60x breastwork for 16th I.B. by night. One section at night to 17th I.B. left battalion constructing barrel pier bridge across moat of PORT EGALE farm. Commenced work with civilian labour on retired line; Erected 50x revetment with shelters + commenced digging. Began building sandbag barrier at PORT EGALE level crossing.	
Jan 24th	Company allowed day's rest. Civilians erected 50x on retired line + continued digging.	
Jan 25th	36x for 17th I.B, 90x for 16th I.B. + 50x by civil labour in retired line.	

(9 26 6) W 257—976 100,000 4/12 H W V 79/3298

Army Form C. 2118.

Instructions regarding War Diaries and Intelligence Summaries are contained in F.S. Regs., Part II. and the Staff Manual respectively. Title pages will be prepared in manuscript.

WAR DIARY

~~INTELLIGENCE SUMMARY~~.

(Erase heading not required.)

Hour, Date, Place	Summary of Events and Information	Remarks and references to Appendices
1915 Jan 26th	Section at night to 16th I.B. erecting 100x revetment with dug-outs. One section to 17th I.B. erecting 36x breastwork + continuing building of PORT EGAZE level crossing barrier. Civilians erected 30x in retired line + continued digging.	
Jan 27th	Section to 16th I.B. putting up revetment. One section to 17th I.B. erecting 36x breastwork, completing Rly barrier + putting in shelters. Civilians on retired line erecting 50x + digging.	
Jan 25th	Party under officer to BOIS GRENIER in morning to loophole buildings. Section to 16th I.B. at night erecting 50x breastwork for support to left battalion. 36x for 17th I.B. Civilians erecting 50x + digging.	
Jan 29th	Party to BOIS GRENIER loopholing buildings. Revetting sup=porting line for rt battalion 16th I.B. Section erecting 36x for right battalion 17th I.B. Civilians work as usual – erected 50x new revetment. Went out in evening with B.G.C. 17th I.B. selecting supporting points.	
Jan 30th	Party to BOIS GRENIER to continue loopholing. One officer in morning to 19th I.B. to advise as to defence of localities. One section to RUE DU BOIS in morning putting up revetment. Section to left company 16th I.B at night to put in shelters in trench; one to	

(9 26 6) W 257—976 100,000 4/12 H W V 79/3298

Instructions regarding War Diaries and Intelligence Summaries are contained in F. S. Regs., Part II. and the Staff Manual respectively. Title pages will be prepared in manuscript.

WAR DIARY

~~or~~

~~INTELLIGENCE SUMMARY~~.

(Erase heading not required.)

Army Form C. 2118.

Hour, Date, Place	Summary of Events and Information	Remarks and references to Appendices
30th Jan (contd)	17th I.B. erecting 36" breastwork. Officer with B.G.C. 17th I.B. in evening reconnoitring & selecting supporting points. Civilians on back line as usual – 50x new revetment erected.	
31st Jan.	One section by day & one by night in left company's trenches of 16th I.B. improving + remodelling trench. Remainder of company had a day's rest.	
	31st Jan 1915. [signature] Capt R.E. O.C. 12th Co R.E.	

(9 26 6) W 257—976 100,000 4/12 H W V 79/3298

a99
b710
MT.2

6th Division

121/4505

12th Field Coy: RE

Vol VII. 1–28.2.15

Instructions regarding War Diaries and Intelligence Summaries are contained in F. S. Regs., Part II. and the Staff Manual respectively. Title pages will be prepared in manuscript.

WAR DIARY

~~or~~

~~INTELLIGENCE SUMMARY~~.

(*Erase heading not required.*)

Army Form C. 2118.

17th Fd Co RE

Hour, Date, Place	Summary of Events and Information	Remarks and references to Appendices
1915 1st Feb.	Preparing material for issue to Bdes. One section by night to left company 16th I.B. remodelling trench & putting in dug-outs. One section to rt. Bn: 17th I.B. erecting 36" revetment & shelters for breastwork. Civilian labour erecting 50" revetment & shelters on retired line & digging breastwork. Party to BOIS GRENIER preparing houses for defence.	
2nd Feb.	Party to BOIS GRENIER preparing houses. [One section at night to 16th I.B. continuing work on left trench. One section to 17th I.B. preparing rubbish heap as supporting point.] Civilians on retired line erecting fresh revetment & digging on old. Working party from Div Mtd. Troops also employed on retired line. One civilian killed working on retired line.	
3rd Feb.	Continued work on BOIS GRENIER locality by day & on 16th I.B. left trench & 17th I.B. rubbish heap by night. One officer to artillery observing stations to report on measures for making them splinter-proof.	
~~4th Feb.~~	~~Continued work on BOIS GRENIER. One section at night to 16th I.B.~~ Billets shelled about 5.0 p.m., seven men wounded, two severely, and one building set on fire.	
4th Feb.	Continued work on BOIS GRENIER. Section to 16th I.B. at night completing work on left trench & one party to RUE DU BOIS putting up	

Instructions regarding War Diaries and Intelligence Summaries are contained in F.S. Regs., Part II. and the Staff Manual respectively. Title pages will be prepared in manuscript.

WAR DIARY
or
INTELLIGENCE SUMMARY.
(Erase heading not required.)

Army Form C. 2118.

17th Fd Co RE

Hour, Date, Place	Summary of Events and Information	Remarks and references to Appendices
	revetment + dug-outs on supporting line. One section to 17th I.B. putting up revetment of supporting work between rubbish-heap and railway. Party to Observing Station of Bty improving protection.	
5th Feb:	Work on BOIS GRENIER continued. One section to RUE DU BOIS putting up revetments and replacing dug-outs destroyed by shell fire. One section to 17th I.B. putting up revetment of supporting point.	
6th Feb.	Work on BOIS GRENIER continued. One section at night to left battalion 16th I.B. to improve a length of trench + build in shelters. One to 17th I.B. erecting 36" revetment + shelters for breast-work on left of right battalion. Civilians + cavalry employed on retired line.	
8 Feb.	Sappers and civilians employed on preparing revetments shelters etc. Party at BOIS GRENIER. At night one section to 16 IB and one to 17 IB erecting breastworks. Civilians and cavalry on 2nd line.	
9th Feb	Same work as yesterday.	
10 Feb	Similar work to yesterday	
11th Feb.	Sappers and civilians preparing materials for front line. Party at defended post on LILLE ROAD and partly reclaiming communication trench from Cemetery to Right Bn.	

Instructions regarding War Diaries and Intelligence Summaries are contained in F. S. Regs., Part II. and the Staff Manual respectively. Title pages will be prepared in manuscript.

WAR DIARY
or
~~INTELLIGENCE~~ SUMMARY. / 12 Fd Co

(Erase heading not required.)

Army Form C. 2118.

17th Fd Co RE

Hour, Date, Place	Summary of Events and Information	Remarks and references to Appendices
11th Cont ARMENTIERES	At night civilians and cavalry on second line - one section to 16 IB to make bridge and erect parapet for communication on left of B1C - one section to 17 IB to erect breastwork and prepare Haystack Farm for defence	
12 Feb	Sappers and civilians preparing materials - At night civilians and cavalry on 2 line. One section to 16 IB to put up revetment and shelters to left of Railway and prepare for barricade on road (RUE DU BOIS) - one section to 17 IB to reclaim communication trench by putting trestles and pathway	
13 Feb	Sappers and civilians preparing materials - party on cemetery communication trench - Civilians and cavalry on 2 line by night	
14th Feb	Work by day as usual - At night 1 section to 16 IB to put up revetment behind left trench; 2 sections to 17 IB to reclaim communication trench from Haystack Farm - Lt Hanna wounded	
15 Feb	Work by day as usual. At night cavalry and civilians on 2 line but latter knock off after 1½ hours owing to heavy rain - 1 section to 16 IB to complete revetment behind left trench and to construct bridge over stream - 1 section to 17 IB on communication trench	

(9 26 6) W 257—976 100,000 4/12 H W V 79/3298

Instructions regarding War Diaries and Intelligence Summaries are contained in F. S. Regs., Part II. and the Staff Manual respectively. Title pages will be prepared in manuscript.

WAR DIARY
or
~~INTELLIGENCE SUMMARY.~~
(Erase heading not required.)

12 Field Company

Army Form C. 2118.

12th Fd Co RE

Hour, Date, Place	Summary of Events and Information	Remarks and references to Appendices
Feb 16. ARMENTIERES	Sappers and civilians working by day in making up material. Night – 1 section constructing barricade RUE DU BOIS and flooring dug-outs. 80 Cavalry and civilians on 2 line breastworks	
Feb 17.	Sappers and civilians by day on making up material. At night 1 section with 17 IB in left trenches of left Bn, 1 section to 16 IB to erect revetments, make barricades etc, cavalry and civilians on 2 line breastworks	
Feb 18.	Sappers and civilians by day as usual, N.C.O. instructing Canadian N.C.O. in Field works. At night one section in 17 IB trenches, 1 section to 16 IB to make bridges and erect revetments, 1 officer and 4 N.C.Os superintending Canadian working parties for 17 IB; cavalry and civilians on 2 line breastworks	
Feb 19.	Sappers and civilians by day as usual. Night 1 section to 17 IB left trenches of left Bn and 1 section in trenches of right Bn 16 IB. 3 officers R.C.E. report and accompany sections working in trenches – cavalry & civilians on 2 line	
Feb 20	Sappers and civilians by day making up material – 3 officers R.C.E. leave this afternoon. Night 1 section in 17 IB trenches and 1 section to 16 IB to repair damage done by shell fire and erecting revetments. cavalry & civilians on 2 line	
Feb 21.	Preparing material by day. Cavalry at night on 2 line	
Feb 22.	Sappers and civilians by day as usual – party improving 17 IB communication trench. Night 1 section 17 IB in left trenches of right Bn, 1 section adding to revetment and putting ruined house in state of defence; cavalry & civilians on 2 line	
Feb 23	Sappers & civilians by day making hurdles, footboards, dug outs, peep hole plates etc. Night 1 section 17 IB trenches right Bn revetting, flooring and generally improving – 1 section 16 IB putting up revetment and preparing demolished house for defence. Cavalry and civilians on 2 line	
Feb 24	Sappers and civilians by day as usual, assisting Canadian Infantry etc. Night 1 section 17 IB trenches, 1 section 16 IB putting shelters in fire trench and preparing demolished house for defence. N.C.Os superintending 17 IB digging parties. Cavalry and civilians on 2 line	

Instructions regarding War Diaries and Intelligence Summaries are contained in F. S. Regs., Part II. and the Staff Manual respectively. Title pages will be prepared in manuscript.

WAR DIARY
or
INTELLIGENCE SUMMARY.
(Erase heading not required.)

12 Field Company

Army Form C. 2118.

17th Fd Co RE

Hour, Date, Place	Summary of Events and Information	Remarks and references to Appendices
ARMENTIERES Feb 25.	Sappers and civilians by day making brushwood hurdles, dug-outs, foot boards, pig hole plates machine gun stands jam-pot grenades etc. By night parties of cavalry infantry and civilians on 2nd line. One section with 16 IB preparing house for defence and erecting scaffolding and plates for snipers rest. One section with 17 IB improving trenches of left Coy Rt Bn	
Feb 26	By day sappers and civilians making up materials - company Canadians instructed in Field Works. By night 1 section 17 IB trenches, 1 section 16 IB preparing demolished house for defence - Cavalry, infantry, civilians on 2 line	
Feb 27	By day sappers and civilians making up materials - one company Canadians instructed in Field Works. By night Infantry, cavalry, civilians on 2 line - one section in 17 IB lines putting up revetments and improving trenches - one section 16 IB paving communication trench near Railway Barrier and preparing demolished house for defence	
Feb 28	Instructing parties of Infantry in Field Works. By night cavalry, infantry and civilian working parties	

A. F. Sargeaunt
Major RE
OC 12 Fd Co

1/3/15

6th Division

12th Field Company RE.

Vol VIII 1-29.3.15

Instructions regarding War Diaries and Intelligence Summaries are contained in F. S. Regs., Part II. and the Staff Manual respectively. Title pages will be prepared in manuscript.

WAR DIARY or ~~INTELLIGENCE SUMMARY~~. of 12 F. Co

(Erase heading not required.)

Army Form C. 2118.

Hour, Date, Place	Summary of Events and Information	Remarks and references to Appendices
March 1st 1915 ARMENTIERES	By day sappers and civilians making fascines, hurdles, footboards, dug-outs, peep hole plates etc. By night No 2 Section putting up traverses for 16 IB at left Coy of Left Bn and preparing house for defence. No 4 Section putting up parados for breastwork behind left Co. of Rt Bn. 17 IB. Cavalry, infantry and civilians employed on second line	
March 2nd	By day sappers and civilians making up materials. At night No 3 Section strengthening house and putting up shelters against shell fire at RUE DU BOIS for 16 IB. No 4 Section erecting parados for breastwork at left Co of Rt Bn 17 IB. No 1 and No 2 Section each 300x entanglement on 2 line. Cavalry, infantry and civilians on 2 line	
March 3	By day sappers and civilians making hurdles, dug outs, footboards, machine gun hatches, peepholes etc. By night No 2 Section commence reclaiming communication trench from FERME DU BIE. No 4 Section improving trenches of left Co. Rt. Bn 17 IB. No 1 and No 3 Sections digging on 2 line. Cavalry, Infantry and civilians on 2 line	
March 4	By day sappers and civilians making up materials. By night No 1 Section FERME DU BIE communication trench and extending shelter in house at RUE DU BOIS. No 3 section improving trenches of Lt Co Rt Bn 17 IB and bridging ditches. Infantry, cavalry and civilians on 2 line.	
March 5	By day sappers and civilians making up materials. By night No 4 Section putting up parados in 17 IB lines. No 2 Section improving communications left 16 IB line. Infantry, cavalry and civilians on 2 line	
March 6	By day sappers and civilians making up materials. By night No 1 Section on 16 IB left communication trench. No 3 Section with 300 Infantry making new communication trench from COUNTEMBU FARM. Cavalry, Infantry, and civilians on 2 line	

Instructions regarding War Diaries and Intelligence Summaries are contained in F. S. Regs., Part II. and the Staff Manual respectively. Title pages will be prepared in manuscript.

WAR DIARY or ~~INTELLIGENCE~~ SUMMARY. of 12 Field Co.

(*Erase heading not required.*)

Army Form C. 2118.

Hour, Date, Place		Summary of Events and Information	Remarks and references to Appendices
ARMENTIERES	March 7.	By day. civilians on 2 line. Lt Turner and 13 men No 1 Section to 16 IB lines for sapping and to live there.	
		By night No 2 Section on 16 IB left communication trench	
	March 8	By day. Civilians on 2 line. Sappers and civilians in shops and making up materials.	
		By night No 3 Section and 300 Infantry on QUATEMBU communication trench and putting up parados to breastwork in orchard for 17 IB. ½ No 1 Section on 16 IB left communication trench, No 4 Section RUE DU BOIS.	
	March 9	By day. Civilians on 2 line, sappers and civilians making up materials. No 4 Section improving communications 17 IB.	
		By night No 2 Section putting in shelters and traverses at 21 & 21 G 16 IB.	
		No 4 Section and 2 reliefs Infantry (300 each) on 17 IB communication trench	
	March 10.	By day. Civilians on 2 line. No 1 Section sapping in 16 IB lines and No 4 Section on 17 IB communication trench. CRE orders all sections to remain in tonight and all men to be recalled	
	March 11	Worked in morning as usual	
		During night took part with N Staffs in attack on L'EPINETTE. Paraded at 10pm and reported at 11 pm to O.C. N STAFFS at BARRIER on L'EPINETTE Road. Distributed company as follows:- Lt Turner and 10 men of No 1 Section with right assaulting column; the remainder of No 1 Section accompanied the working parties of right column. Lt Jackson and 10 men No 2 Section with left assaulting column; remainder of No 2 Section with working parties of left Column. No 3 Section followed Right Column to assist in consolidating new line. No 4 Section assisted in consolidating left of new line.	

(9 26 6) W 257—976 100,000 4/12 H W V $\frac{79}{3298}$

Instructions regarding War Diaries and Intelligence Summaries are contained in F. S. Regs., Part II. and the Staff Manual respectively. Title pages will be prepared in manuscript.

WAR DIARY
or
INTELLIGENCE SUMMARY. 1/12 Field Co

(Erase heading not required.)

Army Form C. 2118.

Hour, Date, Place		Summary of Events and Information	Remarks and references to Appendices
ARMENTIERES	March 11 (continued)	Capt Noble supervised working parties of 2 London Regt who worked on new line between BARRIER and L'EPINETTE. Both assaulting columns encountered barbed wire entanglement but this was not of a formidable nature and was successfully cut through. As soon as all buildings on new line had been occupied all sappers assisted in strengthening the houses and joining up between houses. The Co had 2 men wounded and 1 missing during the operations	Capture of L'Epinette
	March 12	All sections all night of 12/13 at L'EPINETTE, whole of new line wired, barricade built on road at No 5 house; shelters put in trenches, houses, trenches and communications improved.	
	March 13	Civilians by day on 2 line. During afternoon sappers prepare materials for night work By night. No 2 Section bridging gap on LILLE ROAD and damming ditch Remainder of company making splinter proof shelters in trenches at L'EPINETTE	
	March 15	By day. Civilians on 2 line sappers making up materials and No 3 Section on communication trench from COUNTEMBU. By night 4 sections at L'EPINETTE with Infantry working parties improving trenches and communications, putting in shelters, and wire entanglement.	
	March 16.	By day civilians on 2 line; sappers and civilians making up materials By night No 2 Section erecting 300^x wire entanglement in front of breastwork line to right of L'EPINETTE. No 1 Section improving communications and making bridge to right of L'EPINETTE.	

(9 26 6) W 257—976 100,000 4/12 H W V 79/3298

Instructions regarding War Diaries and Intelligence Summaries are contained in F. S. Regs., Part II. and the Staff Manual respectively. Title pages will be prepared in manuscript.

WAR DIARY
or
~~INTELLIGENCE~~ SUMMARY.
(Erase heading not required.)

12 Fd. Co

Army Form C. 2118.

Hour, Date, Place		Summary of Events and Information	Remarks and references to Appendices
ARMENTIERES	March 17.	By day Civilians on 2 line. No 4 Section on COUNTEMBU communication trench, sappers and civilians making up materials. By night No 3 Section at L'EPINETTE making communications across road and through houses, No 4 Section on COUNTEMBU communication trench	
	March 18	By day civilians on 2 line. No 1 Section erecting revetment for communication trench behind DU BIE Farm; remainder making up materials By night No 2 Section erecting revetment behind left trench 16 IB. No 4 Section improving COUNTEMBU communication trench.	
	March 19	By day Civilians on 2 line. No 1 Section erecting revetment for communication trench behind DU BIE FARM, No 2 Section lowering foot boards in same trench No 3 Section on COUNTEMBU communication trench By night No 2 Section erecting traverse to protect communication trench No 3 Section erecting bridges and blindages at L'EPINETTE.	
	March 20	Day civilians on 2 line. No 1 Section on FERME DU BIE communication trench. Night - No 1 Section communication trench and traverse No 3 Section at L'EPINETTE improving and making communication No 4 Sections on COUNTEMBU communication trench.	
	March 21	Civilians on 2 line. No 2 Section on FERME DU BIE communication trench. 1/1 N. Midland Fd Co report for work	
	March 22	Civilians on 2 line No 1 Section FERME DU BIE Night No 1 Section filling lines RUE DU BOIS - No 2 Section erecting revetment on left com trench 16 IB. No 3 Section wiring in front of WATERWHEEL HB No 4 Section COUNTEMBU com. trench	

Instructions regarding War Diaries and Intelligence Summaries are contained in F. S. Regs., Part II. and the Staff Manual respectively. Title pages will be prepared in manuscript.

WAR DIARY or ~~INTELLIGENCE SUMMARY.~~

(*Erase heading not required.*)

1/2 Fd. Co.

Army Form C. 2118.

Hour, Date, Place		Summary of Events and Information	Remarks and references to Appendices
ARMENTIERES.	March 23.	Civilians on 2 line. No 2 Section 16 DB com. trench. remaining sappers and civilians making up materials. Night No 1 section at RUE DU BOIS putting up splinter proof shelters No 4 Section at L'EPINETTE.	
	March 24	Civilians on 2 line. Nos 1 and 2 sections on DU BIE com.-trench. Night No 3 Section building sandbag breastworks at L'EPINETTE	
	March 25	Civilians on 2 line. No 2 Section on DU BIE com trench, remaining sappers and civilians making up materials and constructing 30' range. Night No 4 Section at WATERWHEEL FARM building breastworks and erecting splinter proof shelters. No 1 Section making 2 bridges over stream and putting up shelters at RUE DU BOIS.	
	March 26	No 2 Section DU BIE communication trench. Civilians on 2 line. Sappers and civilians making up materials Night No 3 Section at L'EPINETTE making parades for right flank and traverses	
	March 27.	No 2 Section com. trench and No 1 Section erecting parados FERME DU BIE. Civilians on 2 line Night No 1 Section erecting revetment to cover com. trench, No 4 Section L'EPINETTE loop holing wall, making breastwork behind wall and making shelters	
	March 29	Civilians on 2 line. No 2 Section DU BIE com. trench; remaining sappers and civilians making up materials Night No 1 Section erecting revetment to cover communication trench No 4 Section at L'EPINETTE making machine gun emplacement erecting shelters building traverses etc	

A F Sargeaunt Major RE
OC 1/2 Fd Co

31/3/15

(9 26 6) W 257—976 100,000 4/12 H W V 79/3298

6th Division

121/5195

12th Field Coy: R.E.

Vol IX 30.3 — 30.4.16

Instructions regarding War Diaries and Intelligence Summaries are contained in F. S. Regs., Part II. and the Staff Manual respectively. Title pages will be prepared in manuscript.

Army Form C. 2118.

WAR DIARY
or
~~INTELLIGENCE SUMMARY.~~
(Erase heading not required.)

1/12 Field Company

Hour, Date, Place	Summary of Events and Information	Remarks and references to Appendices
March 30. ARMENTIERES and March 31 to April 6	Sappers and civilians making up materials – footboards, dug-outs, box loopholes, peep-hole plates, chevaux de frise ~~etc~~, bridges, ladders etc. At night one section taking down trees behind 17 I.B., one section strengthening L'EPINETTE, one section on communications.	
April 7 to April 11	Take over 19th I.B. lines in addition to 16 I.B. Civilians on second line. Sappers and civilians making up materials. By night two sections putting up box revetment and bridges for communications behind the 16 I.B. and 19 I.B. lines.	
April 12 to April 18	Civilians on 2 line. Sappers and civilians making up materials. By night putting up breastworks behind CHARD FARM, box revetment on communication trenches, and making bridges, repairing railway to RUE DU BOIS damaged by shell fire.	
April 19 to April 21	Return to 16 and 17 I.B. lines. Civilians on 2 line. Sappers and civilians making up materials and bombs. Night one section box revetment on communication trench to CHARD FARM, one section building trench and barrier on main line to LILLE to join fire trenches across railway.	
April 22 and April 23	Civilians on 2 line. Sappers and civilians making footboards, dug-outs, bombs, machine gun stands, box loopholes, rifle grenade stands, bomb carriers etc. By night box revetment on communication trench to CHARD FARM, strengthening L'EPINETTE	
April 24 to April 26	Sappers and civilians by day as before. By night one section putting up revetment to support trench to right of Lechan 16 I.B., one section revetting communication trench in front of PORT EGALE	
April 27	Sappers and civilians by day as before. By night one section at L'EPINETTE repairing machine gun emplacement and strengthening defences at No 5 house. One section putting up box revetment and cages at head of communication trench to CHARD FARM	

(9 26 6) W 257—976 100,000 1/12 H W V (79) 3298

Instructions regarding War Diaries and Intelligence Summaries are contained in F. S. Regs., Part II. and the Staff Manual respectively. Title pages will be prepared in manuscript.

WAR DIARY or ~~INTELLIGENCE~~ SUMMARY. of 12th Field Company

(*Erase heading not required.*)

Army Form C. 2118.

Hour, Date, Place	Summary of Events and Information	Remarks and references to Appendices
ARMENTIERES April 28	Civilians on 2 line. Sappers and civilians making up materials By night one section at L'EPINETTE strengthening defences at No 5 House one section putting up breastwork to right of railway RUE DU BOIS	
April 29.	Sappers and civilians as before By night one section making bridge in trench in front of SWAN FARM, and blowing up rails to give through communication. One section extending revetment to right of breastwork behind CHARD FARM, one section making Poste de Commandant for 16 IB.	
April 30.	Sappers and civilians as before Receive orders 12.30 pm to work with the 16 and 19 IB instead of 16 and 17 IB. By night putting up barrier on road by ALLE POST and one section fix revetment behind SWAN FARM for communication trench to "B" work	
	1/5/15 A H Sargeaunt Major RE OC 12 F Co	

(9 26 6) W 257—976 100,000 4/12 H W V 79/3298

121/5614

6th Division

No 12 Field Coy: RE

Vol X 1 — 31.5.15.

Instructions regarding War Diaries and Intelligence Summaries are contained in F. S. Regs., Part II. and the Staff Manual respectively. Title pages will be prepared in manuscript.

WAR DIARY
or
INTELLIGENCE SUMMARY. of 12 Field Company

(*Erase heading not required.*)

Army Form C. 2118.

Hour, Date, Place	Summary of Events and Information	Remarks and references to Appendices
May 1st to May 6 ARMENTIERES	By day Civilians employed on digging communication trenches Sappers and civilians making up materials, hurdles, footboards, dug-outs, fixed rifle rests, loop holes etc. By night: wire entanglement in front of breastwork behind CHARD FARM construct Poste de Commandant on LILLE ROAD, box revetment for communication trenches	
	Take over trenches of 18 I B at LE TOUQUET N. of River LYS	
May 7 to May 12	Civilians on communication trenches at LE TOUQUET and behind 16 I B Sappers and civilians making up material. 2 Sections LE TOUQUET erecting overhead cover in houses used as communication trench, boarding trenches, sapping new trenches in front of our line By night one section putting up box revetment at LE TOUQUET. Receive Search Light Equipment and overhaul same	
May 13 to May 18	Civilians on communication trenches at LE TOUQUET and behind 16 I B Sappers and civilians making up materials 2 Sections LE TOUQUET deepening and boarding trenches, putting in traverses, making splinter proof shelters at The FORT, continue sapping By night one section continue box revetment for communication trenches at LE TOUQUET.	

(9 26 6) W 257—976 100,000 4/12 H W V 79/3298

Instructions regarding War Diaries and Intelligence Summaries are contained in F. S. Regs., Part II. and the Staff Manual respectively. Title pages will be prepared in manuscript.

WAR DIARY
or
~~INTELLIGENCE SUMMARY~~. of 12th Field Company

(*Erase heading not required.*)

Army Form C. 2118.

Hour, Date, Place	Summary of Events and Information	Remarks and references to Appendices
May 19 to May 26 ARMENTIERES.	Civilians on communication trenches at LE TOUQUET and behind 16 Bde	
	Sappers and civilians making up materials: dugouts, footboards, hurdles, spraying nozzles, gongs, braziers, fixed rifle rests, loop-holes, ladders, bridges etc	
	2 sections at LE TOUQUET covering and boarding trenches, mining houses in THE FORT, traverses	
	Night one section putting up box revetment, rebuilding parapet at THE FORT, roofing 'Forward Post' with splinter proof cover	
10 am May 26	Receive verbal intimation that 6 Division is to leave on 29th to relieve 27th Division	
May 27	Packing up etc preparatory to moving	
9 am May 28	2/Wessex R.E. arrive to take over. Leave Asylum at 2.45 pm and march via NIEPPE to farms 1 mile S.W of BAILLEUL	
May 29.	BAILLEUL.	
5.30 am May 30.	Leave BAILLEUL and march to WINTERHOEK where company bivouacs — OC with Brig 18 Bde to Canal to see GOC 9 Bde and viewing the trenches which are to be taken over by 18 Bde	
May 31.	Leave WINTERHOEK and march to huts in Area B Camps 1 m N.W of YPRES. Officers go round trenches after dusk	

A G Sargeaunt Major RE
OC 12 Fd Co

9/6

(9 26 6) W 257—976 100,000 4/12 H W V 79/3298

6th Division

121/5871

12th Field Coy: R.E.

Vol XI 1 – 30.6.15

Instructions regarding War Diaries and Intelligence Summaries are contained in F. S. Regs., Part II. and the Staff Manual respectively. Title pages will be prepared in manuscript.

Army Form C. 2118.

WAR DIARY
or
~~INTELLIGENCE SUMMARY.~~ of 12 Field Company.
(Erase heading not required.)

Hour, Date, Place	Summary of Events and Information	Remarks and references to Appendices
June 1. YPRES.	Superintend digging of dug-outs for 18 I.B. H.Q. and collecting timber for same. At night 2 sections erecting wire entanglement in front of 18 I.B. trenches	
June 2.	Continue 18 I.B. dug-outs At night 2 sections wiring in front of trenches	
June 3.	O.C. to POTIJZE re defence. At night 2 sections wiring in front of trenches, one section sandbagging trench to Forward Houses, superintending 2 Co Inf digging left com. trench.	
June 4.	Arrange to make foot boards for trenches in [illegible] factory in YPRES At night 2 sections wiring in front of fire trenches, one section sandbagging trench to forward houses infantry parties on com trench	
June 5.	2 sections making foot boards, chevaux de frize, ladders etc One section erecting and filling box revetment to Forward houses by night No 4 section moves to dug-outs on Canal to take charge of all bridges.	
June 6	One section making up materials By night 2 sections putting wire entanglement round A.B.C.D. works behind 2 line. 2 platoons digging POTIJZE	
June 7.	To POTIJZE and SAINT-JEAN re defences. Sappers making foot boards etc. Night at ST JEAN 2 platoons digging Night 2 sections wiring at POTIJZE, 1 Co Inf digging trenches	
June 8.	Sappers making up materials Night at POTIJZE, 2 sections wiring, 1 section pulling down houses. 2 platoons Inf digging trenches At ST JEAN 2 platoons digging	

(9 26 6) W 257—976 100,000 4/12 H W V 79/3298

Army Form C. 2118.

Instructions regarding War Diaries and Intelligence Summaries are contained in F. S. Regs., Part II. and the Staff Manual respectively. Title pages will be prepared in manuscript.

WAR DIARY
or
~~INTELLIGENCE~~ SUMMARY. 1/12 Field Company

(Erase heading not required.)

Hour, Date, Place		Summary of Events and Information	Remarks and references to Appendices
YPRES	June 9	Company moves from huts to billet 200^x N of X roads VLAMERTINGHE Evening No 4 Section repairing holes in main road through YPRES 2 platoons Infantry digging at POTIJZE.	
	June 10	Civilians making chevaux de frize No 1 Section pulling down houses POTIJZE, No 3 and No 4 sections wiring at POTIJZE — 1 Co. Inf at POTIJZE and 1 Co at St JEAN.	
	June 11	No 2 Section moves to dug-outs on Canal to join No 1 Section. Civilians making canvas hurdles and chevaux de frize Night No 1 Section demolishing at POTIJZE No 4 Section sandbagging trenches at St JEAN 1 Co Inf POTIJZE, 1 Co Inf St JEAN.	
	June 12	Sappers and civilians making hurdles, chevaux de frize, footboards. Night 16 civilians POTIJZE, No 2 and No 3 Section at St JEAN wiring and completing trenches. At midnight No 4 Section called out to cope with fire in VLAMERTINGHE the church having been set on fire by shell fire. 1 Co. Inf St JEAN, 1 Co at POTIJZE	
	June 13.	Sappers making hurdles and footboards. CRE calls afternoon to say whole company to be at disposal of 18 IB for special work Four Sections ~~[illegible]~~ with 2 Coys. Infy improving trenches along ROULERS railway for use as assembly trenches.	
	June 14	Civilians making revetments etc. 17 civilians night work at POTYZE. Carpenters making ladders — Civilians ditto Four Sections preparing new assembly trenches near Railway wood with two Companies of Infantry to assist 20 civilians — night work at POTYZE.	Major Sargeant went on leave.

Instructions regarding War Diaries and Intelligence Summaries are contained in F. S. Regs., Part II. and the Staff Manual respectively. Title pages will be prepared in manuscript.

WAR DIARY
or
~~INTELLIGENCE SUMMARY.~~ 12th Fd. Co. R.E.
(Erase heading not required.)

Army Form C. 2118.

Hour, Date, Place	Summary of Events and Information	Remarks and references to Appendices
YPRES June 15	Carpenters and civilians making floorboards for trenches 22 civilians night work at POTYZE. Work in connection with projected attack by 3rd Div in direction of BELLEWAARDE FARM as follows. No 1 Section improving dugouts near RAILWAY WOOD for dressing station No 2 " dug themselves in near railway. This section to remain with supporting battalion of 18th Bde during following day. No 3 Section ~~[illegible]~~ Removed wire in front of No 10 Trench (3rd Div) No 4 Section Put new sandbag barrier across railway connecting "switch" with 3rd Div. trenches. 100 Infantry assisted with above work – filling sandbags etc	
June 16	Attack by 3rd Div. started at 4.15 am. after bombardment. No 2 Section were not called on to do anything but had 3 men wounded. They were relieved at dusk by No 1 Section who replaced some of the wire in front of No 10 trench (3rd Div) Nos 3 + 4 sections – day off. Carpenters + civilians making floor boards. Civilians would not go out to night work on account of shelling	
June 18th to 20th	3 Sections per night continue defences of POTIJZE and St JEAN with 100 Infantry and 50 civilians Sappers and civilians making footboards, collecting and repairing pumps etc	

(9 26 6) W 257—976 100,000 4/12 H W V 79/3298

Instructions regarding War Diaries and Intelligence Summaries are contained in F. S. Regs., Part II. and the Staff Manual respectively. Title pages will be prepared in manuscript.

WAR DIARY
or
~~INTELLIGENCE~~ SUMMARY. 1/2 Fd. Co

(Erase heading not required.)

Army Form C. 2118.

Hour, Date, Place		Summary of Events and Information	Remarks and references to Appendices
YPRES	June 21	By day Sappers and civilians making up materials Night 2 sections with 100 Infantry at St JEAN - 1 section wiring at POTIZE - 100 Infantry and 50 civilians POTIZE	
	June 22	Sappers and civilians working by day making up materials. Cancel night work owing to attack on right of railway.	
	June 23.	Day work as usual. Night 2 sections with 100 Infantry St JEAN. Trench marked out 80" in front of fire trench to right of SHERWOOD FARM - 150 Infantry dig this trench and 1 section wires in front of it - 400 Infantry commence new evacuation trench to right of POTIZE ROAD.	
	June 24.	B Gen Hill visits POTIZE and St JEAN - No 2 Section returns to HQ and No 3 Section to Canal - Sappers and civilians making up materials - Night 1 section POTIZE - 1 section continues wire in front of forward trench - 150 Infantry on this trench and 400 on evacuation trench	
	June 25.	By day work as usual - Night 2 sections with 100 Infantry St JEAN - one section at POTIZE making way through houses - ~~?~~ com. trenches to forward trench taped out	
	June 26.	Sappers and civilians making up materials. Engine and circular saw set going Night 2 sections and 100 men St JEAN - one section at POTIZE making defences near Shrine - 100 Infantry on trenches at POTIZE + 50 civilians - 400 Infantry commence com trench on right for 14th Division	

(9 26 6) W 257—976 100,000 4/12 H W V 79/3298

Instructions regarding War Diaries and Intelligence Summaries are contained in F.S. Regs., Part II. and the Staff Manual respectively. Title pages will be prepared in manuscript.

WAR DIARY
or
~~INTELLIGENCE~~ SUMMARY. 1/2 Fd Co

(Erase heading not required.)

Army Form C. 2118.

Hour, Date, Place	Summary of Events and Information	Remarks and references to Appendices
YPRES. June 27.	Work by day as usual Night 2 sections and 150 men ST JEAN 400 Infantry on right com trench	
June 28.	Work by day as usual Night 1 section and 40 men at ST JEAN - one section POTIJZE putting up 100 hurdles on evacuation trench 400 Infantry on this trench - 400 Infantry on right com trench - 100 Infantry on trench from Shrine - 50 civilians frommy ff trenches POTIJZE	
June 29.	Sappers and civilians making footboards hurdles etc - Pulley for circular saw breaks - Collecting pumps from YPRES and repairing them for trenches. Night - One section ST JEAN with 40 Inf. one section box-hurdling evacuation trench and 200 Inf improving this trench - one section with 800 Infantry on post to left of POTIJZE WOOD - 400 Infantry on right communication trench	
June 30.	Sappers and civilians making footboards, hurdles, bulls-eye boards etc. Night - No 2 Section Box-hurdling right communication trench across railway with 200 Infantry - 100 Inf and 60 civilians at POTIJZE digging new trenches and sand bagging those already dug - one section and 100 Inf ST JEAN - Lt BAINES tapes out forward trench to left of VERLORENHOEK	
	1/7/15 A.T. Sargeaunt Major RE (?) Lt Col OC 1/2 Fd Co	

(9 26 6) W 257—976 100,000 4/12 H W V 79/3298

6th Division.

121/6242

12th Field Coy RE

Vol XII

June July 15

WAR DIARY

OF

12th (7th) Co R.E

FROM 1.7.15 TO 31.7.15.

Instructions regarding War Diaries and Intelligence Summaries are contained in F. S. Regs., Part II. and the Staff Manual respectively. Title pages will be prepared in manuscript.

WAR DIARY or ~~INTELLIGENCE SUMMARY~~

(*Erase heading not required.*)

1/2 Field Company

Army Form C. 2118.

Hour, Date, Place	Summary of Events and Information	Remarks and References to Appendices
YPRES July 1	By day sappers and civilians making footboards, repairing pumps, making hurdles etc. Night No 3 Section with 100 Infantry continue St JEAN defences; No 1 Section with 100 Infantry and 50 civilians continue POTIJZE defences; No 2 Section making M.G. emplacements and finishing off trenches at POTIJZE; 100 Infantry dig new trench to left of VALORENHOEK.	
July 2.	Sappers and civilians making up materials; party collecting light rails in YPRES, make sample parapet-shelter for trenches 6'6" long x 3' broad. Afternoon wagons to Canal to load up 2 pontoons and superstructure. Night one section wiring new trench to left of VALORENHOEK whilst 100 Infantry continue digging. No 1 and No 2 sections with 130 Infantry continue defences of POTIJZE village, digging drains, making shelters, M.G. emplacements; 50 civilians sand bagging trenches at POTIJZE. Lt BAINES wounded by bullet in right hand	
July 3.	Sappers and civilians making up materials. Captain SHANNON to Canal to take charge of No 3 Section. O.C. shows Capt SHANNON work required at POTIJZE. No 1 Section and 75 civilians continue work on shelters and trenches at POTIJZE by night. 1st London Fd Co take over St JEAN.	
July 4.	Sappers making up materials. O.C. accompanies Brigadier round 1st Bn trenches. At night. No 1 Section continues shelters, No 2 machine gun emplacements and demolishing houses No 3 M.G. emplacements in wood with 50 Infantry all at POTIJZE	
July 5	Sappers and civilians making footboards hurdles etc. O.C. accompanies Brigadier round centre and left Bns trenches. At night No 4 Section box making & communication trench No 3 Section making M.G. emplacements and finishing trenches POTIJZE. 120 Inf and 50 civilians working at POTIJZE. Tape out support trenches to left of POTIJZE ROAD and 200 Inf dig on this trench	

Instructions regarding War Diaries and Intelligence Summaries are contained in F. S. Regs., Part II. and the Staff Manual respectively. Title pages will be prepared in manuscript.

WAR DIARY
or
INTELLIGENCE SUMMARY

(*Erase heading not required.*)

~~Intelligence Summary~~ 1/12 Field Company

Army Form C. 2118.

Hour, Date, Place	Summary of Events and Information	Remarks and References to Appendices
YPRES. July 6.	Sappers and civilians making hurdles, footboards etc. CSM and Sgt Bowyer superintend Infantry digging party making road (High St) in wood (A.30). Capt SHANNON to advise 24 Bn R.F.A. re forward emplacements. 2Lt FRECHEVILLE reports for duty. Night. No 2 Section demolishing houses at POTIJZE, No 1 Section making shelters and No 3 Section M.G. emplacements and trenches with 40 Inf at POTIJZE. 60 Inf digging communication trenches and shelters under 2Lt SIBETH at POTIJZE. Capt Shannon superintending marking out and digging of support trenches behind left Bn with 200 Inf for digging. O.C. reconnoitring line for com. trench from left of rt. Bn with O.C. Bn. 60 Inf continue work POTIJZE. 1 Lance Corporal and 1 Sapper to each of 3 Bns in Front Line to live with them to assist in erecting dug-outs	
July 7.	O.C. with C.R.E. to defended localities. Sappers and civilians making hurdles footboards etc. 2 Sappers to 2 Londons to advise re drainage of trenches. Night No 1 Section and No 3 Section continue work at POTIJZE with 80 civilians. 20 civilians clearing BELLEWARDE BEKE	
July 8.	Sappers and civilians making footboards, hurdles etc. Lt Jackson makes sketch of POTIJZE defences. Night. No 1 Section shelters and No 4 Section sandbagging trenches POTIJZE with 80 civilians. O.C. lays out communication trench between B and C redoubts and 100 Inf ~~continue digging~~ commence digging this. 50 Inf to POTIJZE to live there and to work under RE in completing defences. 20 civilians on clearing BEKE	
July 9.	8 Sappers to assist Inf at POTIJZE. Sappers and civilians making footboards, hurdles, jam-pot bombs etc. Lt Playfair and 5 men to lay out defences of 6 Div H.Q. Night. No 2 Section demolishing houses, 1 and 3 Sections defences POTIJZE. 100 Inf dig communication trench between B and C Redoubts. 80 civilians continue	

Army Form C. 2118.

Instructions regarding War Diaries and Intelligence Summaries are contained in F. S. Regs., Part II. and the Staff Manual respectively. Title pages will be prepared in manuscript.

WAR DIARY or ~~INTELLIGENCE SUMMARY~~ 1/12th Fd. Co.

(Erase heading not required.)

Hour, Date, Place	Summary of Events and Information	Remarks and References to Appendices
YPRES July 10.	Sappers and Civilians making footboards, hurdles, bombs etc. Small party to POTIJZE Road to make shelter for M.F. Police. Lt PLAYFAIR superintending Infantry digging defences of 6 Div H.Q. Night half section putting overhead cover to M.G. emplacements POTIJZE – 2 Lt FRECHEVILLE superintending 90 Inf on trench between B and C Redoubts – 80 Inf. at POTIJZE and 20 on Beek.	
July 11.	Major and Lt Col. A.F. Sargeaunt proceeds to 14 Div to take up duties of CRE and hands over 12 Fd. Co to Captain Campbell. Sappers & civilians making up material in yard. LT PLAYFAIR superintending infantry at VLAMERTINGHE CHATEAU. LIEUT SIBETH & 8 Sappers completing dugouts at POTIJZE.	
July 12.	Visited left of line with brigade [illegible] for officers & [illegible] concrete emplacement. LIEUT SIBETH at POTIJZE. Sappers & civilians making up material in yard. Night visited POTIJZE. LIEUT SIBETH [illegible] one section on improvements. LIEUT FRECHEVILLE [illegible] [illegible] with one section; civilians sandbagging [illegible]. LIEUT JACKSON [illegible] section erecting hurdles on (Q) communication trench. CAPT SHANNON [illegible] RA with dugout in second line.	
July 13.	Visited front line South of YPRES – POTIJZE road with LIEUT JACKSON & O.C. Batts. Arranged for completion of two [illegible] M.G. emplacements also for [illegible] & maintenance of communication trench. At night visited POTIJZE and proposed support trench South of road. Morning. Sappers and civilians making up material. LIEUT PLAYFAIR acting adjutant. CAPT SHANNON [illegible] with rate of PICCADILLY communication trench & [illegible] with infantry & maintenance. LIEUT SIBETH at night with section improving POTIJZE. LIEUT PLAYFAIR at night demolishing cottage at POTIJZE.	

(9 26 6) W 257—976 100,000 4/12 H W V 79 / 3298

Instructions regarding War Diaries and Intelligence Summaries are contained in F. S. Regs., Part II. and the Staff Manual respectively. Title Pages will be prepared in manuscript.

WAR DIARY
or
INTELLIGENCE SUMMARY
(Erase heading not required.)

Army Form C. 2118

Place	Date	Hour	Summary of Events and Information	Remarks and references to Appendices
YPRES.	4.7.15	9.AM.	Visited Brigade HQ and sections in canal bank arranged supply of material. Went to POTIJZE met OC RF and went round right of his front line up right communication trench and back of centre. Arranged for material and creation of splinter proofs in front line. Company and civilians making material in yard. LIEUT JACKSON to LEINSTERS in afternoon. CAPT SHANNON to communication trenches. LIEUT PLAYFAIR assisting CRE. NIGHT LIEUT SIBETH POTIJZE defences 1 section. CAPT SHANNON & LIEUT FRECHEVILLE one section boarding PICCADILLY communication trench. LIEUT PLAYFAIR assisting CRE. One section resting on account of inoculation.	
	15.7.15	9.AM	Visited Brigade HQ, sections on Canal bank & clearance of BELLEWARDE BEEK. AG	
		2.15PM	Visited second line with Brigade Machine Gun Officer to choose sites for Machine Guns.	
		8.PM	To second line to set out work on M.G. emplacements. DAY L^T JACKSON & section concreting M.G. emplacements in front line & framing dugouts. 2nd L^T FRECHEVILLE framing dugouts front line. NIGHT LT PLAYFAIR & section boarding PICADILLY communication trench. 2nd LT SIBETH POTIJZE defences with section & 100 Infantry. CAPTAIN SHANNON & one section M.G. emplacements second line. Civilians POTIJZE defences and clearing BELLEWARDE BEEK.	
	16/7/15	9AM 8P.M	Brigade HQ. Went to front line of RB Leinsters & RF returning at 3PM & MG emplacements in second line. AG. CAPTAIN SHANNON MG emplacement second line. LIEUT JACKSON dugouts & MG emplacement LEINSTERS. LIEUT PLAYFAIR arrangements for dugouts RB. LIEUT FRECHEVILLE dugouts RF & communication works A & B at night. LT SIBETH POTIJZE. AG	

1875 Wt. W593/826 1,000,000 4/15 J.B.C. & A. A.D.S.S./Forms/C. 2118.

Instructions regarding War Diaries and Intelligence Summaries are contained in F. S. Regs., Part II. and the Staff Manual respectively. Title Pages will be prepared in manuscript.

WAR DIARY
or
INTELLIGENCE SUMMARY
(Erase heading not required.)

Army Form C. 2118

Place	Date	Hour	Summary of Events and Information	Remarks and references to Appendices
YPRES	17.7.15	9. AM	To Brigade H.Q. + POTIJZE. Saw work at POTIJZE and discussed splinterproofs with OC R.F.	
			Company Day. LIEUT JACKSON + 1 Section concreting M.G. emplacements + framing dugouts front line. LEINSTERS.	
			LIEUT SIBETH POTIJZE defences.	
			LIEUT PLAYFAIR + 100 O.R. splinterproofs for R.B.	
			2nd Lt FRECHEVILLE + 8 O.R. " R.F.	
			Small parties in repairing communication trenches + M.G. emplacements 2nd line.	
			Remainder making up material	
			Night LIEUT ~~JACKSON~~ PLAYFAIR splinterproofs in new front line with 1 section.	
			small party with CAPTAIN SHANNON on M.G. emplacements 2nd line	
			C.G.	
	18.7.15	9. AM.	To Brigade H.Q. thence to new front line at junction of right and centre battalions. Inspected BOND STREET + HAYMARKET communication trenches + M.G. emplacements second line. Also M.G. emplacements concreting in front line	
			Company DAY Lieut Sibeth POTIJZE with 1 Section	
			Lieut Playfair + 100 O.R. Splinter proofs of right battalion	
			Lieut Jackson + 1 Section. Concreting M.G. emplacements + framing dugouts centre battalion	
			2nd Lt Frecheville + 8 O.R. framing dugouts centre battalion.	
			Small parties in M.G. emplacements second line + repairing communication trenches.	
			NIGHT LIEUT SIBETH with infantry garrison + 100 working party POTIJZE defences.	
			CAPT SHANNON with small party concreting emplacements for M.G. second line	
			Two sappers assisting in splinterproofs of new front line centre battalion	
			C.G.	

1875 Wt. W593/826 1,000,000 4/15 J.B.C. & A. A.D.S.S./Forms/C. 2118.

Instructions regarding War Diaries and Intelligence Summaries are contained in F. S. Regs., Part II. and the Staff Manual respectively. Title Pages will be prepared in manuscript.

WAR DIARY
or
INTELLIGENCE SUMMARY
(Erase heading not required.)

Army Form C. 2118

Place	Date	Hour	Summary of Events and Information	Remarks and references to Appendices
YPRES	19.7.15	9 AM	To Brigade HQ thence POTIJZE new front line of right & centre battalions & M.G. emplacements of centre battalion. CAPT SHANNON communication trenches & assisting R.A. Lt JACKSON & section night & day shifts emplacements of centre battalion. Lt PLAYFAIR framing dugouts right battalion. 2nd Lt FRECHEVILLE " left battalion. 2nd Lt SIBETH POTIJZE Remainder in yard. Cyclists by night at POTIJZE & PICCADILLY communication trench	
	20.7.15	9 AM. 8 PM.	To Brigade HQ thence to front line left battalion. To PICCADILLY communication trench. DAY CAPTAIN SHANNON communication trenches LIEUT JACKSON M.G. emplacements & dugouts centre battalion ½ Section LIEUT PLAYFAIR dugouts right battalion 10 O.R. 2nd Lt SIBETH POTIJZE 1 Section 2nd Lt FRECHEVILLE dugouts left battalion 8 O.R. Remaining sappers & cyclists making up material in yard. NIGHT - LIEUT JACKSON & ½ section M.G. emplacements centre battalion. 2nd Lt Sibeth with infantry POTIJZE 2nd Lt FRECHEVILLE with 18 O.R. hurdling PICCADILLY communication trench One man wounded	
	21.7.15	9 AM.	To Brigade HQ thence with G.O.C. to inspect front line of centre and right. Went up BOND STREET & back HAYMARKET. G.O.C. not in favour of commencing new work till new front line and communication trenches completed. DAY as on 20th except that LT PLAYFAIR commenced [illegible] PICCADILLY. NIGHT. LIEUT JACKSON & ½ section M.G. emplacements 2nd LT SIBETH with infantry POTIJZE LIEUT PLAYFAIR assisting infantry new front line	

Instructions regarding War Diaries and Intelligence Summaries are contained in F. S. Regs., Part II. and the Staff Manual respectively. Title Pages will be prepared in manuscript.

WAR DIARY
or
INTELLIGENCE SUMMARY
(Erase heading not required.)

Army Form C. 2118

Place	Date	Hour	Summary of Events and Information	Remarks and references to Appendices
YPRES	22/7/15	10 AM	Conference on measures required to modify defences for winter campaign.	
		2 PM	To PICADILLY communication trench and POTIJZE defences.	
			Company. DAY. CAPTAIN SHANNON communication trenches.	
			LIEUT PLAYFAIR + section new front line centre + ~~left~~ right bn	
			battalions + piling PICADILLY.	
			LIEUT JACKSON M.G. emplacements + dugouts centre battalion.	
			2nd Lt SIBETH POTIJZE.	
			2nd Lt FRECHEVILLE dugouts left battalion.	
			NIGHT. LIEUT JACKSON M.G. emplacements centre battalion.	
			2nd Lt SIBETH. POTIJZE.	
			Heavy rain from 4 P.M.	
			AG	
	23/7/15	9 AM.	To Brigade HQ then to new front line of right and centre battalions. Saw O.C. left battalion re works and drainage.	
		8 P.M	To PICADILLY communication trench.	
			Company. DAY. Captain Shannon communication trenches.	
			Lieut Playfair + section new front line centre + right batts.	
			Lieut Jackson + section M.G. emplacements + dugouts centre battalion.	
			2nd Lt SIBETH + section POTIJZE	
			2nd Lt FRECHEVILLE + 80R. dugouts left battalion.	
			NIGHT. O.C + 2nd Lt FRECHEVILLE setting out infantry working parties on PICADILLY. communication trench. CAPTAIN SHANNON with infantry cutting drain for STRAND communication trench. 2nd Lt SIBETH POTIJZE, 2nd Lt JACKSON M.G. emplacements centre battalion.	
			AG	

Instructions regarding War Diaries and Intelligence Summaries are contained in F. S. Regs., Part II. and the Staff Manual respectively. Title Pages will be prepared in manuscript.

WAR DIARY
or
INTELLIGENCE SUMMARY
(Erase heading not required.)

Army Form C. 2118

Place	Date	Hour	Summary of Events and Information	Remarks and references to Appendices
YPRES.	24/7/15	9.AM	To brigade HQ. then round left battalion with OC Bn. Inspected drainage of right of second line. Decided realignment of communication trenches. Company DAY CAPTAIN SHANNON supervising maintenance of communication trenches with 2 sappers per trench. LIEUT PLAYFAIR + section digouts new front line right + centre battalions; siting PICADILLY communication trench. LIEUT JACKSON + ½ section M.G. emplacements centre battalion 2nd Lt SIBETH + section POTIJZE. 2nd Lt FRECHEVILLE + 100R digouts left battalion Remainder making up material in yard. Civilians making up material & clearing BELLEWARDE BEEK. NIGHT LIEUT PLAYFAIR + 100 infantry widening PICADILLY. LIEUT JACKSON assisting infantry communication trenches centre battalion 2nd Lt FRECHEVILLE + ½ section hurdling PICADILLY and supervising 50 infantry clearing drains. 2nd Lt SIBETH POTIJZE. AG	
	25/7/15	9.AM	To Brigade HQ. Then with CRE round POTIJZE and left battalion. CRE decided that practically the whole of STRAND & FLEET STREET would have to be realigned. Company DAY. CAPTAIN SHANNON paying civilians & supervising in camp. LIEUT PLAYFAIR + section digouts centre + left battalions & siting PICADILLY. LIEUT JACKSON + section digouts + M.G. emplacements centre & preparation of Canal maps. 2nd Lt FRECHEVILLE digouts left battalion. 2nd Lt SIBETH POTIJZE NIGHT CAPTAIN SHANNON + 150 infantry clearing BELLEWARDE BEEK. LIEUT PLAYFAIR + 110 infantry widening PICADILLY + carrying hurdles 2nd Lt SIBETH POTIJZE Civilians not working except a few in yard. AG	

1875 Wt. W593/826 1,000,000 4/15 J.B.C. & A. A.D.S.S./Forms/C. 2118.

Instructions regarding War Diaries and Intelligence Summaries are contained in F. S. Regs., Part II. and the Staff Manual respectively. Title Pages will be prepared in manuscript.

WAR DIARY
or
INTELLIGENCE SUMMARY
(Erase heading not required.)

Army Form C. 2118

Place	Date	Hour	Summary of Events and Information	Remarks and references to Appendices
YPRES	26/7	9. AM	To Brigade HQ then to left battalion & part of Centre. Inspected CHEAPSIDE FLEET STREET, STRAND B & BOND STREET.	
			Company DAY CAPTAIN SHANNON communication trenches.	
			LIEUT JACKSON with OC & pickaxes for WARWICK LINE.	
			2nd Lt SIBBETH POTIJZE.	
			2nd Lt FRECHEVILLE dugouts left battalion.	
			Remainder making up material in yard.	
			NIGHT LIEUT JACKSON & section WARWICK LINE.	
			LIEUT PLAYFAIR hurdling PICADILLY.	
			Civilians POTIJZE.	
			No infantry digging on account of reliefs. [initials]	
	27/7	9. AM.	To Brigade HQ then with G.O.C. round new front line of centre and right back centre and HEDDON ST. After leaving G.O.C. visited each battalion HQ.	
		9. P.M.	To POTIJZE and swamp where PICADILLY crosses BELLEWAARDE BEEK.	
			Company with DAY CAPTAIN SHANNON communication trenches and to arrange with relieving battalions for maintenance fatigues.	
			LIEUT JACKSON to HQ of ~~right~~ battalion to arrange for night work.	
			2nd Lt SIBBETH POTIJZE	
			2nd Lt FRECHEVILLE & det dugouts left battalion	
			NIGHT CAPTAIN SHANNON with 185 infantry clearing BELLEWAARDE BEEK	
			2nd Lt FRECHEVILLE and small detachment hurdling new front line centre battalion	
			2nd Lt SIBBETH & 100 infantry POTIJZE	
			LIEUT JACKSON & section WARWICK LINE	
			[initials]	

1875 Wt. W593/826 1,000,000 4/15 J.B.C. & A. A.D.S.S./Forms/C. 2118.

Instructions regarding War Diaries and Intelligence Summaries are contained in F. S. Regs., Part II. and the Staff Manual respectively. Title Pages will be prepared in manuscript.

WAR DIARY
or
INTELLIGENCE SUMMARY
(Erase heading not required.)

Army Form C. 2118

Place	Date	Hour	Summary of Events and Information	Remarks and references to Appendices
YPRES.	28/7	9 AM. 9 P.M.	Conference with CRE. Then to Brigade HQ. + POTIJZE to PICADILLY and to show works A + B to Sergt ROUSE	
			Company DAY. CAPTAIN SHANNON Communication trenches. LIEUT PLAYFAIR piling PICADILLY. LIEUT JACKSON + section Support 17th IB. 2nd Lt SIBETH + section POTIJZE. 2nd Lt FRECHEVILLE Supports left battalion. Remainder making up material in yard. Work hampered for want of planks + nails.	
			NIGHT. CAPTAIN SHANNON with 25 infantry clearing BELLEWAARDE BEEK. O.C. with 125 infantry widening PICADILLY and getting up material for piling. LIEUT PLAYFAIR + section heading PICADILLY and front trench of Centre battalion. LIEUT JACKSON + section WARWICK LINE. 2nd Lt SIBETH with 100 infantry + part of garrison POTIJZE. 2nd Lt FRECHEVILLE breastworks left battalion. AG	
	29.7	9 AM.	With CRE to see GOC Divn who decided that only shelters of regiments etc were to be made in new front line + WARWICK LINE. Shelters in the front line and concrete emplacements to be pushed on. Then to Brigade HQ. At night with Brigade major choosing line for fire trenches to right of PICADILLY in rear of BELLEWAARDE BEEK.	
			Company DAY. As on 28th except that LIEUT JACKSON + section worked on WARWICK LINE by day.	
			NIGHT. CAPTAIN SHANNON Communications + drainage. LIEUT PLAYFAIR new front line. 2nd Lt SIBETH POTIJZE wiring (no infantry except Johnson). SERGT ROUSE Redoubts A + B.	
			AG	

1875 Wt. W593/826 1,000,000 4/15 J.B.C. & A. A.D.S.S./Forms/C. 2118.

Instructions regarding War Diaries and Intelligence Summaries are contained in F. S. Regs., Part II. and the Staff Manual respectively. Title Pages will be prepared in manuscript.

WAR DIARY
or
INTELLIGENCE SUMMARY
(Erase heading not required.)

Army Form C. 2118

Place	Date	Hour	Summary of Events and Information	Remarks and references to Appendices
YPRES	30/7/15	9 AM.	To Brigade H.Q. and all battalion H.Q. Inspected PICADILLY and part of HAYMARKET BOND ST + CHEAPSIDE. Arranged for collection of brickbats for two Concrete M.G. Emplacements	
		9 P.M.	Laid out two trenches in support of right flank, inspected work in new front line near CRUMP FARM.	
			Company work DAY. 2nd Lt SIBETH + ½ Section POTISZE. Remainder as on 29th greatly hampered by want of timber + nails.	
			NIGHT. LIEUT JACKSON + section WARWICK LINE. 2nd Lt SIBETH POTISZE. 2nd Lt FRECHEVILLE left battalion. LIEUT PLAYFAIR assisting O.C.	
			Civilians POTISZE.	
			CAPTAIN TURNER arrived. NG	
	31/7/15	9 AM.	With CAPTAIN TURNER to Brigade H.Q. then to POTIZE, CHEAPSIDE, STRAND + STINK HOUSES. Saw O.C. left + centre battalions.	
		9 P.M.	To work in WARWICK LINE north of CHEAPSIDE.	
			Company DAY. CAPTAIN SHANNON left for ENGLAND. CAPTAIN TURNER with O.C. LIEUT JACKSON + section 17th I.B. dugouts + preparing for night work. LIEUT PLAYFAIR + 2nd Lt FRECHEVILLE to left + centre battalion. 2nd Lt SIBETH POTISZE with section.	
			Civilians + remainder of sappers in yard. Civilians clearing BELLEWAARDE BEEK and clearing line for tramway.	
			NIGHT LT PLAYFAIR + det. new front line centre battalion. 2nd Lts SIBETH + FRECHEVILLE with 2 sections wiring WARWICK LINE. LIEUT JACKSON + section WARWICK LINE. Work delayed for want of timber + nails. LIEUT JACKSON wounded at night. NG	[signature] O.C. 12th Coy R.E.

1875 Wt. W593/826 1,000,000 4/15 J.B.C. & A. A.D.S.S./Forms/C. 2118.

6th Division

121/6587

12th Field Coy: RE

Vol XIII

From 1 - 31. 8. 15

WAR DIARY

OF

12th (3d) Co R.E.

FROM 1. 8. 15 to 31. 8. 15.

Instructions regarding War Diaries and Intelligence Summaries are contained in F. S. Regs., Part II. and the Staff Manual respectively. Title Pages will be prepared in manuscript.

WAR DIARY
or
INTELLIGENCE SUMMARY
(Erase heading not required.)

Army Form C. 2118

Place	Date	Hour	Summary of Events and Information	Remarks and references to Appendices
YPRES.	1/8/15	9AM	To Brigade HQ then to parts of front line of left & centre battalions. Work of company reduced to minimum to allow for bathing. Parties out at night wiring WARWICK LINE, completing [illegible] of WARWICK LINE, and [illegible] of new front line. AG	
	2/8/15	9AM 12.30.	To 18th IB. HQ Orders recd that company would work with 16th IB. Issued orders recalling Canal sections & all men from 17th IB. [illegible] Company making up material & demolishing house to clear foreground for VLAMERTINGHE CHATEAU defences AG	
	3/8/15	9AM. [illegible] 3P.M	To see CRE To see G.O.C. 16th IB. To see CRE 14th Div, GOC 18th IB & 42 [illegible] Company. 1 section demolishing house, 2 sections dugouts at Co HQ. remainder making up material. Night. 1 section wiring trenches near MENIN [illegible] roads	
	4/8/15	10AM.	With Brigade Major 16th IB to see part of new line. AG Company at HQ completing dugouts demolishing house and making M.G. emplacement. Detachment at night preparing forward dumps. AG	
	5/8/15.	9AM.	To CRE, Brigade HQ then round whole of new area of 16th IB returning at 4 P.M. Got general outline (verbally) of plans of G.O.C. 16th IB Sent reconnaissance to ramparts of YPRES with CAPTAIN TURNER 72nd LT [illegible] PROCHEVILLE. 1½ sections at night on Brigade Battle Station AG	

1875 Wt. W593/826 1,000,000 4/15 J.B.C. & A. A.D.S.S./Forms/C. 2118.

Army Form C. 2118

Instructions regarding War Diaries and Intelligence Summaries are contained in F. S. Regs., Part II. and the Staff Manual respectively. Title Pages will be prepared in manuscript.

WAR DIARY
or
INTELLIGENCE SUMMARY
(Erase heading not required.)

Place	Date	Hour	Summary of Events and Information	Remarks and references to Appendices
YPRES.	6/8/15	9.A.M.	To Brigade H.Q. then with G.O.C. to see O.C. Y&L & O.C. K.S.L.I. with 2/Lt SIBETH to cutout on MENIN ROAD close to HALFWAY COTTAGES.	
		8P.M.	To Brigade H.Q. then to lay out assembly trenches in rear of front line SOUTH of MENIN ROAD. Returned at 1.A.M.	
			Sent SERGT ROUSE & section to ramparts. Men at H.Q. making up material.	
			2 sections at night on Brigade battle stations.	
			2/Lt SIBETH & 2/Lt CROFTON with 600 infantry carrying to forward dumps.	
YPRES.	7/8/15	9.A.M.	To VLAMERTINGHE to arrange about stores.	
		2P.M.	To OXFORD STREET to inspect and arrange for improvement.	
		8P.M.	Two sections improving battle stations and laying footboards in OXFORD ST.	
	8/8/15	2P.M.	Brought up 4th section to Ramparts.	
		8.30P.M.	Nos 1 & 3 sections under CAPTAIN TURNER 2/Lt SIBETH & 2/Lt FRECHEVILLE with 24 extra NCOs & sappers for [illegible] parties marched to [illegible] infantry. Lt PLAYFAIR & det. footboards OXFORD ST. SERGT ROWSE & det. clearing UNION ST.	
	9.8.15	6A.M.	Wounded from attack began to come in. Collected information during day from those returning. All officers hit but work being successfully carried out in front of captured trenches. Sappers worked on reversing parapets and digging communications but work not satisfactory owing to heavy shell fire. From reports it seems doubtful whether sappers were usefully employed after work completed.	
			Casualties: Officers — K: —, W: 2, M: 1; O.R. — K: 10, W: 18, M: 9	
			Went up at night with remainder of company but found trenches too full of wounded to allow of useful work being done.	

1875 Wt. W593/826 1,000,000 4/15 J.B.C. & A. A.D.S.S./Forms/C. 2118.

Instructions regarding War Diaries and Intelligence Summaries are contained in F. S. Regs., Part II. and the Staff Manual respectively. Title Pages will be prepared in manuscript.

WAR DIARY
or
INTELLIGENCE SUMMARY
(Erase heading not required.)

Army Form C. 2118

Place	Date	Hour	Summary of Events and Information	Remarks and references to Appendices
YPRES.	10/8.		Company resting by day. O.C. and C.S.M. Cowley with detachment of Sappers and 200 infantry clearing communication trenches where blown in and assisting infantry near CRATER. Work unsatisfactory owing to shell fire and relief. Found Sapper Garland wounded and got him in. Found Sapper EASTON dead and got his disc. Casualties 1 N.C.O. + 1 man wounded. AG	
	11/8.		Company resting by day. Nos 1 + 3 Sections still shaky owing to shelling on 9/8. Left them in camp at night. O.C. by day with officers of infantry to detail work on improving UNION + CASTLE STREET communication trenches. 300 infantry on this by night. 2nd Lt WOOD joined for duty. Lt PLAYFAIR + 2nd Lt WOOD to CRATER with 2 + 4 sections to wire in close to fire trench and generally improve position. AG	
	12/8.		O.C. with G.O.C. 17th I.B. to CRATER. Held up by heavy shell fire for 2 hours. Lt PLAYFAIR + det to CRATER by night wiring, infantry clearing communication trenches.	
	13/8	2 P.M.	O.C. + 2nd Lt WOOD with B.M. 17th I.B. to CRATER by day.	
		8 P.M.	O.C. + 2nd Lt WOOD laying out deviation of communication trench (?) to CRATER. SERGT ROWSE with detachment wiring at CRATER and digging sites for [illegible]. 2nd Lts LESLIE + BUDDEN joined for duty.	
	14/8.	2 P.M.	O.C., Lt PLAYFAIR + 2nd Lt BUDDEN to MUDDY LANE. O.C. + 2nd Lt BUDDEN to CRATER.	
		8 P.M.	SERGT ROWSE + det CRATER. O.C. + 2nd Lt BUDDEN with 2 Cos (15th) infantry on deviation of communication trench. All infantry parties delayed till 12 M.N. on account of shelling. 1 N.C.O. + 1 Sapper wounded. AG	

1875 W: W593/826 1,000,000 4/15 J.B.C. & A. A.D.S.S./Forms/C. 2118.

Instructions regarding War Diaries and Intelligence Summaries are contained in F. S. Regs., Part II. and the Staff Manual respectively. Title Pages will be prepared in manuscript.

WAR DIARY
or
INTELLIGENCE SUMMARY
(Erase heading not required.)

Army Form C. 2118

Place	Date	Hour	Summary of Events and Information	Remarks and references to Appendices
15/8/15.		2PM	O.C. & 2nd Lt BUDDEN to LEINSTER H.Q. LT PLAYFAIR & 2nd Lt LESLIE to CRATER.	
		8PM	LT PLAYFAIR 2nd Lts BUDDEN & WOOD with LONDON REGT (350) 1 Co carrying 1 Co digging deviation of communication trench 1 Co improving support trench 1 Co improving fire trench Work fairly satisfactory. Infantry 12 casualties. Sappers nil	
16/8/15.		2PM	O.C. LT PLAYFAIR & 2nd Lt LESLIE to CRATER	
		8PM.	O.C. 2nd Lts BUDDEN LESLIE & WOOD with LONDON REGT & 1 Co STAFFORDS. SERGT ROUSE with sappers making [illegible] in and near crater. Work on communication trench continued also repairs to support & fire trenches. Billet heavily shelled between 8.30–9 PM. Casualties 5 killed 8 wounded. [initials]	
17.8.15.		10AM	O.C to Brigade H.Q. then to see O.C. NORTH STAFFORDS. O.C. with LT PLAYFAIR & 2nd Lt WOOD to reconnoitre line for new communication between H12 & firing line. Ind line utilizing old saps.	
		8PM	LT PLAYFAIR 2nd Lts WOOD, BUDDEN & LESLIE 2nd Bn LONDON REGT & 1 Co LEINSTERS. Communication trench in rear of H12 completed. New fire trench dug to 3'x3' except 2 bays. [initials]	

1875 Wt. W593/826 1,000,000 4/15 J.B.C. & A. A.D.S.S./Forms/C. 2118.

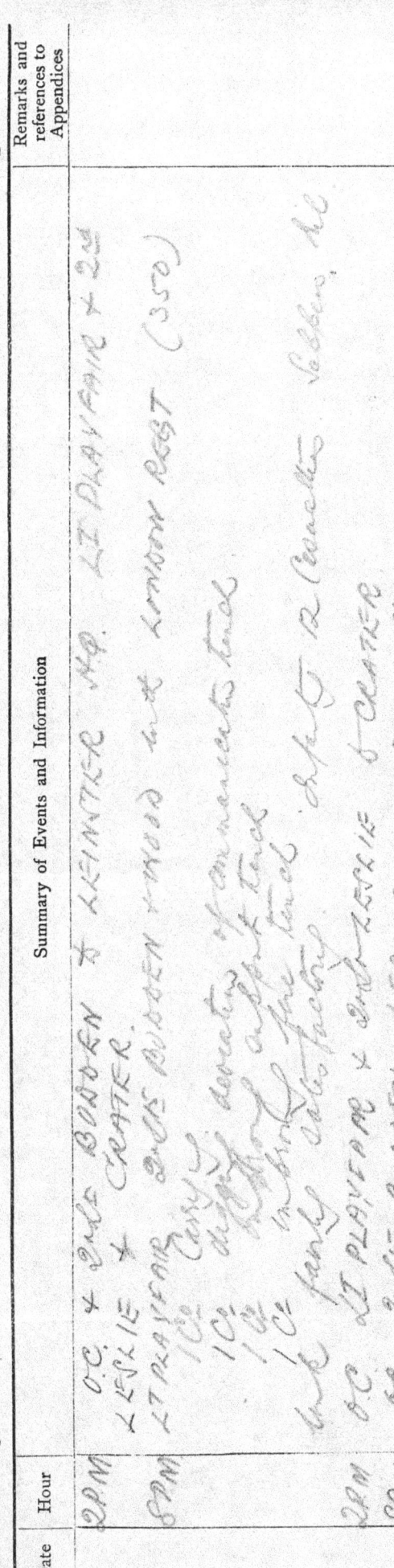

Instructions regarding War Diaries and Intelligence Summaries are contained in F. S. Regs., Part II. and the Staff Manual respectively. Title Pages will be prepared in manuscript.

WAR DIARY
or
INTELLIGENCE SUMMARY
(Erase heading not required.)

Army Form C. 2118

Place	Date	Hour	Summary of Events and Information	Remarks and references to Appendices
YPRES	18/8	2PM	With G.O.C. 17th I.B. to CRATER. Got badly shelled. G.O.C. gave orders to concentrate work on dugouts.	
		8PM	O.C. & 2nd Lt LESLIE to lay out dugouts. 2nd Lts LESLIE & WOOD with 2/ LONDON REGT to dig. 2nd Lt LESLIE wounded & Sapper CURTIS killed while laying out. Work delayed owing to this & casualties among infantry. Progress poor. AG	
	19/8	11.30AM	O.C. & Lt PLAYFAIR to reconnoitre work for night.	
		8PM	Lt PLAYFAIR 2nd Lts BUDDEN & WOOD & 2nd LONDON REGT digging & erecting dugouts with 2 Sections Sappers. Three RE dugouts erected in forward parts, one large dugout in CRATER & 4 dugouts in rear of front line. 2nd Lt WOOD wounded.	
	20/8	2PM	O.C. to reconnoitre work in CRATER.	
		8PM	O.C. & Lt BUDDEN 2 Sections RE & 2nd Bn LONDON REGT. Sandbagged parapet of new support trench. Sandbagged in CRATER. [illegible] dugouts in crater & [illegible] forward parts. 2 men wounded in billets by shell fire in day.	
	21/8		Consolidating position. Sandbagging support trench. Opening out new communication in front of H12.	
	22/8	9AM	To CRATER with G.O.C. 17th I.B.	
		8PM	O.C. & 2nd Lt BUDDEN, 4 Sections RE, LONDON REGT & [illegible] in front of CRATER, dugouts [illegible]	

1875 Wt. W593/826 1,000,000 4/15 J.B.C. & A. A.D.S.S./Forms/C. 2118.

Army Form C. 2118

WAR DIARY
or
INTELLIGENCE SUMMARY
(Erase heading not required.)

Instructions regarding War Diaries and Intelligence Summaries are contained in F. S. Regs., Part II. and the Staff Manual respectively. Title Pages will be prepared in manuscript.

Place	Date	Hour	Summary of Events and Information	Remarks and references to Appendices
	22/8		in Crater. Completing new communication trench. 2nd Lt RUDDEN + 1 NCO wounded near support trench. Sapper wounded working in front of CRATER. P.C.	
	23/8.	9 P.M.	O.C. to CRATER by day.	
		8 P.M.	O.C. + Section of Indian Regt. Completed CRATER. Completed 5 dugouts in rear of support trench. Cleared parados of support trench and thickened ditto + parapet for bomb pits	
	24/8 to 31/8		Company resting near HOUTKERQUE.	

A. [illegible] Capt.
O.C. 12th Co. R.E.
31/8/15

1875 Wt. W593/826 1,000,000 4/15 J.B.C. & A. A.D.S.S./Forms/C. 2118.

R.E.

6th Division

121
6973

12th Field Coy: R.E.

Vol XIV

Sept 15

29/10/15

WAR DIARY

OF

12th (Fd) Co R.E.

FROM 1.9.15 TO 30.9.15

Army Form C. 2118

WAR DIARY
or
~~INTELLIGENCE SUMMARY~~
(Erase heading not required.)

Instructions regarding War Diaries and Intelligence Summaries are contained in F. S. Regs., Part II. and the Staff Manual respectively. Title Pages will be prepared in manuscript.

Place	Date	Hour	Summary of Events and Information	Remarks and references to Appendices
YPRES DIST.	1/9/15	to 3/9/15	Company in rest billets WEST of POPERINGHE. Moved by bus on evening of 3/9/15 HQ + 2 Sections to CANAL BANK. 2 Sections to Camp in Square A29 AG	
	4/9/15		Sappers employed repairing and constructing dugouts for their own use in CANAL BANK. Went with RE officer to choose sites for Bn dugouts in front line trenches. Very wet and little or no signs of any new work having been done since company left them at end of July. AG	
	5/9/15		Sunday. Company resting. AG	
	6/9/15		At work on Bn dugouts by day. No party taking tea[?] place in communication trenches by night	
	7/9/15		As on 6/9. 100 Infantry commenced drainage scheme by night AG	
	8/9/15		As on 7/9. 100 infantry on drainage. 25 Company[?] for Bn dugouts AG	
	9/9/15		As on 8/9. Commenced [illegible] of GORDON STREET by day. No infantry at night on account of reliefs. AG	
	10/9/15		As on 9.9 AG	
	11/9/15		As on 10/9. 200 infantry by night on drainage scheme. LIEUT JACKSON reported from hospital AG	
	12/9/15		Sunday. Sappers resting. 150. infantry on drainage by night AG	
	13/9/15		Sappers on Bn emblacements[?] to aid [illegible] GORDON STREET. Commenced experimental [illegible] to reclaim front line. 150 infantry on drainage by night. AG	
	14/9/15		As on 13/9.	
	15/9/15		As on 14/9. No infantry at night on account of reliefs AG	
	16/9/15		Commenced main drain of left sector. Work as usual. AG	

1875 Wt. W593/826 1,000,000 4/15 J.B.C. & A. A.D.S.S./Forms/C. 2118.

Instructions regarding War Diaries and Intelligence Summaries are contained in F. S. Regs., Part II. and the Staff Manual respectively. Title Pages will be prepared in manuscript.

WAR DIARY
or
INTELLIGENCE SUMMARY
(Erase heading not required.)

Army Form C. 2118

Place	Date	Hour	Summary of Events and Information	Remarks and references to Appendices
YPRES DIST	17/9/15		Got more M.G. dugouts in hand. 120 infantry on main drains of left sector by night. 30 infantry with det. of Sappers completing main drains of Right sector. AG	
	18/9/15		As before. Commenced siting of two more communication trenches. AG	
	19/9/15		Sunday. Company resting. AG	
	20/9/15		As before. AG	
	21/9/15		As before. AG	
	22/9/15		Received instructions to push on erection of dugouts & assist infantry. Took Sappers off drainage work at 1 PM and sent out 4 detachments to erect by night [illegible]. Shelters made of 3 special frames, 5 rafters & corrugated iron roof most successful. Re-[illegible] existing shelters for sentries in front line on extreme right. New X line commenced with 95 infantry. AG	
	23/9/15		As on 22/9. Progress fair. Bridge No 2 broken by shell fire and party employed on repair. Heavy rain brought [illegible] work. 2nd LIEUT MACKINNON RE reported for duty. AG One wounded AG	
	24/9/15		Revetting front line (small parties completing piece in hand). Small parties finishing GARDEN & BOND STREETS. All work suspended at night except parties erecting shelters for sentries. AG	
	25/9/15		Completing in dugouts awaiting development of action on right. No work done. AG	
	26/9/15		Sunday. Company resting. No infantry parties available.	
	27/9/15		Siting communication trenches resumed. All dugouts in hand. No infantry available on account of reliefs.	

1875 Wt. W593/826 1,000,000 4/15 J.B.C. & A. A.D.S.S./Forms/C. 2118.

Army Form C. 2118.

WAR DIARY
or
INTELLIGENCE SUMMARY
(Erase heading not required.)

Instructions regarding War Diaries and Intelligence Summaries are contained in F. S. Regs., Part II. and the Staff Manual respectively. Title pages will be prepared in manuscript.

Hour, Date, Place		Summary of Events and Information	Remarks and References to Appendices
YPRES DIST	28/9	On 27.9 Infantry attack at night on X line but work delayed by rain. ABS	
	29.9	Commenced a new [illegible] but infantry line remainder of work as before. 150 infantry on new X line but work delayed by rain. ABS	
	31/9	Work as before. No infantry at night on account of relief.	

A. D. [illegible]
Capt.
O.C. [illegible] Co. R.E.
30/9/15

(9 26 6) W 257—976 100,000 4/12 H W V 79/3298

1

6th Division

121/7333

12th Field Coy: RE

Vol XV

Oct 15

WAR DIARY

OF

12th (Fd) Co R.E.

FROM 1 10 15.

TO 31-10-15.

Instructions regarding War Diaries and Intelligence Summaries are contained in F. S. Regs., Part II. and the Staff Manual respectively. Title Pages will be prepared in manuscript.

WAR DIARY
or
~~INTELLIGENCE SUMMARY~~
(Erase heading not required.)

Army Form C. 2118

Place	Date	Hour	Summary of Events and Information	Remarks and references to Appendices
YPRES DISTRICT	1/10/15 to 12/10/15		Company distributed, 1 section in back billets 3 sections on CANAL. Back billets on manufacture of material for trenches. CANAL BANK sections improving communication trenches, erecting sample revetments in front line, dugouts for machine guns in front and second line dugouts on CANAL BANK. AG	
	12/10/15		Work as usual but hampered by shelling at night. Trench tramway on ST JEAN road commenced. AG	
	13/10/15 to 14/10/15		Work as for 12th with addition of trench tramway. One section of 2/2 West Riding Fd Co attached for instruction. AG	
	15/10/15		Work as usual marked out first part of WARWICK LINE. AG	
	16/10/15 to 20/10/15		Work as usual. 2nd Lt THRELFALL wounded on night of 20th. AG	
	21/10/15		Work as usual. Drainage of WIELTJE POND completed. AG	
	22/10/15 to 25/10/15		Company transferred to work on right sector. Work of same nature as before. 2nd Lt G. H. IVORY reported for duty on 25/10/15. Commenced trench tram down POTIJZE ROAD. One sapper wounded night of 25th/26th. AG	
	26/10/15 to 29/10/15		Work as usual. Progress on 29.10 practically nil on account of shelling. AG	
	30/10/15 31/10/15		Work as usual. AG	

A. Campbell Captain RE
O.C. 12th Co R.E.
31/10/15

1875 Wt. W593/826 1,000,000 4/15 J.B.C. & A. A.D.S.S./Forms/C. 2118.

6th Division

12th Fd. Co. R.E.

Nov.

Vol XVI

WAR DIARY

OF

121/7655

12th (Fd) Co R E

FROM 1. 11. 15. TO 30. 11. 15.

Instructions regarding War Diaries and Intelligence Summaries are contained in F. S. Regs., Part II. and the Staff Manual respectively. Title Pages will be prepared in manuscript.

WAR DIARY
or
INTELLIGENCE SUMMARY
(Erase heading not required.)

Army Form C. 2118

Place	Date	Hour	Summary of Events and Information	Remarks and references to Appendices
YPRES DISTRICT	1/11/15		Company distributed. HQ + 3 Sections YPRES CANAL 1 Section + Workshops YPRES - POPERINGHE ROAD Mounted Section ELVERDINGHE - POPERINGHE ROAD Sections on CANAL employed in sector VERLOREN HOEK ROAD & MENIN ROAD. Work mainly drainage & reclamation of communication trenches, construction of trench tram on POTIJZE ROAD, dugouts on CANAL BANK. Progress poor, infantry working parties cancelled by Brigade. [initials]	
	2/11/15		Work as usual. Progress poor on account of heavy rains which had caused many slips in trenches. [initials]	
	3/11/15		Work as usual. Progress poor at night on account of lack of infantry who were not available on account of reliefs. [initials]	
	4/11/15		Work as usual. Progress better. [initials]	
	5/11/15		Work as usual. Works at POTIJZE hampered by shelling. Reserve party employed at night clearing debris of trees etc on POTIJZE ROAD after shelling. [initials]	
	6/11/15		Work as usual. [initials]	
	7/11/15		Sunday. Company resting & bathing. [initials]	

Instructions regarding War Diaries and Intelligence Summaries are contained in F. S. Regs., Part II. and the Staff Manual respectively. Title Pages will be prepared in manuscript.

WAR DIARY
or
INTELLIGENCE SUMMARY
(Erase heading not required.)

Army Form C. 2118

Place	Date	Hour	Summary of Events and Information	Remarks and references to Appendices
YPRES DIST	8/11		Work as usual. Commenced excavating site for new "Bench" dugouts on CANAL BANK. AG	
	9/11		Works as usual. AG	
	10/11		Handed over sector GULLY to MENIN ROAD to another division and took over extreme left of divisional line. Found trenches on new line very wet. Employed one party at night on commencement of drainage. No infantry available for this sector. AG	
	11/11		Works as usual AG	
	12/11		Works as usual AG	
	13/11		Works as usual. Commenced experimental revetment of drained trench in left sector. AG	
	14/11		Company resting. 320 infantry on drainage of left, & 100 on drainage of right sector by night. AG	
	15/11		Work as usual AG	
	16/11		Works as usual but delayed by hostile shelling. AG	
	17/11		Works as usual AG	

1875 Wt. W593/826 1,000,000 4/15 J.B.C. & A. A.D.S.S./Forms/C. 2118.

Instructions regarding War Diaries and Intelligence Summaries are contained in F. S. Regs., Part II. and the Staff Manual respectively. Title Pages will be prepared in manuscript.

WAR DIARY
or
INTELLIGENCE SUMMARY
(Erase heading not required.)

Army Form C. 2118

Place	Date	Hour	Summary of Events and Information	Remarks and references to Appendices
YPRES DIST.	18/11		Division relieved. Company moved back to rest billets. A.G.	
	19 – 30th		Company in rest billets. Part at first on POPERINGHE – YPRES ROAD but finally main body on POPERINGHE ELVERDINGHE ROAD. Sappers employed in improving their own + infantry rest billets. A.G.	

A. O. Abell
Capt RE
O.C. 12th Co RE
30/11

1875 Wt. W593/826 1,000,000 4/15 J.B.C. & A. A.D.S.S./Forms/C. 2118.

6th Div

WAR DIARY

OF

12th (Fd) Co R E

FROM 1-12-15

Vol XVII

TO 31. 12. 15

Instructions regarding War Diaries and Intelligence Summaries are contained in F. S. Regs., Part II. and the Staff Manual respectively. Title Pages will be prepared in manuscript.

WAR DIARY
or
~~INTELLIGENCE SUMMARY~~
(Erase heading not required.)

Army Form C. 2118

Place	Date	Hour	Summary of Events and Information	Remarks and references to Appendices
YPRES. DISTRICT.	1/12/15 to 15/12/15		Company in rest billets on POPERINGHE – ELVERDINGHE ROAD. Sappers employed on improving hutting accomodation in rest camps erecting huts making baths & making furniture. Weather generally rough and wet but not cold. Marched two sections to CANAL BANK on night of 15/16 and took over old dugouts which were occupied in Sept. Oct. Novr. AG	
	16/12/15		Made reconnaissance of line and arranged with Brigadier as to what work should first be put in hand. Found trenches rather wet throughout and in places so wet as to be unfit for occupation. LIEUT PLAYFAIR slightly wounded by fragment of shell. Sent him to back billet to rest after anti-tetanus injection. AG	
	17/12/15		Commenced work on revetting derelict bays in X line and construction of dugouts for accomodation of additional infantry on CANAL BANK. AG	
	18/12/15		Work as usual AG	
	19/12/15		Enemy turned on gas between 5AM & 6AM. Sections in dugouts used tube helmets for about an hour and were not any the worse. Enemy continued to shell heavily all day and did not attempt any work at night. Decision not to work proved wise as all roads were heavily shelled at night and bombardment did not slack off till morning of 20th AG	
	20/12/15		Work as usual except on CANAL BANK where dugout building was suspended as situation was uncertain and shelling still rather dangerous. AG	

1875 Wt. W593/826 1,000,000 4/15 J.B.C. & A. A.D.S.S./Forms/C. 2118.

Instructions regarding War Diaries and Intelligence Summaries are contained in F. S. Regs., Part II. and the Staff Manual respectively. Title Pages will be prepared in manuscript.

WAR DIARY
or
~~INTELLIGENCE SUMMARY~~
(Erase heading not required.)

Army Form C. 2118

Place	Date	Hour	Summary of Events and Information	Remarks and references to Appendices
YPRES DIST	21/12		Work as usual. Shelling less by day but roads shelled at night. Working parties shelled at POTIJZE VILLAGE. 2nd Lt REGNARD & 15 O.R. slightly wounded. 2nd Lt REGNARD & 2 OR at duty. 3 OR to Fd Ambulance. AG	
	22/12		Work as usual. One section employed wiring in front of front line NORTH of VERLORENHOEK ROAD. Quiet night. AG	
	23/12		Work as usual. One section employed wiring in rear of POTIJZE WOOD. One sapper severely wounded. AG	
	24/12		Work as usual. Relieved one section by section from rear billet. AG	
	25/12		Commenced reclamation of derelict bays in front line SOUTH of VERLORENHOEK ROAD. Employed one section on this one in X line near POTIJZE. Quiet night but enemy made no attempt to fraternize. AG	
	26/12		Work as usual. Continued reclamation of front & X line. Work slow and difficult on account of mud. AG	
	27/12		Work as usual. Reclamation proceeds slowly. AG	
	28/12		Work as usual. Party in front line wounded by snipers. One sapper killed. One infantry died of wounds.	
	29/12		Work as usual AG	

1875 Wt. W593/826 1,000,000 4/15 J.B.C. & A. A.D.S.S./Forms/C. 2118.

Instructions regarding War Diaries and Intelligence Summaries are contained in F. S. Regs., Part II. and the Staff Manual respectively. Title Pages will be prepared in manuscript.

WAR DIARY
or
INTELLIGENCE SUMMARY
(Erase heading not required.)

Army Form C. 2118

Place	Date	Hour	Summary of Events and Information	Remarks and references to Appendices
YPRES DIST.	30/12		Work by day as usual. No work at night on account of relief of infantry. Relieved one section. AG	
	31/12.		Work as usual. Snipers active on front line where three of infantry party were hit. One sapper slightly wounded in X line. AG	

A. O. Abell Capt RE
O.C. 12 Co RE.
31/12/15

6th DIV.

R.E.

No. 12 Field Coy

Jan – Dec 1916.

Index

SUBJECT.

No.	Contents.	Date.
	12/D.L.I. July - Oct, 1916	

(63,965). Wt.15,820—176. 2000. 9/21. Gp.164. A.&E.W.

6

WAR DIARY

OF.

12th Fd. Co. R.E. 6th Div.

Jan

Vol XVIII

FROM. 1.1.16. TO 31.1.16.

Instructions regarding War Diaries and Intelligence Summaries are contained in F. S. Regs., Part II. and the Staff Manual respectively. Title pages will be prepared in manuscript.

WAR DIARY

or

~~INTELLIGENCE SUMMARY.~~

(*Erase heading not required.*)

Army Form C. 2118.

Place	Date	Hour	Summary of Events and Information	Remarks and references to Appendices
YPRES DISTRICT	1/1/16		Company distributed 2 Sections on YPRES CANAL. 2 Sections at Sawmills near BRANDHOEK on YPRES-POPERINGHE ROAD. Advanced sections for work on trenches, reserve sections resting and doing day work on hutting etc. Work on hand dugouts on CANAL BANK and reclaiming flooded trenches. Employed 70 infantry by day 105 by night. AG	
	2/1/16		Work as above. Employed 20 infantry by day 100 by night. AG	
	3/1/16		Work as above. Progress on reclaiming front line slow owing to flooded state of trench and necessity of shutting hurdles. 115 Infantry at night. AG	
	4/1/16		No work at night as brigade relieved. Employed 72 infantry on dugouts by day. AG	
	5/1/16		Commenced footway along abandoned front line and suspended full reclamation. Reclaiming bad bays on extreme left of sector (A8). 70 Infantry by day 160 by night. AG	
	6/1/16		As on 5/1/16. Progress on footway improving as sappers get used to work. Infantry DAY 85 NIGHT 115	
	7/1/16		Work as before. Infantry DAY 103 NIGHT 115. AG	
	8/1/16		Work as usual. AG	

1577 Wt. W10791/1773 500,000 1/15 D. D. & L. A.D.S.S./Forms/C. 2118.

Instructions regarding War Diaries and Intelligence Summaries are contained in F. S. Regs., Part II. and the Staff Manual respectively. Title pages will be prepared in manuscript.

WAR DIARY
or
INTELLIGENCE SUMMARY.
(Erase heading not required.)

Army Form C. 2118.

Place	Date	Hour	Summary of Events and Information	Remarks and references to Appendices
YPRES DIST.	9.1.16		No work at night owing to relief. AG	
	10/1/16		Both sections on piled footway & bush work on. 100 yards completed. Infantry DAY 83 NIGHT 175.	
	11/1/16		Completed piled footway (about 900 yds) commenced on 5/1. Infantry DAY 100 NIGHT 120 AG	
	12/1/16		One Section reclaiming on left of front line one section on left of X line Infantry DAY 105 NIGHT 120 AG	
	13/1/16		Brigade relief. No work at night 90 infantry on CANAL dugouts by day AG	
	14/1/16		Work as before Continued reclamation of trenches commenced on 12/1	
	15/1/16		Work as on 14th. Delay on X line owing to failure of infantry party Infantry DAY 85 NIGHT 60. AG	
	16/1/16		Continued same trenches Infantry day NIL NIGHT 83. AG	
	17/1/16		Continued same trenches. Infantry Day 90 NIGHT 85 AG	

1577 Wt. W10791/1773 500,000 1/15 D. D. & L. A.D.S.S./Forms/C. 2118.

Army Form C. 2118.

Instructions regarding War Diaries and Intelligence Summaries are contained in F. S. Regs., Part II. and the Staff Manual respectively. Title pages will be prepared in manuscript.

WAR DIARY
or
INTELLIGENCE SUMMARY.
(Erase heading not required.)

Place	Date	Hour	Summary of Events and Information	Remarks and references to Appendices
YPRES DIST.	18/1/16		Both sections on front line at night 'Shudder' work. Made good progress. Infantry DAY 85 NIGHT 120 AG	
	19/1/16		No work at night owing to infantry reliefs. Rebuild bridge No 7 by day. 50 Infantry on dugouts by day AG	
	20/1/16		One section at night on extreme right of X line reclaiming. One section reclaiming support in rear of CRUMP FARM. Infantry DAY 64 NIGHT 135 AG	
	21/1/16		Work continued on same trenches as 20/1. Infantry DAY 60 NIGHT 140 AG	
	22/1/16		One section on support area O0 + O1st. One section revetting on front line. Infantry DAY 50 NIGHT 130 AG	
	23/1/16		Sunday. No work on dugouts. Sections at work at night on same trenches as 22nd. Infantry NIGHT 120. AG	
	24/1/16		Work by night as on 23rd. Infantry DAY NIL Night 120. Supply of steel for dugouts running short so infantry party discontinued and work done by civilians only AG	
	25/1/16		Infantry reliefs no night work except a few sappers laying footboards in support line AG	

Army Form C. 2118.

Instructions regarding War Diaries and Intelligence Summaries are contained in F. S. Regs., Part II. and the Staff Manual respectively. Title pages will be prepared in manuscript.

WAR DIARY
or
INTELLIGENCE SUMMARY.
(Erase heading not required.)

Place	Date	Hour	Summary of Events and Information	Remarks and references to Appendices
YPRES DIST	26/1/16		Commenced reclamation of Support trench S6A continued reclamation of support to SOUTH from CRUMP FARM 120 Infantry at NIGHT. 2nd Lt J.A. RENNIE who had gone missing from rest billet on night of 24th 25th was found in POPERINGHE on 25th and transferred to BASE as a "mental case". Nothing known to account for this. AG	
	27/1/16		Continued as on 26/1/16. Commenced reclaiming CANAL LINE trenches by civilian labour. Infantry at night 150. AG	
	28/1/16		Scheme of work upset as wagons were not allowed down on account of expected retaliation. Used 200 infantry thickening parapet in Support X line. AG	
	29/1/16		Reclaiming trenches as on 26th & 27th. Employed 180 infantry at night. AG	
	30/1/16		Infantry reliefs. No work at night. AG	
	31/1/16		Work continued as on 26th, 27th & 29th. Employed 85 infantry. AG	

A. [illegible]
Captain RE
OC 12th Co RE
31/1/16

WAR DIARY.

OF

12th (Fd) Co. R.E.

From 1.2.16. —— To. 29.2.16.

Vol XIX

Instructions regarding War Diaries and Intelligence Summaries are contained in F. S. Regs., Part II. and the Staff Manual respectively. Title pages will be prepared in manuscript.

WAR DIARY
or
INTELLIGENCE SUMMARY.
(Erase heading not required.)

Army Form C. 2118.

Place	Date	Hour	Summary of Events and Information	Remarks and references to Appendices
YPRES DISTRICT	1/2/16		Distribution of Company 2 Sections in dugouts on bank of YPERLEE NORTH of YPRES 2 Sections at workshops on YPRES - POPERINGHE ROAD near BRANDHOEK. Forward sections reclaiming trenches back sections in training etc. Reclaiming S6A + S5. Employed 170 Infantry by night. AG	
	2/2/16		Reclaiming S5. Employed 200 Infantry at night. AG	
	3/2/16		Reclaiming S5. Infantry 200. Small party in dugouts in SOTNLE WOOD. AG	
	4/2/16		" " " 185	AG
	5/2/16		Infantry relief. No night work. AG	
	6/2/16		Commenced reclamation of S4. 150 Infantry at work. AG	
	7.2.16		Continued reclamation of S5 S4. 140 Infantry at work. 30 Cyclists at work on repair of CANAL LINE. AG	
	8/2/16		Continued reclamation & CANAL LINE. Infantry & Cyclists as on 7.2.16. AG	
	9/2/16		Continued reclamation of S5 S4. 160 Infantry employed, a few Sappers by day revetting CANAL LINE. No Cyclists. AG	
	10/2/16		Infantry relief. No night work. AG	
	11/2/16		Reclaiming S5 S4. Progress poor as much material used in repair of work already done which had been shelled in. AG	
	12/2/16		Heavy shelling to SOUTH. Working parties recalled by Brigade. AG	

1577 Wt. W10791/1773 500,000 1/15 D. D. & L. A.D.S.S./Forms/C. 2118.

WAR DIARY
or
INTELLIGENCE SUMMARY.
(Erase heading not required.)

Army Form C. 2118.

Instructions regarding War Diaries and Intelligence Summaries are contained in F. S. Regs., Part II. and the Staff Manual respectively. Title pages will be prepared in manuscript.

Place	Date	Hour	Summary of Events and Information	Remarks and references to Appendices
YPRES DIST.	13/2/16		Reclaiming S5 S4. Work of party shelled shortly after beginning work. Lieut IVORY wounded, 1 NCO killed, 9 NCOs & Sappers wounded, 19 of infantry wounded. Work abandoned. AG	
	14/2/16		Heavy shelling. Work of parties cancelled by Brigade. AG	
	15/2/16		Infantry reliefs. No night work. AG	
	16/2/16		Reclaiming S3. Strengthening S4 & S5. Repairing POTIJZE DEFENCES. 100 Infantry at work. AG	
	17.2.16		Repairing S3. Improving S5 S4. POTIJZE DEFENCES. 100 Infantry AG	
	18/2/16		Rest in H 2 AG	
	19/2/16		Repair of POTIJZE DEFENCES. Reclaiming S3. 105 Infantry at work. AG	
	20/2/16		Infantry reliefs. AG	
	21/2/16		Repair of POTIJZE DEFENCES. Reclaiming & revetting S3 S4. 130 Infantry AG	
	22/2/16		Cutting new Communication trench S4 to A4. 120 infantry AG	
	23/2/16		Reclaiming S4. [illegible] Sentries AG	
	24/2/16		Reclaiming S4 & revetting in CANAL LINE. AG	
	25/2/16		Infantry Reliefs. Snow. AG	

T2134. Wt. W708–776. 500000. 4/15. Sir J. C. & S.

Army Form C. 2118.

Instructions regarding War Diaries and Intelligence Summaries are contained in F. S. Regs., Part II. and the Staff Manual respectively. Title pages will be prepared in manuscript.

WAR DIARY
or
INTELLIGENCE SUMMARY.
(Erase heading not required.)

Place	Date	Hour	Summary of Events and Information	Remarks and references to Appendices
YPRES DIST	26/2/16		Relaying S4. Tidying breaches AG	
	27/2/16		Relaying S4 & Improving HAYMARKET. 165 Inf party AG	
	28/2/16		Relaying S5 & DUKE STREET damaged by shelling. 70 Inf party AG	
	29.2.16		Revetting & picket of S5 & repairing damages. Relaying and Strengthening HAYMARKET & DUKE STREET. 150 Inf party AG	

A. O. Abell
Capt R.E.
O.C. 12th Coy R.E.
1/3/16

T2134. Wt. W708 – 776. 500000. 4/15. Sir J. C. & S.

6

Vol XX

WAR DIARY

OF

12th (Fd) Co R.E.

FROM 1.3.16 TO 31.3.16.

Instructions regarding War Diaries and Intelligence Summaries are contained in F. S. Regs., Part II. and the Staff Manual respectively. Title pages will be prepared in manuscript.

WAR DIARY
or
~~INTELLIGENCE SUMMARY.~~
(*Erase heading not required.*)

Army Form C. 2118.

Place	Date	Hour	Summary of Events and Information	Remarks and references to Appendices
YPRES DISTRICT	1/3/16		Distribution of Company. 2 Sections in dugouts on YPERLEE NORTH of YPRES. 2 Sections and workshops at BRANDHOEK on POPERINGHE - YPRES road. Horses on POPERINGHE ELVERDINGHE ROAD about 1½ miles from POPERINGHE. Working sections reclaiming derelict trenches, [illegible] sections on hutting & [illegible] of trench stores. [illegible] of [illegible] at work on CANAL LINE. [illegible] shelled [illegible] 6.00. AG	
	2/3/16		[illegible] and widening [illegible] of support line & communication trenches. Employed 160 Infantry [illegible] revetting CANAL LINE. AG	
	3/3/16		Revetting & improving support line & communications. Progress poor owing to bad weather. Employed 80 Infantry. AG	
	4/3/16		Reclaiming support line, improving communications, revetting CANAL LINE. AG	
	5/3/16		Reclaiming support line. Infantry parties very weak on account of reliefs. AG	
	6/3/16		Improving support line. AG	
	7/3/16		Heavy snow. Employed infantry on sandbagging communications where not in direct view from front. AG	
	8/3/16		Clearing drainage of front & support lines. Snow still hampering work. AG	
	9/3/16 to 16/3/16.		Continued drainage of support & front lines. Collected material for M.G. emplacements at [illegible] and completed [illegible] of one emplacement. AG	

T2134. Wt. W708-776. 500000. 4/15. Sir J. C. & S.

Instructions regarding War Diaries and Intelligence Summaries are contained in F. S. Regs., Part II. and the Staff Manual respectively. Title pages will be prepared in manuscript.

WAR DIARY
or
INTELLIGENCE SUMMARY.
(Erase heading not required.)

Army Form C. 2118.

Place	Date	Hour	Summary of Events and Information	Remarks and references to Appendices
YPRES DISTRICT.	15/3/16		Advanced sections withdrawn at night to BRANDHOEK AC	
	16/3/16		Marched to rest billets at HERZEELE. AC	
	17/3/16		Rest. AC	
	18/3/16		Route marching AC	
	19/3/16		Sunday. AC	
	20/3/16		Route marching. AC	
	21/3/16		Pontoon & section drill. C in C inspected billets. AC	
	22 – 24		Instruction classes for infantry. Officers on water supply project AC	
	25/3/16		Drill AC	
	26/3/16		Sunday. AC	
	27/3/16		Marched HOPAUDT and entrained for CALAIS. AC	
	28/3/16		Drill AC	
	29/3/16		Brigade route march AC	
	30/3/16		Drill AC	
	31/3/16		Short route march & drill AC	

A. Campbell Capt RE
OC 12t Co RE 31/3/16

T2134. Wt. W708-776. 500000. 4/15. Sir J. C. & S.

6

WAR. DIARY.

OF.

12th (Fd) Co R.E.

Vol XXI

FROM. 1-4-16

TO. 30-4-16

WAR DIARY
or
INTELLIGENCE SUMMARY.
(Erase heading not required.)

Army Form C. 2118.

Instructions regarding War Diaries and Intelligence Summaries are contained in F. S. Regs., Part II. and the Staff Manual respectively. Title pages will be prepared in manuscript.

Place	Date	Hour	Summary of Events and Information	Remarks and references to Appendices
CALAIS and HERZEELE	1/4/16 – 16/4/16		Company resting. Marched from CALAIS to HERZEELE. Daily routine route marching & drills employed after [illegible] [illegible] to camps as required. AG	
YPRES DISTRICT	17/4/16.		Sent two sections to take over back billets of company relieved. AG	
	18/4/16		Took over front billet and marched remaining sections into back billet. AG	
	19/4/16		No work as brigade still taking over line. AG	
	20/4/16.		Heavy shelling no work possible till midnight. AG	
	21/4/16		Heavy shelling no work. AG	
	22/4/16		100 infantry repairing front line sappers and infantry wiring X line. Sappers & infantry wiring support line. AG	
	23/4/16.		No infantry available sappers wiring X line. AG	
	24/4/16.		Repairing SKIPTON ROAD & wiring X line. 110 infantry. AG	
	25/4/16		Repairing BARNSLEY ROAD. Wiring X line. 110 infantry. Shelled out of back billet on night of 24/25. AG	
	26/4/16.		Repairing BARNSLEY, wiring X line. 110 infantry. AG	
	27.4.16.		As on 26/4. AG	
	28/4/16		As on 26 + 26. AG	

Instructions regarding War Diaries and Intelligence Summaries are contained in F. S. Regs., Part II. and the Staff Manual respectively. Title pages will be prepared in manuscript.

WAR DIARY
or
INTELLIGENCE SUMMARY.
(Erase heading not required.)

Army Form C. 2118.

Place	Date	Hour	Summary of Events and Information	Remarks and references to Appendices
YPRES DISTRICT	29/4/16.		Commenced reclamation of line of 'Butts'. Infantry (100) mainly on drainage of trenches & clearance of ships. Sappers wiring & line. AC	
	30/4/16.		Continued reclamation and wiring AC	

A. Campbell
Capt. RE
OC 12 [illegible] RE
30/4/16

T2134. Wt. W708-776. 500000. 4/15. Sir J. C. & S.

6

Vol 22

WAR DIARY.
OF.
12th (F.d) Coy R.E.

FROM. 1-5-16 TO 31-5-16

Instructions regarding War Diaries and Intelligence Summaries are contained in F. S. Regs., Part II. and the Staff Manual respectively. Title Pages will be prepared in manuscript.

WAR DIARY
or
INTELLIGENCE SUMMARY
(Erase heading not required.)

Army Form C. 2118

Place	Date	Hour	Summary of Events and Information	Remarks and references to Appendices
YPRES DISTRICT	1/5/16		Distribution of Co. 2 Sections on YPERLEE in dugouts. 2 sections & transport in huts on POPERINGHE – ELVERDINGHE ROAD. Workshops with HQ sections. Wiring reserve line. Constructing support line. 150 Infantry. AG	
	2/5/16		Infantry reliefs. Relieved one section on CANAL. AG	
	3/5/16		Wiring reserve line, constructing support line. Clearing drainage of communication to right of front line. AG	
	4/5/16		As above. Used party on communication & repairs "minenwerfer" craters on extreme left. 110 Infantry. AG	
	5/5/16		As above. Repairs to bridge damaged by shell fire. 80 Infantry. AG	
	6/5/16		Clearance of drainage of right communication trench, support line & wiring of reserve line. 70 Infantry. AG	
	7/5/16		Infantry reliefs. Relieved one section. AG	
	8/5/16		Support line, wiring reserve line. MG emplacements. 150 Infantry. AG	
	9/5/16		1 Co Pioneers commenced work BARNSLEY ROAD–COLNE VALLEY. 150 Infantry on work as 8/5. AG	
	10/5/16		No work done. All parties recalled owing to uncertainty of situation. AG	
	11/5/16		1 Co Pioneers SKIPTON ROAD new trench and improvement of old, started. 1 Co Pioneers HUDDERSFIELD. Clearing old trench carrying material for revetment. 1 Co Pioneers BARNSLEY ROAD–COLNE VALLEY. Revetting & raising parapets. 150 Infantry. Reserve line, support line & MG emplacements. AG	

Army Form C. 2118

WAR DIARY
or
INTELLIGENCE SUMMARY
(Erase heading not required.)

Instructions regarding War Diaries and Intelligence Summaries are contained in F. S. Regs., Part II. and the Staff Manual respectively. Title Pages will be prepared in manuscript.

Place	Date	Hour	Summary of Events and Information	Remarks and references to Appendices
YPRES DIST	12/5/16		Infantry relief. Relieved one section. 3 Pioneer Co at work as on 11/5/16. Commenced new alignment of HUDDERSFIELD. AG	
	13/5/16		3 Pioneer Co at work as before. Infantry as before. Sapper wounded. AG	
	14/5/16		3 Pioneer Cos & Infantry as before. AG	
	15/5/16		3 Pioneer Cos. 125 Infantry. Communication trenches support & reserve lines. MG emplacements. AG	
	16/5/16		3 Pioneer Cos. 120 Infantry. Work as before. AG	
	17/5/16		2 Pioneer Cos at work. 1 Pioneer Co resting. Infantry relief relieved one section. AG 1 Sapper wounded. AG	
	18/5/16		1 Pioneer Co. BARNSLEY RD – COLNE VALLEY. 100 Infantry. MG emplacements, support lines. AG	
	19/5/16		1 Pioneer Co as above. Infantry as usual. AG	
	20/5/16		LIEUT JACKSON slightly wounded night of 19–20. At duty. Pioneer Co on communication trench. 110 Infantry as before. AG	
	21/5/16		Work as usual. 150 Infantry. AG	
	22/5/16		No pioneers in ... Infantry as usual. Continued repairs of trench ... AG	
	23/5/16		1 Co Pioneers BARNSLEY RD – COLNE VALLEY. Infantry as usual. AG	

1875 Wt. W593/826 1,000,000 4/15 J.B.C. & A. A.D.S.S./Forms/C. 2118.

Instructions regarding War Diaries and Intelligence Summaries are contained in F. S. Regs., Part II. and the Staff Manual respectively. Title Pages will be prepared in manuscript.

WAR DIARY
or
INTELLIGENCE SUMMARY
(Erase heading not required.)

Army Form C. 2118

Place	Date	Hour	Summary of Events and Information	Remarks and references to Appendices
	24/5/16		Pioneer Co moved to SKIPTON ROAD. Infantry relief. Relieved one section. AG One sapper wounded AG	
	25/5/16		Pioneers SKIPTON ROAD. Infantry 150 as before AG One sapper killed AG	
	26/5/16		Pioneers as before but moved to HUDDERSFIELD. Infantry as usual. One sapper wounded AG	
	27/5/16		As before. One Lance Corpl wounded. AG	
	28/5/16		Infantry relief. Relieved one section. Pioneers HUDDERSFIELD AG	
	29/5/16		Work as usual. AG	
	30/5/16		Pioneers & infantry as usual. ~~[illegible] WHITE TRENCH~~ AG One sapper wounded AG	
	31/5/16		Pioneers & infantry as usual. Sect Co of Pioneers on WHITE TRENCH	

A. [illegible] Capt RE
O.C. [illegible] Co RE
31/5/16

1875 Wt. W593/826 1,000,000 4/15 J.B.C. & A. A.D.S.S./Forms/C. 2118.

6

WAR. DIARY.

OF.

12th (7th) Co R.E.

Vol 23

FROM. 1-6-16 To 30-6-16

Instructions regarding War Diaries and Intelligence Summaries are contained in F. S. Regs., Part II. and the Staff Manual respectively. Title Pages will be prepared in manuscript.

WAR DIARY
or
INTELLIGENCE SUMMARY
(Erase heading not required.)

Army Form C. 2118

Place	Date	Hour	Summary of Events and Information	Remarks and references to Appendices
YPRES DISTRICT	1/6/16		Distribution of Co. 2 Sections on CANAL BANK in dugouts on EAST of YPERLEE. 2 Sections, workshops & transport near POPERINGHE-ELVERDINGHE ROAD about 1½ miles EAST of POPERINGHE. [illegible] Sections in rear [illegible] & making up material. Sections in front assisting infantry. 1 Co. Pioneers on communication trenches. 1 Co. Pioneers sandbagging front line. AG	
	2/6/16		1 Co. Pioneers sandbagging front line. Infantry carrying material. AG	
	3/6/16		Infantry advance in trenches commenced 9.15 but final objective not reached till 11 P.M. Employed one section to assist Pioneer Co. in opening up old communication trench to front line. This work was started at 10 P.M. [illegible] not useful in clearing entanglements out of trench. One section working to connect left flank of advance to original front line. Ground very bad and sniping heavy. This party succeeded in laying out trench wire along the [illegible] connect the [illegible] also [illegible] digging party in rear.	
	4/6/16		One Co. Pioneers continued communication trench. ½ Co. carrying to working party which was working [illegible]. ½ Co. [illegible] front line. 2nd Lt OSMASTON wounded. AG	

1875 Wt. W593/826 1,000,000 4/15 J.B.C. & A. A.D.S.S./Forms/C. 2118.

Instructions regarding War Diaries and Intelligence Summaries are contained in F. S. Regs., Part II. and the Staff Manual respectively. Title Pages will be prepared in manuscript.

WAR DIARY
or
INTELLIGENCE SUMMARY

(Erase heading not required.)

Army Form C. 2118

Place	Date	Hour	Summary of Events and Information	Remarks and references to Appendices
	5/6/16		Working on left flank had to be drawn back as trenches on left were found to be untenable. Half section with covering & carrying parties employed on this. Progress slow as ground was very difficult to work on. Half section repairing bridge over canal damaged by shell fire. 1/2 Co Pioneers improving communication trench to new front line. One party on old emplacements. AG	
	6/6/16		Continued work on left. Progress good. 1/2 Co Pioneers sandbagging front line. 1 Co Pioneers improving communication to front line. Parties on old emplacements. AG	
	7/6/16		Relieved both sections. One Co Pioneers [illegible] communication trench AG	
	8/6/16		Commenced opening up old support line in rear of new front line. Employed both Pioneer Cos on this assisted by sappers. [illegible] on Bty emplacements & dugouts. AG	
	9/6/16		As on 8th AG	
	10/6/16		As on 9th, footboarding new communication AG	
	11/6/16		1 Co Pioneers resting, other as on 10th AG	

Instructions regarding War Diaries and Intelligence Summaries are contained in F. S. Regs., Part II. and the Staff Manual respectively. Title Pages will be prepared in manuscript.

WAR DIARY
or
INTELLIGENCE SUMMARY
(Erase heading not required.)

Army Form C. 2118

Place	Date	Hour	Summary of Events and Information	Remarks and references to Appendices
	[illegible]/6/16		One section worked on night of 11–12th. The Co Pioneers [illegible] other on communication trench & Indian Sappers working on part of new support line. Infantry draining. AG	
	13/6/16		Heavy rains. Continued drainage & work of support line AG	
	14/6/16		Heavy rains. Work as on 13th. AG	
	15/6/16		Marched back 2 sections to rest camp. AG	
HERZEELE	16/6/16		Company marched to HERZEELE AG	
HERZEELE	17/6/16		Resting at HERZEELE AG	
VOLKERINGHOVE	18/6/16		Marched HERZEELE – VOLKERINGHOVE AG	
"	19/6/16		Company resting. Employed 600 Infantry on practice trenches. AG	
"	20/6/16		Company in infantry drill. Employed 1100 infantry on practice trenches AG	
"	21/6/16		Company in route march. 1650 infantry on practice trenches	
"	22/6/16		Company in drill 1650 Infantry on practice trenches AG	

1875 Wt. W593/826 1,000,000 4/15 J.B.C. & A. A.D.S.S./Forms/C. 2118.

Instructions regarding War Diaries and Intelligence Summaries are contained in F. S. Regs., Part II. and the Staff Manual respectively. Title Pages will be prepared in manuscript.

WAR DIARY

or

~~INTELLIGENCE SUMMARY~~

(Erase heading not required.)

Army Form C. 2118

Place	Date	Hour	Summary of Events and Information	Remarks and references to Appendices
VOLKERING HOVE	23/6/16		Company in drill. 1100 working party of [illegible] section of sappers in practice trenches which were attached [illegible]	
	24/6/16		Drill AmJ	
VOLKERING HOVE.	25/6/16		Company church parade. AmJ	
"	26/6/16		Drill & physical training. AmJ	
"	27/6/16		Drill & physical training and weapon drill AmJ	
"	28/6/16		Brigade training. AmJ	
"	29/6/16		Brigade training. AmJ	
"	30/6/16		Brigade training. AmJ	

July 1. 1916

A M Jackson Lt RB
for O.C. 12th Co RB

1875 Wt. W593/826 1,000,000 4/15 J.B.C. & A. A.D.S.S./Forms/C. 2118.

Vol 24

WAR DIARY

OF

12th (70) Co R E

FROM 1. 7. 16 TO 31. 7. 16

Instructions regarding War Diaries and Intelligence Summaries are contained in F. S. Regs., Part II. and the Staff Manual respectively. Title pages will be prepared in manuscript.

WAR DIARY
or
INTELLIGENCE SUMMARY.
(Erase heading not required.)

Army Form C. 2118.

Place	Date	Hour	Summary of Events and Information	Remarks and references to Appendices
VOLKERINGHOVE to HERZEELE	1/7/16		Marched from VOLKERINGHOVE to HERZEELE AG	
HERZEELE to YPRES	2/7/16		Marched from HERZEELE leaving transport WEST of HOOTKERQUE. Billetted in defences WEST of YPRES. AG	
WEST of YPRES	3/7/16		Working on defences and dugouts in YPERLEE. Supervising work of 2 Pioneer Co's on communication trenches. Employed 300 infantry. AG	
"	4/7/16		Work as on 3/7 AG	
"	5/7/16		Work as on 4/7 but infantry short in numbers owing to their being missed trains AG	
"	6/7/16		Works as usual. AG	
"	7/7/16		Works as usual. AG	
"	8/7/16		Works as usual got orders late at night billeting company WEST of POPERINGHE. AG	
W of POPERINGHE	9.7.16		Marched at 5AM to camp WEST of POPERINGHE AG	
	10/7/16 to 14/7/16		Resting WEST of POPERINGHE. Employed two sections on defences AG	
	15/7/16		Marched two sections to billets in cellars of YPRES. 2 sections near BRANDHOEK Horses in POPERINGHE - ELVERDINGHE ROAD AG	

T2134. Wt. W708-776. 500000. 4/15. Sir J. C. & S.

Instructions regarding War Diaries and Intelligence Summaries are contained in F. S. Regs., Part II. and the Staff Manual respectively. Title pages will be prepared in manuscript.

WAR DIARY
or
INTELLIGENCE SUMMARY.
(Erase heading not required.)

Army Form C. 2118.

Place	Date	Hour	Summary of Events and Information	Remarks and references to Appendices
YPRES.	16/4/16		Work mainly on reserve line & drainage. Working reserve line, filling revetments on reserve line already erected. Drainage for proposed support line. 285 Infantry employed. AG	
	17/4/16		Work as on 16/4. 290 Infantry. 1 Co. Pioneers on communication trench. AG	
	18/4/16		Work as on 17/4. AG 290 Infantry. AG	
	19/4/16		Infantry relief. Relieved our section. Remainder resting. Pioneers at work as usual. AG	
	20/4/16		Work as before. AG	
	21/4/16		Work as before. 300 infantry at work. AG	
	22/4/16		Work as usual. AG	
	23/4/16		Brigade relief. Relieved our section. AG	
	24/4/16		Commenced work with new brigade. Brigade Pioneer Co. commenced sites for dugouts behind wall NORTH of POTIJZE. Commenced thickening parapet of reserve line with width of 10' thickness at top. 370 infantry in addition to Brigade Pioneer Co. AG	
	25/4/16		Work as on 24/4. AG	

Army Form C. 2118.

Instructions regarding War Diaries and Intelligence Summaries are contained in F. S. Regs., Part II. and the Staff Manual respectively. Title pages will be prepared in manuscript.

WAR DIARY
or
INTELLIGENCE SUMMARY.
(Erase heading not required.)

Place	Date	Hour	Summary of Events and Information	Remarks and references to Appendices
YPRES.	26/7/16		Work as on 25/7. NC	
"	27/7/16		Battalion rested sections except for a few offloading stores NC	
"	28/7/16		Work as usual. 420 Infantry in addition to Brigade Pioneer Co. NC	
"	29.7.16		Work as usual 450 Infantry NC	
	30/7/16		Work as usual 420 Infantry NC	
	31/7/16		Reached two sections from back billet to rest camp WEST of POPERINGHE NC	

N.C. [illegible]
[illegible]
OC 125 Coy RE
31.7.16

T2134. Wt. W708–776. 500000. 4/15. Sir J. C. & S.

6th Divisional Engineers

12th FIELD COMPANY R. E.

AUGUST 1 9 1 6

Instructions regarding War Diaries and Intelligence Summaries are contained in F. S. Regs., Part II. and the Staff Manual respectively. Title Pages will be prepared in manuscript.

WAR DIARY
or
~~INTELLIGENCE SUMMARY~~
(Erase heading not required.)

Army Form C. 2118

Place	Date	Hour	Summary of Events and Information	Remarks and references to Appendices
YPRES DISTRICT	1/8/16		Resting in Camp K. NG	
"	2/8/16		Resting in Camp K. NG	
BEAUVAL	3/8/16		Marched at 2AM entrained at PROVEN, detrained CANDAS – FIENVILLERS Marched to BEAUVAL arrived 8.30 P.M. NG	
ARQUEVES	4/8/16		Marched BEAUVAL – ARQUEVES NG	
ARQUEVES	5/8/16		Halted ARQUEVES.	
ENGELBELMER	6/8/16		Marched to billet on ENGELBELMER – MARTINSART ROAD. Horses except those wanted for work left at ARSAU. NG	
"	7/8/16		Relief completed. Company on mining at dugouts in chalk. Reliefs of 6 hours actual work on face. NG	
	8/8/16		Work as usual NG	
	9/8/16		Work as usual. NG	
	10/8/16		Work as usual NG	
	11/8/16		Work as usual NG	
	12/8/16		Work as usual NG	
	13/8/16		Work as usual NG	

1875 Wt. W593/826 1,000,000 4/15 J.B.C. & A. A.D.S.S./Forms/C. 2118.

Army Form C. 2118

Instructions regarding War Diaries and Intelligence Summaries are contained in F. S. Regs., Part II. and the Staff Manual respectively. Title Pages will be prepared in manuscript.

WAR DIARY
or
INTELLIGENCE SUMMARY
(Erase heading not required.)

Place	Date	Hour	Summary of Events and Information	Remarks and references to Appendices
SOUTH of ENGELBELMER on road to MARTINSART	14/8		Work as usual AG	
	15/8		Work as usual AG	
	16/8		Work as usual AG	
	17/8.		Company employed on "strong points" in new assembly Trench. Heavily trench mortared and had to abandon attempt. 10 Sappers wounded AG	
	18/8		Rested company. AG	
	19/8		Work as usual. AG	
	20/8		Work as usual AG	
	21/8		Work as usual. AG	
	22/8		Work as usual AG	
	23/8		Work as usual AG	
	24/8		Work as usual AG	
	25/8		Work as usual AG	

1875 Wt. W593/826 1,000,000 4/15 J.B.C. & A. A.D.S.S./Forms/C. 2118.

Instructions regarding War Diaries and Intelligence Summaries are contained in F. S. Regs., Part II. and the Staff Manual respectively. Title Pages will be prepared in manuscript.

WAR DIARY
or
INTELLIGENCE SUMMARY
(Erase heading not required.)

Army Form C. 2118

Place	Date	Hour	Summary of Events and Information	Remarks and references to Appendices
BERTRANCOURT	26/8		Handed over units and marched to BERTRANCOURT AG	
AMPLIER	27/8		Marched BERTRANCOURT - AMPLIER AG	
GEZAINCOURT	28/8		Marched AMPLIER - GEZAINCOURT AG	
VIGNACOURT	29/8		Marched GEZAINCOURT - VIGNACOURT AG	
VIGNACOURT	30/8		Resting. Inspection of kit etc. AG	
VIGNACOURT	31/8		Company route march. O.C. with CRE to ALBERT & lines in vicinity of CARNOY - MARICOURT. AG	

A. [illegible] Capt RE
O.C. 125 Co RE
31/8/16

1875 Wt. W593/826 1,000,000 4/15 J.B.C. & A. A.D.S.S./Forms/C. 2118.

6th Divisional Engineers

12th FIELD COMPANY R. E.

SEPTEMBER 1916.

Vol 26

WAR DIARY

OF

12th (Fd) Co R. E

FROM

1. 9. 16

TO

30/9./16.

Instructions regarding War Diaries and Intelligence Summaries are contained in F. S. Regs., Part II. and the Staff Manual respectively. Title Pages will be prepared in manuscript.

WAR DIARY
or
~~INTELLIGENCE~~ SUMMARY
(Erase heading not required.)

Army Form C. 2118

Place	Date	Hour	Summary of Events and Information	Remarks and references to Appendices
VIGNACOURT	1/9/16		Drill & training AG	
"	2/9/16		Drill & training AG	
"	3/9/16		Drill & training AG	
"	4/9/16		Drill & training AG	
"	5/9/16		Drill & training AG	
RANNEVILLE	6/9/16		Marched VIGNACOURT – RANNEVILLE AG	
SAILLY-LE-SEC	7/9/16		Marched RANNEVILLE – SAILLY LE SEC AG	
"	8/9/16 to 10/9/16		Halted SAILLY LE SEC. Drill & training AG	
SANDPITS	11/9/16		Marched SAILLY LE SEC to SANDPITS AG	
CITADEL	12/9/16		Marched SANDPITS – CITADEL AG	
"	13/9/16		Halted CITADEL AG	
MONTAUBAN	14/9/16		Marched to assembly area, bivouaced & marched on in early morning to valley in front of BRIQUETERIE near MONTAUBAN AG	
	15/9/16		Stood fast all morning. Sent out road repair party after 2 PM. AG	
	16/9/16		Roadmaking to right of GUILLEMONT AG	

1875 Wt. W593/826 1,000,000 4/15 J.B.C. & A. A.D.S.S./Forms/C. 2118.

Instructions regarding War Diaries and Intelligence Summaries are contained in F. S. Regs., Part II. and the Staff Manual respectively. Title Pages will be prepared in manuscript.

WAR DIARY
or
INTELLIGENCE SUMMARY
(Erase heading not required.)

Army Form C. 2118

Place	Date	Hour	Summary of Events and Information	Remarks and references to Appendices
Near MONTAUBAN	17/9/16		Roadmaking SOUTH of GUILLEMONT. 4 men wounded by explosion of bomb in road. AG	
"	18/9/16		Sent one section to form strong point in captured line. Casualties 1 slightly wounded. Work easy as shelling not serious. AG	
MEAULTE	19/9/16		Marched to MEAULTE. Very heavy march across wet mud roads. AG	
"	20/9/16		Halted MEAULTE. AG	
TRONES WOOD	21/9/16		2 sections by lorry to GUILLEMONT to prepare Brigade HQ. 2 sections by road to TRONES WOOD. Bivouaced at TRONES WOOD. AG	
"	22/9/16		Preparing brigade HQ. AG	
"	23/9/16		Preparing brigade HQ. AG	
GUILLEMONT	24/9/16		Preparing brigade HQ. 2 sections to assembly trenches. 2 sections to GUILLEMONT. AG	
	25/9/16		2 sections making strong points by day. Casualties 3K. 7W. 2 sections wiring front by night. Casualties NIL. AG	

1875 Wt. W593/826 1,000,000 4/15 J.B.C. & A. A.D.S.S./Forms/C. 2118.

Instructions regarding War Diaries and Intelligence Summaries are contained in F. S. Regs., Part II. and the Staff Manual respectively. Title Pages will be prepared in manuscript.

WAR DIARY
or
INTELLIGENCE SUMMARY
(Erase heading not required.)

Army Form C. 2118

Place	Date	Hour	Summary of Events and Information	Remarks and references to Appendices
GUILLEMONT	26/9/16		2 sections working front by night. 2 sections resting. [illegible]	
	27/9/16		4 sections working front + second lines [illegible]	
	28/9/16		Marched to bivouac in rear of BRIQUETERIE near MONTAUBAN [illegible]	
	29/9/16		Marched MEAULTE [illegible]	
	30/9/16		Marched MEAULTE — VILLE SUR ANCRE	
			[illegible signature] Capt. OC [illegible] 30/9/16	

1875 Wt. W593/826 1,000,000 4/15 J.B.C. & A. A.D.S.S./Forms/C. 2118.

Vol 27

WAR. DIARY

OF.

12th (Fd) Co R.E.

FROM. 1-10-16

To 31-10-16

Instructions regarding War Diaries and Intelligence Summaries are contained in F. S. Regs., Part II. and the Staff Manual respectively. Title pages will be prepared in manuscript.

WAR DIARY
or
INTELLIGENCE SUMMARY.
(Erase heading not required.)

Army Form C. 2118.

Place	Date	Hour	Summary of Events and Information	Remarks and references to Appendices
MERICOURT	1/10/16		Moved on evening of 30/9. Halted resting. AG	
"	2/10/16		Resting & refitting AG	
"	3/10/16		Training AG	
"	4/10/16		Training AG	
	5/10/16		Training AG	
	6/10/16		Training. Sent one section to make brigade dugouts AG	
CITADEL	7/10/16		Marched to CITADEL AG	
LONGUEVAL	8/10/16		Marched to dugouts in rear of LONGUEVAL very wet AG	
"	9/10/16		LONGUEVAL dugouts improved. All company on dugouts for brigade. 1 Section attempted wiring front line. Sniping too heavy for progress. AG	
"	10/10/16		Mining dugouts for brigade. 1 Section wiring support line. Casualties Off. 1 wounded OR 2 killed AG	
	11/10/16		Mining dugouts for Brigade HQ. Making Bn HQ in PEN TRENCH. Sent one section to accompany attack on 12/10 AG	

T2134. Wt. W708–776. 500000. 4/15. Sir J. C. & S.

Instructions regarding War Diaries and Intelligence Summaries are contained in F. S. Regs., Part II. and the Staff Manual respectively. Title pages will be prepared in manuscript.

WAR DIARY
or
INTELLIGENCE SUMMARY.
(Erase heading not required.)

Army Form C. 2118.

Place	Date	Hour	Summary of Events and Information	Remarks and references to Appendices
LONGUEVAL	12/10		Moving dugout for Brigade H.Q. Constructing dressing station. OR 1 wounded in attack. Section consolidating at night. OR 1 wounded. RG	
"	13/10		2 Sections resting. 1 Section moving dugouts for Brigade. Section on dressing station. RG	
"	14/10		1 Section in reserve. 2 Sections at night to attack. Section moving dugouts for Brigade. RG	
"	15/10		Sections with attack troops. OR 1 killed 2 wounded. Continued on Brigade dugouts. RG	
"	16/10		Brigade dugouts. RG	
"	17/10		In reserve. RG	
	18/10		In reserve. RG	
CITADEL	19/10		To CITADEL. RG	
CITADEL	20/10		Halted. RG	
MERICOURT	21/10		To MERICOURT. RG	
MERICOURT	22/10		Handed over to Lt REGNARD at 9 AM. RG [illegible] O.C. 12 Coy [illegible]	

Instructions regarding War Diaries and Intelligence Summaries are contained in F. S. Regs., Part II. and the Staff Manual respectively. Title pages will be prepared in manuscript.

WAR DIARY
or
INTELLIGENCE SUMMARY.
(Erase heading not required.)

Army Form C. 2118.

Place	Date	Hour	Summary of Events and Information	Remarks and references to Appendices
MERICOURT	22/10		Took over from Captain Campbell D.S.O. at 9 A.M. To ALLERY by train Transport by road L.F.R.	
"	23/10		Resting & refitting L.F.R.	
"	24/10		Training L.F.R.	
"	25/10		Training L.F.R.	
"	26/10		Training L.F.R.	
"	27/10		Training L.F.R.	
"	28/10		Training L.F.R.	
"	29/10		Coy entrained for CHOQUES & marched to MARLES-LES-MINES L.F.R.	
"	30/10		Resting & refitting L.F.R.	
"	31/10		Training with Brigade L.F.R.	

L. [illegible]
Lt R.E.
O.C. 12th Field Coy R.E.
31/10/16

1577 Wt. W10791/1773 500,000 1/15 D. D. & L. A.D.S.S./Forms/C. 2118.

Vol 28

WAR DIARY

OF

12th (Fd) Co R.E.

FROM 1-11-16 TO 30-11-16

Instructions regarding War Diaries and Intelligence Summaries are contained in F. S. Regs., Part II. and the Staff Manual respectively. Title pages will be prepared in manuscript.

WAR DIARY
or
INTELLIGENCE SUMMARY.
(Erase heading not required.)

Army Form C. 2118.

Place	Date	Hour	Summary of Events and Information	Remarks and references to Appendices
MARLES-LES-MINES	1/11/16		Training, pontooning etc. - L.A.R.	
"	2/11/16		Training. L.A.R.	
"	3/11/16		Training. L.A.R.	
"	4/11/16		Training. L.A.R.	
"	5/11/16		Church parade, route march. L.A.R.	
"	6/11/16		Coy left MARLES-LES-MINES.. 1 section to MAROC remainder	
"			of Coy. MAZINGARBE.	
MAZINGARBE	7/11/16		Took over work in reserve line of 24th Div area L.A.R.	
"	8/11/16		1 section making 2 groups dug outs in 129th Fld Coy area (reserve line)	
			1 section making 2 groups dugouts in 104th Fld Coy area (reserve line)	
			2 sections making 4 groups dug outs in 103rd Fld Coy area (reserve line) L.A.R.	
"	9/11/16		deep dug outs as on the 8th. L.A.R.	
"	10/11/16		Construction of deep dug outs L.A.R.	
"	11/11/16		Construction of deep dug outs L.A.R.	
"	12/11/16		Construction of deep dug outs L.A.R.	
"	13/11/16		Construction of deep dug outs. Handed over to Captain A.M. JACKSON. R.E at 3 p.m. L.A.R. Lt. R.E. O.C. 129th Fld Coy. R.E.	

Instructions regarding War Diaries and Intelligence Summaries are contained in F. S. Regs., Part II. and the Staff Manual respectively. Title pages will be prepared in manuscript.

WAR DIARY
or
~~INTELLIGENCE SUMMARY~~.
(Erase heading not required.)

Army Form C. 2118.

Place	Date	Hour	Summary of Events and Information	Remarks and references to Appendices
MAZINGARBE	14.11.16		Construction of deep dugouts.	Amf
	15.11.16		As on 14.11.16	Amf
	16.11.16		As on 15.11.16	Amf
	17.11.16		As on 16.11.16	Amf
	18.11.16		As on 17.11.16	Amf
	19.11.16		As on 18.11.16	Amf
	20.11.16		As on 19.11.16	Amf
	21.11.16		As on 20.11.16	Amf
	22.11.16		As on 21.11.16.	Amf
	23.11.16		As on 22.11.16	Amf
	24.11.16		As on 23.11.16	Amf
	25.11.16		As on 24.11.16	Amf
	26.11.16		Coy (less No 2 section) ceased work on deep dugouts 6 pm.	Amf
	27.11.16		O.C. went round line with 126 Fd Co RE	Amf
	28.11.16		O.C. went round line with 98 Fd Co RE One section moved to BEUVRY	Amf
BEUVRY	29.11.16		Coy less 3 sections moved to BEUVRY. One section moved to CAMBRIN	Amf

WAR DIARY
or
INTELLIGENCE SUMMARY
(Erase heading not required.)

Instructions regarding War Diaries and Intelligence Summaries are contained in F. S. Regs., Part II. and the Staff Manual respectively. Title Pages will be prepared in manuscript.

Place	Date	Hour	Summary of Events and Information	Remarks and references to Appendices
BEUVRY	30.11.16	—	One Section to CAMBRIN. Work started on 18 Inf Bde sector on Commns trenches to front line and also work on support line. Infantry working parties night of 30/1 — 136. Inf.	

A M Jackson Capt RE
OC. 12th Fd Co RE.

Vol 29

War. Diary.

OF. 12th Fd Coy. R.E.

From 1-12-16. To 31-12-16

Army Form C. 2118.

Instructions regarding War Diaries and Intelligence Summaries are contained in F. S. Regs., Part II. and the Staff Manual respectively. Title pages will be prepared in manuscript.

WAR DIARY
or
INTELLIGENCE SUMMARY.
(Erase heading not required.)

Place	Date	Hour	Summary of Events and Information	Remarks and references to Appendices
1	1.12.16 to 8.12.16		Right sector working on front line FORFAR ST and Boyau 6 and Dundee walk. also junction of HIGH ST with Boyau 6.	AMJ
			Left sector work on Boyaux and junctions of HIGH ST with boyaux	AMJ
	8.12.16		One company of Pioneers report for work. Clearing HIGH ST to ~~left~~ right AMJ. of Boyau 8	AMJ
	8.12.16 to 13.12.16		As above. Rear work Hutting started. 60' huts 20' span for D.A.C. and D/38th RFA.	AMJ
	13.12.16 to 16.12.16		All working parties working on front line.	AMJ
	16.12.16		No 2 section returns from detachment with 24th Divn.	AMJ.
H.Q. of Coy. BEUVRY. Advanced section HQ CAMBRIN. Work in Cambrin sector	16.12.16 to 21.12.16		Working in trenches as above. YMCA hut erected at BEUVRY.	
	21.12.16 to 31.12.16		All working parties on front line except small parties on Boyaux 6, 15, 16 and 19.	AMJ

31.12.16

A M Jackson Capt RE
O.C. 12th Fd. Co RE.

1577 Wt. W10791/1773 500,000 1/15 D. D. & L. A.D.S.S./Forms/C. 2118.

6th Division

10th Field Coy

R. Es.

January to December

1917

Vol 30

WAR DIARY

January 1917

12th Fd Co RE

Instructions regarding War Diaries and Intelligence Summaries are contained in F. S. Regs., Part II. and the Staff Manual respectively. Title pages will be prepared in manuscript.

WAR DIARY
or
INTELLIGENCE SUMMARY.
(Erase heading not required.)

Army Form C. 2118.

Place	Date	Hour	Summary of Events and Information	Remarks and references to Appendices
H.Q. at BEUVRY. Advanced sections (2) at CAMBRIN. Work in CAMBRIN Sector	1.1.17. to 9.1.17.		Preparing posts in front line at heads of Boyau 2, 6, 8, 10 and 15. Work on ADS CAMBRIN, AID POST ROBERTSONS ALLEY, TM Emplacement.	Amf
			Digging berms on communication trenches with any extra digging parties. Two sections back billet on hutting and making up material.	Amf
	9.1.17.		As above. Work started on MG "battle" emplacements in VILLAGE LINE.	Amf
	10.1.17.		As above. Work started on front line on left of Boyau 21	Amf
	12.1.17 to 19.1.17		As above. One of back sections starts work on dugouts (repairing) in OLD BOOTS TRENCH. Work discontinued on front line Boyau 2 and 6.	Amf
	19.1.17. to 23.1.17.		Work commenced on HIGH ST (right of Boyau 21) making new Coy HQ & clearing trench. also work commenced on RESERVE line clearing berm & revetting. Work discontinued on Boyaux 15 and 10.	Amf
	24.1.17.		2nd Lt OCH Osmaston arrives. Work as above.	Amf
	25.1.17.		Frost makes ground very hard & ~~work~~ progress becomes slow.	Amf
	27.1.17.		Lt WILLIAMSON takes over duties of 2nd in command vice Lt L F REENARD	Amf.
	27.1.17 to 31.1.17		RE and Bde working parties employed on repairing the Reserve line. Pioneers wiring reserve line.	Amf.

AM Jackson Major RE
OC 12th Co RE.

Army Form C. 2118.

12 Fd Coy R.E.

Vol 31

Instructions regarding War Diaries and Intelligence Summaries are contained in F. S. Regs., Part II. and the Staff Manual respectively. Title pages will be prepared in manuscript.

WAR DIARY
or
INTELLIGENCE SUMMARY.
(Erase heading not required.)

Place	Date	Hour	Summary of Events and Information	Remarks and references to Appendices
H.Q. at BEUVRY Advanced section at CAMBRIN Work in CAMBRIN Sector.	1.2.17 to 13.2.17		Work on Reserve line (OLD BOOTS TRENCH) average working parties 250 daily Improving dugouts in OLD BOOTS TRENCH) Wiring Reserve line Construction of new A.D.S. CAMBRIN. Repair of Heavy Trench Mortar Emplacements.	
	13.2.17		Company moved to GUARBECQUE	
	13.2.17 to 25.2.17		Training Drill – Pontooning – Route marching – Field Works. do do	
	25.2.17		Company moved to GONNEHEM.	
	26.2.17 to 28.2.17		Training Drill	
	28.2.17		Company moved to BÉTHUNE.	

A. Williamson Capt RE
for O.C. 12th Field Coy RE

1577 Wt. W10791/1773 500,000 1/15 D. D. & L. A.D.S.S./Forms/C. 2118.

Vol 32

WAR Diary

12th Co R.E

March 1917

Instructions regarding War Diaries and Intelligence Summaries are contained in F. S. Regs., Part II. and the Staff Manual respectively. Title pages will be prepared in manuscript.

WAR DIARY
or
INTELLIGENCE SUMMARY.
(Erase heading not required.)

Army Form C. 2118.

Place	Date	Hour	Summary of Events and Information	Remarks and references to Appendices
BÉTHUNE to LES BREBIS	1 3/17		Coy moved into LES BREBIS, where Hd. Qrs. & No 1 Section billeted at L 29-c-8-0. and	
LES BREBIS and TRENCHES	1 3/17		Nos 2, 3 & 4 Sections moved into Forward billets in LOOS, the Brigade front running	
			from ~~[illegible]~~ H·31·c·2·0 to H·19·a·3·7. Work was principally	
			on repair of RESERVE LINE along the whole front, and in clearing chief communication trenches	
			– RAILWAY and POSEN ALLEYS; other work being T.M. Emplacements & Dug-outs. etc	
LES BREBIS and TRENCHES (LOOS)	8 3/17		No 1 Section moved into LOOS and relieved No 3. Section.	
	16 3/17		Commenced installing Gas Cylinder Boxes along Brigade Front Line with all available Infy Working Parties	
	17 3/17		No 3 Section moved into LOOS and relieved No 4 Section. Capt Williamson on Special Leave to England	
	24 3/17		All Infy Working Parties taken off Gas preparation and put on to repair of SCOTS ALLEY. The	
			Gas preparation being carried on by party of 100 Special Coy RE.	
	25 3/17		2/Lieut Langley. RE evacuated to No 27 General Hospital, suffering from German Measles.	
	26/27 3/17		Brigade Front readjusted from H·31·c·5·1 to H·13·c·2·5 on night of 26/27	
	27 3/17		Capt. Williamson returned to Coy from Special Leave.	
	29 3/17		No 4 Section moved into LOOS and relieved No 2 Section	
	31 3/17			

A Williamson
Capt. RE
for O.C. 12th Field Coy RE

T2134. Wt. W708–776. 500000. 4/15. Sir J. C. & S.

Vol 33

WAR DIARY

APRIL 1917

12th Fd Co RE

Instructions regarding War Diaries and Intelligence Summaries are contained in F. S. Regs., Part II. and the Staff Manual respectively. Title pages will be prepared in manuscript.

WAR DIARY
or
INTELLIGENCE SUMMARY.
(Erase heading not required.)

Army Form C. 2118.

Place	Date	Hour	Summary of Events and Information	Remarks and references to Appendices
LES BREBIS and TRENCHES (LOOS)	1		2nd Lieut C A Langley, M.C., R.E., returned from Hospital. 2nd Lieut G W Tack was relieved from duty in LOOS on account of ill health.	
	2nd		Capt A M Williamson took over No 1 Section in LOOS	
	4		Capt Williamson to Back Billets, 2nd Lieut Langley to LOOS.	
	7		2nd Lieut G W Tack, R.E. to C R E Hd Qrs.	
	11th		No 2 Section relieved No 1 Section in LOOS	
	18		One NCO killed & 1 Spr mortally wounded by Shell fire, the latter dying from wounds following day	
	19		No 1 Section relieved No 3 Section in LOOS. ~~One Sapper wounded in LOOS~~	
	21		One Sapper killed by shell fire and one Sapper wounded in LOOS	
	23		No 4 Section returned to Back Billets (LES BREBIS)	
	22		One Sapper wounded by shell fire in LOOS	
	26		Major A M Jackson, M.C., R.E. wounded by Shell fire in LOOS & died from wounds on the 27th-4-17.	
	27		No 3 Section relieved No 2 Section in LOOS. 2nd Lieut G W Tack to Officers Rest Camp, AIRE.	
	1st to 30th		Work during month includes – Cleaning & making good main Communication Trenches; Repairs to Roads, & bridges over trenches etc, into LOOS, for Artillery and Transport; Extension & maintenance of water supply to Front Lines; Trench Mortar Emplacements	

T2134. Wt. W708–776. 500000. 4/15. Sir J. C. & S.

Instructions regarding War Diaries and Intelligence Summaries are contained in F. S. Regs., Part II. and the Staff Manual respectively. Title pages will be prepared in manuscript.

WAR DIARY
or
INTELLIGENCE SUMMARY.
(Erase heading not required.)

(Continued) 2.

Army Form C. 2118.

Place	Date	Hour	Summary of Events and Information	Remarks and references to Appendices
	1st to 30th		Fixing Special boxes in parapet of Front line trenches for Gas installation; Construction of O.P.s and Dugouts; Tramway maintenance; etc. etc.	

A Williamson
Capt RE.

Confidential

WAR DIARY Vol 34

12th Field Co RE

MAY 1917

Instructions regarding War Diaries and Intelligence Summaries are contained in F. S. Regs., Part II. and the Staff Manual respectively. Title pages will be prepared in manuscript.

WAR DIARY
or
INTELLIGENCE SUMMARY.
(Erase heading not required.)

Army Form C. 2118.

12th FIELD COMPANY, R.E.
No. ......
Date ......

(1)

Place	Date	Hour	Summary of Events and Information	Remarks and references to Appendices
	MAY			
LES BREBIS	2nd		2/Lieut T Johnson rejoined from 6th Div School	
and	3		Inspection of Horses & Horse Lines by C.R.E. 2 Sappers & 1 Shoeing Smith joined Coy from No 1 Reinforcement Coy	
TRENCHES (LOOS)	"		2/Lieuts. Johnson & Newcombe to Adv. Billet (LOOS); 2/Lieut Osmaston to Back Billet (LES BREBIS)	
	"		Board of Survey held on Horse Rugs.	
	4		1 N.C.O. & 2 Sappers rejoined from Div. School. 1 Sapper joined from No 1 Wing R E Base Depot	
	5		1 NCO & 1 Sapper to BOULOGNE on Escort duty for Spr Catchpole, arrested by M.P. (Drunkenness)	
	6		3 Sappers joined from No 7 Reinforcement Coy. 1 Spr wounded (slight) LOOS 2/Lieut Johnson to LES BREBIS	
	7		2/Lieut Johnson to 1st Corps School as Instructor. 12 Horses L.D. & 7 Drivers to C.R.E. Hd Qrs.	
	"		Escort returned with Spr Catchpole from BOULOGNE.	
	8		2 Horses L.D. to Mobile (from C.R.E. Hd Qrs)	
	9		Dr Gibson rejoined from R.E. Hd Qrs. 6th Div. 1 Horse Riding from C.R.E.	
	10		2/Lieut Osmaston to LOOS; 2/Lieut Langley to LES BREBIS. Nos 2 & 4 Sections to LOOS; Nos 1 & 3 Sections to LES BREBIS.	
	11		2/Lieut G.H. Tack re rejoined from 1st Corps Rest Station. 2 Sappers joined from No 1 Reinforcement Coy.	
	12		1 Shoeing Smith joined from Base. 1 Dr wounded (slight) LES BREBIS, splinter from own Anti-Air shell	
	13		1 Platoon (2 NCOs & 23 men) attached this Coy from each Infy Battn in 18th Brigade for training & work.	
	"		3 Platoons to LOOS for Working Parties; 1 Platoon LES BREBIS for training.	

T2134. Wt. W708-776. 500000. 4/15. Sir J. C. & S.

Instructions regarding War Diaries and Intelligence Summaries are contained in F. S. Regs., Part II. and the Staff Manual respectively. Title pages will be prepared in manuscript.

WAR DIARY
or
INTELLIGENCE SUMMARY.
(Erase heading not required.)

Army Form C. 2118.

12th FIELD COMPANY, R. E.
No. ....
Date ....

Place	Date	Hour	Summary of Events and Information	Remarks and references to Appendices
	MAY.		(2)	
LES BREBIS	14th		1 Sapper to Hospital (Sick). 2 Sappers joined from No 7 Reinforcement Coy. 2/Lieut Newland to LOOS;	
and			2/Lieut Newcombe to LES BREBIS. Searchlight arrived from 31st AT Coy RE, with attendant.	
TRENCHES	15th		1 of Attached Infy (Sussex) to Hospital	
(LOOS)	17		2/Cpl Christian wounded (slight) LOOS. Continues on duty	
	19		1. O.R. to England on leave 20/7 to 30/7.	
	20th		4 Sappers joined from No 1 Reinforcement Coy. Attached Infy Platoon (2nd D.L.I) to LOOS; platoon	
	"		(1st W. Yorks) to LES BREBIS. 1 O.R. to Hospital	
	23		Sapr Wilson transferred to 31st AT Coy RE	
	25		Dr rejoined from Hospital. 2/Lieut Newland RE wounded (slight) LOOS & sent to Hospital	
			2/Lieuts Langley & Newcombe to LOOS; 2/Lieut Osmaston to LES BREBIS. Nos 1 & 3 Sections to LOOS;	
			Nos 2 & 4 Sections to LES BREBIS.	
	26		Inspection of Horse Lines and Billets by CRE.	
	27		Attached Infy platoon (1st W. Yorks) to LOOS; platoon 14th DLI to LES BREBIS.	
	28		1 NCO & 2 Drs to Base for remounts.	
	29		1 Spr returned from Course of Cold Shoeing.	
	30		2/Lieut Osmaston to LOOS; 2/Lieut Langley to LES BREBIS. 1 Driver left for Course in Cold Shoeing.	

T2134. Wt. W708 – 776. 500000. 4/15. Sir J. C. & S.

Instructions regarding War Diaries and Intelligence Summaries are contained in F. S. Regs., Part II. and the Staff Manual respectively. Title pages will be prepared in manuscript.

WAR DIARY
or
INTELLIGENCE SUMMARY.
(Erase heading not required.)

Army Form C. 2118.

12th FIELD COMPANY, R.E. No. .... Date ....

(3)

Place	Date	Hour	Summary of Events and Information	Remarks and references to Appendices
	MAY			
LES BREBIS	31st		1 Lieut Langley & 2 Sappers leave to England 1.6/17 to 10.6/17.	
and TRENCHES (LOOS)			During the month work has been carried on in reclaiming, deepening & hurrying the following trenches. - RESERVE LINE; ENGLISH ALLEY; SCOTS ALLEY; BOYAUX 47, 46 & 44; SUPPORT LINE between ENGLISH ALLEY and CAMERON ALLEY; FRONT LINE between BOYAU 46 and Sap to CAMERON CRATER; BLACK WATCH ALLEY. The latter trench had new traverses cut and was wired in. SAPS were cut from front line to THE HUMP; to CAMERON CRATER, and continued to German Front Line; and for over 100 yds in front of BOYAU 45. New Galleries & excavations for new MTM Emplacements (double ones) at SCOTS ALLEY and BOYAU 49. ADS at ENCLOSURE fitted up, & new Mortuary built near ST PATRICKS. Repairs & extensions to ST PATRICK'S ADS & to Regtl A.P. at the CRUCIFIX. New bridge to take heavy transport erected over SOUTH ST on the LENS ROAD. Maintenance of TRAMWAYS and 2" Water Supply Pipe Line. Repairs to various Dug-outs, MG Emplacements & T.M.E.s damaged by shell fire. Work on LOOS DEFENCES (B and C KEEPS). Commencement of new 4" Water Supply Pipe Line, etc. etc.	
			A Williamson Major RE OC 12th Field Coy RE	

T2134. Wt. W708-776. 500000. 4/15. Sir J. C. & S.

Confidential

WAR DIARY

Vol 35

June 1917.

12th Fd Co RE.

Instructions regarding War Diaries and Intelligence Summaries are contained in F. S. Regs., Part II. and the Staff Manual respectively. Title pages will be prepared in manuscript.

WAR DIARY
or
INTELLIGENCE SUMMARY.
(Erase heading not required.)

Army Form C. 2118.

12th FIELD COMPANY, R.E.
No. ....
Date ....

(1)

Place	Date	Hour	Summary of Events and Information	Remarks and references to Appendices
	JUNE			
LES BREBIS	1		1 Sapper wounded night of 31/1 LOOS	
and	2		2/Lieut H.N. OBBARD, RE joined Coy from Base. 1 Spr rejoined from Hospital	
TRENCHES	3		3 men 11th Essex joined as Reinforcement to Attached Infy	
(LOOS)	4		1 Driver wounded in LOOS, – sent to Hospital. 1 Spr slightly wounded, LOOS – remained on duty with Coy.	
	5		1 NCO & 1 man 2nd DLI joined as Reinforcement to Attached Infy. 8 mules arrived.	
	7		2/Lieut G.W. JACK, RE leave to U.K. 2/Lieut A.K. NEWLAND, RE, rejoined from 1st Corps Rest Station. 1 Driver struck off strength of Unit	
	8		No 2 & 4 Sections to LOOS. No 1 & 3 Sections to Hd Qrs, LES BREBIS.	
	9		A/Sergt DOWE, ~~returned~~ rejoined Coy from Base	
	10		11th Essex, attached Infy, to LOOS; 2nd DLI, attached Infy, to Hd Qrs LES BREBIS	
	12		1 – 14th DLI to Hospital. 3 Horses L.D. to Mobile	
	15		2/Lieut C.A. LANGLEY, MC RE returned from Leave	
	16		2/Lieut A.K. NEWLAND, RE leave to U.K.	
	17		2nd DLI, attached Infy, to LOOS; 1st West Yorks, attached to Hd Qrs.	
	18		3 Horses, L.D. struck off strength of Coy.	

T2134. Wt. W708–776. 500000. 4/15. Sir J. C. & S.

Instructions regarding War Diaries and Intelligence Summaries are contained in F. S. Regs., Part II. and the Staff Manual respectively. Title pages will be prepared in manuscript.

WAR DIARY
or
INTELLIGENCE SUMMARY.
(Erase heading not required.)

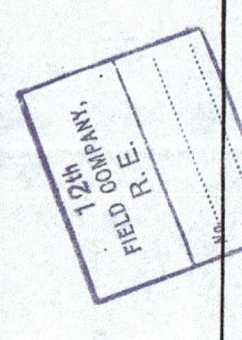

12th FIELD COMPANY, R. E.
No. ....
Date ....

Army Form C. 2118.

(2)

Place	Date	Hour	Summary of Events and Information	Remarks and references to Appendices
	JUNE			
LES BREBIS and TRENCHES (LOOS)	18/19		Night of 18/19 the Brigade sideslipped one Batt^n Sector to the South, taking over portion of 46th Division Sector. 18th Bde new boundary was;- North - RAILWAY ALLEY (inclusive); South - CITE ST AUGUSTE - DOUBLE CRASSIER Railway (inclusive)	
	19		2nd Lieut G W JACK returned from leave. 4 men 14th D L I (Attached) wounded, LOOS.	
	20		1 man 11th Essex (Attached) to Hospital	
	23		2nd Lieut OSMASTON MC, RE, leave to U.K. Nos 1 & 3 Sections to LOOS; No 4 Section to H^d Qrs. 1 man 1st West Yorks (Attached) as Reinforcement	
	25		a/ L^e Cpl & 2 Sappers wounded, LOOS. 5 men killed, 2 wounded, of 2nd D L I (Attached) LOOS; 1 man 11th Essex (Attached) wounded, LOOS; 1 Sgt killed, 1 man wounded 1st West Yorks (Attached) LOOS.	
	27		1 D^r to Hospital	
	28		2nd Lieut A.K NEWLAND, returned from leave.	
			During the month work has been carried on in reclaiming, deepening & making good, ~~the following trenches:-~~ two main Communication Trenches, the whole of the Reserve, Support & Front Lines and the Subsidiary Communication	

T2134. Wt. W708-776. 500000. 4/15. Sir J. C. & S.

Instructions regarding War Diaries and Intelligence Summaries are contained in F. S. Regs., Part II. and the Staff Manual respectively. Title pages will be prepared in manuscript.

WAR DIARY
or
INTELLIGENCE SUMMARY.
(Erase heading not required.)

Army Form C. 2118.

12th FIELD COMPANY, R.E.
No. ....
Date. ....

Place	Date	Hour	Summary of Events and Information	Remarks and references to Appendices
			(3)	
			trenches between these. In addition a new large Dressing Station has been constructed for the Bde Field Ambulance; the construction of a pump-house & 4" main for a new water supply from deep well at foot of Crassier, 'LOOS', is well in hand; and many minor works. For the latter half of the month working parties have been supplied by the 4th Batt The West India Regt.; & also by the 11th Leicesters (Pioneers), & the 9th Batt Suffolks.	
			A Williamson Major, R.E. O.C. 12th (Field) Coy. R.E.	

T2134. Wt. W708-776. 500000. 4/15. Sir J. C. & S.

WAR DIARY Vol 36

12th Company R.E.

July. 1917.

Instructions regarding War Diaries and Intelligence Summaries are contained in F. S. Regs., Part II. and the Staff Manual respectively. Title pages will be prepared in manuscript.

WAR DIARY
or
INTELLIGENCE SUMMARY.
(Erase heading not required.)

(1)

Army Form C. 2118.

Place	Date	Hour	Summary of Events and Information	Remarks and references to Appendices
	JULY			
LES BREBIS	1		11th Essex attached Infy, to ~~LOOS~~ LES BREBIS; 14th D.L.I. Attached Infy to LOOS. Sergt Brown	
and			14th D.L.I. Attached, killed, & 1 Pte wounded.	
TRENCHES	2		2 Sappers wounded, one slightly & remains on duty. 1 Pte 14th D.L.I. Attached, wounded.	
(LOOS)	3		No 2 Section to LES BREBIS. 1 Pte 14th D.L.I. Attached, wounded.	
	5		Major Williamson leave to U.K. 2nd Lieut Ormaston returned from leave.	
	6		No 4 Section to LOOS; No 1 returned to LES BREBIS. 2nd Lieut Ormaston to LOOS; 2nd Lieut Ubbard to LES BREBIS.	
	7		30th Labour Battn (44 O.R.) attached for rations.	
	8		1 Spr returned from Hospital. 1 reinforcement from R.E. Base Depot. 1-11th Essex Attached to Hospital	
			2nd D.L.I. attached to LES BREBIS; 11th Attached Essex to LOOS.	
	9		One 11th Attached Essex joined as reinforcement. 1-14th D.L.I. attached to Hospital	
	10		1 Spr to 1st Corps School of Instruction. 1-2nd D.L.I. Attached to Hospital. 1-West Yorks	
			attached as reinforcement. 1 Spr from 31st A.T. Coy to run Searchlight.	
	11		1 Driver reinforcement from R.E. Base Depot.	
	12		L/Corp (Mounted) to Horse Transport Depot, ABBEVILLE. - Course of Instruction.	
			4 Sappers to Signalling School DROUVIN on Course.	
	13		2nd D.L.I. attached inspected by A.D.M.S. 1-West Yorks Attached joined as reinforcement	

T2134. Wt. W708-776. 500000. 4/15. Sir J. C. & S.

Instructions regarding War Diaries and Intelligence Summaries are contained in F. S. Regs., Part II. and the Staff Manual respectively. Title pages will be prepared in manuscript.

WAR DIARY
or
INTELLIGENCE SUMMARY.
(*Erase heading not required.*)

(2)

Army Form C. 2118.

Place	Date	Hour	Summary of Events and Information	Remarks and references to Appendices
	JULY			
LES BREBIS and TRENCHES (LOOS.)	12		2nd DLI attached to LOOS & attached to LOOS Commandant for Salvage purposes. 3 L.D Horses from Remount Depot.	
	13		Searchlight returned to 31st AT Coy. Nos 3 & 4 Sections returned to LES BREBIS.	
LABOURSE	14		Attached Infy (1st West Yorks; 11th Essex; 2nd & 14th DLI) return to their Battalions. Coy. move from LES BREBIS to LABOURSE. 1 Officer & 23 O.R. of 30th Labour Battn from LES BREBIS attached for rations & as Working Party.	
"	18		1 Spr joined as reinforcement from No 5 Reinforcement Coy RE.	
"	20		1 Horse (Rider) from 6th Divisional Train.	
"	21		1 Spr to 459 Field Coy RE to work searchlight. 1 Spr returned from Hospital.	
GUESTREVILLE	22		466th Field Coy RE take over from this Coy at LABOURSE. This Coy moves to GUESTREVILLE taking over from 468 Field Coy RE.	
	23		30th Labour Detatchment transferred to 466 Field Coy RE for rations from 23rd inclusive. 3 Sappers (Tradesmen) joined Coy from No 2 Reinforcement Coy RE.	
	24		Major Williamson returned from Sick Leave extension. 1 Spr returned from 459 Coy RE 1 Spr returned from Chiropody Course.	
	28		1 Spr to Hospital	
	29		1 Spr evacuated to CCS. 1 Driver reported from Course of Cold Shoeing, ABBEVILLE.	

Instructions regarding War Diaries and Intelligence Summaries are contained in F. S. Regs., Part II. and the Staff Manual respectively. Title pages will be prepared in manuscript.

WAR DIARY
or
INTELLIGENCE SUMMARY.
(Erase heading not required.)

Army Form C. 2118.

(3)

Place	Date	Hour	Summary of Events and Information	Remarks and references to Appendices
LES BREBIS and TRENCHES (LOOS)	JULY 1 to 14		During this period the special work in the trench Sector included the Completion of the new pump-house in LOOS, the 4" main, and the 1½" branch to HARTS CRATER, and 2" branch to junction of ENGLISH ALLEY and RESERVE LINE (this 2" line only partially completed); FORT GLATZ A.D.S. also practically completed; deepening & A framing of RAILWAY ALLEY from RESERVE LINE to TOSH ALLEY; & cutting Switch trench around the CRUCIFIX. The new RESERVE LINE on Right Sector was wired, & maintenance work on the front & Support trenches generally. At LES BREBIS work was carried on in the improvement of permanent Reserve Batt. Billets, and the different Horse Standings of the Brigade.	
LABOURSE	14 to 22		Repairs to huts at FOSSE 12; 2 D.A.C.; 87th RFA Batty; 43rd & 53rd RFA Batty; the A 147 Batty. Horse Standing improvements for 97 RFA Batty; 10th RFA Batty; 147 B.A.C.; Water Supply Extn to 21st RFA Batty; 87th RFA Batty; 1st Coy Div Train; 17th Field Ambulance. Mortuary in NOEUX-LES-MINES Cemetery; a 30ft Elephant Dug-out for French civilians near the church, NOEUX-LES-MINES. Improving approach road & fittings to Water Cart Filling Point at LABOURSE. Construction of ovens to Cook-house, H.Q. RA. SAILLY-LABOURSE.	
GUESTREVILLE	22 to 31		Improvements to Coy Billets. Commenced Coy. training 25th inst. – Drill & Musketry	

A Williamson
Major, R.E.
O.C. 12th (Field) Coy. R.E.

CONFIDENTIAL

WAR DIARY

of

12th Co RE.

from 1-8-17 to 31-8-17

Instructions regarding War Diaries and Intelligence Summaries are contained in F. S. Regs., Part II. and the Staff Manual respectively. Title pages will be prepared in manuscript.

WAR DIARY
or
INTELLIGENCE SUMMARY.
(Erase heading not required.)

Army Form C. 2118.

12th FIELD COMPANY, R.E.
No. ....
Date ....

Place	Date	Hour	Summary of Events and Information	Remarks and references to Appendices
	AUGUST			
GUESTREVILLE	1		Billets inspected by C.R.E. 1 NCO & 4 O.R. returned from Leave	
	3		1 Spr returned from Hospital; 3 NCOs & 9 O.R. returned from leave. 1 NCO & 9 O.R. on leave to U.K.	
	4		2 NCOs & 8 O.R. Leave to U.K. 1 NCO. to Hospital	
	5		2 NCOs to LA COMTÈ for 3 days Gas Course	
	7		1 NCO from Horse Transport Depot, ABBEVILLE. 1 Rider & 1 L.D. horse to Mobile. 2 Sprs to CRE.	
	8		5 Sprs & 1 attached Infy returned from leave. 1 Spr to Hospital	
	9		2 Lieut Newcombe RE, 4 NCOs & 5 O.R. returned from leave. 2 NCOs returned from Gas Course at LA COMTÈ. Chief Engineer, 1st Army, inspected the Company.	
	10		5 O.R. Leave to U.K.; 1. O.R. returned from Leave.	
	11		1 NCO (Mounted) returned from Veterinary Course at ABBEVILLE. 3. O.R. Leave to U.K.	
	14		1. O.R (RAMC attached 12 Field Coy RE) leave to U.K. 1 Spr to Hospital. 1 Rider to Mobile 1. L.D. horse from No 2 Coy Train	
	15		1 Spr. to Hospital. 1 NCO & 5 O.R. returned from Leave.	
	16		2 NCOs & 5 O.R. returned from Leave. 4 Sprs returned from Course at Divl Signal School.	
	17		5. O.R Leave to U.K.; 6. O.R returned from leave. 1 Spr to Hospital	
	18		1 Spr returned from 1st Corps School of Instruction. 2 O.R Leave to U.K. 2. O.R returned from leave.	

1577 Wt. W10791/1773 500,000 1/15 D. D. & L. A.D.S.S./Forms/C. 2118.

Instructions regarding War Diaries and Intelligence Summaries are contained in F. S. Regs., Part II. and the Staff Manual respectively. Title pages will be prepared in manuscript.

WAR DIARY
or
INTELLIGENCE SUMMARY.
(Erase heading not required.)

12th FIELD COMPANY, R.E.
No.
Date.

Army Form C. 2118.

Place	Date	Hour	Summary of Events and Information	Remarks and references to Appendices
	August			
GUESTREVILLE	20		Bde. Boxing Tournament at VILLERS CHATEL (1st day). 1 NCO returned from Hospital. 1 Reinforcement	
"			joined from No 1 Reinforcement Coy RE.	
"	21		Bde. Boxing Tournamt (2nd day). 1 Spr returned from Hospital. 1 Reinforcemt from No 7 Reinforcemt Coy RE	
"	22		Inspection of 6th Divisional Engineers (Field Coys.) by Maj-Gen T.O. Marden, CMG.	
"	23		Company move by Route March from GUESTREVILLE to LES BREBIS.	
LES BREBIS	24		~~2~~ 2' Lieut FITCH , 11th Essex, and 2' Lieut BREWER, A.G. 14' DLI; with 1 Senior NCO & 25 men	
			from each Battn in the Bde. are attached to the Company. 8 O.R. returned from Leave.	
"	25		Coy take over Billets from 8th Field Coy Canadian Engineers, Nos 1, 2 & 4 Sections RE and Attached	
"			Infy Platoons from 2nd DLI; 14th DLI; & 1st West Yorks, to Advanced Billets at HARTS CRATER	
"			and HARRISONS CRATER. 11 Lieuts, Newland, Osmaston & Newcombe, RE; and 11 Lieuts FITCH and	
"			Brewer, to Harrisons Crater Forward Billets. The 18th I.B. Sector having boundaries on	
"	"		the Right between it & the 3rd Canadian Divn — N-2-b-6-0 — N.2. Central — N.1.d.15.80	
"			(Old German Front Line just South of Junctn of NELSON TRENCH and NASH ALLEY) — M.6.d.75.75	
"			(Junctn of Railways) — Along Rly to Double Crassier — Double Crassier (inclus. to 6th Division)	
"			Boundary between 18 IB and 16th IB = Approx HURRAH ALLEY (incl. to Left Bde) — SCOTS	
"			ALLEY (incl. to Right Bde)	

Instructions regarding War Diaries and Intelligence Summaries are contained in F. S. Regs., Part II. and the Staff Manual respectively. Title pages will be prepared in manuscript.

WAR DIARY
or
INTELLIGENCE SUMMARY.
(Erase heading not required.)

12th FIELD COMPANY, R.E.
No.............
Date...........

Army Form C. 2118.

Place	Date	Hour	Summary of Events and Information	Remarks and references to Appendices
	August			
LES BREBIS and TRENCHES	26		2 Lieut. O.C.H. OSMASTON, M.C., RE, killed by Shell Fire in the trenches, NETLEY TRENCH. Sergt Clarke & 2 Spr wounded, same place. 33 Spr from E & M Coy, and 8 men of Salvage Corps; attached this Coy for Rations. 1 RAMC attached, returned from leave.	
"	27		2 Lieut Obbard to Advanced Billet to Command No 4 Section RE. 1 Remount (L.D.) from 46 Divisional Train	
"	28		Funeral of 2 Lieut Osmaston. MC. at Cemetery, BÉTHUNE.	
"	29		1-14th DLI attached accidently? wounded while cleaning rifle. 3 men of Div. Canteen Staff attached for rations	
"	30		2 Lieut OBBARD wound by Shell fire, HARTS CRATER. 2 Lieut Brewer, 14th DLI, attached from Advanced to Rear Billet. 2 O.R. returned from Leave.	
"	31		3. O.R. returned from Leave.	
GUESTREVILLE	1 to 23.		This time was spent in training the Coy. in the usual subjects, — Squad, Section and Company Drill; Rifle Exercises & Esc. Order Drill; Musketry; Firing (group, application, and rapid); Demolitions; Use of Spars; Pontooning; Weldon trestle; Use of Compass & Field Geometry; Gas Drill; Route Marches; etc, etc	

1577 Wt. W10791/1773 500,000 1/15 D. D. & L. A.D.S.S./Forms/C. 2118.

Instructions regarding War Diaries and Intelligence Summaries are contained in F. S. Regs., Part II. and the Staff Manual respectively. Title pages will be prepared in manuscript.

WAR DIARY
or
INTELLIGENCE SUMMARY.
(Erase heading not required.)

12th FIELD COMPANY, R. E.
No.............
Date.............

Army Form C. 2118.

Place	Date	Hour	Summary of Events and Information	Remarks and references to Appendices
LES BREBIS and TRENCHES	August 23 to 31		Work on clearing Communication Trenches, left in badly shelled condition by our Advance; and work on repair & extension of Dug-outs, bridges, roads, etc —	

A Williamson
Major, R.E.
O.C. 12th (Field) Coy. R.E.

Instructions regarding War Diaries and Intelligence Summaries are contained in F. S. Regs., Part II. and the Staff Manual respectively. Title Pages will be prepared in manuscript.

WAR DIARY
or
INTELLIGENCE SUMMARY
(Erase heading not required.)

12th FIELD COMPANY, R.E.
No. ....
Date 1·10·17

Army Form C. 2118

Vol 38

Place	Date	Hour	Summary of Events and Information	Remarks and references to Appendices
LES BREBIS	September 1		1 Sapper Special Leave to U.K. 1 Sapper returned from Leave. 1 1st West Yorks (attached) to Hospital	
	2		No 3 Section + 11th Essex (attached) to Advance Billet. No 4 Section + 1st West Yorks to Back Billet. 1 1st West Yorks joined.	
	3		Baths for No 4 Section + Mounted Section. 1 14th D.L.I. (attached) proceeds to Busnes as witness at Court martial of Pte Cook 14th D.L.I. (attached) wounded while cleaning rifle. Lieut R J Hall arrived as reinforcement. Took over No 4 section	
	4		71st Infantry Brigade relieved the 18th Infantry Brigade in the Right Section (see Diary August 25th 1917 for Boundaries). Court Martial at Busnes of Pte Cook 14th D.L.I attached wounded while cleaning rifle. 1 sapper returned from ~~leave~~ Hospital. Major Williamson from Advance to Back Billet.	
	5.		1 L/Cpl to 6th Div Signals for Test as Motor Despatch Rider. 1 Driver to Hospital. II/Lieut W.M Veitch arrived as reinforcement	
	6		1 Horse (L D) struck off – died through Gas Poisoning. 1 Horse (L.D) cast as vicious to M.V.S. 1 Officer and 55 O Rs of 120th Labour Batt attached to Coy for Rations from 7th inst. 1 Sapper Killed and 1 sapper wounded (accidently) caused by striking bomb with a pick. 1 2nd D.L.I. (attached) wounded by same cause. 1 Sergt 11th Essex (attached) to Hospital suffering from gas poisoning. 1 2nd D.L.I (attached) to Hospital. 2 Sappers returned from Leave.	
	7.		R.T.O. Les Brebis + servant attached to Coy for Rations. 3 14th D.L.I (attached) admitted to Hospital. 1 Sergt 11th Essex joined as reinforcement. 1 West York (attached) wounded by shell fire. 1 man 11th Essex (attached) reported absent. 1 sapper to Hospital. Major Williamson to Advance Billet. II Lt Brewer 14th D.L.I (attached) to advance, and II Lieut Fitch 11th Essex (attached) to Back Billet. 1 Sapper died of wounds at 7th C.C.S.	

1875 Wt. W593/826 1,000,000 4/15 J.B.C. & A. A.D.S.S./Forms/C. 2118.

Instructions regarding War Diaries and Intelligence Summaries are contained in F. S. Regs., Part II. and the Staff Manual respectively. Title Pages will be prepared in manuscript.

WAR DIARY
or
INTELLIGENCE SUMMARY
(Erase heading not required.)

Army Form C. 2118

12th FIELD COMPANY, R. E.
No. ....
Date 1-10-17

Place	Date	Hour	Summary of Events and Information	Remarks and references to Appendices
LESBREBIS	SEPTEMBER 8.		2 Sappers 1 L/cpl Mounted and 1 Driver leave to U.K. 1 Driver awarded 4 days F.P. No 2 2 West Yorks (attached) arrived as reinforcements 2 2nd D.L.I " " 2 O.R's 2nd D.L.I (attached) Killed and 5 O.R's of 2nd D.L.I (attached) wounded by shell fire 1 Sergt of 14th D.L.I (attached) Killed by shell fire.	
	9		Major A. Williamson, II Lieut Newland, and II Lieut Newcombe from Advance to Back Billet Lieut Hall and II Lieut Veitch to Advance Billet No 1 Section and 2nd D.L.I (attached) from Advance to Back Billet. No 4 Section and 1st West Yorks (attached) to Advance Billet 1 Sapper to Hospital	
	10		1 Sapper evacuated to 1st C.C.S. 1 Cpl 14th D.L.I arrived as reinforcement II Lt Newland to Advance Billet 1 Cpl and 6 men 2nd D.L.I arrived as reinforcements 1 L/cpl (mounted) evacuated to 1st C.C.S Baths – No 1 Section and Mounted Section	
	11.		1 14th D.L.I (attached) returned from Hospital 1 2nd D.L.I " 2 Sappers to Sanitary Section for 2 days instruction	
	12		1 Sapper to Hospital 1 Sapper returned from Hospital	
	13		2 Sappers returned from Sanitary Course 1 Driver to Hospital	
	14.		18th Infantry Brigade relieved the 71st Infantry Brigade in right Section see Diary August 25th for boundaries 1 Sapper to Hospital 1 Sapper returned from Leave	

1875 Wt. W593/826 1,000,000 4/15 J.B.C. & A. A.D.S.S./Forms/C. 2118.

Instructions regarding War Diaries and Intelligence Summaries are contained in F. S. Regs., Part II. and the Staff Manual respectively. Title Pages will be prepared in manuscript.

WAR DIARY
or
INTELLIGENCE SUMMARY
(Erase heading not required.)

12th FIELD COMPANY, R.E.
No. ....
Date 1-10-17

Army Form C. 2118

Place	Date	Hour	Summary of Events and Information	Remarks and references to Appendices
LES BREBIS	SEPTEMBER 15		2 sappers and 2 drivers Leave to U.K. Major Williamson to Advance Billet II/Lt Veitch from Advance to Back Billet	
	16		II Lieut Newland from Advance to Back Billet II Lieut Brewer 14th D.L.I (attached) from Advance to Back Billet. II Lieut Newcombe to Advance Billet II Lieut Fitch 11th Essex attached to Advance Billet. No 2 Section and 14nd D.L.I (attached) from Advance Billet to Back Billet No 1 " " 2nd D.L.I " to " from 1 Sapper wounded and 1 Sapper died of wounds from shellfire 2 men of 509th Coy R.E attached for Rations 1 Driver arrived as Reinforcement from R.E Base Depot	
	17		Baths:- No 2 section - mounted Major Williamson from Advance to Back Billet II Lieut Langley " " No 3 Section 1 Sapper to 1st Corps Workshops 11th Essex (attached) from Advance to Back Billet	
	18.		1 L/cpl (mounted) arrived from 18th C.C.S 1 Sapper evacuated to C.C.S.	
	19		1. 2nd D.L.I (attached) to Hospital 1. 1st West Yorks (attached) wounded.	
	20		2 Drivers returned from Leave. 1 Sapper arrived as Reinforcement from R.E. Base Depot Lieut Hall from Advance to Back Billet II Lieut Veitch to Advance Billet	

Instructions regarding War Diaries and Intelligence Summaries are contained in F. S. Regs., Part II. and the Staff Manual respectively. Title Pages will be prepared in manuscript.

WAR DIARY
or
INTELLIGENCE SUMMARY
(Erase heading not required.)

Army Form C. 2118

12th FIELD COMPANY, R.E.
No. ....
Date 1-10-17

Place	Date	Hour	Summary of Events and Information	Remarks and references to Appendices
LES BREBIS	September 21		78th Infantry Brigade changed its boundaries. Side stepping to the South. Northern Boundary became Nuns Alley inclusive N2.b 5.4 - H 31c 7 4 - H 31 c.2.7 SCOTS ALLEY (exclusive G.36.b.3.1 English Alley inclusive G 29 d 7.1 - G 29 c.7.9 Southern Boundary. Front Line at N.8.b 52 82 - N2c 30.36 - N1d 70.50. thence West along railway	
	22		3 Horses L.D from No 1 Coy Train Captain Jack and 1 Driver Leave to U.K Lieut Hall to back billet C.Q.M.S Dobson transferred to 1st Bn H.A.C	
	23		II Lieut Newland to Advance Billet II Lieut Brewer 14th D.L.I (attached) to Advance Billet II Lieut Fitch 11th Essex (attached) from Advance to Back Billet No 2 Section to Advance Billet 14th DLI (attached)	
	24		1 14th DLI (attached) to Hospital	
	25		Baths:- No 3 section + Mounted	
	26		1 Sapper returned from 1 months leave	
	27		1 Sapper to Hospital 1 11th Essex (attached) joined as reinforcement 2 Sappers + 1 Driver returned from Leave 1 O.R of 2nd D.L.I (attached) to Coy for Trade Test as plumber	

1875 Wt. W593/826 1,000,000 4/15 J.B.C. & A. A.D.S.S./Forms/C. 2118.

Instructions regarding War Diaries and Intelligence Summaries are contained in F. S. Regs., Part II. and the Staff Manual respectively. Title Pages will be prepared in manuscript.

WAR DIARY
or
INTELLIGENCE SUMMARY
(Erase heading not required.)

Army Form C. 2118

12th FIELD COMPANY, R.E.
Date 1·10·17

Place	Date	Hour	Summary of Events and Information	Remarks and references to Appendices
LES BREBIS	September 28		1 Sapper arrived as reinforcements from RE Base Depôt 1 Driver returned from leave	
	29		2 Drivers leave to U.K.	
	30		No 3 Section to Advance No 4 " to Back Billet Lieut Langley to Advance II Lieut Veitch to Back Billet " Fitch 11th Essex (attached) to Advance " Brewer 14th DLI " to Back Billet 11th Essex (attached) to Advance 1st West Yorks " " Back 1 14th DLI joined as reinforcement.	
			Resume of Work for Month of Sept: Deepening + widening and duck-boarding trenches taken over mostly in a destroyed condition due to the shelling in the operations of our advance. Two communication trenches Nestor + Netley have been made good in this sector. An overland Ration track has been built running from Harrison's Crater to the junction of Norel + Netley Trenches. This track is being continued A strong point was completed and wired at the junction of Nelson New Cut + Nuns Alley. Work has been started on 4 Trench Mortar Emplacements for 6" Newton Gun. A new trench ~~joining~~ Essex Lane has been dug joining HAPPY TRENCH and Easter Trench Dug-out accomodation in the sector has been increased	

[signature]
Major, R.E.
O.C. 12th (Field) Coy. R.E.

Instructions regarding War Diaries and Intelligence Summaries are contained in F. S. Regs., Part II. and the Staff Manual respectively. Title Pages will be prepared in manuscript.

WAR DIARY
or
INTELLIGENCE SUMMARY
(Erase heading not required.)

Army Form C. 2118

12 Fd Coy R.E.

Vol 39

Place	Date	Hour	Summary of Events and Information	Remarks and references to Appendices
LES BREBIS	October 1.		Lce Cpl Johnson S. proceeded on Veterinary Course.	
			1 attd Infy 2nd D.L.I. to Hospital.	
	2.		1 Sapper joined Company as reinforcement	
			1 Sapper + 4 Infantry to OSLER SIDING for duty.	
	3.		1 attached 2nd D.L.I. returned from Hospital	
			1 attached 14th D.L.I. admitted to Hospital.	
	4.		1 Sapper and 1 driver from Hospital.	
	5.		1 driver returned from Leave in U.K.	
	6.		2 Sappers Leave to U.K.	
	7.		II Lt Veitch to Advance Billet. II Lt Newcombe to Back Billet II Lt Brewer 14th D.L.I. to Advance	
			II Lt Fitch 11th Essex to Back Billet.	
			No 4 section to Advance Billet	
			No 1 section to Back Billet	
			1st West Yorks attd to Advance	
			2nd D.L.I. attd to Back	
			1 attd 11th Essex wounded by Shell fire	
			1 Sapper + 1 attd to Elvaston Castle on Electric Light Installation.	
	8.		1 attd 11th Essex joined as reinforcement	
	9.		1 att 11th Essex to Hospital sick	
			1 mule to Mobile Veterinary Section	

1875 Wt. W593/826 1,000,000 4/15 J.B.C. & A. A.D.S.S./Forms/C. 2118.

Instructions regarding War Diaries and Intelligence Summaries are contained in F. S. Regs., Part II. and the Staff Manual respectively. Title Pages will be prepared in manuscript.

WAR DIARY
or
INTELLIGENCE SUMMARY
(Erase heading not required.)

Army Form C. 2118

Place	Date	Hour	Summary of Events and Information	Remarks and references to Appendices
LES BREBIS	OCTOBER 10		1 Sapper wounded by Shell fire	
			2 attd 11th Essex wounded by Shell fire	
			1 attd 14th DLI to Hospital sick	
			1 mule to Mobile Veterinary Section	
	11		13 Horses isolated by V.O. Skin disease or suspected Skin disease	
			1 attd Inf 11th Essex Died of wounds in 7 C.C.S.	
			Sappers Lockyer + Hollingsworth to Lillers as witnesses in F.G.C Martial.	
	12		1 O.R. returned from Veterinary course	
			1 O.R. from leave to U.K.	
			1 attd Inf 11th Essex died of wounds in 7 C.C.S.	
			1 attd Inf 14th DLI joined as reinforcement	
			2 attd Inf 11 Essex joined as reinforcement	
	13		C.S.M and 1 O.R. Leave to U.K.	
			Sgt Jones arrived from 2nd Pontoon Park to take over duties of C.Q.M.S.	
			1 driver returned from leave to U.K	
	14.		2/Lt Newcombe to Advance Billet	
			2/Lt R.K. Newland to Back Billet	
			No 1 section to Advance Billet	
			No 2 section to Back Billet.	
			Attd 2nd DLI to Advanced Billet,	
			14th Back Billet.	

1875 Wt. W593/826 1,000,000 4/15 J.B.C. & A. A.D.S.S./Forms/C. 2118.

Instructions regarding War Diaries and Intelligence Summaries are contained in F. S. Regs., Part II. and the Staff Manual respectively. Title Pages will be prepared in manuscript.

WAR DIARY
or
INTELLIGENCE SUMMARY
(Erase heading not required.)

Army Form C. 2118

Place	Date	Hour	Summary of Events and Information	Remarks and references to Appendices
LESBREBIS.	October 15.		II Lt Fitch 11th Essex + servant to Hospital.	
			1 11th ESSEX O.R. joined as reinforcement	
			2 Horses L.D. to Mobile Veterinary section	
			1 Surplus rider to 6th Div Signals.	
	16		1 1st West Yorks joined unit	
			1 1st West Yorks rejoined Battn	
	17.		5 14th D.L.I. joined unit	
			5 14th D.L.I. to Battn.	
			2 sappers joined as reinforcements	
	18		1 L/Cpl 1st West Yorks rejoined Coy	
			1 Horse L.D. to Mobile.	
	19.		2 O.R. returned from Leave	
			1 att to Yorks to Hospital	
	20.		2 O.Rs Leave to U.K.	
			1 O.R. returned from 1st Corps ~~Signals~~ School.	
			1 O.R. and 4 attd from OSLER SIDING	
			Lieut C A LANGLEY to Back BILLET.	

1875 Wt. W593/826 1,000,000 4/15 J.B.C. & A. A.D.S.S./Forms/C. 2118.

Instructions regarding War Diaries and Intelligence Summaries are contained in F. S. Regs., Part II. and the Staff Manual respectively. Title Pages will be prepared in manuscript.

WAR DIARY
or
INTELLIGENCE SUMMARY
(Erase heading not required.)

Army Form C. 2118

Place	Date	Hour	Summary of Events and Information	Remarks and references to Appendices
LES BREBIS.	October 21		2 officers and 3 ORs. 68th Field Company arrived & take over forward Billets	
			II Lts Newcombe & Veitch to B Billet Nos 1, 3, 4 sections to Back Billets attd 2nd DLI [illegible]	
			and 1st West Yorks to Back Billet.	
			Advance Billets handed over to 68th Field Coy.	
	22.		Lieut C A LANGLEY and 3 ORs to new area EQUEDEQUE BILLETING	
			1 1st West York joined as reinforcement.	
			1 OR from 18th I B	
			II Lt Newland to CRE.	
EQUEDEQUES	23.		Coy moved from LES BREBIS to Noeux Les Mines by March Route. Entrained at	
			Noeux Les Mines to Lillers. Route March from Lillers to EQUEDEQUES	
	"		Transport by Road to EQUEDEQUES	
"	24		Inspection of Kits, general clean up.	
			Sapper Wakefield transferred to 6th Divl Signals	
	25		Coy on squad drill, Inspection of tools and stores on toolcarts by section officers	
			1 OR returned from leave to U.K.	
	26		Coy in drill & physical Exercises.	
	27		Coy Baths at Lillers	
			Attd Infy Baths — do —	
			C.S.M. Returned from Leave II Lt A K Newland returned from C.R.E.	

1875 Wt. W593/826 1,000,000 4/15 J.B.C. & A. A.D.S.S./Forms/C. 2118.

Instructions regarding War Diaries and Intelligence Summaries are contained in F. S. Regs., Part II. and the Staff Manual respectively. Title Pages will be prepared in manuscript.

WAR DIARY
or
INTELLIGENCE SUMMARY
(Erase heading not required.)

Army Form C. 2118

Place	Date	Hour	Summary of Events and Information	Remarks and references to Appendices
EQUEDEQUES	October 28		Lt J. C Newcombe granted leave to CANADA and struck off Coy strength Church Parade	
Magnicourt	29.		Coy moved by march route from Equedeques to Magnicourt-en-Comté	
Rullecourt	30		Coy and attached Infantry moved by march route from Magnicourt-en-Comté to Grand Rullecourt.	
	31.		Transport of Headquarters & of Nos 3 + 4 Sections moved by road from GRAND Rullecourt to Achiet le Petit under Lt R. J. Hall. Attd Infy returned to their units —	
			Summary of Work of October. Until the relief of the company from Les Brebis on the 21st October the work done was mainly the clearing and improving of trenches which had got into a very bad state with the rain. NESTOR NERO, NASH & NETLEY Trenches all were laid with duck boards. The overland ration track was carried forward to NASH ALLEY and Brigade Headquarters was improved. A scheme was got out + started for the improvement of the Horse Lines in the Brigade for winter. After relief all time was spent trekking	

A. Williamson [signature] Major RE
O.C. 12th Field Coy RE

1875 Wt. W593/826 1,000,000 4/15 J.B.C. & A. A.D.S.S./Forms/C. 2118.

Instructions regarding War Diaries and Intelligence Summaries are contained in F. S. Regs., Part II. and the Staff Manual respectively. Title Pages will be prepared in manuscript.

WAR DIARY
or
INTELLIGENCE SUMMARY
(Erase heading not required.)

12 1/Fd Coy RE

Vol 40

Army Form C. 2118

Place	Date	Hour	Summary of Events and Information	Remarks and references to Appendices
FINS	1 November		Major A Williamson, Lieut C. A Langley M.C + II Lt Veitch with H. Qrs and No 3 & 4 Sections (dismounted) march route to SAULTY. Entrained at SAULTY and detrained at FINS. Lieut R J Hall with Hd Qrs and Nos 3 & 4 Section Transport by road from ACHIET LE PETIT to NURLU.	
			No 1 & 2 Sections with Transport left at Grande RULLECOURT II Lt Newland i/c.	
	2.		Company employed on their new billets	
	3.		2 sappers returned from Leave. C.Q.M.S Foster joined the company.	
			2 reinforcements joined the Coy.	
			1 Sapper granted Leave to U.K.	
	4.		Work commenced in new area.	
	5.		Transport Lines moved to another site less conspicuous in NURLU.	
	6.		Work commenced on camouflaged billets at Queens Cross. Shelters erected.	
	7.		Work continued	
	8		Work continued	
	9		New work commenced for an advanced D.H.Q in sunken road at W4a 00.50	
	10		II Lieut D.R. Vachell RE joined as reinforcement	
			C.Q.M.S Jones C transferred to 3rd Pontoon Park	

1875 Wt. W593/826 1,000,000 4/15 J.B.C. & A. A.D.S.S./Forms/C. 2118.

2

Army Form C. 2118

Instructions regarding War Diaries and Intelligence Summaries are contained in F. S. Regs., Part II. and the Staff Manual respectively. Title Pages will be prepared in manuscript.

WAR DIARY
or
INTELLIGENCE SUMMARY
(Erase heading not required.)

Place	Date	Hour	Summary of Events and Information	Remarks and references to Appendices
Fins	11 Nov.		1 Driver special leave to U.K.	
			a cpl Thomson to III Corps Inst school 6th Div [illegible]	
	12		1 O.R. leave to U.K. 1 O.R. returned from leave to U.K.	
	13		2 O.R joined as reinforcements	
			2 officers 26 O.R. 14 D.L.I. } rejoined Coy as attached Infy.	
			26 " 2 D.L.I	
			26 " 1st W Yorks	
			28 " 11th Essex	
			2 O.R. 2nd D.L.I admitted to hospital	
	14		Work continued at Queens Cross and D.H.Q.	
	15			
	16.		2/Lt Bruce with the 11th Essex + 1st W Yorks attached to Queens Cross	
			1 N.C.O + 4 sappers of No 4 section to Queens Cross	
			1 O.R. 14th D.L.I. leave to U.K.	
			2 O.R. 2nd D.L.I. returned from Hospl.	
			1 O.R. to hospital.	
	17.		Dismounted of the Company from Fins to Queens Cross	
			1 O.R. to hospital	

1875 Wt. W593/826 1,000,000 4/15 J.B.C. & A. A.D.S.S./Forms/C. 2118.

Instructions regarding War Diaries and Intelligence Summaries are contained in F. S. Regs., Part II. and the Staff Manual respectively. Title Pages will be prepared in manuscript.

WAR DIARY
or
INTELLIGENCE SUMMARY
(Erase heading not required.)

3

Army Form C. 2118

Place	Date	Hour	Summary of Events and Information	Remarks and references to Appendices
QUEENSCROSS	18 Nov.		2 O.R. leave to U.K.	
	19		Lieut Champ 11th Essex joined company	
			2 O.R joined as reinforcements	
			2/Lt Brewer 14th DLI returned to his regiment.	
			3 Trestle wagons all tool carts, water cart, 2 forage carts moved to Queens X	
			6 extra packs for horses drawn giving a total of 10 Pack animals.	
RIBECOURT	20		Company under 18th I.B took part in attack opposite RIBECOURT	
			Major Williamson RE with Brigade Headquarters	
			No 3 Section (Lieut Langley MC.) attached to Brigade Headquarters in Reserve	
			No 2 section (2/Lt Neasland) + 2 sections attached Infy (2/Lt Bruce) 5 Pack animals	
			with wire and No 4 Section 2/Lt Veitch + 2 sections attached Infy 2/Lt Champ	
			5 Pack animals with wire moved forward from Queens Cross at 8 a.m.	
			No 4 section eventually built a strong point at L15 d.10.10.	
			No 2 section commenced one at L20 b 20.30 but had casualties including	
			2/Lt Neasland (afterwards died of wounds at the dressing station) Lieut	
			Langley with No 3 section relieved No 2 section and completed the work.	
			No 1 section 2/Lt Vachell remained in Divisional reserve at Queens Cross under orders from the C.R.E.	

1875 Wt. W593/826 1,000,000 4/15 J.B.C. & A. A.D.S.S./Forms/C. 2118.

Instructions regarding War Diaries and Intelligence Summaries are contained in F. S. Regs., Part II. and the Staff Manual respectively. Title Pages will be prepared in manuscript.

WAR DIARY
or
INTELLIGENCE SUMMARY
(Erase heading not required.)

4

Army Form C. 2118

Place	Date	Hour	Summary of Events and Information	Remarks and references to Appendices
RIBECOURT	20 Nov.		Transport (Lt Hall) 3 trestle wagons loaded picks, shovels, sandbags, wire pickets, 2 tool carts Nos 3+2, moved to RIBECOURT at 12 noon by ARGYLE ROAD through BEAUCAMP from Queens Cross. Trestle wagons offloaded at a captured German pioneer dump and all transport returned to BEAUCAMP.	
			H.Q. + details remained at Queens Cross under C.S.M. Rowe	
			Pontoons + Transport details remained at horse lines NURLU.	
			CASUALTIES	
			Lt A.K. NEWLAND R.E. wounded later died of wounds	
			1 O.R. KILLED	
			2 O.R. 14th D.L.I. died of wounds	
			1 O.R. 2nd D.L.I. KILLED	
			3 O.R. 2nd D.L.I. wounded	
	21st		No 1 Section 2/Lt Vachell joined company at RIBECOURT	
			A third strong point was constructed by No 2 section 2/Lt Veitch between the other two mentioned under Nov 20th covering the inner flanks of the outer two + the valley running N.W from PREMY RIDGE Map reference L 21 a 75.90	

1875 Wt. W593/826 1,000,000 4/15 J.B.C. & A.D.S.S./Forms/C. 2118.

5

Army Form C. 2118

Instructions regarding War Diaries and Intelligence Summaries are contained in F. S. Regs., Part II. and the Staff Manual respectively. Title Pages will be prepared in manuscript.

WAR DIARY
or
INTELLIGENCE SUMMARY
(Erase heading not required.)

Place	Date	Hour	Summary of Events and Information	Remarks and references to Appendices
RIBECOURT	22	Nov	Trestle wagons returned to NURLU loaded up pontoons & returned to BEAUCAMP	
			Nos 1 & 4 tool carts and remainder of transport brought up to BEAUCAMP	
			from QUEENS CROSS	
			H.Q. details joined Coy at RIBECOURT	
			a shell exploding near No 4 section shelter 1 O.R killed & 3 O.R wounded	
	23		Company remained in Reserve at RIBECOURT	
			2 machine gun emplacements made by No 4 section 2/Lt Vietch in the strong	
			points mentioned above	
			1 O.R joined as reinforcement.	
	24		Work commenced on a communication trench between L 15 d 60.70 and	
			L 16 a. 45. 85. Nos 3 & 2 Sections Lieut Langley.	
			1 O.R to hospital.	
	25		Work continued on Communication Trench	
			1 O.R 11th Essex to hospital	
			Sgt Whybrows 11th Essex returned to his regiment.	

Army Form C. 2118

6/

WAR DIARY
or
INTELLIGENCE SUMMARY
(Erase heading not required.)

Instructions regarding War Diaries and Intelligence Summaries are contained in F. S. Regs., Part II. and the Staff Manual respectively. Title Pages will be prepared in manuscript.

Place	Date	Hour	Summary of Events and Information	Remarks and references to Appendices
RIBECOURT	26	Nov	Work on Communication trench continued.	
			Sgt Young 11th Essex joined Coy to replace Sgt Whytrow	
			1 O.R. transferred to No 1 RE workshops	
	27	"	No 3 section Lt Langley and No 1 section 2/Lt Vachell commenced wiring front line in front of CANTAING. F.28.b. and F.28.d.	
			No 4 Section 2/Lt Veitch commenced to O.Ps at PREMYCHAPEL for 6th Divn at L-15-d-3.8. and L-16-c-5.5.	
	28		Nos 3 + 1 sections continued wiring completing 1500x	
			No 4 section completed the O.Ps. Also fitting stretcher racks in RAMC Dressing Station at L-25-b-6.2.	
			1 O.R. 2nd ? Hospital.	
	29		Nos 1 + 4 Sections put additional fence of wire in front of CANTAING, making the wire fence 1500x in length with breadth of 8x. Continued work on RAMC Dressing Station and commenced erection of elephant shelter entrances to dug-outs there	
	30		Lt Hall arrived about 11 am with orders to "Stand-to". Later a ~~verbal~~ message came from CRE about 11-30 am ordering Coy to UNSEEN TRENCH off ARGYLE ROAD at L.31.c.5.35 All kit was got away on a commandeered lorry, the 2 tool carts were manhandled by 2 sections attached Infy up the TRESCAULT Road to about Q-5-b-8-8, where they were afterwards sent for by Coy horse teams. The Coy + remainder attached Infy marched to UNSEEN TRENCH. All Transport out of RIBECOURT were found to be held up by failure of bridges across HINDENBERG LINE on ARGYLE ROAD at L-31-c-0-4 and	

1875 Wt. W593/826 1,000,000 4/15 J.B.C. & A. A.D.S.S./Forms/C. 2118.

Instructions regarding War Diaries and Intelligence Summaries are contained in F. S. Regs., Part II. and the Staff Manual respectively. Title Pages will be prepared in manuscript.

WAR DIARY
or
INTELLIGENCE SUMMARY
(Erase heading not required.)

Army Form C. 2118

E 7

Place	Date	Hour	Summary of Events and Information	Remarks and references to Appendices
RIBECOURT	30 Nov		and at K·36·d-8-0. These bridges were repaired by parties from No 1 and 4 Sections, under enemy shell fire, and all the transport enabled to cross safely. About 2-30 pm orders were received from CRE to proceed to HINDENBERG MAIN LINE across MARDON ROAD and report to Col ROSHER, 14th D.L.I. who was holding a line in L·32. and R-2. This order was duly carried out. A ~~separate~~ maintenance party was left at ARGYLE ROAD to keep the two trench crossings in order.	
			Transport (Lt Hall) received orders from C.R.E to move from BEAUCAMP to METZ at 12 30 PM. This was done with only two casualties horses killed while getting harnessed up.	
			Transport formed up in METZ and returned with the Coy by 8 P.M.	

A Williamson
Major RE
OC 12th Field Coy RE

2-12-17.

1875 Wt. W593/826 1,000,000 4/15 J.B.C. & A. A.D.S.S./Forms/C. 2118.

Instructions regarding War Diaries and Intelligence Summaries are contained in F. S. Regs., Part II. and the Staff Manual respectively. Title Pages will be prepared in manuscript.

WAR DIARY
or
INTELLIGENCE SUMMARY
(Erase heading not required.)

Army Form C. 2118

12 Fd Coy RE
Vol 41

Place	Date	Hour	Summary of Events and Information	Remarks and references to Appendices
RIBECOURT	1 December		Company holding the Line in RIDGE TRENCH from K 31 d 60.00 to R 2 a 40.85	
			2 O R returned from leave to U.K.	
			1 O R to Hospital.	
	2	–	At 1 a.m. Coy moved to old billets at RIBECOURT. Nos 1 + 4 sections + 3 sections of attached Infantry wiring 1200' from L 3 d 2 6 to L 10 a 80 00	
			1 Section attached working on Roads in RIBECOURT.	
			2 O R rejoined from 239 A.T. Coy R.E	
			1 O R wounded.	
	3.		At 3 P.M. Company relieved 2 coys 2nd D.L.I in trenches from L 20 a 80.80 to L 20 d 00.00 at 8-30 P.M. company was relieved by A + D Coys 2nd D.L.I. and the company took over those trenches vacated by these D.L.I companies between L 27 a 3.6 and L 27 c 8-9. Company's front was afterwards readjusted to get into touch with the flanks and its boundaries were L 20 d 20 to L 27 a 2-0. This move was completed by 5-30 AM 4/12/17 —	
			4 O R joined unit from base.	
	4.		At 8 P.M. No 4 section and Headquarters returned to RIBECOURT remainder + all attached Infantry wired outpost Line from L 20 a 20,40 to L 21 a 80.10. 2000 wire on completion of work returned to RIBECOURT.	
	5		3 Sections RE and 2 sections attached wired close support from L 20 a 2 4 to L 21 a 2.4 1000' also taped Line of trench for Infantry to dig.	
			2/Lt J M Noble joined unit from base No 2 reinforcement Coy RE	

1875 Wt. W593/826 1,000,000 4/15 J.B.C. & A. A.D.S.S./Forms/C. 2118.

Instructions regarding War Diaries and Intelligence Summaries are contained in F. S. Regs., Part II. and the Staff Manual respectively. Title Pages will be prepared in manuscript.

WAR DIARY
or
INTELLIGENCE SUMMARY
(Erase heading not required.)

Army Form C. 2118

Place	Date	Hour	Summary of Events and Information	Remarks and references to Appendices
MOLE TRENCH. K36 b 9.7	5 Dec	(contd)	Company moved from RIBECOURT to dug outs in K.36.b. (Mole Trench)	
	6		No 3 section (Lieut Langley M.C. + 2/Lt Noble) destroyed 2 tanks one at L 20 d 5.1 and the other at L 20 a 8.1 These tanks were destroyed with guncotton.	
			Nos 4 + 1 sections + 2 sections of attached commenced wire between L 19 b 90 45 and L 13 c 50 60	
	7		2 ORs returned from leave.	
			Trench taped out from L 20 a 4.4 to L 13 b 4 2 ~~....~~ 2 sections + 2 sections attached Infy wired in front of this Line.	
			5 O.R. to hospital sick	
			3 O.R. " " gassed	
			1 O.R. " " wounded	
	8		2 sections R.E. and 2 sections attached continued wiring as above (7th)	
			1 O.R. to hospital sick	
			1 O.R. " – gassed	
			1 a/E Cpl to R.E Base Depot for 2 months course	
	9		3 Sections R.E. and 3 sections attached continued wiring as above	
	10		2 OR returned from Hospital	
			1 officer and 3 O.R leave to U.K. – (Lt Langley)	
ETRICOURT	11		Dismounted H.Q. and attached moved from MOLE TRENCH, via METZ to ETRICOURT on relief by 82nd Field Coy R.E. Mounted from METZ to ETRICOURT. Moves complete by 6 PM. Capt Jack struck off with effect from 4-10-17	

Instructions regarding War Diaries and Intelligence Summaries are contained in F. S. Regs., Part II. and the Staff Manual respectively. Title Pages will be prepared in manuscript.

WAR DIARY
or
INTELLIGENCE SUMMARY
(Erase heading not required.)

Army Form C. 2118

Place	Date	Hour	Summary of Events and Information	Remarks and references to Appendices
HENDECOURT	12	DEC.	Dismounted from ETRICOURT to HENDECOURT by Motor Bus –	
			Transport followed by road –	
			Coy billeted in rest camp –	
	13		2 att Infy returned from Hospital =	
			Coy cleaning up	
	14		Coy moved to another camp in same village	
			1 reinforcement arrived from 11th Essex –	
			2nd c/pl Cox arrived to relieve Sgt Caulfield –	
			1 o.R. joined as reinforcement –	
			2 o.R. returned from leave –	
	15.		[illegible] arrived to Relieve [illegible]	
	16		1 o.R. returned from Hospital	
	17.		[illegible] sick. 1 o.R. sick to U.K. struck off strength [illegible]	
	18.		Sgt Caulfield [illegible] 1 o.R. leave to U.K.	
	19.		[illegible] 1 o.R. leave to U.K.	
	20		3 o.R. returned from leave U.K.	
	22		1 o.R. hospital [illegible]	
	23.		2 o.R. returned from hospital	
	24		Coy moved by march Route to BAPAUME attached Infantry [illegible] HENDECOURT	
	25.		Scheme got out for two camps each to accommodate 1 Battalion pioneers + 1 Field Coy R.E.	

1875 Wt. W593/826 1,000,000 4/15 J.B.C. & A. A.D.S.S./Forms/C. 2118.

Instructions regarding War Diaries and Intelligence Summaries are contained in F. S. Regs., Part II. and the Staff Manual respectively. Title Pages will be prepared in manuscript.

WAR DIARY
or
INTELLIGENCE SUMMARY
(Erase heading not required.)

Army Form C. 2118

Place	Date	Hour	Summary of Events and Information	Remarks and references to Appendices
25 DEC	BAPAUME		one camp in I 13 b, the other in I 29 b (Sheet 57c). Comprising NISSEN HUTS, shelters + revetting. Work to be done under C.E. IV corps	
26			Work commenced on above scheme. 2 sections I 13 2 sections I 29	
27			1 O.R. to hospital sick. 2 O.R returned from leave.	
28			1 O.R. to hospital	
29			Capt C.A. Langley M.C. returned from leave	
30			Capt C.A. Langley M.C. to G.H.Q school BLENDECQUES for course	
31			2/Lt J.M. Noble leave to U.K.	
			1 O.R to hospital	
			Work on Camps continued as from Dec. 25th.	

R. J. Hall Lieut
a/ O.C. 12th (Field) Coy. R.E.

1875 Wt. W593/826 1,000,000 4/15 J.B.C. & A. A.D.S.S./Forms/C. 2118.

6th Divisional Engineers.

WAR DIARY

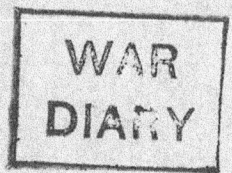

12th FIELD COMPANY R. E.

MARCH 1 9 1 8

Instructions regarding War Diaries and Intelligence Summaries are contained in F. S. Regs., Part II. and the Staff Manual respectively. Title pages will be prepared in manuscript.

17

WAR DIARY
or
INTELLIGENCE SUMMARY.
(Erase heading not required.)

Army Form C. 2118.

12 Fd Coy RE 6

Vol 44

Place	Date	Hour	Summary of Events and Information	Remarks and references to Appendices
C29C 0.5. (Sheet 57C).	7		2nd LT. D.R. Vachell. R.E. proceeded on leave to U.K.	
	18		[redacted] Major Williamson. R.E. returned from leave to Paris.	
	1–20.		Work carried out by Company in PRONVILLE SECTOR of the Line. Main work consisted in improvements + extension of accomodation in the Sector. Shelters (splinter proof) 20 erected in the Reserve Line. 17 erected in Support Line. Dugouts. 1 for 14 men completed in Reserve Line 2 more commenced. 2 commenced in Support Line. Deep dugout for R.A.P. completed. 2 deep dugout completed at Company Billets (C29C0.5) for 100 men. 2 dugouts at Battery positions enlarged 2 more commenced. All dugouts in Brigade Sector fitted with Gas Blankets Trenches. 35 firebays were put in in the Reserve Line. 12 in Support Line. A little work on drainage + maintenance. On the nights of the 11th/12th + 12th/13th 4 Minefields for Defence against Tanks were put out. 850 mines being laid in all. Brigade H.Q. A new Bde H.Q. was erected for 18th Inf Bde at I 17 a 7,10 } Completed in 1 week with all furniture and fittings. A new Bde H.Q. was erected for 2nd Bde R.F.A. at I 17 a 7.10. }	
	21.		Company was ordered to stand to in the Corps Line in front of MORCHIES at 5.30 a.m. At 5.a.m while Company was proceeding to Corps Line enemy opened an intensive barrage all along the Line. ~~that~~ Major A. Williamson RE. was killed almost immediately. LT Charlton, attached Infantry, also became a casualty. Section Officers rallied their men and got them into position in the Corps Line. About 12 NOON Capt C.P. Langley, R.E. arrived from Transport Lines and took over Command of the Company. About 6.p.m. Corps Line had become the front line and three five parties were sent out to close gaps in the wire and later parties of the enemy approaching over wire were driven off with rifle fire.	

A7092). Wt. W12839/M1297 750,000. 1/17. D. D & L., Ltd. Forms/C2118/14.

Instructions regarding War Diaries and Intelligence Summaries are contained in F. S. Regs., Part II. and the Staff Manual respectively. Title pages will be prepared in manuscript.

WAR DIARY
or
INTELLIGENCE SUMMARY.
(Erase heading not required.)

Army Form C. 2118.

Place	Date	Hour	Summary of Events and Information	Remarks and references to Appendices
	21		2 LT. J.C. Newcombe was wounded about 3.p.m and later killed while being carried to Dressing station.	
			About 11.p.m. Corps line was reorganized and Company was withdrawn into Reserve in VAULX-BEUGNY Rd at I 16 a.0.7.	
			Casualties suffered. 2 Officers killed. 12 O.R. killed 30 wounded, 7 missing.	
			Attached Infantry. 1 Officer missing. 6 O.R. wounded 12 missing	
	22		At 5.30.a.m. Company moved back to I 15 a 6.0. and there in conjunction with detachments from 459 + 509 Field Companies constructed a Strong Point for 200 men and wired in the North flank wire being drawn from BEUGNY. RE Yard.	
			At about 11.a.m. Company received orders to form a defensive flank across VAULX-BEUGNY Road about I 9 a + b. This was carried out the Company being on the North of the road with the detachments from 459 + 509 Companies on the SOUTH of the road.	
			At about 2 p.m. Front line retired to this position + detachments from 459 + 509 were withdrawn to the Strong Point. Front line troops were reorganized + formed a line across VAULX-BEUGNY Road with Company on the right flank facing North East.	
			Troops on the left continued to retire and therefore left flank was brought back till it faced North West.	
			By 4.P.m. troops on the right + left ~~were with~~ had retired and Company remained in a position in I 9 a with about 60 Infantry of various Regiments under command of the O.C.	
			Parties of the enemy advancing from VAULX-MORCHIES Road were held up + heavy fire was directed against large bodies of the enemy advancing up the valley to the S.E. of VAULX.	
			At 6.30.p.m. Company was withdrawn to the Army line owing to lack of ammunition and the flanks of the position having become very exposed.	

A7092). Wt. W12839/M1297 750,000. 1/17. D. D & L., Ltd. Forms/C2118/14.

Instructions regarding War Diaries and Intelligence Summaries are contained in F. S. Regs., Part II. and the Staff Manual respectively. Title pages will be prepared in manuscript.

WAR DIARY
or
INTELLIGENCE SUMMARY.
(Erase heading not required.)

Army Form C. 2118.

Place	Date	Hour	Summary of Events and Information	Remarks and references to Appendices
ACHIET-LEGRAND	22.		At 11 p.m. Transport proceeded to BUCHANAN CAMP ACHIET-LE-GRAND.	
	23.		At 12 MIDNIGHT. Company left ~~[illegible]~~ Army Line and ~~proceeded~~ marched to BUCHANAN CAMP. ACHIET-LEGRAND and arrived there at 3.30 A.M.	
	24.		Company marched to PUISIEUX and there entrained for MONDICOURT.	
MONDICOURT	25.		Transport marched direct by road to MONDICOURT. Company arrived at MONDICOURT at 8.a.m. Company with transport entrained for PESELHOEK.	
ELVERDINGHE	26.		Company arrived detrained at PESELHOEK and marched into Camp at ELVERDINGHE.	
ST JAN-TER-BREZEN	27.		Company marched to ST JAN-TER-BIEZEN. 2/LT. D.R. Vachell. R.E. returned from leave.	
~~EECKE~~ EECKE.	28		Company marched to EECKE.	
	30.		Company and attached Infantry were inspected by Army Commander II Army.	

[illegible] Capt RE
O.C. 12th Field Company R.E.

A7092). Wt. W12839/M1297 750,000. 1/17. D. D & L., Ltd. Forms/C2118/14.

6th Divisional Engineers

12th FIELD COMPANY R. E.

APRIL 1918.

Army Form C. 2118.

12 Fd Coy R.E.

Vol 45

Instructions regarding War Diaries and Intelligence Summaries are contained in F. S. Regs., Part II. and the Staff Manual respectively. Title pages will be prepared in manuscript.

Apl 18

WAR DIARY
or
INTELLIGENCE SUMMARY.

(Erase heading not required.)

Place	Date	Hour	Summary of Events and Information	Remarks and references to Appendices
EECKE (Ref Sheet 27)	1		II LIEUT. J.M.T. Horne R.E. + 7 O.R arrived from Base as reinforcements.	
SAPPER CAMP I9a5,9. (Sheet 28)	2 3		Company (Dismounted Personnel) moved by tactical train to YPRES + thence marched to SAPPER CAMP I9a5,9, (Ref Sheet 28). Transport moved by road to H23C7,6. (Sheet 28)	
	3.4		Commenced work on the Corps Line.	
	6.		Capt F.W. MOORE M.C. R.E. took over Command of the Company from Capt. C.A. LANGLEY M.C. RE. 45 O.R joined Company from Base as reinforcements.	
	10.		Company stood to in Billets at 3.a.m. owing to anticipated enemy attack. IILT A. L. Handley R.E. to Hospital Sick.	
	11.		2 Horses (Rides) killed, 2 wounded by shell fire 1 O.R wounded.	
	13.		Transport moved to H21 b 3,3. (Sheet 28).	
	14		Transport moved to H15C3,7. (Sheet 28)	
	16.		Transport moved Camp 43 H8C 6,0. (Sheet 28). Headquarters Nos 1+2 Sections RE + 1 Section attached Infantry moved from Sapper Camp to Camp 43. Nos 3+4 Sections R.E. + 2 Sections Attached Infantry moved to new billets in the Ramparts YPRES near the LILLE GATE.	
	21.		Section Relief. Nos 1+2 Sections R.E. + 1 Section Attached Infantry from Camp 43 to Ramparts YPRES. Nos 3+4 Sections RE + 1 Section attached Infantry from YPRES to Camp 43.	

D. D. & L., London, E.C.
(A8001) Wt. W1771/M2031 750,000 5/17 Sch. 52 Forms/C2118/14

Instructions regarding War Diaries and Intelligence Summaries are contained in F. S. Regs., Part II. and the Staff Manual respectively. Title pages will be prepared in manuscript.

WAR DIARY
or
INTELLIGENCE SUMMARY.
(*Erase heading not required.*)

Army Form C. 2118.

Place	Date	Hour	Summary of Events and Information	Remarks and references to Appendices
I 9 a 5,9. ~~Camp~~ (Sheet 28).	21		4 O.R. killed 5. O.R. wounded by Bomb at Advance Billet	
			7. O.R. Attached Infantry gassed at Advance Billet.	
	22.		Nos 1 & 2 Sections RE. + 2 Sections Attached Infantry withdrawn from Ramparts YPRES to Camp 43.	
	23.		1. O.R. wounded. 2/Lt F.F. Wood RE joined Company from the Base.	
	25.		Company stood to in Billets owing to an enemy attack	
			1 O.R. wounded	
			1. O.R. gassed.	
	28.		Transport moved from Camp 43 to G 10 C 9,3. (Sheet 28.)	
G 10 C 9,3. (Sheet 28)	29.		Company stand to owing to enemy attack.	
			1. O.R. wounded.	
			Company moved at night to A 30 Central (Sheet 28) Headquarters Section came back to Transport Lines.	
			2/Lt A.L. Handley R.E. rejoined the Company.	
	30.		Company withdrew to Camp at G 10 C 9,3. after work.	
			<u>Summary of Work.</u>	
			Period 4th to 9th. Work on Concrete Pill Boxes in Corps Front + Reserve Lines.	
			Do 10th No work. Company stand to all day.	
			Do 11th to 14th New Support Line was dug for the Corps Front Line. Wire was repaired + Trench revetted	

D. D. & L., London, E.C.
(A8001) Wt. W1771/M2031 750,000 5/17 Sch. 52 Forms/C2118/14

Instructions regarding War Diaries and Intelligence Summaries are contained in F. S. Regs., Part II. and the Staff Manual respectively. Title pages will be prepared in manuscript.

WAR DIARY
or
INTELLIGENCE SUMMARY.
(Erase heading not required.)

Army Form C. 2118.

Place	Date	Hour	Summary of Events and Information	Remarks and references to Appendices
G10 C9,2. (Sheet 28.)			Summary of Work (Contd).	
			Period 11th to 14th (Contd). All Bridges and Causeways across YPRES-COMMINES CANAL ~~were prepared~~ between Bridge at I13a 7,4. (inclusive) + Bridge at I19d 5,7. (exclusive)	
			Period 15th to 30th. During this period a series of new lines of Trenches were dug + wired.	
			A new front line was dug + wired from I21c 80,00 to I16c 00,20 with a support line behind it.	
			A new reserve line was dug along YPRES-COMMINES CANAL from I13a 8,5 to I13d 1,5. + thence to I19a 3,2. with a Support line behind it.	
			A new outpost line to the new front line was dug + wired from I17c 2,4 through DORMY HOUSE at I23a 7,4 to I23c 3,6.	
			A new line was dug + wired from H17a 5,0 to H17c 7,0.	
			A new line was dug + wired from ~~H~~ H15c 3,8 to H14d 3,2.	
			During this period a large number of huts were salved from the forward area.	
			All bridges + Causeways across the Moat at YPRES were prepared for demolition + the sluice gates to ZILLEBEKE LAKE were destroyed.	
			J. W. Moore Major R.E. O.C. 127th Fd Coy. R.E.	

D. D. & L., London, E.C.
(A8004) Wt. W1771/M2031 750,000 5/17 Sch. 52 Forms/C2118/14

Instructions regarding War Diaries and Intelligence Summaries are contained in F. S. Regs., Part II. and the Staff Manual respectively. Title pages will be prepared in manuscript.

WAR DIARY
or
INTELLIGENCE SUMMARY.
(Erase heading not required.)

12 Fd Coy R.E.
Vol 46

Army Form C. 2118.

Place	Date	Hour	Summary of Events and Information	Remarks and references to Appendices
G10d1,9 (Sheet 28)	4.		Company stood to in billets owing to expected enemy attack.	
	13.		A Lewis Gun Course was commenced at Company Billet for men of the Company.	
	20.		A Course in R.E. Work for Infantry Officers was commenced at Rear Brigade HQ (18th I.B.) Lectures + practical work given by various officers of the Company.	
	22		C.Q.M.S. FOSTER proceeded to England for a Cadet's Course.	
	~~27~~		~~Company stood to at 4.15 am owing to enemy attack~~	
	25.		Company commenced work for the 16th I.B. on the relief of 18th I.B by ~~the~~ 16th I.B	
	27.		Company stood to at 4.15 am owing to enemy attack.	
			Summary of Work	
			Forward Area.	
			Work mainly consisted in the improvement + gas protection of dugouts in the area. Brigade Headquarters have been improved + strengthened + all headquarters + important dugouts in the area have been fitted with gas curtains. All bridges + causeways along YPRES-COMMINES Canal have been prepared for demolition + a permanent party left in charge of them. The sluice at Zillebeke Lake was destroyed and all the water drained out of it	

D. D. & L., London, E.C.
(A8001) Wt. W1771/M2031 750,000 5/17 Sch. 52 Forms/C2118/14

Instructions regarding War Diaries and Intelligence Summaries are contained in F. S. Regs., Part II. and the Staff Manual respectively. Title pages will be prepared in manuscript.

WAR DIARY
or
INTELLIGENCE SUMMARY.
(Erase heading not required.)

Army Form C. 2118.

Place	Date	Hour	Summary of Events and Information	Remarks and references to Appendices
			The top portion of SWANCHATEAU I 19 c 3,6 (Sheet 28) was destroyed so as not to form an aiming point for the enemy. A ~~B~~ Brigade Battn was constructed at I 17 c 9,5 (Sheet 28). ROADS. A large amount of work has been done screening roads from observation from KEMMEL HILL. The road from H14 b 40,75 (Sheet 28) to H16 b 1,1 has been completely screened & also the road from H17 c 7,0 to H18 d 5,3, and the road between these two parts is in hand at present. BACK AREA. Work here consisted in the erection of a Brigade H.Q at G 9 b 6,3 (Sheet 28). Consists of English shelters protected so as to be proof against 5.9" Shells. J. W. Moore Major R.E. O.C. 12th Fd. Co. R.E.	

D. D. & L., London, E.C.
(A8001) Wt. W1771/M2031 750,000 5/17 Sch. 52 Forms/C2118/14

Instructions regarding War Diaries and Intelligence Summaries are contained in F. S. Regs., Part II. and the Staff Manual respectively. Title pages will be prepared in manuscript.

WAR DIARY
or
INTELLIGENCE SUMMARY.
(Erase heading not required.)

Army Form C. 2118.

12TH FIELD COMPY R.E. 30-6-18

Vol 47

Place	Date	Hour	Summary of Events and Information	Remarks and references to Appendices
G.10 d 1, 9. Sheet 28.	1st		IIL^T Veitch MC RE. proceeded on a Course to No 4 Veterinary Hospital Calais.	
			IIL^T Horne R.E. + 13 O.R. proceeded to Cormette Camp. near St Omer.	
	3rd.		Major F.W. Moore MC RE. proceeded on special leave to England and Capt Langley, MC RE. took over Command of the Company.	
	7.		On relief of Division by the 33rd Division all work etc in the Company Sector was handed over to the 11th Field Company R.E. At 2 p.m. the Company marched out of Camp + proceeded to Camp taken over from the 11th Field Coy RE. Camp at L 9 d 0.1 Sheet 27 Transport lines at L 15 b 8.5	
L 9 d 0.1 Sheet 27.	8.		Commenced training today.	
	9.		IIL^T Horne + party returned to the Company from Cormette Camp.	
	12.		Commenced work on the Vlamertinghe line for 4 days. ~~Sector from~~ Work consisted in Completing the revetment of Front + Support Lines, completion of parapet + parados + strengthening of the wire.	
	~~16~~ 15		Handed over work on Vlamertinghe Line to 507 Field Coy RE	
	16		Commenced training again.	
	17.		Commenced a programme of Company Sports to be carried out each afternoon.	
	19.		Commenced work on the EAST Poperinghe Reserve Line. Sector from POPERINGHE – BUSSEBOOM Road to SOUTH CORPS Boundary. Work consisted in Completing wire, revetment + parapet + parados.	

D. D. & L., London, E.C. (A8001) Wt. W1771/M2031 750,000 5/17 Sch. 52 Forms/C2118/14

Instructions regarding War Diaries and Intelligence Summaries are contained in F. S. Regs., Part II. and the Staff Manual respectively. Title pages will be prepared in manuscript.

WAR DIARY
or
INTELLIGENCE SUMMARY.
(*Erase heading not required.*)

12TH FIELD COMPANY, R.E.
No.
Date 30.6.18

Army Form C. 2118.

Place	Date	Hour	Summary of Events and Information	Remarks and references to Appendices
L9d 0.1. Sheet 27.	22.		Handed over work on East Poperinghe Reserve line to 509 Field Coy. R.E. All Attached Infantry returned to their Battalions.	
	24		Recommenced training. Held a Driving Drill Competition + a Section Drill Competition. C.R.E. came down + judged same	
	25.		Capt Langley with 3 Section Officers reported at H.Q. 46th French Division and from there went to H.Q. of the 28/3 ~~Compagnie de genie~~ Compagnie de genie. Then proceeded round the line + took over the work in the DICKEBUSCH sector.	
	26		H.Q. + Nos 2+3 Sections R.E. took over the billets of 28/3 Compagnie de genie at G.10.d.9.2. No 4 Section RE took over forward billet at H.14.d.1.2.	
	29		~~Mj~~ Major F.W. Moore M.C. R.E. returned from leave + resumed Command of the Company.	
			Summary	
			During this period the Company has been out in rest for the majority of the time.	
			The training carried out has been largely hampered by the work which had to been carried out 4 days each week and also by the large amount of sickness owing to the epidemic of Influenza.	
			Training consisted of Drill and Musketry in the mornings followed by Sports in the afternoon.	

[signature] Major, R.E.
O.C. 12th (Field) Company R.E.

D. D. & L., London, E.C.
(A8001) Wt. W1771/M2031 750,000 5/17 Sch. 52 Forms/C2118/14

Instructions regarding War Diaries and Intelligence Summaries are contained in F. S. Regs., Part II. and the Staff Manual respectively. Title pages will be prepared in manuscript.

WAR DIARY
or
INTELLIGENCE SUMMARY.
(Erase heading not required.)

Army Form C. 2118.

12 Fd Coy R.E.

Vol 48

Place	Date	Hour	Summary of Events and Information	Remarks and references to Appendices
G.10.d.9.2	1/7/18		Coy in Billets as follows. H.Q. + 2 + 3 Sections at G.10.d.7.2, No 4 Section forward at H.20.d.3.3 (both these Sheet 28) + No 1 Sec + Transport at L.18.a.0.3. (Sheet 27.)	
	2/7/18	2 P.M.	Hd.Qrs. + Nos 1, 2 + 3 Sections move to LANBOUVER FARM 28 N.W. G.21.b.3.3. No 4 remains forward.	
	3/7/18		Capt C.A. LANGLEY M.C. RE left Coy to take up duties of Adjutant to C.R.E. 6th Division. Lt J.M. NOBBS taking over from him. No. 1 Section relieved No 4 on forward work	
	8/7/18		1 Lt R.L. WINN (1st Batt W.Y.R.) and 30 men from 18th INF. BDE. are attached to company as the Company's attached infantry party.	
	12/7/18		1 Lt A.L. HANDLEY RE proceeded on 14 days leave to U.K.	
	14/7/18		No. 2 Section relieved No. 1 ~~Sec~~ Sec on Forward work.	
	15/7/18		ENEMY shelled H.Q. billets heavily all day. one casualty only, exceptionally lucky.	
	16/7/18		Enemy gas shelled H.Q. billets during night 16/17th.	
	22/7/18		Enemy attack expected. Coy. "Stand To" at 4 A.M. "Stand Down" at 10 A.M. "Stand to" was in Billets.	
	23/7/18		Enemy shelled Billets heavily once more. Two Sergts of attached Infantry party killed. No 3 Section relieved No 2 for forward work + billets.	
	25/7/18		One platoon of American Engineers attached to Coy for instruction. Half platoon proceeded to forward Billets + half remained at H.Q. Billet. This platoon is 1st Plat. "F" Coy. 102nd American Engrs.	
	28/7/18		American half sections change over.	
	30/7/18		1 Lt A.L. HANDLEY RE rejoined from leave. Enemy shelled H.Q. Billets heavily.	
	31/7/18		The attached American platoon rejoins its Battn being relieved by 3rd Plat. of "D" Coy of 102nd American Engineers who all remain at Rear Billets (i.e. H.Q. Billet.	
			WORK.	
			During this month the Coy. has been working in the LEFT Bde Sector of the 6TH Div. Front (DICKIEBUSCH SECTOR).	

D. D. & L., London, E.C.
(A8001) Wt. W1771/M2031 750,000 5/17 Sch. 52 Forms/C2118/14

Instructions regarding War Diaries and Intelligence Summaries are contained in F. S. Regs., Part II. and the Staff Manual respectively. Title pages will be prepared in manuscript.

WAR DIARY
or
INTELLIGENCE SUMMARY.
(Erase heading not required.)

Army Form C. 2118.

Place	Date	Hour	Summary of Events and Information	Remarks and references to Appendices
			During this period the 18TH INF BDE. held this sector until the night of the 16/17th when they were relieved by the 16TH INF. BDE.	
			The work has consisted chiefly of the following.	
			M.G.E's at H 29 c 8.4 (concrete) H.26 d 8.1. + two MOIR MGE's at H 26 d 5.2 + H.27. a 7.0.	
			R.A.P. at H 29. c 2.5.	
			A.D.S. at H. 24. b 8.4 also one at G 16 c 3.6.	
			Mined Accomodation in DICKIEBUSCH BUND at H 34 b 3.6.	
			DICKIEBUSCH RESERVE and SUPPORT LINES.	
			Strong dugouts at Post "B" (H 26 d 3.3) Post "C" (H 27 a 2 3) + Post "D" (H.20.d 3 3)	
			Battn HQrs at INDUS FARM (H.28 a 2 0)	
			Rear Bde HdQrs at DE DREI GOEN FARM. G 24 b 8.	
			Coy. Billets have been considerably improved at H 20 d 3.3 + G 21 b 3 3.	
			Coy. H.Qrs for Res. Coy. of Left Battn at H 34 central.	
			Map Reference. Sheet 28 N.W. 1/20000	

12TH FIELD COMPANY, R.E.
No.
Date 31-7-18.

J W Munro [signature]
Major. R.E.
O.C. 12th Field Company R.E.

D. D. & L., London, E.C.
(A8001) Wt. W1771/M2031 750,000 5/17 Sch. 52 Forms/C2118/14

Instructions regarding War Diaries and Intelligence Summaries are contained in F. S. Regs., Part II. and the Staff Manual respectively. Title pages will be prepared in manuscript.

WAR DIARY
or
INTELLIGENCE SUMMARY.
(Erase heading not required.)

Army Form C. 2118.

12 Fd Coy R.E. Vol 49

Place	Date	Hour	Summary of Events and Information	Remarks and references to Appendices
	1918 August			
28/G21b33.	1		No 3 Section returned to H.Q. all work in the Left Bde. Section handed over to the 459th Field Co RE. work in the Reserve Bde. area (WESTOUTRE - GOED MOET MILL line) taken over from 459th Coy RE	
	3		Transport moved from 27/L18a03 to 27/L15c49.	
	4		1 officer +9 O.R. attended Commemoration Service	
	6		one platoon 103rd American Engineers rejoined its battalion being relieved by another platoon of the same battalion	
	12		one platoon 103rd American Engineers rejoined its battalion & was relieved by another platoon of the same battalion.	
	15		Enemy shelled Coy H.Q at Midnight. Sergt. SMITH A.W. RE severely wounded	
	18		one platoon 103rd American Engineers rejoins its battalion	
	20		C.S.M Bennett F.G. RE joins Coy from R.E. Base	
27/L15c49	21	3pm	Coy moved back to 27/L15c4.9 after handing over all work in Reserve Bde area to "F" Coy 1st Batt. 103rd American Engineers.	
	23		1 officer +30 O.R. proceeded to WIZERNES as advance party for billeting	
	24	7.41 AM	Coy (less transport) entrained at WATOU detraining at ST. MOMELIN Transport marched to WIZERNES. Billets as follows sheet 36 D.N.E H.Q F3d60.95 transport F3c30.30.	
	25		Lt D.R. VACHELL RE attached to C.R.E. as acting adjutant.	

D. D. & L., London, E.C.
(A8001) Wt. W1771/M2031 750,000 5/17 Sch. 52 Forms/C2118/14

Instructions regarding War Diaries and Intelligence Summaries are contained in F. S. Regs., Part II. and the Staff Manual respectively. Title pages will be prepared in manuscript.

WAR DIARY
or
INTELLIGENCE SUMMARY.
(Erase heading not required.)

Army Form C. 2118.

12TH FIELD COMPANY, R.E.
No. .... Date 1-9-18

Place	Date	Hour	Summary of Events and Information	Remarks and references to Appendices
	1918 AUGUST 28		Coy proceeded to LUMBRE rifle ranges for firing practice.	
	29		" Marched from WIZERNES to MOULLE sheet 27A SE, billets as follows	
			H.Q. Q17b75 Transport Q5c.6.3.	
	31st		Received urgent orders for move which were cancelled at point of departure	
			WORK.	
			From 1-21 the coy has been working in the Reserve Bde. Sector of 6th Div front.	
			During this period the 16th Inf Bde held this sector until relieved by the 18 Inf Bde	
			The work was chiefly of the following:-	
			WESTOUTRE - GOED MOET Mill line Huts for DADOS 27/K18c99	
			A Frank camouflage	
			MERSEY CROSS Res Bde H.Q. G23c9525	
Sheet 28			MGE Main bell line H26d59	
			2nd Bde R.F.A H.Q. shelters G3c6505	
			24th " " " " G24a2040	
			Signal DO. Dominion Farm ← Strengthening dugout	
			LANBOUVER FM. Improving accommodation G21b33	
			Bath. H.Q. G24c05	
			Coy " 36a1.6	
			HALIFAX KEEP Signal DO H.14c80.20	

[signature] Major R.E.
O.C. 12th (Field) Company R.E.

D. D. & L., London, E.C.
(A8001) Wt. W1771/M2031 750,000 5/17 Sch. 52 Forms/C2118/14

Instructions regarding War Diaries and Intelligence Summaries are contained in F. S. Regs., Part II. and the Staff Manual respectively. Title pages will be prepared in manuscript.

9

WAR DIARY
or
INTELLIGENCE SUMMARY.
(Erase heading not required.)

Sept 1918

Army Form C. 2118.

12 Fd Coy R.E.

Vol 50

Place	Date	Hour	Summary of Events and Information	Remarks and references to Appendices
MOULLE	1/10/18		Entrained at ARQUES and left at 21-37 hrs	
BONNAY	2/10/18		Arrived BONNAY 13-30 hrs. fixed baths Sanitary arrangements.	
	3rd		Training in section drill musketry Field levels Instruments Map reading.	
	4th		O.C. to C.R.E. 2/Lt A.L. HANDLEY to hospital.	
	5th		3 O R from RE.B.D. Coy Reconnoissance of District. Cpl BEDFORD from RETS.	
	6th		Spr THOMAS to hospital & 1.O.R. leave to U.K	
	7th		Sgt CHRISTIAN to RETS for course. 2.O.R leave to U.K.	
	8th		2 O R to hospital. 2 OR leave to U.K.	
	9th		2 O R from RE B.D 1.OR to hospital.	
	11th		left BONNAY 14-30 hrs for VAUX SUR SOMME	
VAUX SUR SOMME	12th		left VAUX SUR SOMME 9.00 hrs arrived TERTRY 15.00 hrs by bus arrived in billets 0001 hrs 62d	
TERTRY	13th		No 1 Sect. to Forward Billet/X 8 c 2/Lt D.R. VACHELL from R.E Hqrs.	
	14th		Reconnoissance parties roads & booby traps.	
	15th		Clearing tracks for R.F.A	
	16th		C.R.E. conference 9.0 AM.	
	17th		O.C to Forward Section. Spr DAVIDSON wounded.	
	18th		Div. Attack No3 & 4 Sections with R.F.A for tracks & bridges	
	19th		No1 Sect. to Rear Billet. 3 & 4 Sections up to Forward Billet	
	20th		O.C to Works & C.R.E.	

D. D. & L., London, E.C.
(A8001) Wt. W1771/M2031 750,000 5/17 Sch. 52 Forms/C2118/14

Instructions regarding War Diaries and Intelligence Summaries are contained in F. S. Regs., Part II. and the Staff Manual respectively. Title pages will be prepared in manuscript.

WAR DIARY
or
INTELLIGENCE SUMMARY.
(Erase heading not required.)

Army Form C. 2118.

Place	Date	Hour	Summary of Events and Information	Remarks and references to Appendices
TERTRY	Sept 21st		Nos 1 & 2 Sect 27 Leicesters work on New Div HQrs	
contd	23rd		O.C. to works with old & new C.R.E.s.	
	27th		Coy HQrs moved to late Forward Section Billet.	
	28th		O.O. from 71 I.B. prepared to move	
	29th		moved with TRANSPORT to Q31 c 8 5 at 7.0 PM & made bivouacs.	
			TRAINING & WORK	
			From 1st–12th Coy has been training (including reconnaissance, pontoon & trestle bridging.	
			Work began on 13th & consisted mainly of the following	
			Clearing tracks making bridges & gelbarding for R.A. & Inf.	
			Reconstructing & repairing wells & dug outs	
			Reconnoitring for mines & booby traps.	
			New Div. HQrs. W 8 b central.	
			New Div. Baths at CAULAINCOURT	

12TH FIELD COMPANY, R.E.
No. ....
Date 30-9-18

J.W. [illegible] Major
O.C. 12th Fd Co R.E.

(A8001) Wt. W1771/M2031 750,000 5/17 Sch. 52 Forms/C2118/14
D. D. & L., London, E.C.

Army Form C. 2118.

WAR DIARY
or
INTELLIGENCE SUMMARY.
(Erase heading not required.)

Instructions regarding War Diaries and Intelligence Summaries are contained in F. S. Regs., Part II. and the Staff Manual respectively. Title pages will be prepared in manuscript.

12th [illegible] 57

Place	Date	Hour	Summary of Events and Information	Remarks and references to Appendices
	1918		October 1918	
BELLINGLISE	4		Coy. moved to 62B/G 28 c 6.7. 1 NCO proceeded to 4th Army School of Musketry.	
MAGNY-la-FOSSE	6	07.00	Coy (less transport) - 62B/G 30 c 3 3. CRE conference 17.00 No. 1 + 4 sections moved into gun pits at 62B/H 26 b 8.3 Shelters made in trenches. Cpl EVANS to R.E.T.S. ROUEN.	
	7		O.C. moved into adv. billet.	
	8		Div. attacked successfully gaining all objectives + exploiting same. The Right was held up for sometime but recovered. The Coy assisted Div Artey to move forward with two Sections, the Remainder were in Divisional Reserve + not called on.	
MONTBREHAIN	9		Coy moved to 62B/I. 7 c 4 8 1/Lt. F.F. WOOD proceeded on leave to U.K.	
	10		No 4 Section moved forward to join 16th I.B. + be attached to them.	
BOHAIN	11	15.30	Coy moved to BOHAIN. 62B/D 15 c 4 7	
	12		Constructing road deviations round craters in BOHAIN. 1/Lt. J.W. HANSTOCK RE	
	13		Joined Coy as reinforcement	
	14		Filling in craters. Reconnaissance of BOHAIN for wells, cellars + booby traps. CAPT. J.M. NOBLE returned from leave to U.K.	
	15		Road deviation at 62B/D 14 c 8 2 and D 13 c 1 1. 1/Lt. W.M. VEITCH proceeded to U.K. on leave	
	16	17.00	CRE. conference.	
	17		Div. attacked 4 parties attached to RFA. for removing obstacles + Remainder on Reconnaissance	
	18		Coy moved into fresh billets 62B D 21 b 10 05	
ST. SOUPLET	20	08.15	" " to 57B/Q 33 b 2.2 arrived 14.00	
	21		Forward area reconnoitred roads, wells + cellars	
	22		Repairs to roads round ARBRE GUERNON + FARM 57B/R 25 b. Taping out direction tapes for Inf. 1/Lt. J.M.T. HORNE wounded.	

D. D. & L., London, E.C.
(A8001) Wt. W1771/M2031 750,000 5/17 Sch. 52 Forms/C2118/14

Instructions regarding War Diaries and Intelligence Summaries are contained in F. S. Regs., Part II. and the Staff Manual respectively. Title pages will be prepared in manuscript.

WAR DIARY
or
INTELLIGENCE SUMMARY.
(Erase heading not required.)

Army Form C. 2118.

Place	Date	Hour	Summary of Events and Information	Remarks and references to Appendices
	1918			
	23		Div. attacked O.C. proceeded to Right Bde. H.Q. & stayed during operations.	
	24		CRE conference. Wells, cellars & roads reconnoitred.	
	25		Repairs to metre gauge rly. along CATILLON - BAZUEL ROAD	
	26		do wells roads & cellars reconnoitred N. of CATILLON - BAZUEL Road. Coy. billets shelled during the night	
	27		Road repairs ARBRE GUERNON - BAZUEL Road obstruction in well at farm 57D/ R17c located. Gas curtain frames constructed at Right Bde H.Q. R14a 5095 & at Batt H.Q. R27a 17.	
	28		Fixing gas curtains on above frames. Repairs to road ARBRE GUERNON - BAZUEL Road	
	29		Constructing floating footbridge. Repairs to ARBRE - GUERNON - BAZUEL road	
	30		do. do. do. 2/Lt J.W. HANSTOCK wounded in billets and died on admission to Dressing Station.	
	31		Coy. Paraded at 05.45 hours & marched into Rest Billets at FRESNOY LE GRAND at I.17.d.9.4	
			WORK	
			Clearing tracks, making bridges & signboarding for R.A.	
			Reconnoitring & repairing wells, dugouts, cellars & roads	
			" for mines & booby traps	
			Gas curtains at Bde & Batt H.Q.	
			Making floating foot bridges for Infantry	

J.M. Moore
Major, R.E.
O.C. 12th (Field) Company R.E.

(A8001) Wt. W1771/M2031 750,000 5/17 Sch. 52 Forms/C2118/14 M. D. & L. London, E.C.

Instructions regarding War Diaries and Intelligence Summaries are contained in F. S. Regs., Part II. and the Staff Manual respectively. Title pages will be prepared in manuscript.

WAR DIARY
or
~~INTELLIGENCE SUMMARY.~~
(Erase heading not required.)

Army Form C. 2118.

12 Fd Coy RE
Vol 52

Place	Date	Hour	Summary of Events and Information	Remarks and references to Appendices
	1918 Nov			
FRESNOY LE GRAND	1		Coy H.Q. ST QUENTIN 18 1E 9033 Targets made & erected in 71st Bde training area. Training commenced	
"	2		Fixing targets for 71st Bde. Erecting disinfector for 18th Fld Amb. 2/Lt W.M. NEITCH MC RE returned from leave to U.K.	
"	3		Erecting disinfector, repairing drains & floor at bathhouse for 18th Fld Amb. 2/Lt D.R. VACHELL RE proceeded on leave	
"	4		Making & erecting targets for 18th Inf Bde training area. Constructing concrete floor for 18th Fld Amb.	
	5	10.45 15.00	Moved from FRESNOY to BUSIGNY Coy HQ VALENCIENNES 12 6F 6353	
	6		Cleaning billets wagons & training	
	7	11.00	Moved to CATILLON Coy HQ 15.00 hrs VALENCIENNES 12 5G 7389 Conference at CRE office.	
CATILLON	8		2 pontoons & 2 trestles handed over to the 46th Div complete with equipment. 2/Lt F.F. WOOD RE returned from leave to U.K. Lt M.C. CARR-GOMM RE joined the Coy as a reinforcement from 4th Army H.Q. Repairing road CATILLON - PRISCHES & filling in craters.	
"	9		Repairs to CATILLON - PRISCHES road, also culvert at 5G 8296 CRE conference 18.00 hrs	
	10		Moved to AUTREPPE VALENCIENNES 12 5K 1023	
AUTREPPE	11		Hostilities ceased at 11.00 hrs. Reconnaissance of roads forward of CARTIGNY filling in craters on CARTIGNY - BOULOGNE road. 2/Lt W.L. KERR RE joined the Coy as reinforcement from RERD.	
"	12	10.00	Moved to AVESNES VALENCIENNES 12 5L 1852	
AVESNES	13		Sent back to CARTIGNY pontoons & trestles equipment.	

D. D. & L., London, E.C.
(A8001) Wt. W1771/M2031 750,000 5/17 Sch. 52 Forms/C2118/14

Army Form C. 2118.

Instructions regarding War Diaries and Intelligence Summaries are contained in F. S. Regs., Part II. and the Staff Manual respectively. Title pages will be prepared in manuscript.

WAR DIARY
or
~~INTELLIGENCE SUMMARY.~~

(Erase heading not required.)

Place	Date	Hour	Summary of Events and Information	Remarks and references to Appendices
	1918 NOV.		Moved to FELLERIES Coy HQ. NAMUR 8 5A 3484 removing obstruction at 5A4181	
FELLERIES	14	10.00	filling in craters at 5A 2068 and 5A 70.82, 5A 3875	
"	15-19		filling in above craters	
	20	09.25	moved to SOLRE-ST-GERY NAMUR 8 4C9657	
	21		scraping SOLRE-ST-GERY — BARBENCON road. Unloading mines at bridge 4C 9361	
	22	09.00	Moved to ERPION Coy HQ NAMUR 4E3258	
	23	09.00	MAJOR F.W. MOORE MC RE proceeded on leave to UK. Moved to SILENRIEUX NAMUR 8 4E9772. March to the Rhine Southern Route signboarded to FLORENNES. Reconnaissance of roads forward of FLORENNES	
ST. AUBIN	24	10.10	Moved to ST. AUBIN HQ. NAMUR 8 4G9699 Reconnaissance of roads & sign-boarding continued	
"	25-28		Training commenced.	
"	29	09.30	G.O.C. 6th Division Inspection.	

WORK

The coy was resting from the 1st to 4th. The chief of the work has been repairing bridges, roads, filling craters & moving obstructions destroyed by the retreating enemy. From the 20 - end of month chief work has been road reconnaissance in addition to repair of roads.

J.M.[illegible] Capt
~~Major,~~ R.E.
a/O.C. 12th (Field) Company R.E.

D. D. & L., London, E.C.
(A8001) Wt. W1771/M2031 750,000 5/17 Sch. 52 Forms/C2118/14

Instructions regarding War Diaries and Intelligence Summaries are contained in F. S. Regs., Part II. and the Staff Manual respectively. Title pages will be prepared in manuscript.

WAR DIARY ~~or~~ INTELLIGENCE SUMMARY.

(Erase heading not required.)

Army Form C. 2118.

12 Fd Coy RE

Vol 53

Place	Date 1918	Hours	Summary of Events and Information	Remarks and references to Appendices
ST. AUBIN	DEC 1	08.35	Moved to ERMITON - SUR - BIERT. HQ NAMUR/100,000 3I6257.	
ERMITON - SUR BIERT	2		Roads reconnoitred forward of ERMITON	
	3		" " " " , villages signboarded.	
	4	09.00	Moved to EVREHAILLES NAMUR8 3L0185	
	5	0900	" " CHAU. DE FONTAINE, EMPTINNE MARCHE9 3B5887	
	6	"	" " HAVELANGE MARCHE9.2C6867	
	7	"	Road reconnoitred forward of HAVELANGE	
	8	"	Moved to TERWAGNE MARCHE 9 1E1735	
	9	8.40	" " COMBLAIN - LA-TOUR MARCHE 9 1G7849.	
	11		" " LORCE " 9 2I79.99.	
	12		" " STAVELOT GERMANY 1M 2L1477	
	13		" " WIESMES " 1M 3E2547	
	14		" " ELSENBORN Barracks 1L. Block 17	
	15-19		roads reconnoitred forward of ELSENBORN	
	19		Moved to MONTJOIE GERMANY 1L. 11G1036	
	20		" " OLEF " 1L 11J1531	
	21		" " ROGGENDORF " 1L 10L7132	
	22		" " ELSIG " 1L 8N4318	
	23		" " ERP " 1L 6N2122 March to the Rhine completed.	

D. D. & L., London, E.C.
(A8001) Wt. W1771/M2031 750,000 5/17 Sch. 52 Forms/C2118/14

Army Form C. 2118.

Instructions regarding War Diaries and Intelligence Summaries are contained in F. S. Regs., Part II. and the Staff Manual respectively. Title pages will be prepared in manuscript.

WAR DIARY
or
~~INTELLIGENCE SUMMARY.~~

(Erase heading not required.)

Place	Date 1918	Hour	Summary of Events and Information	Remarks and references to Appendices
ERP	DEC 24-31		Training, reconnoitring 1st Inf Bde area. Industries, works, factories &c.	
			WORK	
			Reconnoitring roads, signboarding villages. March to the Rhine completed	
			Training from 24th to 31st	

12TH FIELD COMPANY, R.E.
No. ....
Date 31-12-18.

[illegible]
Major, R.E.
O.C. 12th (Field) Company R.E.

D. D. & L., London, E.C.
(A8001) Wt. W1771/M2031 750,000 5/17 Sch. 52 Forms/C2118/14

Jan - Apl 1919

Instructions regarding War Diaries and Intelligence Summaries are contained in F. S. Regs., Part II. and the Staff Manual respectively. Title pages will be prepared in manuscript.

WAR DIARY 12th Field Coy R.E. or ~~INTELLIGENCE~~ SUMMARY.

(Erase heading not required.)

Army Form C. 2118.

~~12~~

VR 54

Place	Date 1919	Hour	Summary of Events and Information	Remarks and references to Appendices
	JAN			
ERP	1		Training	
	2		Moved to BORR GERMANY 1L 7N 4651	
BORR	4		1 section attached to 16th Inf. Bde. at KETTENHEIM GERMANY 1L 6L 3109	
			1 " " " 18 " " " LECHENICK " 5N 6930	
	13		Temp Capt (A/Major) F.W. MOORE, M.C. RE left Coy to proceed to ENGLAND for demobilization. Command of Coy taken over by Temp Lt. (A/Major) J.M. NOBLE RE.	
	25		TEMP LTS. T.E. HULL RE & Y.D. SOAR RE joined Coy as reinforcements from 181st Tunnelling Co.	
	28		Command of Coy. taken over by Capt (A/Major) R.M.W. Marsden M.C. R.E.	
			WORK.	
			During the month the company has made a complete reconnaissance of the 16th & 18th Inf. Bde areas as regards Roads, waterways, electricity & water supply, railways & stations and bridges.	
			Signboarding has been completed.	
			Disinfestors have been constructed at BLESSEM, ZULPICH, LECHENICH & VETTWEISS	
			Incinerator stations are being erected for all the units in both Bde. areas.	

R.M.W. Marsden
Major, R.E.
O.C. 12th (Field) Company R.E.

12TH FIELD COMPANY, R.E.
No. ....
Date ....

D. D. & L., London, E.C.
(A8001) Wt. W1771/M2031 750,000 5/17 Sch. 52 Forms/C2118/14

Instructions regarding War Diaries and Intelligence Summaries are contained in F. S. Regs., Part II. and the Staff Manual respectively. Title pages will be prepared in manuscript.

WAR DIARY
or
~~INTELLIGENCE SUMMARY.~~
(Erase heading not required.)

Army Form C. 2118.

Vol 55

Place	Date	Hour	Summary of Events and Information	Remarks and references to Appendices
	1919			
BORR	FEB.		Company at BORR during the whole month, except for detachments as in January. All employed on works as detailed below.	
	25.		2/LT. A.M. STEWART R.E. joined Company from R.E.B.D. on first commission from R.M.A WOOLWICH	
			WORK	
			During the month further reconnaissance was carried on in the 16th and 18th Inf. Bde. areas, to obtain fuller details of Roads, waterways, water supply and bridges.	
			Further baths, incinerators, latrines, etc have been erected for the troops in the 16th and 18th Inf Bde areas.	
			A Large Church Army Hut was commenced at ERP.	
			Work in connection with 6th Div. Races was carried out on the RÖMERHOF race course and erection of Totalisator office, Judges Boxes, notice boards, etc.	
			R. M. W. [illegible] Major, R.E. O.C. 12th (Field) Company R.E.	

D. D. & L., London, E.C.
(A8001) Wt. W1771/M2031 750,000 5/17 Sch. 52 Forms/C2118/14

CONFIDENTIAL

WAR DIARY

of

12th FIELD COY. R.E.

From. April. 1st 1919   To. April. 30th 1919.

Capt. R.E.
[redacted]
O.C. 12th (Field) Company R.E.

April - 1919

Instructions regarding War Diaries and Intelligence Summaries are contained in F. S. Regs., Part II. and the Staff Manual respectively. Title pages will be prepared in manuscript.

WAR DIARY
or
~~INTELLIGENCE SUMMARY.~~
(Erase heading not required.)

Army Form C. 2118.

Place	Date	Hour	Summary of Events and Information	Remarks and references to Appendices
LECHENICH	1		Company on work at LECHENICH, ERP & GYMNICH AS	
	2		Company preparing to move. CAPT. S.C. SAWARD attached from 509 Field Coy. R.E. AS.	
BRUHL	3.		Company proceeded by march route to BRUHL. "Lt. KERR and 8 O.R remained to hand over work and billets to 93rd Field Coy. R.E. AS.	
	4.		Cleaning wagons and equipment. AS.	
	5		Company inspected by G.O.C MIDLAND DIVISION. Farewell address to company by LT. Col. H.A.L. HALL M.C. R.E. AS	
	6.		93rd Field Coy R.E arrived at LECHENICH. AS.	
	7.		Retainable men of Company transferred as follows - 21 O.R to 509 Field Coy. R.E. 20 O.R. to 459 Field Coy. R.E. Attached for demobilisation - 11 O.R. to 509 Field Coy R.E. 10 O.R. to 459 Field Coy R.E. Horses - 6 transferred to 509 Field Coy R.E and 6 transferred to 459 Field Coy. R.E. "Lt. W.L.KERR rejoined Coy from LECHENICH. AS.	
	8		25 horses sent to 93rd Field Coy. R.E. CAPT. J.M. NOBLE + "LT. W.L.KERR left to join 509 Field Coy R.E.	AS.
	9.		Cleaning and checking harness. Lt J. DUNLOP left for U.K. for demobilisation. AS	
	10.		Work as for 9th. "LT. W.L.KERR posted to 206 Field Coy. R.E. AS.	
	11.		11 O.R. and 8 horses attached to 509 Field Coy R.E. - 9 O.R. + 8 horses attached to 459 Field Coy R.E. LTs. J.D. BERESFORD + A.G SAMUEL rejoined from leave. R.E Band played at BRÜHL. AS	
	12.		Cleaning up yard and billets. AS.	
	13		Company inspection AS.	

D. D. & L., London, E.C.
(A8001) Wt. W1771/M2031 750,000 5/17 Sch. 52 Forms/C2118/14

April 1919.

Instructions regarding War Diaries and Intelligence Summaries are contained in F. S. Regs., Part II. and the Staff Manual respectively. Title pages will be prepared in manuscript.

WAR DIARY
or
~~INTELLIGENCE~~ SUMMARY.

(Erase heading not required.)

Army Form C. 2118.

Place	Date	Hour	Summary of Events and Information	Remarks and references to Appendices
BRÜHL	14th		Company working on checking equipment, erecting jumps and cookhouses. SS	
	15th		Work as for 14th. Lt. A.G. SAMUEL posted to 148 A.T. Coy. R.E. SS	
	16th		Work as for 15th Lt. J.D. BERESFORD left for U.K. for demobilisation SS	
	17th		Cadre all employed on cleaning, checking and re-packing tools, and equipment SS	
	18th		GOOD FRIDAY. Mobilisation stores + equipment checked by D.A.D.O.S. Coy. reported down to Cadre 'A'. SS	
	19th		Packing stores and cleaning wagons contd. "Lt. B. FURNESS to hospital. SS	
	20th		Rifle inspection and Church parade SS	
	21st		Work on wagons and jumps. Balance of Imprest a/c handed in to Field Cashier IX Corps. SS	
	22nd		Work on jumps completed SS	
	23rd		7 O.R. left for Chatham (to join unit for Russia) Work on cleaning harness + erecting cookhouse. SS	
	24th		Work as for 23rd. "Lt. B. FURNESS rejoined from hospital. SS	
	25th		Work on repairs to wagons and repainting. SS	
	26th		Kit inspection and pay parade SS	
	27th		Rifle inspection + church parade SS	
	28th–30th		Company working on repairing + repainting wagons SS	
	30th		Party worked under D.A.P.M on raid at BADORF. Search for concealed arms etc. SS	

D. D. & L., London, E.C.
(A8004) Wt. W1771/M2031 750,000 5/17 Sch. 52 Forms/C2118/14

Instructions regarding War Diaries and Intelligence Summaries are contained in F. S. Regs., Part II. and the Staff Manual respectively. Title Pages will be prepared in manuscript.

WAR DIARY
or
INTELLIGENCE SUMMARY
(Erase heading not required.)

Army Form C. 2118

12 Fd Coy R.E.

Vol 42

Place	Date	Hour	Summary of Events and Information	Remarks and references to Appendices
BAPAUME.	1st January		Continued work on Camps at I 13 + I 29 (Sheet 57c)	
	2nd		Nos 2+4 Sections " Lt Handley to Camp I 13. Nos 1+3 Sections " Lt Noble to Camp I 29.	
			Continued work as above. 1. O.R. leave to U.K.	
	3rd		2 Officers (Lt Champ 11th ESSEX + " Lt Bruce 14th D.L.I) + 76. Attached Infantry rejoined Company.	
			Work as above	
			1. O.R returned from leave to U.K	
			1. O.R returned from Hospital.	
	4th		2 Officers + 76. O.R Attached Infantry to Camps at I 29 + I 13. Work as above.	
	5th		Major A. Williamson. R.E. returned from leave to U.K.	
			1. O.R. returned from leave. Work as above	
	6th		Lieut R.J. Hall leave to U.K.	
			7. O.R. leave to U.K. Work as above.	
			1. O.R. to Hospital Sick.	
	8th		3. O.R 11th ESSEX Attd Infantry leave to U.K.	
	9th		Camp at I 13 handed over to 25th Divisional Pioneers. Accomodation 2 Nissen Huts + 15 French shelters. Camp fitted up with Cookhouses, latrines etc.	
			No 4 Section RE to Back Billet Bapaume.	
			Lt Champ + 1st W. Yorks attached Infantry to Back Billet Bapaume.	
	10th		1. O.R. returned from leave	
			1. O.R. W. YORKS leave to U.K.	

1875 Wt. W593/826 1,000,000 4/15 J.B.C. & A. A.D.S.S./Forms/C. 2118.

Instructions regarding War Diaries and Intelligence Summaries are contained in F. S. Regs., Part II. and the Staff Manual respectively. Title Pages will be prepared in manuscript.

WAR DIARY
or
INTELLIGENCE SUMMARY
(Erase heading not required.)

Army Form C. 2118

Place	Date	Hour	Summary of Events and Information	Remarks and references to Appendices
BAPAUME	January			
	11th		5 O.R. 1st W. YORKS joined as reinforcements.	
			6 O.R. 2nd D.L.I. Do Do	
			4 O.R. 14th D.L.I. Do Do	
			2 O.R. 14th D.L.I. returned from leave	
			13 O.R. 1st W. YORKS to Advance Billet at I29	
	13th		6 O.R. leave to U.K.	
			Lieut Champ to Advance Billet	
			2/Lieut Brown to Back Billet	
	15th		1 O.R. returned from leave to U.K.	
			3 O.R. 1st W. YORKS leave to U.K.	
			1 O.R. 14th D.L.I. leave to U.K.	
			Lieut Champ to Back Billet	
			No 2 Section RE + 11th Essex attached Infantry to Back Billet	
			Camp at I29 completed. Accomodation 13 NISSEN HUTS. Camp fitted up with cookhouse latrines, ablution, benches etc.	
	16th		Lieut Champ leave to U.K.	
			3 O.R. 11th Essex leave to U.K.	
			1 O.R. 2nd D.L.I. leave to U.K.	
			2/Lieut Vockell + Handley with Nos 1 + 3 Sections RE + 2nd + 14th D.L.I. attd Infantry to Back Billet at Bapaume. Small party left at Camp I29 to hand over Camp to 459 Field Company R.E.	

Instructions regarding War Diaries and Intelligence Summaries are contained in F. S. Regs., Part II. and the Staff Manual respectively. Title Pages will be prepared in manuscript.

WAR DIARY
or
INTELLIGENCE SUMMARY
(Erase heading not required.)

Army Form C. 2118

Place	Date	Hour	Summary of Events and Information	Remarks and references to Appendices
BAPAUME	January			
"	17th		1. O.R returned from Hospital.	
			Camp at I29 handed over to 451 Field Company R.E	
"	19th		1. O.R 14th D.L.I returned from leave.	
			ii Lieuts Noble + Handley RE with Nos 2,3 + 4 Sections RE to Camp I29 taking over from 451 Coy RE	
			ii Bruce with 2nd D.L.I + 14th D.L.I Attached Infantry to Camp I29.	
			Advance party took over Horse Lines in BEUGNY from 401st Field Company. R.E	
LABUCQUIERE	20th		12 O.R leave to U.K	
			1 O.R returned from leave to U.K.	
			Capt C.A. Langley MC R.E. returned from Course at R.E. School BLENDECQUES.	
			O.C with Company HdQrs No 1 Section RE + 1st W. YORKS Att Infantry moved by march route from BAPUME to Camp I29 LABUCQUIERE. Camp at Bapaume handed over to 307 RE Company, RE	
			Transport under ii Lieut Veitch moved by march route from BAPAUME to BEUGNY taking over Horse Lines vacated by 401st Field Company R.E.	
			ii Lieut Noble + ii Lieut Handley with Nos 2,3 + 4 Sections R.E. ~~moved~~ ii Lieut Bruce with 2nd D.L.I. moved to new Forward Billets at J5C.3.8. (Sheet 57C N.E) taking over Billets from 404th Field Coy. RE.	
			Company took over work in the Line from 404th Field Company RE.	

1875 Wt. W593/826 1,000,000 4/15 J.B.C. & A. A.D.S.S./Forms/C. 2118.

Army Form C. 2118

Instructions regarding War Diaries and Intelligence Summaries are contained in F. S. Regs., Part II. and the Staff Manual respectively. Title Pages will be prepared in manuscript.

WAR DIARY
or
INTELLIGENCE SUMMARY
(Erase heading not required.)

Place	Date	Hour	Summary of Events and Information	Remarks and references to Appendices
LABUCQUIERE.	January			
	21st		2 O.R. 11th Essex Attd leave to U.K.	
	22nd		Lieut Hall, R.E. + 7. O.R. returned from leave to U.K.	
			O.C. to Advance Billet	
			2/Lieut Veitch to Advance Billet	
			2. O.R. to R.E. Base Depot	
BEUGNY	23rd		Company, HdQrs No1 Section (2/Lieut Vackell) 14th D.L.I. Attd + 1st W. YORKS Attd moved from Camp I 29 to BEUGNY taking over Billets vacated by 507 Company, R.E. Camp at I 29 handed over to 507 Field Cy, R.E.	
	24th		OC from Advance Billet to BEUGNY.	
			2/Lieut Veitch from Advance Billet to BEUGNY.	
			Capt C.A. Langley from BEUGNY to Advance Billet.	
			2. O.R joined as reinforcements.	
			5 Horses to Mobile.	
	25th		2/Lieut Veitch 8 O.R. leave to U.K.	
			3 O.R 11th Essex returned from leave.	
			1 O.R. 1st W. YORKS returned from leave	
	26th		14th D.L.I. attd to Advance Billet.	
	27th		Lieut R.J. Hall, R.E. to Advance Billet.	
			2/Lieut Breeze with 14th D.L.I. + 1st W. YORKS. to new billet at J 7 d 9 8 (Sheet 57c N.E)	

Army Form C. 2118.

Instructions regarding War Diaries and Intelligence Summaries are contained in F. S. Regs., Part II. and the Staff Manual respectively. Title pages will be prepared in manuscript.

WAR DIARY
or
INTELLIGENCE SUMMARY.
(*Erase heading not required.*)

Place	Date	Hour	Summary of Events and Information	Remarks and references to Appendices
BEUGNY	January 28th		2/Lieut Vachell with No 1 Section R.E. to Advance Billet	
			2/Lieut Hambley with No 2 Section R.E. to BEUGNY	
			2/Lt Esseville to Advance Billet.	
			2nd D.L.I. Attd to BEUGNY	
			Capt. C.A. Langley R.E. to BEUGNY	
	29th		2 O.R. 1st W. YORKS leave to U.K.	
	30th		Lieut R.T. Hall with No 4 Section R.E. to BEUGNY	
	31st		15 O.R. Leave to U.K	
			2/Lieut Bruce with 14th D.L.I. attached Infantry returned to Battalion.	
			1st W.Yorks to BEUGNY.	

The work in the Line since going into the Sector on 20 inst. has principally consisted of clearing the trenches which had fallen in badly on the break up of the frost, cutting drains, trimming sides, clearing berms & raising footboards. A new trench for joining up Batt. H.Q. through Posts 28, 27 & 26 to RABBIT ALLEY (J.3.a & J.3.f) has been commenced. Dugouts at Coy Adv. Billets, in RABBIT SUPPORT & in ROOK ALLEY are in hand. A new Bde H.Q. at J-7-b-9-0.

[signature] Major, R.E.
O.C. 12th (Field) Coy. R.E.

12th FIELD COMPANY, R. E.
No. ....
Date 31-1-18

A5834 Wt. W4973/M687 750,000 8/16 D. D. & L. Ltd. Forms/C.2118/13.

Army Form C. 2118.

12 7a Coy

Vol 43

WAR DIARY
or
INTELLIGENCE SUMMARY.
(Erase heading not required.)

Instructions regarding War Diaries and Intelligence Summaries are contained in F. S. Regs., Part II. and the Staff Manual respectively. Title pages will be prepared in manuscript.

Place	Date	Hour	Summary of Events and Information	Remarks and references to Appendices
BEUGNY	1		2 O.R. 2nd D.L.I. leave to U.K.	
			LT. R.J. Hall. R.E. transferred to 459 Field Coy. R.E.	
	2.		No 4 Section R.E. to Advance Billet.	
			3 O.R. 11th Essex returned from leave.	
			3 O.R. 11th Essex leave to U.K.	
			2 O.R. 1st W. YORKS leave to U.K.	
	3		2 L.D. Horses to Mobile.	
	4		2nd LT Handley with No 2 Section to Advance Billet.	
			2nd LT. Noble with No 3 Section to BEUGNY	
			1 O.R. joined as reinforcement	
			1 Rider S.L.D. received.	
	5		11 O.R. returned from leave to U.K.	
	6		Capt. C.A. Langley, M.C. R.E. to Advance Billet	
	7		1 O.R. W. YORKS joined as reinforcement	
			1 L.D. Horse returned from CRE	
	7.		1 O.R. joined as reinforcement.	
	8		Capt C.A. Langley, M.C. R.E. to BEUGNY	
			12 O.R. leave to U.K.	
	9.		1 O.R. 11th Essex returned from leave.	
	10.		O.C. + 1 other officer from 400th Field Coy. R.E. arrived to take over works in the line. 2 Lieuts Handley + [illegible] with Nos 1, 2 + 4 Sections R.E. 11th Essex + 1st W. Yorks Attached Infantry to BEUGNY. Advance Billet at J.5.a.3.8 (Sheet 57c N.E.) handed over to 400th Coy. R.E.	

A5834 Wt. W4973/M687 750,000 8/16 D. D. & L. Ltd. Forms/C.2118/13.

Instructions regarding War Diaries and Intelligence Summaries are contained in F. S. Regs., Part II. and the Staff Manual respectively. Title pages will be prepared in manuscript.

WAR DIARY
or
INTELLIGENCE SUMMARY.

(*Erase heading not required.*)

Army Form C. 2118.

Place	Date	Hour	Summary of Events and Information	Remarks and references to Appendices
BEUGNY	10.		2nd Lt. Veitch R.E. returned from leave.	
			2 O.R. returned from leave.	
C.29.c.0.4. (Sheet 57c N.W.)	11.		Company Billets and Transport lines at BEUGNY handed over to 401st Field Coy R.E.	
			Transport moved to FAVREUIL Camp No 10 H.16.b.05.05. (Sheet 57c N.W.) taking over	
			Transport lines vacated by 105th Field Coy RE.	
			Headquarters & dismounted moved to C.29.c.0.4. taking over Billets vacated by 105th Coy RE	
			RE work in the PRONVILLE Section of the line taken over from 105th Coy. RE.	
			4 O.R. returned from leave.	
			Lieut L. Champ 11th Essex returned from leave.	
			1 Horse L.D. to Mobile	
	12		1 O.R. returned from leave	
			Lieut R.A. Hudson RE attached from 459 Field Coy RE	
	13.		1 L.D. received.	
	14		1 O.R. 1st W. Yorks returned from leave	
	15th		3 O.R. 11th Essex leave to U.K	
			12 O.R. leave to U.K.	
			Pontoon & Bridging equipment sent to No 8 Pontoon Park for storage with [illegible]	
	16		1 O.R. returned from leave	
			2nd Lieut Noble RE with 2 O.R. to Bridging School Aire for Course of Heavy Bridging.	

Instructions regarding War Diaries and Intelligence Summaries are contained in F. S. Regs., Part II. and the Staff Manual respectively. Title pages will be prepared in manuscript.

WAR DIARY
or
INTELLIGENCE SUMMARY.
(Erase heading not required.)

Army Form C. 2118.

Place	Date	Hour	Summary of Events and Information	Remarks and references to Appendices
C29C.0.4. (Sheet 57C N.W.)	17		15 O.R. returned from leave	
	19		2 O.R. joined as reinforcements	
	20		1 O.R. returned from leave	
			1 O.R. to R.E. Base Depot	
			5 O.R. 2nd D.L.I. 5 O.R. 1st W. Yorks. 5 O.R. 11th Essex attached to Company bringing strength of Attached Infantry Sections to 30 each	
	22		12 O.R. leave to U.K.	
			1 O.R. to Hospital	
			2 O.R. returned from Hospital	
	25		6 O.R. returned from leave	
	26		3 O.R. returned from leave	
			Major A Williamson R.E. leave to Paris.	
			3 O.R. 11th Essex returned from leave.	
			1 O.R. attached to 174 Tunnelling Coy R.E.	
			1 Horse L.D. to Mobile	
	27.		2 O.R. 2nd D.L.I. returned from leave	
			2 O.R. 1st W. Yorks returned from leave	
			1 O.R. 11th Essex returned from leave	
			1 O.R. R.E. wounded.	
			1 O.R. 2nd D.L.I. died of wounds 1 O.R. 2nd D.L.I. wounded	

A5834 Wt. W4973/M687 750,000 8/16 D. D. & L. Ltd. Forms/C.2118/13.

Instructions regarding War Diaries and Intelligence Summaries are contained in F. S. Regs., Part II. and the Staff Manual respectively. Title pages will be prepared in manuscript.

WAR DIARY
or
INTELLIGENCE SUMMARY.

(*Erase heading not required.*)

Army Form C. 2118.

Place	Date	Hour	Summary of Events and Information	Remarks and references to Appendices
C.29.c.0.4. Sheet (57c N.W.)	28		1.O.R to Hospital.	
			Summary of Work.	
			Period from 1st to 10th	
			Main feature of work during this period in the LOUVERVAL Sector was the [illegible] up of the Intermediate line from Post 28 on the left Boundary to RABBIT ALLEY. This trench was dug through [illegible] and trench boards laid down. Maintenance work was continued in the C.T's. firebays were put in the SUPPORT LINE. Work continued on Dugouts, [illegible] in the support line, [illegible] Rock Alley + [illegible] advance Coy Billets.	
			Work in the back area consisted of the completion of Divisional Baths at BEUGNY + general improvements to Camps.	
			Period from 11th to 28th	
			Work in the PRONVILLE SECTOR of the line. Support line from LEECH AVENUE to the left Brigade boundary has been dug through, but is not completed yet. Main work in the line has been the [illegible] of splinter proof shelters in Support line + Reserve line, firebays in the Support line, extension of Dugout in Leech Avenue, new Dugout in Reserve line Post 30, and fitting all Dugouts with gas curtains + repairing old ones. Extension of R.A.P. Dugout + D.25 [illegible].	
			Work in back area. From 11th to 17th 2 Sections [illegible] were employed working for R.F.A. making new dugouts at Battery Positions + extending old ones also construction of O.P.s. On 18th work for R.F.A. Bde was handed over to 50 [illegible] Coy R.E.s. A new Brigade H.Q. commenced at I.17.a.6.4 nearly completed. 2 Dugouts at Company Billets extended.	

C Haughey Capt ~~Major~~, R.E.
O.C. 12th (Field) Coy. R.E.

28.2.18.

A5834 Wt. W4973/M687 750,000 8/16 D. D. & L. Ltd. Forms/C.2118/13.

WO95/1599 (2)

6th Division

38th Fld Coy. R.E.

Aug 1914 — Mar 1915

To 28 DIV TROOPS

6th Divisional Engineers

Disembarked ST.NAZAIRE 10.9.14.

38th FIELCD COMPANY R. E.

AUGUST 1914.

—

Mar 1915

Instructions regarding War Diaries and Intelligence Summaries are contained in F. S. Regs., Part II. and the Staff Manual respectively. Title pages will be prepared in manuscript.

WAR DIARY
or
~~INTELLIGENCE~~ ~~SUMMARY.~~
(Erase heading not required.)

Army Form C. 2118.

Hour, Date, Place	Summary of Events and Information	Remarks and references to Appendices
CORK . 5-8-14	Orders to mobilise received at 6pm on 4th August. Ten reservists joined unit & mobilisation stores were fetched from ~~Queenstown~~ QUEENSTOWN by a party of company sent for the purpose	[illegible] Major
CORK 6-8-14	Seventy six reservists joined & were equipped. Ammunition & explosives stored at ~~Haulbowline~~ HAULBOWLINE were received today	[illegible] Major
CORK 7-8-14	144 Reservists in all joined & equipped. 29 Horses received from Depot & were shod & Harness fitted. Arrangements made with Civilian Farrier for assistance in shoeing owing to large horses supplied. Store shoes were too small. Two civilian Farriers employed in accordance with para 43 Mobilisation Regulations	[illegible] Major
CORK 8-8-14	Reservists arrived ~~sufficient~~ 14 in excess of requirements of unit. 32 bicycles received from Advance incomplete. All horses received & being shod. Reservists being trained in Drill & marching	[illegible] Major
CORK 9-8-14	Six noncommissioned officers equipment required for 32 Bicycles. Otherwise mobilisation complete. Men & Horses being trained	[illegible] Major
CORK 10-8-14	above still required to complete. Men & Horses being trained in marching & drill	[illegible] Major
CORK 11-8-14	as for 10-8-14	[illegible] Major

Instructions regarding War Diaries and Intelligence Summaries are contained in F. S. Regs., Part II. and the Staff Manual respectively. Title pages will be prepared in manuscript.

WAR DIARY
or
INTELLIGENCE SUMMARY.
(Erase heading not required.)

Army Form C. 2118.

Hour, Date, Place	Summary of Events and Information	Remarks and references to Appendices
CORK 12-8-14	are non commissioned officers arrived also parts of equipment required for 32 bicycles. Training of men & horses in progress	HMB Major
CORK 13-8-14	As no puncture outfit was received with bicycles this was purchased locally by orders of CRE 6th Division & account to be forwarded to ~~Ordnance~~ ORDNANCE OFFICER. Training in use of Trestles, marching drill in progress	HMB Major
CORK 14-8-14	All personnel & equipment complete, except one FARRIER SERGEANT, whose services are not available (authority Officer i/c RE Records) CHATHAM). Received orders from CRE 6th DIVISION to be in readiness to march at 6-am on 16th AUGUST	HMB Major
CORK 15-8-14	Training of Company proceeding. Orders received to proceed by march route to QUEENSTOWN at 6-20 am on 16th ~~AUGUST~~	HMB Major
CORK 16-8-14	Company paraded ready to move at 7-45 am when order was received to stand fast. Whole company marched out & practised getting into bivouacs & awaited orders	HMB Major
CORK 17-8-14	awaiting orders to move which were received at 7pm to be at QUEENSTOWN at 12 noon on 18-8-14	HMB Major
CONEMARA SS ~~CALORIC~~ 18-8-14	Company marched from CORK to QUEENSTOWN & embarked by half companies on S.S CALORIC & CONEMARA leaving QUEENSTOWN at 6pm	HMB Major

(9 29 6) W 3332—1107 100,000 10/13 H W V Forms/C. 2118/10.

Instructions regarding War Diaries and Intelligence Summaries are contained in F. S. Regs., Part II. and the Staff Manual respectively. Title pages will be prepared in manuscript.

WAR DIARY
or
INTELLIGENCE SUMMARY.

(*Erase heading not required.*)

Army Form C. 2118.

Hour, Date, Place	Summary of Events and Information	Remarks and references to Appendices
LIVERPOOL 19-8-14	On arrival at HOLYHEAD boats were signalled to proceed to LIVERPOOL where CONEMARA arrived at 3 pm & CALORIC at 6 pm. ~~Both~~ Each parties embarked in separate trains & proceeded to CAMBRIDGE arriving at 3 AM & 6 AM on 20th respectively.	HMM Major
CAMBRIDGE 20-8-14	Proceeded to wet CAMP at JESUS COMMON & having pitched camp received orders to move to BOTTS GREEN & having struck camp received further orders to stand fast until another site was selected. Proceeded to camp at LAMMAS GREEN arriving at 3 pm & pitched camp	HMM Major
	Camp	
CAMBRIDGE 21-8-14	in wet camp. Instruction given in extended order drill & rifle exercises packing & unpacking pontoons & launching boats	HMM Major
CAMBRIDGE 22-8-14	Unit took part in route march of Divisional troops remainder of day camp fatigues	HMM Major
CAMBRIDGE 23-8-14	Troops attended Church parade	

(9 29 6) W 3332—1107 100,000 10/13 H W V Forms/C. 2118/10.

Instructions regarding War Diaries and Intelligence Summaries are contained in F. S. Regs., Part II. and the Staff Manual respectively. Title pages will be prepared in manuscript.

WAR DIARY
or
~~INTELLIGENCE SUMMARY.~~
(Erase heading not required.)

Army Form C. 2118.

Hour, Date, Place	Summary of Events and Information	Remarks and references to Appendices
CAMBRIDGE 24-8-14	The unit took part in Divisional Route march leaving Camp at 8-40 & arriving at RENDEZVOUS at 9-45 am. The route followed was about 10 miles to point of Dispersal and returning to Camp at 3 pm	F.M.M. Major
CAMBRIDGE 25-8-14	Unit was practised in pontooning & trestle bridging on R. CAM at PIKE & EEL 2½ miles from Camp	F.M.M. Major
CAMBRIDGE 26-8-14	Unit took part in Brigade Tactical exercise in the neighbourhood of TRUMPINGTON. Company marched near head of main body. Two officers & four cyclists were sent ahead to reconnoitre. Exercise was abandoned before completion & unit was not employed	F.M.M. Major
CAMBRIDGE 27-8-14	Unit was practised in Pontooning, Trestle bridging, barrel piering & use of spars	F.M.M. Major
CAMBRIDGE 28-8-14	The four Sections were practised independently. No 1 Section Defence of post No 2 Section Bridging with Company Equipment No 3 Section Preparation of Rear Guard position No 4 Section preparation of Rear Guard position	F.M.M. Major

(9 29 6) W 3332—1107 100,000 10/13 H.W.V. Forms/C. 2118/10.

Instructions regarding War Diaries and Intelligence Summaries are contained in F. S. Regs., Part II. and the Staff Manual respectively. Title pages will be prepared in manuscript.

WAR DIARY
or
~~INTELLIGENCE SUMMARY.~~

(Erase heading not required.)

Army Form C. 2118.

Hour, Date, Place	Summary of Events and Information	Remarks and references to Appendices
CAMBRIDGE 29-8-14	Two sections of Company took part in Brigade Group exercise. This consisted in the attack of a position. The remainder of Company took part in night operation with 18th Infantry Brigade. The Company was ordered to prepare a scheme for making good the first position taken with a view to covering a possible retirement. The line was reconnoitred by two officers & one section [illegible] sent to each flank & estimate of Infy working party required submitted. No 3 Section started work on right of position above. 7.15 pm work was stopped at 8 pm & a ~~preparation~~ orders for assault given. All wire cutters & cutting tools were taken by sections & carts & horses left behind. The Company advanced in rear of right centre of line of advance but were not called upon to carry out any work. Clearing gaps which would have been necessary if it had been permitted. Company returned to camp at 6 am.	HMB Major
CAMBRIDGE 30-8-14	Company paraded for Church.	HMB Major
CAMBRIDGE 31-8-14	Company was exercised in digging on C.U.R.A. RIFLE RANGE	HM Major

[illegible]

(9 29 6) W 3332—1107 100,000 10/13 H W V Forms/C. 2118/10.

6th Divisional Engineers

38th FIELD COMPANY R. E.

SEPTEMBER 1914.

Instructions regarding War Diaries and Intelligence Summaries are contained in F. S. Regs., Part II. and the Staff Manual respectively. Title pages will be prepared in manuscript.

WAR DIARY
or
~~INTELLIGENCE SUMMARY.~~
(Erase heading not required.)

Army Form C. 2118.

Hour, Date, Place	Summary of Events and Information	Remarks and references to Appendices
CAMBRIDGE 1-9-14	Company paraded with Pontoons of 12th W.B. R.E. & bridged R. CAM E of MILTON. The company troops crossed bridge which was then dismantled & unit returned home via FEN DITTON	[illegible] Major
CAMBRIDGE 2-9-14	Company was employed in erecting water troughs etc & moving latrines for camps	[illegible] Major
CAMBRIDGE 3-9-14	Company took part (less pontoons) in Brigade Scheme which formed part of rear guard action. Parties were employed in demolishing bridges & blocking roads & preparing delaying position	[illegible] Major
CAMBRIDGE 4-9-14	Unit was instructed in extended order drill use of spars lashings etc	[illegible] Major
CAMBRIDGE. 5-9-14	Two sections employed in erecting camp structures. Two sections in bridging R. CAM & forming covering parties	[illegible] Major
CAMBRIDGE 6-9-14	The company attended Church parade	[illegible] Major

(9 29 6) W 3332—1107 100,000 10/13 H W V Forms/C. 2118/10.

Instructions regarding War Diaries and Intelligence Summaries are contained in F.S. Regs., Part II. and the Staff Manual respectively. Title pages will be prepared in manuscript.

WAR DIARY
or
~~INTELLIGENCE SUMMARY.~~
(*Erase heading not required.*)

Army Form C. 2118.

Hour, Date, Place		Summary of Events and Information	Remarks and references to Appendices
CAMBRIDGE	7-9-14	The company was exercised in extended order movements	[signature] Major
S.S. ARCHIMEDES	8-9-14	The company entrained complete at CAMBRIDGE by 6.35 am & proceeded to SOUTHAMPTON embarking there on S.S. ARCHIMEDES by 4 pm.	[signature] Major
SS ARCHIMEDES	9-9-14	On board S.S ARCHIMEDES	
St NAZAIRE	10-9-14	Disembarked at St NAZAIRE by 1-30 am & proceeded to rest camp	[signature] Major
IN TRAIN	11-9-14	entrained at St NAZAIRE at 11-30 am & left at 1.55 pm	[signature] Major
MERLES	12-9-14	disembarked at MERLES at 6-30 pm & proceeded into bivouac & billets	[signature] Major
FRAMOUTIERS	13-9-14	proceeded at 10-15 am to FRAMOUTIERS arriving at 2 pm & went into billets (10 miles)	[signature] Major
BIERCY	14-9-14	marched at 7-30 am to billets in BIERCY arriving at 3 pm (15 miles) & pontoons of 12th (new) Coy attached to unit	[signature] Major
BEZOET	15-9-14	marched at 8-15 am to rendezvous with 17th I B group halted from 2-15 pm to 5-15 pm A Z & proceeded to billets at BEZOUET arriving at 10 pm very wet (21 miles)	[signature] Major

Army Form C. 2118.

Instructions regarding War Diaries and Intelligence Summaries are contained in F. S. Regs., Part II. and the Staff Manual respectively. Title pages will be prepared in manuscript.

WAR DIARY
or
~~INTELLIGENCE SUMMARY.~~

(*Erase heading not required.*)

Hour, Date, Place		Summary of Events and Information	Remarks and references to Appendices
VILLE MONTOIRE	16-9-14	Continued march of Division [illegible] 7-30 am & proceeded to bivouac at VILLE MONTOIRE arriving at 5 pm	[illegible] Major
VILLEBLAIN	17-9-14	Marched at 9 am & proceeded to billet at VILLEBLAIN arriving 12-45 pm (6 miles) very wet & bad roads	[illegible] Major
VILLEBLAIN	18-9-14	In billet at VILLEBLAIN. Officers employed in reconnaissance [illegible] to MOULIN DES ROCHES to take over Pontoon bridge. Two Pontoons returned to 12th (Field) Coy RE	[illegible] Major
PAARS	19-9-14	Marched at 1 pm to billets in PAARS (12 miles) arriving 8 pm	[illegible] Major
PAARS	20-9-14	In billets at PAARS [illegible] from MOULIN DES ROCHES [illegible]	[illegible] Major
BOURG	21-9-14	Marched from PAARS at 2 pm to report to CRE 2nd Division for work & went into billets at BOURG	[illegible] Major
BOURG	22-9-14	Company employed in making corduroy road along tow path of AISNE CANAL. Timber obtained from barges & [illegible] from roadside	[illegible] Major
BOURG	23-9-14	Continuing work on corduroy roads	[illegible] Major

(9 29 6) W 3332—1107 100,000 10/13 H W V Forms/C. 2118/10.

Instructions regarding War Diaries and Intelligence Summaries are contained in F.S. Regs., Part II. and the Staff Manual respectively. Title pages will be prepared in manuscript.

WAR DIARY
or
~~INTELLIGENCE SUMMARY.~~
(*Erase heading not required.*)

Army Form C. 2118.

Hour, Date, Place	Summary of Events and Information	Remarks and references to Appendices
BOURG 24-9-14	Company employed on making & improving approaches to Bridges etc	[signature]
BOURG 25-9-14	As on 24-9-14	[signature]
BOURG 26-9-14	Two sections proceeded to COURTONNE to clear the front & entangle a defensive position there. Work not being completed sections billetted at COURTONNE. Remainder of company on roads & approaches at BOURG	[signature]
BOURG 27-9-14	As on 26-9-14. Work being completed on defensive position. Two sections returned to BOURG at 7-30 pm	[signature]
BOURG 28-9-14	Two sections to SOUPIR to make bridge for Infantry over R AISNE. Span trestle bridge of 105' span commenced from material on the spot. Remainder at BOURG as before	[signature]
BOURG 29-9-14	Company Bridging Equipment sent to SOUPIR also 5 Trestles belonging to 1st Bridging Train for use in bridge. Company employed as on 28-9-14 also in maintaining all bridges at BOURG. Two sappers wounded by shell fire at SOUPIR	[signature]
BOURG 30-9-14	Bridge at SOUPIR completed except for approaches. Five [illegible] trestles & four spare trestles were used in the bridge. Remainder of company on bridges & roads at BOURG	[signature]

[signature]
O.C. 38 (Field) C.R.E.

6th Divisional Engineers

----9----

38th FIELD COMPANY R. E.

OCTOBER 1914.

Instructions regarding War Diaries and Intelligence Summaries are contained in F. S. Regs., Part II. and the Staff Manual respectively. Title pages will be prepared in manuscript.

WAR DIARY
or
INTELLIGENCE SUMMARY.
(Erase heading not required.)

Army Form C. 2118.

Hour, Date, Place	Summary of Events and Information	Remarks and references to Appendices
BOURG 1-10-14	Two sections at SOUPIR working on approaches to bridge. Remainder at BOURG on roads, bridges & approaches. Shrapnel fire on picket lines & working party in afternoon. One horse badly hit & had to be destroyed one horse slightly hit also one driver	[illegible]
DHUISY 2-10-14	Company received orders to rejoin the 6th Division & marched to VAUXTIN arriving at 11 am halted till 7pm when the march was continued & went into billets at DHUISY arriving at 2 am	[illegible]
DHUISY 3-10-14	Company employed in erecting water troughs for watering horses also in excavating trenches constructed by 5th Division	[illegible]

(9 29 6) W 3332—1107 100,000 10/13 H W V Forms/C. 2118/10.

Instructions regarding War Diaries and Intelligence Summaries are contained in F. S. Regs., Part II. and the Staff Manual respectively. Title pages will be prepared in manuscript.

WAR DIARY
or
INTELLIGENCE SUMMARY.
(Erase heading not required.)

Army Form C. 2118.

Hour, Date, Place	Summary of Events and Information	Remarks and references to Appendices
DHUISY - 4-10-14	Company employed in continuing defensive position prepared by 5th Division south of LACROUTELLE. This consisted of digging rifle pits & clearing the undergrowth of a wood. A party of 2 officers & 12 men sent to CONDE-SUR-AISNE to prepare for demolition the towpath over the R VESLE. The bridge was of reinforced concrete of 3 spans of 17 feet. The supports consisted of 4 piers (13" square) each. Roadway was carried on girders cased in reinforced concrete. A charge of 8lbs was fixed to the four piers of one support. Two charges of 10lbs & 12lbs respectively fastened to cased girders one of which was deeper than the other & a charge of 18lbs fixed under centre of roadway. Detonators were fixed in charges at the piers & leads taken on shore. As the orders were to prepare bridge for demolition by night the remaining detonators would have been fixed when orders were received to demolish bridge.	[illegible signature]

(9 29 6) W 3332—1107 100,000 10/13 H W V Forms/C. 2118/10

Instructions regarding War Diaries and Intelligence Summaries are contained in F. S. Regs., Part II. and the Staff Manual respectively. Title pages will be prepared in manuscript.

WAR DIARY
or
INTELLIGENCE SUMMARY.
(Erase heading not required.)

Army Form C. 2118.

Hour, Date, Place	Summary of Events and Information	Remarks and references to Appendices
DHUISY 5-10-14	Company employed on defensive position as before. Orders received to demolish bridge at CONDÉ SUR AISNE & to be ready to move. These orders subsequently cancelled	[illegible]
COUTREMAIN 6-10-14	Company standing by ready to move. Moved at 8-45 pm from billets to COUTREMAIN arriving at 12-30 am (9 miles) One officer & 4 men to bridge at CONDÉ SUR AISNE to bring back guncotton placed in bridge there. It was found to have been entirely removed by the enemy except 4 lbs guncotton which was brought back.	[illegible]
LARGNY. 7-10-14	Company standing by ready to move. Moved at 7 p.m from billets at COUTREMAIN and marched to LARGNY. Arrived 3.30 a.m on 8th & went into billets distance 17 miles.	[illegible]

(9 29 6) W 3332—1107 100,000 10/13 H W V Forms/C. 2118/10.

Instructions regarding War Diaries and Intelligence Summaries are contained in F. S. Regs., Part II. and the Staff Manual respectively. Title pages will be prepared in manuscript.

WAR DIARY
or
~~INTELLIGENCE SUMMARY.~~

(Erase heading not required.)

Army Form C. 2118.

Hour, Date, Place	Summary of Events and Information	Remarks and references to Appendices
La BREVIERE (COMPEIGNE FOREST) 8.10.14	Left LARGNY at 2 p.m. at head of 18th I.B. and marched to La BREVIERE arriving at 7 p.m. distance 14 miles. Went into Billet.	HMM major
COMPÉIGNE 9.10.14	Lft La BREVIERE at 6 a.m. and marched to COMPÉIGNE arriving 8 a.m. Went into French barracks and stayed there the night of 9th 10th.	HMM major
ARQUES ~~HAZEBRUCK~~ 11-10-14	entrained at 8am on 10th & disentrained at WIZERNES at 6am on 11th went into billets at BLANDECQUES till 3-30pm moved into billets at ARQUES arriving at 4-0pm	HMM major
HAZEBRUCK 12-10-14	moved with transport of 18th Infantry Brigade to HAZEBRUCK arriving at 10-30am (9 miles) went into billets at 3 pm	HMM major

Instructions regarding War Diaries and Intelligence Summaries are contained in F. S. Regs., Part II. and the Staff Manual respectively. Title pages will be prepared in manuscript.

WAR DIARY
or
~~INTELLIGENCE SUMMARY.~~
(Erase heading not required.)

Army Form C. 2118.

Hour, Date, Place	Summary of Events and Information	Remarks and references to Appendices
VIEUX BERQUIN - 13-10-14	Marched with 18th Inf. Brigade as Right Column to attack line BLEU - LES 3 FERMES. This line was held by Brigade at night. Company was kept in reserve & went into billets at 6pm	[illegible]
LES TROIS - FERMES 14-10-14	Marched with 18th Inf. Brigade & went into billets at LES TROIS FERMES (distance 3 miles)	[illegible]
SAILLY - 15-10-14	Advanced with 18th Inf. Brigade on SAILLY. Two officers sent on to reconnoitre bridge at SAILLY which was found broken. Centre span of bridge a suspension pattern both end spans broken. Two sections employed on making good for infantry traffic which was completed at 5 am by making ramps at either end. Went into billets	[illegible]
SAILLY 16-10-14	Two pontoons of 12th (Field) Company were received & a	

(9 29 6) W 3332—1107 100,000 10/13 H W V Forms/C. 2118/10

Instructions regarding War Diaries and Intelligence Summaries are contained in F. S. Regs., Part II. and the Staff Manual respectively. Title pages will be prepared in manuscript.

WAR DIARY
or
~~INTELLIGENCE SUMMARY.~~
(*Erase heading not required.*)

Army Form C. 2118.

Hour, Date, Place	Summary of Events and Information	Remarks and references to Appendices
16-10-14 (contd)	a medium pontoon bridge of 1 trestle & four pontoons was made with approaches about ~~100~~ 50x above broken bridge	[illegible]
FLEURBAIX 17-10-14	Ten pontoons of 2nd Bridging Train joined unit & a second medium pontoon bridge & approaches was constructed about 50 yards below broken bridge. One section left at SAILLY to maintain bridges. Remainder of company marched to FLEURBAIX & were employed in putting village in state of defence by blocking roads & clearing etc trenches dug by civilian population. Went into billets at 9pm	[illegible]
RUE-DU-BOIS 18-10-14	Marched to RUE-DU-BOIS (distance 5 miles) & bivouaced	[illegible]

Army Form C. 2118.

Instructions regarding War Diaries and Intelligence Summaries are contained in F. S. Regs., Part II. and the Staff Manual respectively. Title pages will be prepared in manuscript.

WAR DIARY
or
~~INTELLIGENCE SUMMARY.~~
(Erase heading not required.)

Hour, Date, Place	Summary of Events and Information	Remarks and references to Appendices
LEQUESNE 19-10-14	The three sections marched to FETUS to join 18th Infantry Brigade & were employed as follows 1 Section to RAILWAY bridge 3/4 mile SE of LA VALLEE & constructed a breastwork across line with approaches & cleared front 1 Section making barricade & communication trench at E end of ENNETIERES also placing wire entanglement in front of trenches at this place 1 Section making communication through houses in ENNETIERES	[signature]
GRANDE FLAMENGERIE 20/10/14	One section to BOIS BLANCS placing wire entanglement in front of position being prepared then to BRIDOUX where trenches were dug	

Army Form C. 2118.

WAR DIARY
or
INTELLIGENCE ~~SUMMARY.~~
(Erase heading not required.)

Instructions regarding War Diaries and Intelligence Summaries are contained in F. S. Regs., Part II. and the Staff Manual respectively. Title pages will be prepared in manuscript.

Hour, Date, Place	Summary of Events and Information	Remarks and references to Appendices
	One section at LEQUESNE blocking road and clearing in connection with position. This section was afterwards employed as infantry to assist in repelling attack of enemy in LAVALLEE. One section cutting pickets at GRANDE FLAMENGRIE	H Morgan
BOIS GRENIER 21-10-14	One section to BRIDOUX to erect wire entanglements block roads etc. The remaining two sections to RUE DU BOIS & LEQUESNE ~~[illegible]~~ for purpose of erecting wire in front of trenches. As work was impossible during day this work was attempted at night. That at LEQUESNE was successful but firing too heavy at RUE DU BOIS & Lt Evans was severely wounded.	H Morgan

Instructions regarding War Diaries and Intelligence Summaries are contained in F. S. Regs., Part II. and the Staff Manual respectively. Title pages will be prepared in manuscript.

WAR DIARY
or
INTELLIGENCE SUMMARY.
(*Erase heading not required.*)

Army Form C. 2118.

Hour, Date, Place	Summary of Events and Information	Remarks and references to Appendices
BOIS GRENIER 22-10-14	Two section employed with 19th Infantry Brigade extending position to ROUGES BANCS. One section on night work at RUE DU BOIS owing to shell fire the billets had to be shifted in BOIS GRENIER. One driver & three horses slightly wounded	HMB
BOIS GRENIER 23-10-14	Two sections on night work placing wire in front of trenches of 19th I.B. Sniping on left flank. One section with 16th I.B. half employed w/ infantry remainder erecting wire in front of trenches occupied by Leicester Regt. Capt Kelly mortally wounded	HMB

Instructions regarding War Diaries and Intelligence Summaries are contained in F. S. Regs., Part II. and the Staff Manual respectively. Title pages will be prepared in manuscript.

WAR DIARY
or
~~INTELLIGENCE~~ SUMMARY.
(Erase heading not required.)

Army Form C. 2118.

Hour, Date, Place	Summary of Events and Information	Remarks and references to Appendices
BOIS GRENIER 24-10-14	Three sections went to work with 16th + 19th I.B. but owing to heavy firing no work was possible. No 4 Section relieved No 2 at SAILLY	HMS major
BOIS GRENIER 25-10-14	One section to RUE-DU-BOIS to improve trenches held by E YORKS. Two sections digging on the retired position in the section allotted to 18th Brigade	HMS major
BOIS GRENIER 26-10-14	One section to RUE-DU-BOIS as before. One section erecting wire in front of trenches occupied by Royal Fusiliers at ROUGES BANCS. One section employed on demolishing chimney of factory on RIV: DES LAYES, which served as aiming mark for enemy. A portion of bottom of chimney was cut away & two pieces cut by guncotton. The demolition was quite successful. Section from SAILLY rejoined company	HMS major

(9 29 6) W 3332—1107 100,000 10/13 H W V Forms/C. 2118/10.

Army Form C. 2118.

Instructions regarding War Diaries and Intelligence Summaries are contained in F. S. Regs., Part II. and the Staff Manual respectively. Title pages will be prepared in manuscript.

WAR DIARY
or
~~INTELLIGENCE~~ SUMMARY.
(*Erase heading not required.*)

Hour, Date, Place	Summary of Events and Information	Remarks and references to Appendices
BOIS GRENIER ~~FLEURBAIX~~ 27-10-14	One Section to erect wire in front of trenches of R. W. Fusiliers no work possible owing to firing One Section erecting flares in front of trenches of Cameronians One Section supplied pickets & wire to W. Yorks	[illegible]
FLEURBAIX 28-10-14	Move billets of company into FLEURBAIX Capt W H KELLY RE joined Company for temporary duty One section erecting wire in front of trenches of R W Fusiliers little work possible owing to firing One section preparing positions for "snipers" in rear of second line And two sections digging an advanced line S of DES PLANCHES FERME	[illegible]

(9 29 6) W 3332—1107 100,000 10/13 H W V Forms/C. 2118/10.

Instructions regarding War Diaries and Intelligence Summaries are contained in F. S. Regs., Part II. and the Staff Manual respectively. Title pages will be prepared in manuscript.

WAR DIARY
or
~~INTELLIGENCE SUMMARY.~~
(Erase heading not required.)

Army Form C. 2118.

Hour, Date, Place	Summary of Events and Information	Remarks and references to Appendices
FLEURBAIX 29-10-14	Three sections digging on second line in front of RUE PETILLON One section erecting wire in front of trenches of R.W. Fusiliers	J.M. Brown
FLEURBAIX 30-10-14	Two sections employed in erecting wire in front of trenches occupied by MIDDLESEX REGT very little work possible owing to firing.	J.M. Brown
FLEURBAIX 31-10-14	Capt KELLY left the unit to reform 2nd bridging train. Three sections employed on digging second line in front of RUE PETILLON One section erecting wire in front of trenches occupied by R. W. Fusiliers work interrupted by firing	J.M. Brown

J.M. Brown [illegible]
O.C. 38 (Indi) Co. R.E.

(9 29 6) W 3332—1107 100,000 10/13 H W V Forms/C. 2118/10.

5th Divisional Engineers

38th FIELD COMPANY R. E.

NOVEMBER 1914.

Army Form C. 2118.

Instructions regarding War Diaries and Intelligence Summaries are contained in F. S. Regs., Part II. and the Staff Manual respectively. Title pages will be prepared in manuscript.

WAR DIARY
or
~~INTELLIGENCE SUMMARY.~~

(Erase heading not required.)

Hour, Date, Place	Summary of Events and Information	Remarks and references to Appendices
FLEURBAIX 1.11.14	Company employed in preparing pickets and erecting wire; clearing field of fire in front of Strategic line.	H. Eyre
FLEURBAIX 2.11.14	Two sections clearing field of fire and two sections erecting wire in front of strategic line. 2/Lt Osborn R.E. joined the company for duty. One section putting up wire in front of trenches occupied by York & Lancs by night.	H. Eyre
FLEURBAIX 3.11.14.	Three sections employed in demolishing houses. One section collecting pickets and wire & cutting to clear field of fire in front of Strategic line. 38th Coy take over supervising Civil labour from 20th Coy.	H. Eyre

(9 29 6) W 3332—1107 100,000 10/13 H W V Forms/C. 2118/10.

Army Form C. 2118.

Instructions regarding War Diaries and Intelligence Summaries are contained in F. S. Regs., Part II. and the Staff Manual respectively. Title pages will be prepared in manuscript.

WAR DIARY
or
INTELLIGENCE SUMMARY.
(Erase heading not required.)

Hour, Date, Place	Summary of Events and Information	Remarks and references to Appendices
FLEURBAIX 4.11.14.	Three sections employed in demolishing houses to clear field of fire. One section cutting to clear field of fire in front of strategic line.	Company supervise Civilian Labour each day. H. Eyre
FLEURBAIX 5.11.14.	Company clearing field of fire in front of strategic line. One section putting up wire, in front of trenches occupied by York & Lancs, by night.	H. Eyre
FLEURBAIX 6.11.14.	Three sections constructing shelters for supports behind the strategic line. One section clearing field of fire. Two sections putting up entanglement in front of line occupied by R. Fusiliers & Buffs, by night.	H. Eyre
FLEURBAIX 7.11.14	Company constructing shelters for supports behind the strategic line.	H. Eyre.

(9 29 6) W 3332—1107 100,000 10/13 H W V Forms/C. 2118/10.

Instructions regarding War Diaries and Intelligence Summaries are contained in F.S. Regs., Part II. and the Staff Manual respectively. Title pages will be prepared in manuscript.

WAR DIARY
or
~~INTELLIGENCE SUMMARY.~~
(Erase heading not required.)

Army Form C. 2118.

Hour, Date, Place	Summary of Events and Information	Remarks and references to Appendices
FLEURBAIX 8.11.14.	Three sections making shelters for supports in rear of strategic line S.W. of FLEURBAIX and superintending civil labour. One section erecting wire at night in front of trenches occupied by York & Lancs.	H. Syme
FLEURBAIX 9.11.14.	All sections employed ~~in~~ obtaining pickets and rolling barbed wire in convenient lengths. At night all sections employed erecting low wire entanglement in front of second line S. of CROIX MARECHAL	H. Syme.
FLEURBAIX 10.11.14.	Company employed obtaining pickets & rolling wire during day. At night erecting low wire entanglement in front of second line S of CROIX MARECHAL & RUE PETILLON. Superintending civilian labour	[illegible signature]

(9 29 6) W 3332—1107 100,000 10/13 H W V Forms/C. 2118/10.

Instructions regarding War Diaries and Intelligence Summaries are contained in F. S. Regs., Part II. and the Staff Manual respectively. Title pages will be prepared in manuscript.

WAR DIARY
or
INTELLIGENCE SUMMARY.
(Erase heading not required.)

Army Form C. 2118.

Hour, Date, Place	Summary of Events and Information	Remarks and references to Appendices
FLEURBAIX 11-11-14	Superintending civilian labour. by day preparing wire & pickets. at night all company employed in erecting low wire entanglement in front of second line of trenches N of RUE DAVID & also S of RUE PETILLON	[signature]
RUE DU - QUESNOY 12-11-14	Superintending civilian labour. moved billets from FLEURBAIX which had been shelled the previous day. Company employed by day in preparing wire & pickets Capt Noble CSM Cowley 12 Sappers & 1 Driver joined as reinforcements	[signature]
RUE DU QUESNOY 13-11-14	Superintending civilian labour. By day preparing wire & pickets. At night all company employed in erecting low wire entanglements in front of second line of trenches S of LE CRON BALLOT & S of RUE PETILLON	[signature]
RUE DU QUESNOY 14-11-14	Superintending civil labour. By day preparing wire & pickets. By night 3 sections employed in erecting low wire entanglements in front of second line of trenches S of LE CRON BALLOT. Low wire completed from BOIS-GRENIER — TOUQUET road to road running S.E. from R of RUE-PETILLON	[signature]

Instructions regarding War Diaries and Intelligence Summaries are contained in F. S. Regs., Part II. and the Staff Manual respectively. Title pages will be prepared in manuscript.

WAR DIARY
or
~~INTELLIGENCE SUMMARY.~~
(*Erase heading not required.*)

Army Form C. 2118.

Hour, Date, Place	Summary of Events and Information	Remarks and references to Appendices
RUE-DU-QUESNOY 15-11-14	Supervising civilian labour on third line of trenches & cutting brushwood & making fascines for use in trenches	H.M.B. Major
RUE-DU-QUESNOY 16-11-14.	Supervising civilian labour binding wire, cutting brushwood & preparing fascines	H.M.B. Major
ARMENTIERES 17-11-14	One Section to ESTAIRES to repair bridge. Company moved billets to ARMENTIERES to left of line held by 6th Division. One officer & six men to 17th I.B. to lay out communication trenches. Supervising civilian labour	H.M.B. Major
ARMENTIERES 18-11-14	Civilian labour employed in cutting & collecting brushwood for fascines. Company employed in making fascines. Hot water apparatus. One section at night to Cameronians trenches. One officer & six men laying out communication trenches for 17th I.B.	H.M.B. Major

Instructions regarding War Diaries and Intelligence Summaries are contained in F. S. Regs., Part II. and the Staff Manual respectively. Title pages will be prepared in manuscript.

WAR DIARY
or
~~INTELLIGENCE SUMMARY.~~
(Erase heading not required.)

Army Form C. 2118.

Hour, Date, Place	Summary of Events and Information	Remarks and references to Appendices
ARMENTIERES 19-11-14	Civilian Labour cutting brushwood Company employed making fascines, gabions, footboards for trenches, hot water apparatus, loophole plates one section at night to R Fusiliers trenches for connecting trenches.. Snow & frost.	HMB major
ARMENTIERES 20/11/14	Civilian Labour cutting brushwood Company employed making fascines, footboards for trenches, hot water apparatus, loophole & lookout plates, handbarrows. Eight N.C.O.s & men in trenches of R.W. Fusiliers superintending making shelters one party to Argyll & Sutherland Highlanders to put up barbed wire across road	HMB major
ARMENTIERES 21/11/14	Civilian Labour cutting brushwood. Company employed as above one section to A & S trenches to erect low wire entanglement	HMB major

(9 29 6) W 3332—1107 100,000 10/13 H W V Forms/C. 2118/10.

Army Form C. 2118.

Instructions regarding War Diaries and Intelligence Summaries are contained in F. S. Regs., Part II. and the Staff Manual respectively. Title pages will be prepared in manuscript.

WAR DIARY
or
~~INTELLIGENCE SUMMARY.~~
(Erase heading not required.)

Hour, Date, Place	Summary of Events and Information	Remarks and references to Appendices
ARMENTIERES 22/11/14	Civilian labour cutting brushwood for fascines Company employed on making fascines, footboards for trenches, hot water apparatus loopplate & lookout plates, handbarrows	J.M. Major
ARMENTIERES 23/11/14	Civilian labour cutting brushwood for fascines Company employed as above	J.M. Major
ARMENTIERES 24/11/14	Civilian labour cutting brushwood for fascines Company employed as above.	J.M. Major
ARMENTIERES 25/11/14	Civilian Labour cutting brushwood No 3 Section rejoined from ESTAIRES. Company employed in making fascines, handbarrows & footboards for trenches also hand grenades.	J.M. Major
ARMENTIERES 26/11/14	Civilian labour cutting & carting brushwood Company employed as above	J.M. Major

(9 29 6) W 3332—1107 100,000 10/13 H W V Forms/C. 2118/10.

Instructions regarding War Diaries and Intelligence Summaries are contained in F. S. Regs., Part II. and the Staff Manual respectively. Title pages will be prepared in manuscript.

WAR DIARY
or
~~INTELLIGENCE SUMMARY.~~
(*Erase heading not required.*)

Army Form C. 2118.

Hour, Date, Place	Summary of Events and Information	Remarks and references to Appendices
ARMENTIERES 27/11/14	Civilian labour carting & cutting brushwood Company employed in making fascines, pontoons & handbarrows & hand grenades	[signature]
ARMENTIERES 28/11/14	Civilian labour cutting & carting brushwood Company employed as above. G.O.C. 6th Div. inspected hand grenades & methods of throwing from trench. Also effect of machine gun on low wire entanglement. 200 rounds at a range of 400x had good effect & cleared a portion of entanglement. Gun moved to 300x but went out of action & experiment could not be continued	[signature]
ARMENTIERES 29/11/14	Civilian labour cutting & carting brushwood Company employed as above. One section at night blew down with guncotton a house in front of line held by Argyle & Sutherland Highlanders	[signature]
ARMENTIERES 30/11/14	Civilian labour cutting & carting brushwood Company employed as above & mending pumps in trenches occupied by 17th I.B.	[signature]

[signature]
O.C. 38th (Field) Coy

1/12/14

6th Divisional Engineers

38th FIELD COMPANY R. E.

DECEMBER 1914.

Army Form C. 2118.

Instructions regarding War Diaries and Intelligence Summaries are contained in F. S. Regs., Part II. and the Staff Manual respectively. Title pages will be prepared in manuscript.

WAR DIARY
or
~~INTELLIGENCE SUMMARY~~.
(Erase heading not required.)

Hour, Date, Place	Summary of Events and Information	Remarks and references to Appendices
ARMENTIERES 1-12-14	Civilian labour cutting & carting brushwood Company employed in making fascines footboards handbarrows	F M Brice major
ARMENTIERES 2-12-14	The company paraded as strong as possible for inspection by H.M. The King. practically no work was done. one party at night to trenches of R. Fusiliers to make communication in walls. Experiments carried out in cutting various forms of barbed wire entanglement by machine gun fire Civilian labour cutting & carting brushwood	F M B major
ARMENTIERES 3-12-14	Civilian labour cutting & carting brushwood Company employed in making fascines, footboards handbarrows & stand for rifle grenade. Two sections at night erecting low wire entanglement in front of trenches of 1st Middlesex Regt	F M Brice major

(9 29 6) W 3332—1107 100,000 10/13 H W V Forms/C. 2118/10.

Instructions regarding War Diaries and Intelligence Summaries are contained in F. S. Regs., Part II. and the Staff Manual respectively. Title pages will be prepared in manuscript.

WAR DIARY
or
~~INTELLIGENCE~~ SUMMARY.

(*Erase heading not required.*)

Army Form C. 2118.

Hour, Date, Place	Summary of Events and Information	Remarks and references to Appendices
ARMENTIERES 4-12-14	Civilian labour cutting & carting brushwood Company employed in making fascines, chevaux de frises & footboards for trenches	[illegible] Major
ARMENTIERES 5-12-14	Company & civilians employed as above	[illegible] Major
ARMENTIERES 6-12-14	no civilian labour Company paraded for bathing in Divisional Bathing Establishment. In afternoon making fascines, footboards etc. One section at night employed in revetting with timber the trenches occupied by R.W. Fusiliers	[illegible] Major
ARMENTIERES 7-12-14	Civilians cutting & carting brushwood Company employed making fascines, chevaux-de-frises & footboards Six men assisting in North Stafford trenches One section at night blinding communication trench to R.B. trenches One section at night revetting trenches of R.W. Fusiliers	[illegible] Major

(9 29 6) W 3332—1107 100,000 10/13 H W V Forms/C. 2118/10.

Army Form C. 2118.

Instructions regarding War Diaries and Intelligence Summaries are contained in F. S. Regs., Part II. and the Staff Manual respectively. Title pages will be prepared in manuscript.

WAR DIARY
or
~~INTELLIGENCE SUMMARY~~.

(*Erase heading not required.*)

Hour, Date, Place	Summary of Events and Information	Remarks and references to Appendices
ARMENTIERES 8-12-14	Civilian Labour cutting & carting brushwood. Company employed on fascines & footboards & making trench mortar & chevaux-de-frises. One section at night revetting trenches of R.W. Fusiliers	[illegible] Major
ARMENTIERES 9-12-14	as on 8-12-14	[illegible] Major
ARMENTIERES 10-12-14	as on 9-12-14	[illegible] Major
ARMENTIERES 11-12-14	Civilian Labour cutting & carting brushwood. Company employed in making fascines chevaux de frises & footboards repairing pumps in R.B. trenches. One section at night revetting trenches of R.W. Fusiliers	[illegible] Major

(9 29 6) W 3332—1107 100,000 10/13 H W V Forms/C. 2118/10.

Instructions regarding War Diaries and Intelligence Summaries are contained in F. S. Regs., Part II. and the Staff Manual respectively. Title pages will be prepared in manuscript.

WAR DIARY
or
~~INTELLIGENCE SUMMARY.~~
(Erase heading not required.)

Army Form C. 2118.

Hour, Date, Place	Summary of Events and Information	Remarks and references to Appendices
ARMENTIERES 12-12-14	Civilian labour carting & cutting brushwood & making fascines Company employed in making fascines footboards chevaux de frises etc	[illegible] Major
ARMENTIERES 13-12-14	Civilian labour as above Company employed in making fascines footboards & chevaux de frises One section at night netting trenches of RW Fusiliers	[illegible] Major
ARMENTIERES 14-12-14	Civilian labour as above Company employed in making fascines, footboards One section at night netting trenches of RW Fusiliers One section erecting low wire entanglement in front of trenches of 1st Middlesex Regt	[illegible] Major
ARMENTIERES 15-12-14	Civilian labour as above Company employed in making fascines footboards hot water apparatus	[illegible] Major

(9 29 6) W 3332—1107 100,000 10/13 H W V Forms/C. 2118/10.

Instructions regarding War Diaries and Intelligence Summaries are contained in F. S. Regs., Part II. and the Staff Manual respectively. Title pages will be prepared in manuscript.

WAR DIARY
or
~~INTELLIGENCE SUMMARY.~~
(Erase heading not required.)

Army Form C. 2118.

Hour, Date, Place	Summary of Events and Information	Remarks and references to Appendices
ARMENTIERES 16-12-14	Civilian labour cutting & carting brushwood & making fascines. Company employed in making fascines & footboards one party erecting pumps in trenches of Rifle Brigade	[illegible]
ARMENTIERES 17-12-14	Civilian labour as above Company employed in making fascines, footboards & sand bag forks	[illegible]
ARMENTIERES 18-12-14	Civilian labour as above. Company employed in making fascines, footgratings, and sand bag forks for infantry. Officer inspecting communication trenches of 17th I. B. with view to draining them.	[illegible]

(9 29 6) W 3332—1107 100,000 10/13 H W V Forms/C. 2118/10

Instructions regarding War Diaries and Intelligence Summaries are contained in F. S. Regs., Part II. and the Staff Manual respectively. Title pages will be prepared in manuscript.

WAR DIARY
or
~~INTELLIGENCE SUMMARY.~~
(*Erase heading not required.*)

Army Form C. 2118.

Hour, Date, Place	Summary of Events and Information	Remarks and references to Appendices
ARMENTIERES 19.12.14	Civilian labour cutting and loading brushwood. Company employed in making fascines + foot-gratings for trenches. Calibrating trench gun made by Coy and experimenting with various types of hand grenades.	H. Syme Lt.
ARMENTIERES 20.12.14.	The Company bathed in the Div: bathing establishment in the morning. In the afternoon they were employed in making fascines and footgratings	H. Syme Lt.
ARMENTIERES 21-12-14.	Civilian labour cutting + carting brushwood. The company was employed in making fascines, footgratings, chevaux-de-frises and ladders to get out of trenches.	H. Syme Lt.

(9 29 6) W 3332—1107 100,000 10/13 H W V Forms/C. 2118/10.

Instructions regarding War Diaries and Intelligence Summaries are contained in F.S. Regs., Part II. and the Staff Manual respectively. Title pages will be prepared in manuscript.

WAR DIARY
or
~~INTELLIGENCE~~ SUMMARY.
(*Erase heading not required.*)

Army Form C. 2118.

Hour, Date, Place	Summary of Events and Information	Remarks and references to Appendices
ARMENTIERES 22·12·14	Civilian labour cutting brushwood + loading. Company employed in making fascines and foot-gratings. Hot water apparatus for heating water. Wiring 'chevaux de frises' for 19th I.B. making ladders for trenches. Two pumps were fixed at night in a wet trench of 2nd R.W. Fusiliers.	H. Eyre Lt.
ARMENTIERES 23·12·14	Civilian labour as above. Company was employed in making fascines, footgratings and hot water apparatus: also rifle rests for firing grenades for 17th I.B.	J. W. Noble Capt RE
ARMENTIERES 24·12·14	Civilian labour as above. Company making fascines footgratings and materials (hurdles + 'dug-outs') for breastwork for 17th I.B. One Officer and party laying out 2nd Line trenches for 19th I.B. by night.	J. W. Noble Capt RE.

(9 29 6) W 3332—1107 100,000 10/13 H W V Forms/C. 2118/10.

Army Form C. 2118.

Instructions regarding War Diaries and Intelligence Summaries are contained in F. S. Regs., Part II. and the Staff Manual respectively. Title pages will be prepared in manuscript.

WAR DIARY
or
~~INTELLIGENCE SUMMARY.~~

(*Erase heading not required.*)

Hour, Date, Place	Summary of Events and Information	Remarks and references to Appendices
ARMENTIERES 25-12-14	Civilian labour cutting brushwood & loading. Only urgent work carried out. Church parade C of E 9.30 a.m. R.C. 8.45 a.m.	K S Noble Capt RE
ARMENTIERES 26-12-14.	Civilian labour as above. Company making fascines, footgratings and materials for breastwork trench for 17th I.B. One Officer to G.H.Q. re Trench Mortar. Two officers and one Section to reconnoitre Riviere des Layes with a view to clearing it out. One Officer to 3rd R.B. resiting trenches.	K S Noble Capt RE.
ARMENTIERES 27-12-14.	Civilian labour as above. Three sections making fascines footboards and materials for breastwork for 17th I.B. One section with Civilians clearing Riviere des Layes. One officer tracing course of above river ~~the~~ through ARMENTIERES. One Officer reconnoitring for cutting power cables ARMENTIERES–LILLE. One Officer to D.L.I. re improving trenches. One officer instructing parties from 16th & 17th I.Bs in use of trench Mortars.	K S Noble Capt RE

(9 29 6) W 3332—1107 100,000 10/13 H W V Forms/C. 2118/10.

Instructions regarding War Diaries and Intelligence Summaries are contained in F. S. Regs., Part II. and the Staff Manual respectively. Title pages will be prepared in manuscript.

WAR DIARY
or
~~INTELLIGENCE SUMMARY.~~
(Erase heading not required.)

Army Form C. 2118.

Hour, Date, Place	Summary of Events and Information	Remarks and references to Appendices
ARMENTIERES 28-12-14	Civilians cutting brushwood, loading and making fascines. Company (less three parties) making fascines, hurdles, and Materials for 17th I.B. breastwork. Party, at night, working with and instructing D.L.I. in revetting trench. One officer and party cutting Power cables LILLE-ARMENTIERES, using explosives. One officer and party reconnoitring and clearing drains between HOUPLINES and CHAPELLE d'ARMENTIERES. Officer with party of Civilians clearing Riviere des Layes. One Officer instructing Infantry parties in firing trench mortar	W Noble Capt RE
ARMENTIERES 29-12-14.	Civilians as above. Company making fascines, footboards & materials for breastwork. One officer with Civilians clearing drains near CHAPELLE d'ARMENTIERES. One Officer reconnoitring blockage in flow of water from W. Yorks trenches. Experiments with various patterns of hand grenades.	W Noble Capt RE

(9 29 6) W 3332—1107 100,000 10/13 H W V Forms/C. 2118/10.

Army Form C. 2118.

Instructions regarding War Diaries and Intelligence Summaries are contained in F. S. Regs., Part II. and the Staff Manual respectively. Title pages will be prepared in manuscript.

WAR DIARY
or
~~INTELLIGENCE SUMMARY.~~

(Erase heading not required.)

Hour, Date, Place	Summary of Events and Information	Remarks and references to Appendices
ARMENTIERES 30-12-14.	Civilians cutting brushwood, loading & making fascines. Company employed making fascines, hurdles, pickets, foot-boards. Two Officers and 1 Section and party of Civilians clearing drains running towards trenches. Officers class from 19th I.B. instructed in use & throwing of hand grenades. Materials for breastwork for 17th I.B. transported to CHAPELLE d'ARMENTIERES and handed over to 12th Coy. One Officer and party clearing culvert in 18th I.B. trenches by night.	W Noble Capt RE
ARMENTIERES 31-12-14	Civilian labour as above. Company making fascines, hurdles and breastwork trench for 18th I.B. also footboards and "dugouts". One Officer and section clearing drains behind trenches occupied by 18th I.B. One Officer and party instructing 19th I.B in use of hand grenades.	W Noble Capt RE

1.1.15. W Noble Capt RE O.C. 38th Co RE

6th Division

121
4261

Confidential

War Diary

of

38th (Field) Company Royal Engineers

from 1st January 1915 to 31st January 1915

Volume VI 1–31.1.15

Nil

Army Form C. 2118.

Instructions regarding War Diaries and Intelligence Summaries are contained in F. S. Regs., Part II. and the Staff Manual respectively. Title pages will be prepared in manuscript.

WAR DIARY
or
INTELLIGENCE SUMMARY.
(Erase heading not required.)

Hour, Date, Place	Summary of Events and Information	Remarks and references to Appendices
ARMENTIERES 1-1-15	Company was employed in making fascines, hurdles, foot boards, & "Dug outs" for breastworks. Superintending civilians cutting brushwood & making fascines	[illegible]
ARMENTIERES 2-1-15	as above.	[illegible]
ARMENTIERES 3-1-15	as above. One party clearing streams in rear of trenches	[illegible]
ARMENTIERES 4-1-15	Company employed in making fascines & hurdles, footboards & Dug outs" & clearing streams in rear of trenches. Two sections at night erecting breastwork in trenches occupied by N. YORKS. Work much interrupted by shell fire & one Sapper was wounded. Civilians as above.	[illegible]
ARMENTIERES 5-1-15	Company employed in making fascines, hurdles footboards & dugouts, chevaux de frises. Infy of 16th I.B. instructed in throwing hand grenades. One section at night erecting breastwork as above. One Corporal wounded. Civilians as above	[illegible]

Instructions regarding War Diaries and Intelligence Summaries are contained in F. S. Regs., Part II. and the Staff Manual respectively. Title pages will be prepared in manuscript.

WAR DIARY
or
~~INTELLIGENCE SUMMARY~~.
(Erase heading not required.)

Army Form C. 2118.

Hour, Date, Place	Summary of Events and Information	Remarks and references to Appendices
ARMENTIERES - 6-1-15	Company employed in making fascines, hurdles footboards & dugouts. Converting pumps for the trenches Superintending infantry digging breastwork at night. Civilians cutting brushwood & making fascines. clearing drains in rear of line	FMB Major
ARMENTIERES 7-1-15	as above	FMB Major
ARMENTIERES 8-1-15	as above.	FMB Major
ARMENTIERES - 9-1-15	as above	FMB Major
ARMENTIERES - 10-1-15	Company had baths in Divisional Bathing establishment. In afternoon company employed in making fascines, footboards dugouts & hurdles	FMB Major

(9 29 6) W 3332—1107 100,000 10/13 H W V Forms/C. 2118/10

Instructions regarding War Diaries and Intelligence Summaries are contained in F. S. Regs., Part II. and the Staff Manual respectively. Title pages will be prepared in manuscript.

WAR DIARY
or
~~INTELLIGENCE SUMMARY.~~

(Erase heading not required.)

Army Form C. 2118.

Hour, Date, Place	Summary of Events and Information	Remarks and references to Appendices
ARMENTIERES - 11-1-15	Company employed in making hurdles, fascines, dugouts footboards, canvas screens & converting pumps at night one section erecting breastwork in rear of line occupied by SHERWOOD FORESTERS Civilians employed in cutting brushwood & making fascines & clearing drains in rear of trenches	[signature] Major
ARMENTIERES 12-1-15	Company employed in making hurdles, fascines dugouts & footboards, canvas screens, converting pumps. at night a party erecting traverse in trenches occupied by QUEENS WESTMINSTERS Civilians employed as above.	[signature] Major
ARMENTIERES 13-1-15	as above	[signature] Major

Instructions regarding War Diaries and Intelligence Summaries are contained in F. S. Regs., Part II. and the Staff Manual respectively. Title pages will be prepared in manuscript.

WAR DIARY
or
~~INTELLIGENCE SUMMARY.~~
(*Erase heading not required.*)

Army Form C. 2118.

Hour, Date, Place	Summary of Events and Information	Remarks and references to Appendices
ARMENTIERES 14-1-15	Company employed in making fascines, hurdles, dugouts, footboards, canvas screens & converting pumps One section at night erecting breastwork in trenches occupied by Sherwood Foresters Civilians cutting brushwood & making fascines	[illegible]
ARMENTIERES 15-1-15	Company employed in making fascines, hurdles dugouts, footboards canvas screens & converting pumps Civilians cutting brushwood & making fascines, & one party erecting breastwork in second line by day; work interrupted by shell fire & continued at night	[illegible]
ARMENTIERES 16-1-15	Company employed in making fascines, hurdles dugouts, footboards & converting pumps One section at night erecting breastwork behind trenches occupied by Sherwood Foresters Civilians cutting brushwood & making fascines; at night digging breastwork on second line	[illegible]

(9 29 6) W 3332—1107 100,000 10/13 H W V Forms/C. 2118/10.

Army Form C. 2118.

Instructions regarding War Diaries and Intelligence Summaries are contained in F.S. Regs., Part II. and the Staff Manual respectively. Title pages will be prepared in manuscript.

WAR DIARY
or
~~INTELLIGENCE~~ SUMMARY.

(Erase heading not required.)

Hour, Date, Place	Summary of Events and Information	Remarks and references to Appendices
ARMENTIERES 17-1-15	Company employed in making fascines, hurdles, dugouts & footboards & converting pumps. One section at night erecting a breastwork in trenches occupied by W. Yorks. Civilians cutting brushwood & making hurdles. At night digging breastworks in second line	H.M.M. Major
ARMENTIERES 18-1-15	Company employed in making fascines, hurdles, dugouts, footboards & converting pumps. Civilians as above	H.M.M. Major
ARMENTIERES 19-1-15	Company employed in making fascines, hurdles, dugouts, footboards & converting pumps. One section at night erecting parados of breastwork in trenches of Sherwood Foresters. Civilians as above	H.M.M. Major
ARMENTIERES 20-1-15	Company employed in making fascines, hurdles, dugouts, footboards & converting pumps. Civilians as above	H.M.M. Major

(9 29 6) W 3332--1107 100,000 10/13 H W V Forms/C. 2118/10.

Army Form C. 2118.

Instructions regarding War Diaries and Intelligence Summaries are contained in F. S. Regs., Part II. and the Staff Manual respectively. Title pages will be prepared in manuscript.

WAR DIARY
or
INTELLIGENCE SUMMARY.
(*Erase heading not required.*)

Hour, Date, Place	Summary of Events and Information	Remarks and references to Appendices
ARMENTIERES 21-1-15	Company employed in making hurdles, dugouts footboards & converting pumps Civilians cutting brushwood & making hurdles at night digging breastwork in second line	[illegible]
ARMENTIERES 22-1-15	Company employed in making hurdles, dugouts, footboards & converting pumps One section at night erecting parados in breastwork in trenches of West Yorks One section at night erecting traverse in trenches of Queens Westminsters Civilians cutting brushwood, making fascines & hurdles at night digging breastwork in second line	[illegible]
ARMENTIERES 23-1-15	Company employed in making hurdles, dugouts footboards & converting pumps One section at night erecting parados of breastwork in trenches of Sherwood Foresters Civilians as above	[illegible]
ARMENTIERES 24-1-15	Company attended church parade Civilians at night digging breastwork in second line	[illegible]

(9 29 6) W 3332—1107 100,000 10/13 H W V Forms/C. 2118/10.

Instructions regarding War Diaries and Intelligence Summaries are contained in F. S. Regs., Part II. and the Staff Manual respectively. Title pages will be prepared in manuscript.

WAR DIARY
or
~~INTELLIGENCE SUMMARY.~~

(*Erase heading not required.*)

Army Form C. 2118.

Hour, Date, Place	Summary of Events and Information	Remarks and references to Appendices
ARMENTIERES 25-1-15	Company employed in making hurdles, dugouts footboards, & converting pumps One section at night erecting breastwork in trenches of ~~West~~ East Yorks One party at night erecting machine gun platform in trenches of East Yorks Civilians cutting brushwood & making fascines & hurdles, at night digging breastworks in second line	[illegible] Major
ARMENTIERES 26-1-15	Company employed in making hurdles, dugouts footboards & converting pumps One section at night erecting parados to breastworks in trenches of East Yorks One section at night placing a house in a state of defence in rear of Westminsters trenches at HOOPLINES Civilians cutting brushwood & making fascines & hurdles at night digging breastworks in second line	[illegible]
ARMENTIERES 27-1-15	Company employed in making hurdles dugouts footboards, trench anchors & converting pumps Civilians as above	[illegible] Major

(9 29 6) W 3332—1107 100,000 10/13 H W V Forms/C. 2118/10.

Instructions regarding War Diaries and Intelligence Summaries are contained in F.S. Regs., Part II. and the Staff Manual respectively. Title pages will be prepared in manuscript.

WAR DIARY
or
~~INTELLIGENCE SUMMARY.~~
(Erase heading not required.)

Army Form C. 2118.

Hour, Date, Place	Summary of Events and Information	Remarks and references to Appendices
ARMENTIERES 28-1-15	Company employed in making hurdles, dugouts & footboards & converting pumps at night one section loopholing house in rear of line at HOOPLINES Civilians cutting brushwood & making hurdles & fascines at night digging breastworks in second line	[signature]
ARMENTIERES 29-1-15	Company employed in making hurdles, fascines, dugouts footboards & converting pumps Civilians as above	[signature]
ARMENTIERES 30-1-15	Company employed in making hurdles, dugouts, footboards & converting pumps One section placing houses in a state of defence at HOOPLINES One section at night placing houses in a state of defence at CHAPELLE D'ARMENTIERES Civilians as above	[signature]
ARMENTIERES 31-1-15	Company employed in morning in making hurdles dugouts footboards & converting pumps. One section loopholing houses in HOOPLINES. One section at night loopholing houses in lines of 17th Infantry Brigade Civilians as above	[signature]

[signature] Major
O.C. (38th Field) Coy. RE

Confidential

War Diary of 6th Division

38th (Field) Company Royal Engineers

from 1st February 1915 to 28th February 1915

Vol VII

Instructions regarding War Diaries and Intelligence Summaries are contained in F.S. Regs., Part II. and the Staff Manual respectively. Title pages will be prepared in manuscript.

WAR DIARY
or
~~INTELLIGENCE SUMMARY.~~
(Erase heading not required.)

Army Form C. 2118.

38th Fd Co RE

Hour, Date, Place	Summary of Events and Information	Remarks and references to Appendices
ARMENTIERES 1-2-15	Company employed in making hurdles, dugouts footboards & converting pumps one section loopholing houses etc at HOUPLINES one section at night loopholing houses in trenches of 17th IB. Civilians cutting & carting brushwood & making hurdles & fascines at night digging breastworks on the retired line	[signature]
ARMENTIERES 2-2-15	Company employed in making hurdles dugouts converting pumps & making machine gun platforms one section loopholing houses at HOUPLINES at night one officer & 10 men in trenches of 17th IB Civilians as above	[signature]
ARMENTIERES 3-2-15	as on 2-2-15	[signature]
ARMENTIERES 4-2-15	Company making hurdles, dugouts, converting pumps, footboards, & making gun platform apart, at night starting shaft for mine behind trenches of QUEEN'S WESTMINSTERS Civilians as above	[signature]

(9 29 6) W 3332—1107 100,000 10/13 H W V Forms/C. 2118/10.

Instructions regarding War Diaries and Intelligence Summaries are contained in F. S. Regs., Part II. and the Staff Manual respectively. Title pages will be prepared in manuscript.

WAR DIARY
or
INTELLIGENCE SUMMARY.
(Erase heading not required.)

Army Form C. 2118.

38th Fd Co RE

Hour, Date, Place	Summary of Events and Information	Remarks and references to Appendices
ARMENTIERES 5-2-15	Company employed in making hurdles, dugouts, footboards & converting pumps One NCO supervising Infantry party mining Civilians cutting & carting brushwood & making fascines & hurdles. At night digging breastworks on the retired line	[illegible]
ARMENTIERES 6-2-15	Company making hurdles dugouts, footboards & pumps At night one section erecting barbed wire entanglement on retired line Mine had to be abandoned owing to depth of water in the shaft which could not be got out by pumping Civilians as above & also by day clearing out the GHQ line of defence	[illegible] [illegible]
ARMENTIERES 7-2-15	Company paraded for Church & did no work	[illegible]
ARMENTIERES 8-2-15	Company employed as on 6-2-15 Civilians as on 6-2-15	[illegible]
ARMENTIERES 9-2-15	Company & civilians employed as on 8-2-15	[illegible]

Instructions regarding War Diaries and Intelligence Summaries are contained in F. S. Regs., Part II. and the Staff Manual respectively. Title pages will be prepared in manuscript.

WAR DIARY
or
~~INTELLIGENCE SUMMARY.~~
(Erase heading not required.)

Army Form C. 2118.

38th Fd Co RE

Hour, Date, Place	Summary of Events and Information	Remarks and references to Appendices
ARMENTIERES 10-2-15	Company employed in making hurdles, dugouts, footboards & pumps At night one section erecting barbed wire in reserve line Civilians cutting & carting brushwood & making hurdles & fascines. At night digging breastworks in second line	[illegible]
ARMENTIERES 11-2-15	Company & civilians employed as on 10-2-15	[illegible]
ARMENTIERES 12-2-15	Company & civilians employed as on 10-2-15	[illegible]
ARMENTIERES 13-2-15	Company employed in making hurdles, dugouts footboards & pumps. One party loopholing farms etc at HOUPLINES. One party preparing approaches for proposed pontoon bridge Civilians as above	[illegible]
ARMENTIERES 14-2-15	Company paraded for church & did no work	[illegible]
ARMENTIERES 15-2-15	Company & civilians employed as on 13-2-15	[illegible]

Instructions regarding War Diaries and Intelligence Summaries are contained in F. S. Regs., Part II. and the Staff Manual respectively. Title pages will be prepared in manuscript.

WAR DIARY
or
INTELLIGENCE ~~SUMMARY.~~

(*Erase heading not required.*)

Army Form C. 2118.

38th Fd Co RE

Hour, Date, Place	Summary of Events and Information	Remarks and references to Appendices
ARMENTIERES 16-2-15	Company employed in making hurdles, dugouts footboards & pumps. One party loopholing farms & making machine gun emplacements at HOUPLINES. A party making approaches for pontoon bridge. At night a party making machine gun emplacements in second line. Civilians cutting & carting brushwood making hurdles & fascines. At night digging breastworks in second line	H McAnnaym
ARMENTIERES 17-2-15	Company employed in making hurdles, dugouts footboards & pumps. One party loopholing farms at HOUPLINES. Civilians cutting & carting brushwood & making hurdles & fascines. At night digging breastworks in second line. One civilian killed. Capt Noble reported for duty with 12th (Field) Company RE	H McAnnaym
ARMENTIERES 18-2-15	Company employed making hurdles dugouts footboards & pumps & defending houses in HOUPLINES. At night one section erecting a parados in trenches of 18th I.B.	

(9 29 6) W 3332—1107 100,000 10/13 H W V Forms/C. 2118/10

Instructions regarding War Diaries and Intelligence Summaries are contained in F. S. Regs., Part II. and the Staff Manual respectively. Title pages will be prepared in manuscript.

WAR DIARY
or
~~INTELLIGENCE SUMMARY.~~
(Erase heading not required.)

Army Form C. 2118.

31st Fd Co RE

Hour, Date, Place	Summary of Events and Information	Remarks and references to Appendices
ARMENTIERES 18-2-15 (Continued)	Civilians cutting & carting brushwood & making hurdles & fascines, at night digging breastworks in retired line 1st Company of Canadian Engineers were attached to this unit for instruction Parties were employed in workshops & on brushwood work during day At night one party erected a breastwork in retired line & a party worked in trenches erecting a parados	H M Bray Major
ARMENTIERES 19-2-15	Company employed in making hurdles, dugouts footboards & pumps a party at night supervising work in 17th I B trenches Civilians as on 18-2-15 Canadian Engineers were employed in workshops & making brushwood & practising pontooning also making machine gun emplacements in houses in CHAPELLE D'ARMENTIERES. At night continuing breastwork in second line & working in trenches of 17th I B.	H M Bray Major

(9 29 6) W 3332—1107 100,000 10/13 H W V Forms/C. 2118/10.

Instructions regarding War Diaries and Intelligence Summaries are contained in F. S. Regs., Part II. and the Staff Manual respectively. Title pages will be prepared in manuscript.

WAR DIARY
or
INTELLIGENCE ~~SUMMARY.~~
(*Erase heading not required.*)

Army Form C. 2118.

38th Fd Co. RE

Hour, Date, Place	Summary of Events and Information	Remarks and references to Appendices
ARMENTIERES 20-2-15.	Company employed in making hurdles, dugouts, footboards & pumps & machine making gun emplacement for 9.2". At night one party supervising Infantry in 17th I.B. trenches & one section erecting parados in trenches of 18th I.B. Civilians cutting & carting brushwood & making hurdles & fascines. At night digging breastwork in retired line. Canadian Engineers during day in workshops and making brushwood revetments & practising pontooning at night erecting barbed wire in retired line. demolishing a house in connection with this line & a party working in trenches of both 17th I.B. & 18th I.B.	[illegible]
ARMENTIERES 21-2-15	Company by day employed as above in morning no work in afternoon. Bathed in Div. Bathing Establishment. Civilians as above. Canadians practising pontooning. 2nd Lt J.D. Inglis joined for duty with unit.	[illegible] Major

(9 29 6) W3332-1107 100,000 10/13 H W V Forms/C. 2118/10.

Instructions regarding War Diaries and Intelligence Summaries are contained in F. S. Regs., Part II. and the Staff Manual respectively. Title pages will be prepared in manuscript.

WAR DIARY
or
~~INTELLIGENCE SUMMARY.~~
(*Erase heading not required.*)

Army Form C. 2118.

38th Fd Co RE

Hour, Date, Place	Summary of Events and Information	Remarks and references to Appendices
ARMENTIERES 22-2-15	Company employed in making hurdles, dugouts, footboards pumps & concrete gun platform Improving approaches for proposed pontoon bridge making two footbridges over stream at HOUPLINES at night one section working in trenches of 17th I.B. Civilians cutting & carting brushwood & making hurdles & fascines – at night digging breastworks on retired line Canadian Engineers working in workshops, a party loopholing houses & erecting barbed wire entanglement at HOUPLINES one party practised pontooning	H.M. Morgan
ARMENTIERES 23-2-15	Company employed in making hurdles, dugouts, footboards pumps & concrete gun platform & approaches to proposed pontoon bridge at night one section making infantry bridge in front of BUTERNE FARM Civilians as above No3 Con Fld Company Canadian Engineers attached to the unit for instruction	H.M. Morgan
ARMENTIERES 24-2-15	Company employed in making hurdles, dugouts, footboards & pumps – concrete gun platform & approaches for proposed pontoon bridge at night erecting parados in 18th I.B. trenches Civilians as above	

Instructions regarding War Diaries and Intelligence Summaries are contained in F. S. Regs., Part II. and the Staff Manual respectively. Title pages will be prepared in manuscript.

WAR DIARY

or

INTELLIGENCE SUMMARY.

(*Erase heading not required.*)

Army Form C. 2118.

38th Fd Co RE

Hour, Date, Place	Summary of Events and Information	Remarks and references to Appendices
24-2-15 (cont'd)	Canadian Engineers Employed in workshops & making brushwood revetment material At night one section erecting breastwork for 1st London Fd Co At night erecting parados for 12th (Nelo) Co.	[illegible] Major
ARMENTIERES 25-2-15	Company employed in making hurdles, dugouts, footboards & pumps & concrete gun emplacement, erecting trestle in proposed pontoon bridge & making approaches At night preparing machine gun emplacement in 18th I.B trenches Galleries for mines started in trenches of QUEENS WESTMINSTERS Civilians as on 24-2-15 Canadian Engineers employed in workshops & making brushwood revetting materials At night two sections erecting breastworks behind 16th I.B & 17th I.B trenches	[illegible] Major
ARMENTIERES 26-2-15	Company employed as on 25-2-15 Civilians employed as on 25-2-15 Canadian Engineers employed in workshops & making brushwood revetting material - and loopholing houses & making machine	

Instructions regarding War Diaries and Intelligence Summaries are contained in F. S. Regs., Part II. and the Staff Manual respectively. Title pages will be prepared in manuscript.

WAR DIARY
or
INTELLIGENCE SUMMARY.
(*Erase heading not required.*)

Army Form C. 2118.

38th Fd Co RE

Hour, Date, Place	Summary of Events and Information	Remarks and references to Appendices
ARMENTIERES 26-2-15 (contd)	gun emplacements in CHAPELLE D'ARMENTIERES	FMB major
ARMENTIERES 27-2-15	Company employed in making hurdles, screens, footboards, pumps, bombs, concrete gun platform & approaches to pontoon bridge. Mine in trenches of E WORKS commenced. Communicating trenches between breastworks marked for & dug by Infantry at night. Civilians cutting & carting brushwood & making hurdles & fascines. At night making parados to breastworks in second line. Canadian Engineers employed in workshops & making brushwood revetting materials. Loopholing houses on second line. One party practising pontooning. At night two sections erecting wire entanglements on second line behind 17th IB & 16th IB	FMB major
ARMENTIERES 28-2-15	Company paraded for church & did not work. One officer & two NCOs to trenches in connection with mines. Canadian Engineers practised pontooning.	FMB major

F.M. Browne major
OC 5[illegible] (Field) Co RE

(9 29 6) W 3332—1107 100,000 10/13 H W V Forms/C. 2118/10.

6th Division

121/48/4

Confidential

War Diary of

38th (Field) Company Royal Engineers

from 1st March 1915 to 31st March 1915

Volume VIII

Moved to 28th Div 7.4.15.

AG7

DJH

Instructions regarding War Diaries and Intelligence Summaries are contained in F. S. Regs., Part II. and the Staff Manual respectively. Title pages will be prepared in manuscript.

Army Form C. 2118.

WAR DIARY

or

~~INTELLIGENCE SUMMARY.~~

(*Erase heading not required.*)

Hour, Date, Place	Summary of Events and Information	Remarks and references to Appendices
ARMENTIERES 1-3-15	Company employed in making hurdles, fascines, footboards, skew loopholes, miners hammers, bellows & mining frames, pumps, canvas screens, miners candlesticks & bombs a party making approaches to 9.2" emplacements in ARMENTIERES & ERQUINGHEM a party making approaches to proposed pontoon bridges at night one section working in trenches of 17th I. B Civilians cutting & carting brushwood & making hurdles & fascines at night erecting parados to breastworks in second line Canadian Engineers making hurdles screens etc & working in workshops a party practising pontooning at night one party erecting wire entanglements in front of HOUPLINES.	[illegible]
ARMENTIERES 2-3-15	Company employed as above Civilians employed as above Canadian Engineers in the morning a party employed in the workshops in afternoon the unit left the area	[illegible]

(9 29 6) W 3332-1107 100,000 10/13 H W V Forms/C. 2118/10.

Army Form C. 2118.

Instructions regarding War Diaries and Intelligence Summaries are contained in F. S. Regs., Part II. and the Staff Manual respectively. Title pages will be prepared in manuscript.

WAR DIARY
or
~~INTELLIGENCE SUMMARY.~~

(Erase heading not required.)

Hour, Date, Place	Summary of Events and Information	Remarks and references to Appendices
ARMENTIERES 3-3-15	Company employed in making hurdles, screens, footboards, pumps, bombs, mining frames & hammers approaches to 9.2" gun emplacements & pontoon bridges at night one section employed in trenches of 17th IB Civilians cutting & carting brushwood & making hurdles & fascines at night erecting parados to breastworks in second line	HMB Major
ARMENTIERES 4-3-15	Company employed as on 3-3-15 One section also to WESTMINSTER trenches to erect protection mining instruments etc Civilians as on 3-3-15	HMB Major
ARMENTIERES 5-3-15	Company employed in making hurdles, screens, footboards pumps bombs mining frames approaches to pontoon bridges & 9.2" emplacement at night one section to 17th IB trenches. Civilians cutting & carting brushwood & making hurdles & fascines at night thickening parapets & repairing breastworks in 2nd line (two civilians wounded)	HMB Major
ARMENTIERES 6-3-15	Company employed as on 5-3-15 Civilians employed as on 5-3-15	HMB Major

(9 29 6) W 3332—1107 100,000 10/13 H W V Forms/C. 2118/10.

Instructions regarding War Diaries and Intelligence Summaries are contained in F. S. Regs., Part II. and the Staff Manual respectively. Title pages will be prepared in manuscript.

WAR DIARY
or
INTELLIGENCE ~~SUMMARY.~~
(Erase heading not required.)

Army Form C. 2118.

Hour, Date, Place	Summary of Events and Information	Remarks and references to Appendices
ARMENTIERES 7-3-15	Company employed in making hurdles, fascines, mining frames & cases. No work in afternoon. Civilians cutting & carting brushwood & making hurdles & fascines	[signature] Major
ARMENTIERES 8-3-15	Company employed in making hurdles, fascines, mining cases, footboards for screens, pumps, approaches to pontoon bridges & 9.2" emplacement. At night one section working in 17th I.B. trenches. Civilians cutting & carting brushwood & making hurdles fascines. At night thickening parapets of breastworks in second line	[signature] Major
ARMENTIERES 9-3-15	Company employed as on 8-3-15. Civilians employed as on 8-3-15	[signature] Major
ARMENTIERES 10-3-15	Company employed as above & laying concrete to 9.2" emplacement at ERQUINGHEM & starting one at L'ARMEE. At night one section in trenches of 17th I.B. Civilians cutting & carting brushwood & making hurdles & fascines. Civilians confined to their houses at night & no work was done	[signature] Major

(9 29 6) W 3332–1107 100,000 10/13 H W V Forms/C. 2118/10.

Instructions regarding War Diaries and Intelligence Summaries are contained in F. S. Regs., Part II. and the Staff Manual respectively. Title pages will be prepared in manuscript.

WAR DIARY
or
~~INTELLIGENCE~~ SUMMARY.
(Erase heading not required.)

Army Form C. 2118.

Hour, Date, Place	Summary of Events and Information	Remarks and references to Appendices
ARMENTIERES 11-3-15	Company employed in making hurdles, fascines, screens, pattern pumps & mining cases. Finishing approaches to pontoon bridge. Concreting finished of 9.2" emplacement at ERQUINGHEM preparing foundations of 9.2" emplacement at L'ARMEE Levelling site for 15" emplacement at ARMENTIERES at night one section supervising in trenches of 17th I.B. nine sappers to WESTMINSTER Trenches to supervise mining operations Civilians cutting & carting brushwood & making hurdles & fascines. No work after 2 pm	[illegible] Major
ARMENTIERES 12-3-15	Company employed in making hurdles, fascines, screens, footboards - chevaux de frises, ladders & mining cases. continuing 9.2" emplacement at L'ARMEE & 15" at ARMENTIERES at night one party to trenches of 17th I.B. one sapper badly wounded. Civilians cutting & carting brushwood & making hurdles & fascines. At night improving communications & parapets of breastworks in second line	[illegible] Major
ARMENTIERES 13-3-15	Company employed in making hurdles, fascines, screens footboards - chevaux-de-frises. Ladders & mining cases. Concreting completed in 9.2" emplacement at ~~L'ARMEE~~ ERQUINGHEM.	

(9 29 6) W 3332—1107 100,000 10/13 H W V Forms/C. 2118/10.

Instructions regarding War Diaries and Intelligence Summaries are contained in F. S. Regs., Part II. and the Staff Manual respectively. Title pages will be prepared in manuscript.

WAR DIARY
or
INTELLIGENCE ~~SUMMARY.~~
(*Erase heading not required.*)

Army Form C. 2118.

Hour, Date, Place	Summary of Events and Information	Remarks and references to Appendices
13-3-15 (continued)	9.2" emplacement at L'ARMEE in progress 9.2" emplacement at ARMENTIERES commenced work stopped on 15" emplacement in ARMENTIERES at night one section to 17th I.B. mashes Civilians cutting & carting brushwood & making hurdles & fascines. At night revetting communication trenches & thickening parapets on breastwork line	[illegible] Major
ARMENTIERES 14-3-15	Sunday as on 13-3-15 in morning no work in afternoon	[illegible] Major
ARMENTIERES 15-3-15	Company received orders to be prepared to move billets loaded pontoons & made pumps & mining frames & bombs finished 9.2" emplacement at ERQUINGHEM finished concreting 9.2" " at L'ARMEE continued 9.2" emplacement in ARMENTIERES civilians paid off	[illegible] Major
ARMENTIERES 16-3-15	Company employed in making hurdles & fascines pumps & mining cases. one party loopholing houses in HOUPLINES continuing 9.2" emplacements at L'ARMEE & ARMENTIERES no civilians working orders for change of billet cancelled	[illegible] Major

Instructions regarding War Diaries and Intelligence Summaries are contained in F. S. Regs., Part II. and the Staff Manual respectively. Title pages will be prepared in manuscript.

WAR DIARY

or

~~INTELLIGENCE SUMMARY.~~

(*Erase heading not required.*)

Army Form C. 2118.

Hour, Date, Place	Summary of Events and Information	Remarks and references to Appendices
ARMENTIERES 17-3-15	Company employed in making hurdles, fascines, chevaux-de-frises, ladders & pumps Pontoons were unloaded & rafts formed. 9.2" emplacement at L'ARMEE completed. ~~ditto ditto~~ ARMENTIERES foundation completed. 15" emplacement at HOUPLINES commenced. Civilians cutting & carting brushwood at night revetting parapets of communication trenches in Breastwork line	[illegible]
ARMENTIERES 18-3-15	Company employed in making hurdles, chevaux de frises, ladders, pumps & footboards. at night one section in trenches of 17 - 1B one party making footbridge in front of HOUPLINES one section erecting revetting material in communication trench to WESTMINSTER trench. continuing work on 9.2" & 15" emplacements at ARMENTIERES & HOUPLINES. Civilians as on 17-3-15	[illegible]

Instructions regarding War Diaries and Intelligence Summaries are contained in F. S. Regs., Part II. and the Staff Manual respectively. Title pages will be prepared in manuscript.

WAR DIARY
or
~~INTELLIGENCE SUMMARY.~~
(*Erase heading not required.*)

Army Form C. 2118.

Hour, Date, Place	Summary of Events and Information	Remarks and references to Appendices
ARMENTIERES 19-3-15	Company employed in making hurdles, chevaux de frise pumps & footboards. Concreting finished in 9.2" emplacement ARMENTIERES Excavation finished for 15" emplacement HOUPLINES At night one section to 17–18 trenches one section erecting revetting material in communication trench to WESTMINSTERS Civilians cutting & carting brushwood & making hurdles & fascines at night improving approach trenches & breastworks in breastwork line.	[illegible]
ARMENTIERES 20-3-15	Company employed in making hurdles, pumps chevaux-de-frises footboards & dugouts One party loopholing farms at HOUPLINES making iron shod pickets for 15" emplacement at HOUPLINES At night one section to 17–18 trenches one section erecting barbed wire at HOUPLINES one party making blindage in communication trench Civilians cutting & carting brushwood & making hurdles & fascines at night digging & repairing parapets & communications in breastwork line	[illegible]

Instructions regarding War Diaries and Intelligence Summaries are contained in F. S. Regs., Part II. and the Staff Manual respectively. Title pages will be prepared in manuscript.

WAR DIARY

or

INTELLIGENCE ~~SUMMARY.~~

(Erase heading not required.)

Army Form C. 2118.

Hour, Date, Place	Summary of Events and Information	Remarks and references to Appendices
ARMENTIERES 21-3-15	Sunday Company bathed in Divisional Bath House: no work done	H M B Major
ARMENTIERES 22-3-15	Company employed in making hurdles, pumps, dugouts & splinter proof doors for dugouts. One party preparing PONT DE NIEPPE for demolition one party preparing HOUPLINES sluice bridge for demolition 9.2" emplacement ARMENTIERES completed 15" emplacement HOUPLINES completed at night one section to 17th I.B. trenches & one party overhauling pumps at PONT BALLOT	H M B Major
	Civilians cutting & carting brushwood & making hurdles & fascines at night digging trenches at HOUPLINES & on breastwork line	H M B Major
ARMENTIERES 23-3-15	Company employed in making hurdles - chevaux de frise - doors for dugouts & pumps at night one section to 17th I.B. trenches one party erecting bridge in communication trench W PONT BALLOT Civilians as on 24-3-15 Very wet night & little work done	H M B Major

(9 29 6) W3332-1107 100,000 10/13 H W V Forms/C. 2118/10.

Instructions regarding War Diaries and Intelligence Summaries are contained in F. S. Regs., Part II. and the Staff Manual respectively. Title pages will be prepared in manuscript.

WAR DIARY
or
~~INTELLIGENCE SUMMARY.~~
(Erase heading not required.)

Army Form C. 2118.

Hour, Date, Place	Summary of Events and Information	Remarks and references to Appendices
ARMENTIERES 24-3-15	Company employed in making hurdles, dugouts splinter proof doors for dugouts, footboards & pumps preparing bridges for demolition at NIEPPE & HOUPLINES. at night one section to 17-18 trenches one section laying water supply in WESTMINSTER trenches Civilians cutting & carting brushwood & making hurdles & fascines at night digging trenches in breastwork line	HMM major
ARMENTIERES 25-3-15	Company employed as on 24th Civilians employed as on 24th	HMM major
ARMENTIERES 26-3-15	Company employed in making hurdles, dugouts pumps & footboards making holes in piers of NIEPPE & HOUPLINES bridges 9.2" emplacement commenced at GRISPOT but orders received to stop work two 9.2" emplacements commenced at LA TOULETTE at night one section to 17-18 trenches at night one section completing water supply to WESTMINSTERS Civilians cutting & carting brushwood & making hurdles & fascines at night digging trenches at HOUPLINES	HMM major

(9 29 6) W 3332-1107 100,000 10/13 H W V Forms/C. 2118/10.

Instructions regarding War Diaries and Intelligence Summaries are contained in F. S. Regs., Part II. and the Staff Manual respectively. Title pages will be prepared in manuscript.

WAR DIARY
or
~~INTELLIGENCE~~ SUMMARY.

(*Erase heading not required.*)

Army Form C. 2118.

Hour, Date, Place	Summary of Events and Information	Remarks and references to Appendices
ARMENTIERES 27-3-15	<u>Company</u> employed as on 26th. orders received to continue emplacements at GRISPOT <u>Civilians</u> as on 26-3-15	FMB major
ARMENTIERES 28-3-15	<u>Sunday</u> company attended Divine service. No work except on 9·2" emplacements at GRISPOT & LATOULETTE no civilians employed	FMB major
ARMENTIERES 29-3-15	<u>Company</u> employed in making hurdles dugouts, footboards & holes in piers of NIEPPE & HOUPLINES bridges. Continued work on 9·2" emplacements at LATOULETTE and HOUPLINES at night one section to 7th IB trenches <u>Civilians</u> cutting & carting brushwood & making hurdles & fascines at night digging on second line	FMB
ARMENTIERES 30-3-15	<u>Company</u> employed as on 29-3-15 <u>Civilians</u> employed as on 29-3-15	FMB
ARMENTIERES 31-3-15	<u>Company</u> employed in making hurdles, dugouts, footboards & pumps. holes in piers of NIEPPE bridge HOUPLINES bridge completed. loopholing houses at HOUPLINES 9·2" emplacements at GRISPOT & LATOULETTE completed at night one section to 7th IB trenches <u>Civilians</u> cutting & carting brushwood & making hurdles & fascines no work at night	FMB

F M B [illegible] major
OC 38 (Field) Coy

2ND DIVISION

GENERAL STAFF

SEP - OCT 1915

6th Division
Divl Engineers

459

459 Field Co RE

Formerly 2/2nd W.R. Fld Coy. RE.

Oct 1915 ~~to~~ Dec 1916

Vol II.

CONFIDENTIAL

WAR DIARY

OF

2/2 W. R. FIELD Co R.E.

FROM October 8 - 1915 TO October 31 - 1915.

Vol I

2/2ND. FIELD CO. No. W.R. DIV. R.E.

Instructions regarding War Diaries and Intelligence Summaries are contained in F. S. Regs., Part II. and the Staff Manual respectively. Title Pages will be prepared in manuscript.

WAR DIARY
or
~~INTELLIGENCE SUMMARY~~
(Erase heading not required.)

Army Form C. 2118

Place	Date 1915	Hour	Summary of Events and Information	Remarks and references to Appendices
YORK	October 8.		Instructions received for to proceed & entrain for overseas on 1st inst.	
"	" 9.	6. 0 AM	Coy. entrained York for overseas. Detrained Southampton 3·15 p.m. Dockside. Embarked for overseas	
SOUTHAMPTON	" 9.	4. 30 PM	Southampton 4·30 p.m. H.M.T. E6021 "NORTH WESTERN MILLER" (SS)	
LA HAVRE	" 10.	9. 0 AM	Disembarked La Havre & Coy proceeded by march route to No. Large Rest Camp. La Havre	
"	" 11.	10. 0 PM	Coy. entrained at La Havre.	
GODEWAERSVELDE	" 12.	9. 0 PM	Coy. detrained Godewaersvelde (France-Belgian Frontier Station) Coy bivouacked for the remainder of night.	
VLAMERTINGHE	" 13.	8. 0 AM	Coy proceeded by march route via Abeele. Poperinghe to Vlamertinghe (Ypres) joining the 6th DIVISION	
H8 a 5·9. SH. 28 N.W.	" 13.		Coy. inspected by C.R.E. 6th Division. Sections 1 & 2 proceeded to advanced billet Brielen. Ypres	
& YPRES.	" 14.		Sections 1 & 2 employed on St. Jean Tramway & Trench Reclamation in St. Jean - Potijze Sector	
"	" 14.		Sections 3 & 4 employed in Hutting in 6th Divisional Area. SHEET 28 N.W. A.30.	
"	" 15.		Coy. took over from 12th Field Co. R.E. the work in Sector of line in St. Jean - Garden St. Potijze - Bond St. Sector.	
"	" 16.		Sections 1 & 2 reclamation work in Garden St. Bond St. Front Line A7. A8. Section 3 & 4 Hutting A30. 28 N.W.	
"	" 17.		Work as for 16th carried-on work also commenced on Defences of Reigersburg Sool.	
"	" 18.		Work as for 17th carried-on also work on Drainage of Front line Boeschwardbeek.	
"	" 19.		Advanced Billet removed to Petrol Store Kaaie Ypres. work as for 18th carried-on	
"	" 20.		Work as for 19th carried-on	
"	" 21		Work as for 20th carried-on	
"	" 22		Work as for 21st carried-on	
"	" 23		Work as for 22nd carried-on.	
"	" 24		Work as for 23rd carried-on.	
"	" 25		Work as for 24th carried-on	
"	" 26		Work as for 25th carried on.	
"	" 27		Work as for 26th carried-on 1st Casualty to Coy occurs. 1 Other Ranks Died of wounds received during day.	
"	" 28		Sections 1 & 2 relieved by Sections 3 & 4 No work in line	
"	" 29		Sections 3 & 4 at advanced billet carrying on with work as for 27th also constructing Dug-outs W. Bank Yser Canal.	
"	" 30		Work as for 29th carried on also work commenced in X Line Trench between St. Jean Barrier & Potijze.	
"	" 31.		Work as for 30th carried on 2nd Casualties to Coy occur 1 Other Ranks Died of Wounds sustained during day 1 Other Rank wounded.	

[signature] Major
O. C. 2/2 nd. W.R. Div. Field Co.
Royal Engineers. (T. F.)

1875 Wt. W593/826 1,000,000 4/15 J.B.C. & A. A.D.S.S./Forms/C. 2118.

Vol 2

CONFIDENTIAL

WAR - DIARY

OF

2/2 N.R. FIELD Co. R.E. (T)

FROM. November 1st 1915 TO November 30 1915

Vol II

2/2ND FIELD CO.
No.
[illegible] HDG. DIV.

Instructions regarding War Diaries and Intelligence Summaries are contained in F. S. Regs., Part II. and the Staff Manual respectively. Title Pages will be prepared in manuscript.

WAR DIARY
or
~~INTELLIGENCE SUMMARY~~
(Erase heading not required.)

Army Form C. 2118

Place	Date 1915	Hour	Summary of Events and Information	Remarks and references to Appendices
VLAMERTINGHE	NOVEMBER 1st		Sections 1 & 2 erecting hutments in Camp in Wood A30. SHEET 28. N.W. Sections 3 & 4 engaged in Trench Reclamation	
H8. a5.9. 28 N.W.	" 1		in Sector of Front Line A6. A7. A8. BOND ST. GARDEN ST. & constructing new 'X' LINE.	
& YPRES.	" 2.		Work as for the 1st carried on	
	" 3.		Work as for the 2nd carried on	
	" 4.		Work as for the 3rd carried on also Section 3 & 4 repairing Trench Tramway ST JEAN - WIELTJE RD	
	" 5.		Work as for the 4th carried on	
	" 6.		Sections 3 & 4 relieved in line & advanced billet by Section 1 & 2.	
	" 7.		Work as for the 5th carried on	
	" 8.		Work as for the 7th carried on	
	" 9.		Work as for the 8th carried on	
	" 10.		Work as for the 9th carried on	
	" 11.		Work as for the 10th carried on	
	12.		Work as for the 11th carried on	
	" 13.		Work as for the 12th carried on	
	14.	"	Work as for the 13th carried on	
	" 15.		Sections 3 & 4 relieved & returned to Reserve Billet.	
	" 16.		Work in Line handed over to 62nd FIELD Co. R.E. 14th DIVN. Company goes into rest with 6th DIVN.	
	" 16.		Instructions received for 1 Section to proceed to GODEWAERSVELDE to entrain for CALAIS for duty & work then	
	" 17.		Company along with DIVN on REST. Order for Section to proceed to Calais cancelled. Section returns to	
	" 17.	"	Reserve Billet.	
	" 18.		Sections 1. 2 3. 4. engaged in constructing Hutments in Camp in A30. SHEET 28. N.W.	
	" 18.		6 officers 25 N.C.O's of Infantry of 18th Infantry Brigade attached to Coy for course of Military Engineering	
	" 18.	"	instruction.	
	" 19.		Work and course carried on the same as for the 18th inst.	
	" 20.		Work and course carried on the same as for the 19th inst.	
	" 21.		Work and course carried on the same as for the 20th inst.	
	" 22.		Work and course carried on the same as for the 21st inst.	
	" 23.		Work and course carried on the same as for the 22nd inst.	
	" 24.		Work and course carried on the same as for the 23rd inst.	

1875 Wt. W593/826 1,000,000 4/15 J.B.C. & A. A.D.S.S./Forms/C. 2118.

Instructions regarding War Diaries and Intelligence Summaries are contained in F. S. Regs., Part II. and the Staff Manual respectively. Title Pages will be prepared in manuscript.

WAR DIARY
or
~~INTELLIGENCE SUMMARY~~
(Erase heading not required.)

Army Form C. 2118

Place	Date 1915	Hour	Summary of Events and Information	Remarks and references to Appendices
VLAMERTINGHE	Nov. 25.		Work & courses of instruction carried on the same as for 24th inst.	
"	26.		Work & courses of instruction carried on the same as for 25th inst.	
"	27.		Work & courses of instruction carried on the same as for 26th inst.	
"	28.		Work & courses of instruction carried on the same as for 27th inst. Accident at Reserve Billet –	
"	28.		1 Other Ranks sustaining injuries from which he subsequently died.	
"	29.		Work & courses of instruction carried on the same as for 28th inst.	
	30.		Work & courses of instruction carried on the same as for 29th inst.	

R.L. Howard
Major
O. C. 2/2 nd. W.R. Div. Field Co.
Royal Engineers. (T. F.)

1875 Wt. W593/826 1,000,000 4/15 J.B.C. & A. A.D.S.S./Forms/C. 2118.

Vol 3

CONFIDENTIAL

WAR - DIARY

OF

2/2 W. R. FIELD Co. R.E.

FROM:- December 1st 1915 TO:- December 31st 1915

Vol III

Instructions regarding War Diaries and Intelligence Summaries are contained in F. S. Regs., Part II. and the Staff Manual respectively. Title Pages will be prepared in manuscript.

WAR DIARY
or
~~INTELLIGENCE SUMMARY~~

(Erase heading not required.)

Army Form C. 2118

Place	Date 1915	Hour	Summary of Events and Information	Remarks and references to Appendices
VLAMERTINGHE	DEC. 1.		Company on Divl. Rest. Sections 1. 2. 3 & 4 erecting Huts in Camp Wood A 30 Sh 28 N.W. & manufacturing Trench Stores & preparing material in Coy. Workshops & Saw-mill. 6 officers & 25 N.C.O's of infantry of 16th INF. BDE. attached for course of instruction in military & Field Engineering.	
H.Q. a 5.9. Sh 28 N.W. YPRES.				
	2.		Work as for the 1st inst. carried on & including courses of instruction.	
	3.		Work as for the 2nd inst. carried on & including courses of instruction etc. Very inclement weather.	
	4.		Work as for the 3rd inst. carried on & including courses of instruction etc. Very inclement weather.	
	5.		Work as for the 4th inst. carried on & including courses of instruction etc. Very inclement weather.	
	6.		Work as for the 5th inst. carried on & including courses of instruction etc.	
	7.		Work as for the 6th inst. carried on & including courses of instruction etc.	
	8.		Work as for the 7th inst. carried on & including courses of instruction etc.	
	9.		Work as for the 8th inst. carried on & including courses of instruction etc.	
	10.		Work as for the 9th inst. carried on & including courses of instruction etc.	
	11.		Work as for the 10th inst. carried on & including courses of instruction etc. Orders received to relieve 62nd Field Co. R.E. on 15th inst.	
	12		Work as for the 11th carried on including courses of instruction etc.	
	13.		Work as for the 12th carried on including courses of instruction. Preparing equipment for resumption in the Line.	
	14.		All work & duties as for the 13th inst. carried on.	
	15.		Sections 1 & 2 relieved 62nd Field Co. R.E. in advanced billet at Petrol Store Near YPRES & took over work in Section of line LIVERPOOL ST. LA BRIQUE – 89. POTIJZE (inclusive). End of Divl. Rest from line.	
	16.		Sections 1 & 2 engaged in Reclaiming work in GARDEN ST & CONGREVE WALK & constructing dug-outs E. BANK of YSER-CANAL. Sections 3 & 4 erecting Huts in Divl. area & manufacturing trench stores & material at Coy. Idyll's Workshops & Sawmill.	
	17.		All work carried on the same as previous day 16th inst.	
	18.		All work carried on the same as previous day 17th inst.	
	19.		Severe hostile Gas attack opposite Trench 89. followed by intense bombardment of front & support lines, Canal Bank Main Roads & reserve billet area. Work in line suspended.	
	20.		Intense hostile bombardment continued. No work in line.	
	21.		Severe bombardment of Canal Bank & Support lines. No work in line.	
	22.		Sections 1 & 2 relieved by Sections 3 & 4 at advanced billet. No work in line.	

1875 Wt. W593/826 1,000,000 4/15 J.B.C. & A. A.D.S.S./Forms/C. 2118.

Instructions regarding War Diaries and Intelligence Summaries are contained in F. S. Regs., Part II. and the Staff Manual respectively. Title Pages will be prepared in manuscript.

WAR DIARY
or
~~INTELLIGENCE SUMMARY~~
(Erase heading not required.)

Army Form C. 2118

Place	Date	Hour	Summary of Events and Information	Remarks and references to Appendices
	1915			
VLAMERTINGHE	DEC. 23.		Sections 3 & 4 engaged in work reclaiming support & X Line & GARDEN ST which were destroyed by shell fire during the recent bombardments.	
	24.		All work carried on from 23rd inst. also repairing damaged wiring along whole front.	
	25.		All work carried on from 24th inst.	
	26.		Work commenced to restore Front Line at Junction A8 & B9. which were completely destroyed by shell fire.	
	27.		All work carried on from 26th inst.	
	28.		Work as for 27th inst. carried on	
	29.		Work as for 28th inst. carried on. Advanced Battalion Hdqtrs. Commenced in St. Jean.	
	30.		Work as for 29th inst. carried on also 6 Machine Gun Emplacements commenced in front & support line.	
	31.		Sections 1 & 2 relieved sections 3 & 4 in line & advanced billet.	

A. Howard
Major
O. C. 2/2nd. W.R. Div. Field Co.
Royal Engineers. (T. F.)

Vol 4

CONFIDENTIAL

WAR DIARY

OF

2/2 W.R. FIELD Co R.E. (T)

FROM :- January 1st 1916 TO January 31st 1916

Vol IV

212ND. FIELD CO. No. R.E.

Instructions regarding War Diaries and Intelligence Summaries are contained in F. S. Regs., Part II. and the Staff Manual respectively. Title Pages will be prepared in manuscript.

WAR DIARY
or
~~INTELLIGENCE SUMMARY~~
(Erase heading not required.)

Army Form C. 2118

Place	Date	Hour	Summary of Events and Information	Remarks and references to Appendices
	1916			
VLAMERTINGHE H.8.a.5.9. 28 N.W. YPRES.	JAN. 1.		Sections 1 & 2 at advanced billet engaged in work of Reclaiming-GARDEN ST & CONGREVE WALK & Repairing wire in Front line left of sector. Sections 3 & 4 erecting hutments in Devil Area & manufacturing Trench stores at Coy Workshops etc.	
	2.		Work as for 1st carried-on also advanced Battalion Hdqtrs. St Jean re-commenced	
	3.		Work as for 2nd carried-on Heavy bombardment about B10.	
	4.		Work as for 3rd carried-on also Dug-outs in Canal Bank commenced & re-built.	
	5.		Work as for 4th carried-on. Ammunition Dump at H.8.a.5.9 sh 28 N.W. commenced.	
	6.		Work as for 5th carried-on. All.	
	7.		Work as on 6th carried-on. excepting in the line. Sections 3 & 4 relieve Sections 1 & 2 in the line	
	8.		Sections 3 & 4 at advanced billet engaged in laying new wire entanglement between WIELTJE & R of B.11.	
	9.		All work the same as on the 8th inst continued	
	10.		All work the same as on the 9th inst continued including Trench Reclamation as above also making & re-building dug-outs in Front & Support lines.	
	11.		All work & duties as on the 10th inst continued.	
	12.		Work as on the 11th continued. Heavy shelling about sector B9 – B10.	
	13.		Work as on the 12th continued.	
	14.		Work as on the 13th continued. also 3 Machine Gun Emplacements made in X line	
	15.		Sections 1 & 2 relieve Sections 3 & 4 in the line 1 other-Ranks wounded	
	16.		Sections 1 & 2 at advanced billet and in line carry-on with work etc as on 14th Battalion advanced Hdqtrs. Completed	
	17.		All work carried on as for 16th also new Fire Trench commenced from GARDEN ST to ST JEAN-WIELTJE RD	
	18.		All work carried on as for 17th Severe shelling in district of sector B11 – B12	
	19.		Work as for 18th continued	
	20.		Work as for 19th continued	
	21.		Work as for 20th continued Bombardment severe about B9. sector.	
	22.		Sections 3 & 4 relieve Sections 1 & 2 in line	
	23.		Work carried-on. 1st Reinforcement Draft to the Coy arrived 25 Other ranks from 3rd Line Depot Stafford	
	24.		Work carried on. Dismounted portion of Draft proceeds to advanced billet 2 wounded on the way. Heavy Shelling.	

1875 Wt. W593/826 1,000,000 4/15 J.B.C. & A. A.D.S.S./Forms/C. 2118.

Army Form C. 2118

WAR DIARY
or
~~INTELLIGENCE SUMMARY~~
(Erase heading not required.)

Instructions regarding War Diaries and Intelligence Summaries are contained in F. S. Regs., Part II, and the Staff Manual respectively. Title Pages will be prepared in manuscript.

Place	Date	Hour	Summary of Events and Information	Remarks and references to Appendices
	1916			
VLAMERTINGE	JAN. 25.		Work carried on the same as for 24th inst.	
	26.		Work carried on the same as for 25th inst. also reclaiming "X" line North of St Jean	
	27		Work carried on the same as for 26th inst.	
	28		Work carried on the same as for 27th inst.	
	29		Sections 1 & 2 relieve Sections 3 & 4 in the line & advanced billet	
	30		Work carried on in the line by Sections 1 & 2 the same as on 28th inst.	
	31		Work carried on the same as for 30th	

R. A. Howard
Major
O. C. 2/2 nd. W.R. Div. Field Co.
Royal Engineers. (T. F.)

1875 Wt. W593/826 1,000,000 4/15 J.B.C. & A. A.D.S.S./Forms/C. 2118.

Vol 5

CONFIDENTIAL

WAR DIARY

OF

2/2 W.R. FIELD Co R.E. (T)

FROM:- February 1st 1916 TO:- February 29th 1916

Vol V

212ND FIELD CO. No. 40TH DIV. R.E.

Instructions regarding War Diaries and Intelligence Summaries are contained in F. S. Regs., Part II. and the Staff Manual respectively. Title Pages will be prepared in manuscript.

WAR DIARY
or
~~INTELLIGENCE SUMMARY~~

(Erase heading not required.)

Army Form C. 2118

Place	Date 1916.	Hour	Summary of Events and Information	Remarks and references to Appendices
VLAMERTINGHE	FEB. 1.		Sections 1 & 2 at advanced billet & in line reclaiming X Line, N. of S. of [illegible] YPRES. New Fire [illegible] Garden St. [illegible] Sections 3 & 4 at Reserve Billet making Trench Stores & preparing material.	
H.Q. & S.9. [illegible]				
& YPRES.	2.		Work carried on as on the 1st inst. also repairing wire on front of 89. 810.	
	3.		Work carried on as for the 2nd inst.	
	4.		Work carried on as for the 3rd inst.	
	5.		All work carried on the same as on 3 & 4th inst also Reclaiming Garden St. where damaged by shell fire.	
	6.		Sections 3 & 4 relieved Sections 1 & 2 at advanced billet, work in line	
	7.		Sections 3 & 4 at advanced billet reclaiming Garden St & X Line making Dug-out accomodation Canal-Bank & in Front & Support Lines. Sections 1 & 2 at Reserve Billet making Trench Stores & preparing material.	
	8.		All work going on on 7th inst carried on.	
	9.		Work as for 8th inst carried on. Advanced Billet heavily shelled. (district of)	
	10.		Work as for 9th inst. carried on.	
	11.		Work as on 10th inst. continued.	
	12.		Work as on 11th inst continued.	
	13.		Sections 1 & 2 relieved Sections 3 & 4, at advanced billet. no work in line.	
	14.		Sections 1 & 2 at advanced billet engaged in Reclamation work in George St. One Other Rank wounded.	
	15.		Sections carrying on all work as on 14th [illegible] 3 & 4 making Trench Stores etc.	
	16.		All work carried on same as for 15th	
	17.		All work carried on as for 16th also Reclaiming 312. where damaged by Shell-fire.	
	18.		All work carried on as for 17th inst. also Reclaiming of 10.a. where damaged by shell-fire.	
	19.		Work as for 18th continued	
	20.		Sections 3 & 4 relieved Sections 1 & 2. at advanced billet, no work in line, vicinity heavily shelled	
	20		1 Officer Lieut. J.J. Taylor evacuated sick.	
	21.		Sections 3 & 4 at advanced billet carrying on work as for 19th inst.	
			1 Officer Joined for duty from 3rd Line Depôt Sheffield 2/Lt. T. Emmott.	
	22		Work as for 21st inst carried on. vicinity of advanced billet heavily shelled.	
	23.		Work as for 22nd inst carried on.	
	24.		Work as for 23rd inst carried on. also reclaiming "Garden St" & "Drury Lane" trenches.	
	25.		Work as for 24th inst. carried on.	

1875 Wt. W593/826 1,000,000 4/15 J.B.C. & A. A.D.S.S./Forms/C. 2118.

Instructions regarding War Diaries and Intelligence Summaries are contained in F. S. Regs., Part II. and the Staff Manual respectively. Title Pages will be prepared in manuscript.

2/2ND. FIELD CO. No. W. R. DIV. R.E. (T.F.)

WAR DIARY
or
~~INTELLIGENCE SUMMARY~~
(Erase heading not required.)

Army Form C. 2118

Place	Date 1916.	Hour	Summary of Events and Information	Remarks and references to Appendices
VLAMERTINGHE	FEB. 26.		Work as for 25th continued.	
	27.		Sections 1 & 2 relieved Sections 3 & 4 at advanced billet	
	28.		Sections 1 & 2 at advanced billet carrying a with work of reclamation etc. Sections 3 & 4	
	29.		at Reserve billet making trench stores etc.	
	29.		Work as for 27th 28th continued.	

R C Howard
Major
O. C. 2/2 nd. W.R. Div. Field Co.
Royal Engineers. (T. F.)

1875 Wt. W593/826 1,000,000 4/15 J.B.C. & A. A.D.S.S./Forms/C. 2118.

Vol 6

CONFIDENTIAL

WAR DIARY

OF

2/2 W. R. FIELD Co R.E. (?)

FROM:- March 1st 1916 TO:- March 31st 1916

Vol VI

Instructions regarding War Diaries and Intelligence Summaries are contained in F. S. Regs., Part II. and the Staff Manual respectively. Title Pages will be prepared in manuscript.

2/2ND FIELD CO. WEST RIDG. DIV. R.E.

WAR DIARY
or
~~INTELLIGENCE SUMMARY~~
(Erase heading not required.)

Army Form C. 2118

Place	Date	Hour	Summary of Events and Information	Remarks and references to Appendices
	1916.			
VLAMERTINGHE	MARCH. 1		Sections 3 & 4 at advanced billet on work of reclaiming George St. Drury Lane & X. Lines completing through	
H.8.a.5.9.			communication in Congreve walk, wiring Congreve walk making dug-out accomodation Canal Bank	
& YPRES			Sections 1 & 2 manufacturing Trench Mortars at Coy. Workshops & Yard. Advanced billet heavily shelled.	
	2.		Work on 1st continued. Front line heavily shelled. 2 other-ranks killed 1 other-ranks wounded.	
	3.		Work carried on as for 2nd inst.	
	4.		Work carried on as for 3rd inst. heavy shelling of advanced billet etc.	
	5.		Work as for 4th continued also reclaiming 59a & communication trenches.	
	6.		Work as for 5th continued	
	7.		Advanced billet vicinity heavily shelled work carried on also reclaiming S Line & Gowers Farm & St. Jean - Wieltje - Rd	
	8.		All work as on 7th inst. continued.	
	9.		All work continued also wire repaired in front of 39. B12.	
	10.		Orders received (preliminary) to hand over billets & work to 76th Field Co R.E. work continued.	
	11.		All work continued as on 10th inst.	
	12.		Work as for the 11th inst. continued.	
	13.		Work as for the 12th inst. continued.	
	14.		Work as for the 13th inst. continued	
	15.		Work & Land. billets dump. Yard & workshops handed over to 76th Field Co R.E. Guards Divn.	
HOUTKERQUE	16.	11 a.m.	Divisional Rest Period commences. Coy. proceeds by march route to Houtkerque in billets for the night.	
NORD	17.	8.30 a.m.	Coy. proceeds by march route via Herzeele & Wormhoudt to Ledringhem nord. In billets.	
LEDRINGHEM	18		Coy. complete at Ledringhem engaged in General training & rest.	
NORD	19.		Coy. engaged in General Training	
	20		Coy. engaged in General Training	
	21.		Coy. engaged in General Training	
	22.		Coy. engaged in General Training	
	23.		Coy. engaged in General Training	
	24.		Coy. engaged in General Training	
	25.		Coy. engaged in General Training	

1875 Wt. W593/826 1,000,000 4/15 J.B.C. & A. A.D.S.S./Forms/C. 2118.

Instructions regarding War Diaries and Intelligence Summaries are contained in F. S. Regs., Part II. and the Staff Manual respectively. Title Pages will be prepared in manuscript.

212ND. FIELD CO. No. ——— W. RIDG. DIV. R.E. (T.F.)

WAR DIARY

or

~~INTELLIGENCE SUMMARY~~

(Erase heading not required.)

Army Form C. 2118

Place	Date 1916	Hour	Summary of Events and Information	Remarks and references to Appendices
LEDRINGHAM	MARCH 26		Coy engaged in General Training.	
HERZEELE	27		Coy. proceeded by march-route to Herzeele and to take up billets there	
	28		Coy. engaged in General Training.	
	29		Coy. engaged in General Training.	
	30		Coy. engaged in General Training.	
	31		Coy engaged in General Training.	

Major
O. C. 2/2nd. W.R. Div. Field Co.
Royal Engineers. (T. F.)

1875 Wt. W593/826 1,000,000 4/15 J.B.C. & A. A.D.S.S./Forms/C. 2118.

Vol 7

CONFIDENTIAL

WAR DIARY

OF

2/2 W.R. FIELD Co R.E. (T)

FROM:- April 1 1916 TO:- April 30th 1916

Vol VII

Instructions regarding War Diaries and Intelligence Summaries are contained in F. S. Regs., Part II. and the Staff Manual respectively. Title Pages will be prepared in manuscript.

2/2ND FIELD Co. No. WEST RIDG. DIV. R.E.

WAR DIARY
or
~~INTELLIGENCE SUMMARY~~
(Erase heading not required.)

Army Form C. 2118

Place	Date	Hour	Summary of Events and Information	Remarks and references to Appendices
	1916			
HERZEELE	April 1.		Coy. Engaged in General Training.	
NORD	2.		Coy. engaged in General Training.	
	3.		Coy. engaged in General Training.	
	4.		Coy. engaged in General Training.	
	5.		Coy. engaged in General Training orders received to entrain for Calais.	
CALAIS	6.		Coy. proceeded to Poperinghe by march route & entrained at Hopoutre sidings for Calais. Detrained Calais & proceeded from station per march-route to No. 6 Large Rest Camp. occupying tentage with 71st Infantry Brigade Group. Lieut. J. Taylor re-joined Coy (being discharged hospital)	
	7.		Coy. engaged in General Training & rest.	
	8.		Coy. engaged in General Training & rest.	
	9.		Coy. engaged in General Training & rest.	
	10.		Coy. engaged in General Training & rest. Coy inspected by G.O.C. 71st Infantry Brigade	
	11.		Coy. engaged in General Training & rest.	
	12.		Coy. engaged in General Training & rest. Movement orders received.	
ZUTKERQUE	13.		Coy. proceeds per march-route via Calais to Zutkerque [illegible] taking up billets for one night.	
BOLLEZEELE	14.		Coy. proceeds per march-route via Watten to Bollezeele (nord) taking up billets for the night.	
HOUTKERQUE	15.		Coy. proceeds per march-route via Wormhoudt. Herzeele to Houtkerque taking up billets.	
	16.		Coy. at Houtkerque in billets.	
ELVERDINGHE	17.		Coy. proceeds by march-route to Elverdinghe district. Taking over work, dump & billets of 83rd Field Co R.E. at Elverdinghe. taking over work in line from Reserve Field Co. 6th Division.	
AH. 61. C.				
& CANAL BANK	18.		Sections 1 & 2 at advanced billet left sector Canal Bank engaged in building & re-construction Dug-out accomodation Tramway completion repairing of Canal Bridges. Section 3 & 4 commenced	
	19		new Divisional Headqtrs hutting Scheme at Ste Sixte.	
	19.		All work carried on same as for 18th inst.	
	20.		All work carried on as for 19th inst. heavy shelling of front & support lines & Reserve billet areas	
	21.		All work carried on intense bombardment of Reserve billet areas.	
	22		Work continued as for 21st shelling of advanced & reserve billet areas	
	23		Work continued as for 22nd shelling of advanced & reserve billet areas.	

1875 Wt. W593/826 1,000,000 4/15 J.B.C. & A. A.D.S.S./Forms/C. 2118.

Instructions regarding War Diaries and Intelligence Summaries are contained in F. S. Regs., Part II. and the Staff Manual respectively. Title Pages will be prepared in manuscript.

2/2ND. FIELD CO. No. W.R. DIV. R.E. (T.F.)

WAR DIARY
or
~~INTELLIGENCE SUMMARY~~
(Erase heading not required.)

Army Form C. 2118

Place	Date 1916	Hour	Summary of Events and Information	Remarks and references to Appendices
ELVERDINGHE	APRIL 24		Most of work continued as for 23rd. Intense bombardment of reserve billet area 8 other ranks wounded	
(CANAL BANK.			& necessitating transport & horses, mules being transferred further back	
	25		Work in line of Liverpool St. to 316 inc. other work continued, reserve billet area shelled.	
			Coy. took over right sector from 1/1st. London Field Co. R.E.	
	26		All work carried on as for 25th. advanced & reserve billets heavily shelled	
	27		All work carried on as for 26th. Transport lines again transferred owing to continued shelling	
	28		Work carried on as for 27th inst. also reclaiming Threadneedle St. 313-314 315-316-S14 Trenches	
	29		Work carried on as for 28th new reserve billet commenced at Peselhoek	
	30		Sections 3 & 4 relieve sections 1 & 2 in the line (no work in line)	

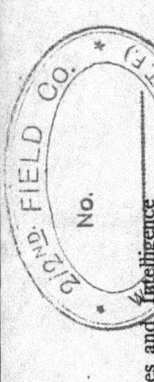

A C Howard
Major
O. C. 2/2nd. W.R. Div. Field Co.
Royal Engineers. (T. F.)

1875 Wt. W593/826 1,000,000 4/15 J.B.C. & A. A.D.S.S./Forms/C. 2118.

Vol 8

CONFIDENTIAL

WAR DIARY

OF

2/2 W.R. Field Co R.E. (T)

From:- May 1 1916 to:- May 31st 1916

Vol VIII

Instructions regarding War Diaries and Intelligence Summaries are contained in F. S. Regs., Part II. and the Staff Manual respectively. Title Pages will be prepared in manuscript.

WAR DIARY
or
~~INTELLIGENCE SUMMARY~~
(Erase heading not required.)

Army Form C. 2118

Place	Date 1916	Hour	Summary of Events and Information	Remarks and references to Appendices
ELVERDINGHE	MAY 1.		Sections 3 & 4 at advanced billet engaged in reclamation of Liverpool St. Skrodowelle St. &c.	
& CANAL BANK.			Sections 1 & 2 engaged in building new Divl. Hdqtrs. Camp. Ste. Sixte & new Reserve Billet	
	2		Work carried on as for 1st. Heavy shelling of front line & advanced billet area.	
	3		Work carried on as for 2nd. also work on B14 B15 & Bridges maintained	
	4.		Work carried on as for 3rd.	
	5.		Work carried on as for 4th. also work on B16 S14 & Bridges	
	6.		Work carried on as for 5th.	
PESELHOEK	7.		Work carried on as for 6th. Coy. moved to new camp at A15 b6.6. Peselhoek	
A15 b6.6.	8.		Coy. completing new camp other work continued as for 7th. Draft of 3 arrived.	
& CANAL BANK.	9.		Work as on 8th inst. continued 1 officer (Major A.C. Howard) wounded 1 other rank wounded.	
	10.		Work as for 9th continued also Machine Gun Emplacements Canal Bank made	
			1 other rank wounded. Heavy shelling & machine gun fire in front line	
	11.		Work as for 10th continued also work in front of B13 & B14 & Dug-out accomodation.	
	12.		Work as for 11th continued also Machine Gun Emplacements on Frascati Posts made	
			1 other rank wounded. Heavy shelling & machine gun fire in front line.	
	13.		Work continued as for 12th inst. Sections 1 & 2 relieve 3 & 4 in the line & at advanced-billet	
	14.		Work continued as for 13th inst. also Machine Gun Emplacements Frascati & Canal Bank.	
	15.		Work continued as for 14th inst.	
	16.		Work continued as for 15th inst.	
	17.		Work continued as for 16th inst. also work on B14. & B15.	
	18.		Work continued as for 17th inst.	
	19.		Work continued as for 18th inst.	
	20.		Work continued as for 19th inst.	
	21.		Work continued as for 20th inst.	
	22.		Work continued as for 21st inst. Major A.C. Howard rejoined Company discharged from Hospital	
	23.		Work continued as for 22nd inst.	
	24.		Work continued as for 23rd inst.	
	25.		Work continued as for 24th inst.	

1875 Wt. W593/826 1,000,000 4/15 J.B.C. & A. A.D.S.S./Forms/C. 2118.

Instructions regarding War Diaries and Intelligence Summaries are contained in F. S. Regs., Part II. and the Staff Manual respectively. Title Pages will be prepared in manuscript.

2/2ND. FIELD CO. * WEST RIDG. DIV. R.E. (T.F.) No.

WAR DIARY
or
~~INTELLIGENCE SUMMARY~~
(Erase heading not required.)

Army Form C. 2118

Place	Date 1916	Hour	Summary of Events and Information	Remarks and references to Appendices
PESELHOEK.	MAY 26		Work continued as for 25th inst.	
A15 L.L.L.	27		Work continued as for 26th inst. Sections 3 & 4 relieve Sections 1 & 2 at advanced billet.	
CANAL BANK.	28		Work continued as for 27th inst.	
	29		Work continued as for 28th inst.	
	30		Work continued as for 29th inst.	

Major
O. C. 2/2 nd. W.R. Div. Field Co.
Royal Engineers. (T. F.)

1875 Wt. W593/826 1,000,000 4/15 J.B.C. & A. A.D.S.S./Forms/C. 2118.

6

Vol 9

CONFIDENTIAL

WAR DIARY

OF

2/2 W.R. FIELD Co R.E. (T)

FROM:- June 1 1916 TO:- June 30 1916

Vol IX

212ND FIELD CO. No.

Instructions regarding War Diaries and Intelligence Summaries are contained in F. S. Regs., Part II. and the Staff Manual respectively. Title Pages will be prepared in manuscript.

WAR DIARY
or
~~INTELLIGENCE SUMMARY~~
(Erase heading not required.)

Army Form C. 2118

Place	Date 1916.	Hour	Summary of Events and Information	Remarks and references to Appendices
DESELHOEK.	June 1		Sections 3 + 4 in the line + at advanced billet engaged in reclamation work in X 9. X 10	
+ CANAL BANK.			S14. B13 Wilsons Farm Garden St Liverpool St. Threadneedle St. Canal Bank	
			Machine Gun Emplacements at Tower Post Hilltop Farm Threadneedle St + Canal Bank etc.	
			Section 1 + 2 at reserve billet making Trench Stores also erecting Huts at	
			Divl Camp Hdqtrs St Sixte almost completed.	
	2.		All work carried on as for 1st inst.	
	3.		All work carried on as for 2nd inst.	
	4.		All work carried on as for 3rd inst.	
	5.		All work carried on as for 4th inst.	
	6.		Work as for 5th continued	
	7.		Work as for 6th continued	
	8.		Work as for 7th continued	
	9.		Work as for 8th continued	
	10.		Sections 1st + 2nd relieve Sections 3 + 4 at advanced billet + work in the line.	
	11.		Work as for 9th continued by Sections 1 + 2 in the line + 3 + 4 at reserve billet making Trench Stores.	
	12.		Work as for 11th	
	13.		Work as for 12th	
	14.		Work as for 13th	
	15.		Work as for 14th	
BURGOMASTER	16.		Sections 1st + 2nd hand over work in line to 55th Field Co. R.E.	
FARM. BRIELEN			Sections 3 + 4 + Hdqtrs move to Burgomaster Farm Brielen. (Sections 1.2 from Canal Bank)	
+ WATOU. K12.	17.		Sections 1. 2. 3. 4. + Hdqtrs at Burgomaster Farm engaged in reclamation work of	
			Halifax Cg + "L" Line Defence Posts - Brielen + Reigersburg	
	18.		Work as for 17th inst. continued	
	19.		Work as for 18th inst. continued	
	20		Work as for 19th inst. continued	
	21		Work as for 20th inst. continued	
	22.		Work as for 21st inst. continued Transport. Hdqrs Section move to K 12 Camp + hand over	
			Deselhoek billet + Yard to 76th Field Co. R.E. Guards Divn.	

1875 Wt. W593/826 1,000,000 4/15 J.B.C. & A. A.D.S.S./Forms/C. 2118.

Instructions regarding War Diaries and Intelligence Summaries are contained in F. S. Regs., Part II. and the Staff Manual respectively. Title Pages will be prepared in manuscript.

WAR DIARY
or
INTELLIGENCE SUMMARY
(Erase heading not required.)

Army Form C. 2118

Place	Date 1916	Hour	Summary of Events and Information	Remarks and references to Appendices
BURGOMASTER FARM.	JUNE 23		Work carried on at Burgomaster Farm by Dismounted portion of Coy. Transport. Mounted Section at K12 Walou.	
	24		Work carried on as for 23rd	
	25		Work carried on as for 24th	
	26		Work carried on as for 25th	
	27		Work carried on as for 26th	
	28		Work carried on as for 27th	
	29		Work carried on as for 28th	
	30		Work carried on as for 29th	

R C Howard
Major
O. C. 2/2nd. W.R. Div. Field Co.
Royal Engineers. (T. F.)

1875 Wt. W593/826 1,000,000 4/15 J.B.C. & A. A.D.S.S./Forms/C. 2118.

CONFIDENTIAL

WAR DIARY

OF

2/2 W.R. FIELD Co. R.E. (T)

6th DIVISION

FROM July 1st 1916 TO July 31st 1916.

VOLUME X

Vol 10

212ND FIELD CO. No. WEST RIDING (T.F.) R.E.

Instructions regarding War Diaries and Intelligence Summaries are contained in F. S. Regs., Part II. and the Staff Manual respectively. Title Pages will be prepared in manuscript.

WAR DIARY
or
~~INTELLIGENCE SUMMARY~~
(Erase heading not required.)

Army Form C. 2118

Place	Date 1916	Hour	Summary of Events and Information	Remarks and references to Appendices
BELGIUM	JULY 1.		Headqtrs. & 4 Sections at BURGOMASTER FARM Engaged in reclamation of HALIFAX RD. –	
SHEET 28. N.W.			Communication Trench, Dug-outs on WEST BANK OF YSER CANAL, Defended Post WEST of	
L8.			YSER CANAL.	
			Mounted Section at (BELGIUM) SHEET 27. K12.C.	
HERZEELE NORD	" 2nd	4.15 a.m.	Headqtrs. & 4 Sections marched to SHEET 27 K12.C & whole Company proceeded by march-route to	
			HERZEELE (NORD) LIEUT. J.T. TAYLOR R.E. Evacuated, Sick	
VOLCKERINCKHOVE NORD.	" 3.	9.0 a.m.	Company proceeded by march-route to VOLCKERINCKHOVE (NORD)	
	" 4.		Company Engaged in tactical exercises & general training	
	" 5.		Company Engaged in tactical exercises & general training	
	" 6.		Company Engaged in tactical exercises & general training	
	" 7.		Company Engaged in tactical exercises & general training 2/LT G. SMITH R.E. joined Coy.	
			from 3rd LINE DEPOT SHEFFIELD	
	" 8.		Company engaged in tactical exercises & general training.	
	" 9.		Company engaged in tactical exercises & general training	
	" 10.		Company engaged in tactical exercises & general training	
	" 11.		Company engaged in tactical exercises & general training	
	" 12.		Company Engaged in tactical exercises & general training Reinforcement of 9 other ranks	
			joined Co. from Base Depot	
	" 13		Company inspected by G.O.C. 6th DIVISION	
	" 14		Company engaged in tactical exercises & general training	
HOUTQUERKE	" 15		Company proceeded by March-route to HOUTKERQUE NORD. bivouacking in field that night.	
VLAMERTINGHE	" 16		Company proceeded by march-route to VLAMERTINGHE SHEET 28 N.W. H8 a 5 9.	
BELGIUM	" 17		Company relieved 83rd FIELD CO. R.E. at VLAMERTINGHE {2/LT. J.H. HARTLEY & 2/LT J. DUNLOP JOINED Coy. from 3rd Line Depot SHEFFIELD}	
SHEET 28 N.W	" 18		Sections 3 & 4 proceeded to YPRES. billeted in 66 RUE DIXMUDE	
H8 a 5.9. & YPRES.	" 19		Sections 3 & 4 engaged in reclaiming KAAIE DEFENCES & preparing billets for MENIN RD.	

1875 Wt. W593/826 1,000,000 4/15 J.B.C. & A. A.D.S.S./Forms/C. 2118.

212ND FIELD CO. No.

Instructions regarding War Diaries and Intelligence Summaries are contained in F. S. Regs., Part II. and the Staff Manual respectively. Title Pages will be prepared in manuscript.

WAR DIARY
or
~~INTELLIGENCE SUMMARY~~
(Erase heading not required.)

Army Form C. 2118

Place	Date 1916	Hour	Summary of Events and Information	Remarks and references to Appendices
BELGIUM	July 20		Sections 3 & 4 engaged in reclaiming KAAIE DEFENCES & preparing billets for MENIN R^D	
SHEET 28 N.W.	" 21		Sections 3 & 4 engaged in reclaiming KAAIE DEFENCES & preparing billets for MENIN R^D	
VLAMERTINGHE	" 22		Sections 3 & 4 engaged in reclaiming KAAIE DEFENCES & preparing billets for MENIN R^D	
H6a5.9	" 23		Sections 3 & 4 engaged in reclaiming KAAIE DEFENCES & preparing billets for MENIN R^D	
& YPRES.	" 23		2/Lt. E.G. HUTSON R.E.(T) evacuated sick	
	" 24		Sections 3 & 4 engaged in reclaiming KAAIE DEFENCES & preparing billets for MENIN R^D	
	" 25		Sections 3 & 4 engaged in reclaiming KAAIE DEFENCES & preparing billets for MENIN R^D	
	" 26		Sections 3 & 4 relieved by Sections 1 & 2. Sections 1 & 2 engaged in reclaiming KAAIE DEFENCES & preparing billets for MENIN R^D	
	" 27		Sections 1 & 2 engaged in reclaiming KAAIE DEFENCES & preparing billets for MENIN R^D	
	" 28		Sections 1 & 2 engaged in reclaiming KAAIE DEFENCES & preparing billets for MENIN R^D	
	" 29		Company relieved by 1/1st. W.R. FIELD COY R.E.(T) Sections 1 & 2 proceeded by March route to VLAMERTINGHE.	
WORMHOUDT.	" 30		Company proceeded by march-route to WORMHOUDT.	
	" 31		Company engaged in general training	

R.C. Howard

Major
O. C. 212 nd. W.R. Div. Field C...
Royal Engineers. (T...

1875 Wt. W593/826 1,000,000 4/15 J.B.C. & A. A.D.S.S./Forms/C. 2118.

6th Divisional Engineers

2/2nd WEST RIDING FIELD COMPANT R. E.

AUGUST 1 9 1 6 ::

Instructions regarding War Diaries and Intelligence Summaries are contained in F. S. Regs., Part II. and the Staff Manual respectively. Title Pages will be prepared in manuscript.

WAR DIARY
or
INTELLIGENCE SUMMARY
(Erase heading not required.)

Army Form C. 2118

2/2 W.R. Fd Coy

Vol XI

Place	Date 1916	Hour	Summary of Events and Information	Remarks and references to Appendices
WORMHOUDT	August. 1.		In billets. Company engaged in General Training	
"	" 2.		In billets. Company engaged in General Training. Orders received for Coy. to entrain at ESQUELBECQ. Aug. 3 1916	
"	" 3.	3 a.m.	Coy. Proceeded by march route to ESQUELBECQ	
AMPLIER (SOMME)	" 3.	4.20 pm	Coy. entrained at ESQUELBECQ and detrained at DOULLENS (SOMME) Coy. proceeded by march route to AMPLIER	
ACHEUX (SOMME)	" 4.	8 am	Coy. proceeded by march route to ACHEUX (SOMME) attached (lead) to 18th INFANTRY BRIGADE.	
ENGLEBELMER	" 5.	1.30 pm	Sections 1. 2. 3. 4. and Hdqtrs of Coy. proceeded by march route to ENGLEBELMER	
"	" 6.	8. 0 am	Work in Sector of line between taken over from 105th FIELD COY. R.E	
"	" 7.		Sections engaged in Trench Reclamation & construction of dug-outs	
"	" 8.		Sections engaged in Trench Reclamation & construction of dug-outs.	
"	" 9.		Sections engaged in Trench Reclamation & construction of dug-outs. Coy. Transport proceeded by march route to LOUVENCOURT.	
"	" 10.		Instruction received to suspend work in line & hand on 11th. to hand over to 75th FIELD Co R.E. This	
"	" 10.		Coy. to go into reserve with 71st INFANTRY BRIGADE. DISTRICT of village heavily bombarded.	
"	" 11.		Coy relieved by 75th FIELD Co R.E at 3 P.M. Coy. Hdqtrs. Sections 1. 2. 3. 4. remain in ENGLEBELMER	
"	" 12.		Sections 1 & 2 engaged in constructing ADVANCED DRESSING STA. at MESNIL. Sections 3 & 4 constructing new-	
"	" 12.		DIVL. BATTLE REPORT STA. at P.23.b.	
"	" 13		Work carried on the same as for 12th no work in the line.	
"	" 14.		Coy. relieved 75th FIELD Co. R.E & took over sector of the line between.	
"	" 15.		No work in the line on account of the Special Brigade of R.E. operation	
"	" 16.		Section No 1. Constructing dugouts in the line. Section No 2 constructing ADVANCED DRESSING STA. MESNIL.	
"	" 16		Section No 3. constructing new DIVL. BATTLE REPORT STA. Section No 4. Trench Reclamation work & widening trench.	
"	" 17.		Work carried on the same as for the 16th	
"	" 18.		Work carried on the same as for the 17th 2/Lieut. M LEEDHAM R.E (T) Joined the unit for duty from 3rd LINE DEPOT.	
"	" 19.		Work carried on the same as for the 18th 2/Lieut. W.W CHAMBERLAIN R.E (T) evacuated sick to C.C.S.	
"	" 20		No work in line, other work carried on the same as for the 19th	
"	" 21.		No work in line, other work carried on the same as for the 20th Village heavily bombarded.	
"	" 22.		Work carried on in line & other work carried on the same as for 19th & 21st	
"	" 23		Work carried on the same as for the 21st	
"	" 24		Work carried on the same as for the 22nd	
"	" 25		Work carried on the same as for the 23rd	
"	" 26		No work in line on account of operations of SPECIAL BRIGADE R.E. Orders received to move to LOUVENCOURT 27th	
LOUVENCOURT	" 27		Hdqtrs & Sections 1. 2. 3. 4. proceeded by march route to LOUVENCOURT to join Coy. Transport	
"	" 27		Work handed over to 225th FIELD Co. R.E.	
BEAUVAL	" 28		Coy proceeded by march route to BEAUVAL with & as part of 71st INF. BDE.	

1875 Wt. W593/826 1,000,000 4/15 J.B.C. & A. A.D.S.S./Forms/C. 2118.

Instructions regarding War Diaries and Intelligence Summaries are contained in F. S. Regs., Part II. and the Staff Manual respectively. Title Pages will be prepared in manuscript.

212ND. FIELD CO. No. W. RIDG. DIV. R.E. (T.F.)

WAR DIARY
or
~~INTELLIGENCE SUMMARY~~
(Erase heading not required.)

Army Form C. 2118

Place	Date 1916	Hour	Summary of Events and Information	Remarks and references to Appendices
FLESSELLES	AUGUST 29th		Coy. proceeded by march route to FLESSELLES with & as part of 71st INF. BDE. GROUP.	
"	" 30		Coy. engaged in General Training.	
"	" 31		Coy. engaged in General Training.	

R C Howard
Major
O. C. 212 nd. W.R. Div. Field Co.
Royal Engineers. (T. F.)
5 Division

1875 Wt. W593/826 1,000,000 4/15 J.B.C. & A. A.D.S.S./Forms/C. 2118.

6th Divisional Engineers

2/2nd WEST RIDING FIELD COMPANY R. E.

SEPTEMBER 1916.

Instructions regarding War Diaries and Intelligence Summaries are contained in F. S. Regs., Part II. and the Staff Manual respectively. Title Pages will be prepared in manuscript.

WAR DIARY
or
~~INTELLIGENCE SUMMARY~~
(Erase heading not required.)

Army Form C. 2118

Place	Date	Hour	Summary of Events and Information	Remarks and references to Appendices
SOMME	1916			
FLESSELLES	SEPT. 1.		Coy. lying at FLESSELLES with & as part of 71st INFANTRY BRIGADE GROUP 6th DIVISION. On Rest & engaged in general training.	
"	2.		Coy. engaged in general training & rest.	
"	3.		Coy. engaged in general training & rest.	
"	4.		Coy. engaged in general training & rest.	
"	5.		Coy. took part in Tactical manoeuvres with & as part of 71st I. BDE GROUP. Orders received for Coy to move with BRIGADE on 6th.	
ALLONVILLE	6.		Coy. with & as part of 71st I.B. Grp. proceeded by march route to ALLONVILLE (SOMME) & occupied Billets	
MERICOURT D'ABBÉ	7.		Coy. with & as part of 71st I.B. Grp. proceeded by march route to MERICOURT D'ABBÉ & occupied Bivouac	
MAULTE	8.		Coy. with & as part of 71st I.B. Grp. proceeded by march route to "SANDPIT" AREA ("HAPPY VALLEY" CAMP) MAULTE & occupied Camp & Bivouacs. Draft of 6 other Ranks arrive from BASE	
"	9.	"	Coy. engaged in general duties & training	
"	10.		Coy. engaged in general duties & training. Orders received for move to ASSEMBLY AREA CARNOY	
CARNOY &	11.		Coy. with & as part of 71st I.B. Grp. proceeded by march route to ASSEMBLY AREA CARNOY	
BRIQUETERIE AREA A.4. b. & 5.		6. pm	Dismounted Sections proceed by march route to BRIQUETERIE AREA A4. b & 5. & occupied Bivouac Trench. Coy. Transport remaining under orders at CARNOY.	
	12	"	Sections 1, 2, 3, 4, & Hdqtrs of Coy. at BRIQUETERIE Bivouac engaged in road making & constructing Advanced Brigade Battle Hdqtrs. at ARROW HEAD COPSE. Great Artillery activity in neighbourhood	
	13		Work & duties of Sections 1, 2, 3, 4, & Hdqtrs as for 12th carried on at BRIQUETERIE (Transport Lines at CARNOY)	
		"	Draft of 5 other Ranks (Drivers) arrive from BASE.	
S.30. b 2.4.	14.		Work as for 13th carried on. Operation Orders for attack by 6th DIVISION received. Dismounted Sections	
		8.0 AM.	proceed from BRIQUETERIE AREA by march route to Bivouac Support Trench ARROW HEAD COPSE S30 b 2. 4.	
	15.	6. 20 AM	Attack by 71st I.B on LESBOEUFS-MORVAL SECTOR commenced accompanied by intense Artillery bombardment	
		8. 0 AM		
			Sections 1 & 4 engaged in making roads & tracks from GUILLEMONT to GINCHY to enable Rations Stores etc to (CONTD.)	

15a

Instructions regarding War Diaries and Intelligence Summaries are contained in F. S. Regs., Part II. and the Staff Manual respectively. Title Pages will be prepared in manuscript.

WAR DIARY
or
~~INTELLIGENCE SUMMARY~~
(Erase heading not required.)

Army Form C. 2118

Place	Date 1916	Hour	Summary of Events and Information	Remarks and references to Appendices
S30 b 2.4	SEPT. 15	CONTD	& Ammunition etc. to be taken to attacking troops. Sections 2 & 3 "stood-to" throughout the day awaiting orders to proceed to 3rd Objective. (LESBOEUFS-MORVAL) as soon as possible when captured by the attacking Infantry, to assist & supervise the work of consolidation. The attack however being held-up at the QUADRILATERAL these Sections were unable to advance to their objective.	
	16		Offensive continues with heavy bombardment by our Artillery. Sections 1 2 3 & 4 engaged in constructing roads & tracks from GUILLEMONT TO GINCHY carrying on work of 15th. 71st I.B. relieved at 10 pm & proceeds to BRIQUETERIE AREA A4 c 6 5	
BRIQUETERIE A4. c6.5.	17		Sections. 1. 2. 3. & 4. & Headqtrs. return to Bivouac-Trench at BRIQUETERIE-AREA 1 Officer 2/Lieut R.L. Box R.E.(T) joined unit for duty from BASE DEPOT SHEFFIELD.	
	18		Dismounted Sections at BRIQUETERIE-AREA as part of reserve Brigade Group to 6th DIVISION also making & repairing roads in vicinity. Very inclement weather prevailing. Orders received for Brigade & Divisional reliefs on the 19th inst.	
VILLE-SUR-ANCRE	19		Coy. as part of & with 71st I.B. Group proceeded by march route to VILLE-SUR-ANCRE for rest, & occupied Billets & Bivouacs.	
	20		Coy. at rest & engaged in general duties. Draft of 2 other Ranks arrived from BASE	
	21		Coy. at rest & engaged in general duties. Orders received for move on 22nd inst.	
CITADEL-AREA CAMP.	22		Coy. as part of & with 71st I.B. Group proceeded by march route to CITADEL-AREA CAMP & occupied Camp & Bivouacs.	
	23		Coy. at CITADEL AREA engaged in General duties. Orders received for move on 24th.	
A8a. A7d.	24		Coy. proceeded by march route to Bivouac in A8 a. Transport proceeding to A7.d. Operation-Orders received for attack by 6th DIVISION on 25th inst. This Coy. to form part of 71st I.B. Group in Reserve.	
TRONES WOOD. S29. d 5. 5.	25		Dismounted Sections proceeded by march-route to Bivouac at ASSEMBLY-AREA. S29 d 5 5. Attack commenced by 6th DIVISION. This Coy in Reserve. LESBOEUFS-MORVAL SECTOR occupied at 12.30 pm by 6th DIVISION Troops, numerous prisoners taken	

1875 Wt. W593/826 1,000,000 4/15 J.B.C. & A. A.D.S.S./Forms/C. 2118.

Army Form C. 2118

Instructions regarding War Diaries and Intelligence Summaries are contained in F. S. Regs., Part II. and the Staff Manual respectively. Title Pages will be prepared in manuscript.

WAR DIARY
or
~~INTELLIGENCE SUMMARY~~
(Erase heading not required.)

Place	Date	Hour	Summary of Events and Information	Remarks and references to Appendices
	1916.	CONTD.		
S.30 A 9 5. (GUILLEMONT.)	SEPT. 26.		This Coy. relieved 1/1st. London Field Co. R.E. (T) at GUILLEMONT on 16th INF. BDE. going into reserve.	
	27.		Section 1. engaged in making Strong-Point N. of MORVAL. Section 4. wiring N of MORVAL road. Section 3. Laying-out 300 YDS. New Trench at T10. a 4.6. – T10. a 4.5. Section 2. making Dug-out accomodation at BRIGADE H.Q. GUILLEMONT & making Tracks N.E. of GINCHY. Draft of 7 other ranks arrived from BASE.	
	28.		Dismounted Sections at GUILLEMONT making Dug-out accomodation at Brigade Hdqtrs., clearing Battle field also Section 1. Laying-out and excavating new communication-trench 600 yards long connecting LESBOEUFS VILLAGE with Front & Support lines	
	29.		Section 1. making Dug-out accomodation at Brigade Hdqtrs. Section 2 3 & 4 making roads between GINCHY & LESBOEUFS.	
	30.		Coy. relieved by 2/2 London Field Co. R.E.(T) at 3 p.m. Sections 1 2 3 & 4 proceeded by march route to Coy. Transport Lines A 7 d.	

A.C. Howard
MAJOR
O.C. 2/2ND. W.R. FIELD Co. R.E. (T).

1875 Wt. W593/826 1,000,000 4/15 J.B.C. & A. A.D.S.S./Forms/C. 2118.

Vol 13

(CONFIDENTIAL)

WAR - DIARY

OF

2/2ND. WEST RIDING FIELD COY. R.E. (T.F.)

FROM:- October 1st 1916 - TO:- October 31st 1916

(VOLUME)
XIII

Instructions regarding War Diaries and Intelligence Summaries are contained in F. S. Regs., Part II. and the Staff Manual respectively. Title Pages will be prepared in manuscript.

WAR DIARY
or
~~INTELLIGENCE SUMMARY~~

(Erase heading not required.)

Army Form C. 2118

Place	Date 1916	Hour	Summary of Events and Information	Remarks and references to Appendices
SANDPIT-AREA MEAULTE	OCT. 1.		Coy. with & as part of 71st Infantry Brigade Group proceeded by march-route to SANDPIT-AREA for rest etc.	
	2.		Coy with & as part of 71st Infantry Brigade Group at SANDPIT-AREA, MEAULTE on rest engaged in general-training & duties.	
	3.		Coy. engaged in general-training & duties.	
	4.		Coy. engaged in general-training & duties. 1 officer evacuated sick (Lt. N. Barlow)	
	5.		Coy. engaged in general-training & duties. No. 4 Section of Coy. under 2/Lt G. Smith proceeded by march-route to GINCHY, to construct Brigade Battle Headquarters.	
	6.		Coy. (less No. 4 Section) continued on rest & general-training & duties at SANDPIT-AREA. No. 4 Section at GINCHY engaged in constructing Brigade Battle Hdqtrs. 1 officer evacuated sick (2/Lt M. Lenham)	
CARNOY	7.		Coy (less No. 4 Section) proceeded by march-route to CARNOY & occupied Camp & Bivouacs.	
MONTAUBAN	8.		Coy. (less No. 4 Section) proceeded by march-route to MONTAUBAN. No. 3 Section proceeding to AREA at T.19.a.1.3. Coy Transport remaining at MONTAUBAN.	
T.19.a.1.3.	9.		Remainder of Coy. (Hdqtrs & Sections 1 & 2) proceeded to T.19.a.1.3. & occupied bivouac-trench & R.E. Dumps at GINCHY & GUILLEMONT. No. 3. Section engaged in night-work constructing "Strong-point" at N.27.b.9.8. One officer killed in action (2/Lt. R.L. Box) & 2 other ranks wounded. at N.27.b.9.8.	
	10.		Coy at T.19.a.1.3. work in line, Brigade Battle Hdqtrs. & on R.E. Dumps continued. No. 2. Section constructing "Strong-point" at N.27.b.9.8. & Assembly trenches close to front-line 2 other ranks wounded.	
	11.		No. 2. Section setting-out communication-trench to front-line 1 other ranks killed 3 other ranks wounded.	
	12.		Attack by 6th Division Sections 2 & 3 consolidating No. 1. Section completing Brigade Battle Hdqtrs	
	13.		Sections 3 & 4 consolidating ground E. of GUEDECOURT. One officer slightly wounded (2/Lt G. Smith) 1 other ranks wounded. Draft of 11 other ranks arrive from BASE.	
	14.		Sections 2 3 & 4 engaged in consolidation ground newly captured. 2 other ranks, (1974 Sergt. Hosnip T. & 2632 Corpl Till F.) awarded "MILITARY MEDAL"	
	15.		Sections 1 & 4 consolidating newly captured Gunpits. N.22.c.3.5. 1 other ranks wounded	
	16.		Sections 1 & 4 engaged in consolidating "GUNPITS" N.22.c.3.5. 2 other ranks killed in action	

1875 Wt. W593/826 1,000,000 4/15 J.B.C. & A. A.D.S.S./Forms/C. 2118.

2/2ND. FIELD CO. No. WEST RID. DIV.

Instructions regarding War Diaries and Intelligence Summaries are contained in F. S. Regs., Part II. and the Staff Manual respectively. Title Pages will be prepared in manuscript.

WAR DIARY

or

~~INTELLIGENCE SUMMARY~~

(Erase heading not required.)

Army Form C. 2118

Place	Date 1916	Hour	Summary of Events and Information	Remarks and references to Appendices
T19a1.3	OCT. 17.		Sections 1 & 2 consolidating 71st Infantry Brigade Front line E. of GUEUDECOURT. 7 other ranks wounded	
	18.		Attack by 6th Division. Sections 3 & 4 consolidating newly-won ground E. of GUEUDECOURT.	
CARNOY	19.		Divisional reliefs. Coy. proceeded by march route to Camp at CARNOY K17. Relieved by 15th Field Co. R.E.	
SANDPIT-AREA MEAULTE.	20.		Coy. proceeded by march route to SANDPIT-AREA MEAULTE. Draft of 8 other ranks arrive from Base.	
CORBIE	21.		Coy. with & as part of 71st Infantry Brigade Group proceeded by march route to CORBIE (SOMME) & occupied billets in Town.	
	22.		Coy. at rest engaged in general training & duties etc.	
	23.		Coy. engaged in general training & duties etc. Coy. Transport proceeded by march route to AILLY	
CORBIE AILLY & DOUDELAINVILLE	24.	12.15 AM.	Coy. with & as part of 71st Infantry Brigade Group proceeded by march route to Entraining point CORBIE STA. & Entrained. Coy. Transport continued by march route to DOUDELAINVILLE.	
		5.45 AM.	Coy. detrained at AIRAINES & proceeded by march route to DOUDELAINVILLE & occupied billets	
	25.		Coy. at rest engaged in general training & duties etc. at DOUDELAINVILLE	
	26.		Coy. engaged in general training & duties etc. Advance-party left for:- FOUQUIERES. BETHUNE	
	27.		Coy. engaged in general training & duties etc. Operation orders received for:- Movement on 29th inst.	
	28.		Coy. engaged in general training & duties etc. 1 AM. Coy. Transport proceeded by march route to:- PONT. REMY.	
PONT REMY	29.	5.15 AM.	Coy. proceeded by march route to PONT REMY (Entraining point) 3 AM Coy. Entrained at PONT. REMY 3.45 Coy. proceeded by train journey.	
FOUQUIERES	30.	1.30 AM.	Coy. arrived at FOUQUEREUIL STA. & detrained, proceeded by march route to FOUQUIERES & occupied billets. During day Coy. engaged in general duties.	
	31.		Coy. at FOUQUIERES engaged in constructing rifle ranges for practice purposes, & general duties in billets.	

A. Howard Major
O. C. 2/2nd. W.R. Div. Field C[illegible]
Royal Engineers. (T. [illegible])

1875 Wt. W593/826 1,000,000 4/15 J.B.C. & A. A.D.S.S./Forms/C. 2118.

Vol 14

CONFIDENTIAL

WAR – DIARY

OF

2/2ND WEST RIDING FIELD COY. R.E. (T)

FROM November 1st 1916 TO November 30th 1916

(VOLUME XIV.)

Instructions regarding War Diaries and Intelligence Summaries are contained in F. S. Regs., Part II. and the Staff Manual respectively. Title Pages will be prepared in manuscript.

WAR DIARY
or
INTELLIGENCE SUMMARY
(Erase heading not required.)

Army Form C. 2118

Place	Date 1916.	Hour	Summary of Events and Information	Remarks and references to Appendices
FOUQUIERES. PAS-DE-CALAIS.	NOV. 1.		Coy. engaged in R.E. Services for 71st Infantry Brigade & general duties. 1 officer 2/Lt. J.H. Hartley R.E. awarded "MILITARY CROSS." (D.R.O's. No. 31/16.)	
	2.		Coy. engaged in R.E. Services for 71st Infantry Brigade & general training.	
AND.	3.		Work & training continued. 2 other ranks 1678 L/Staff Sgt. Ellis D.W. & 2276 Sap: Bellamy H. awarded "MILITARY MEDAL"	(London Gazette dd. Oct 27/16)
VERQUIN.	4.		Work & training continued. Coy. Transport proceeded by march route to VERQUIN & occupied billets & lines	
	5.		Coy. at general duties & training. Orders received for movement to NOYELLES for work in 21st DIVn AREA.	
NOYELLES.	6.		Coy. proceeded by march route to NOYELLES & occupied billets & hutments.	
	7.		Coy. at NOYELLES. Preparing scheme with C.R.E. 21st Division for the construction of series of deep dugouts in 21st DIVn AREA.	
	8.		Coy. commenced work on mine-dugouts in line. Shifts & working parties organised	
	9.		Coy. continued work on mine-dugouts.	
	10.		Coy. continued work on mine-dugouts.	
	11.		Coy. continued work on mine-dugouts.	
	12.		Coy. continued work on mine-dugouts.	
	13.		Coy. continued work on mine-dugouts. 1 officer 2/Lt. A.H. Bassett (Northumbrian R.E.) joined for duty	
	14.		Coy. continued work on mine-dugouts.	
	15.		Coy. continued work on mine-dugouts.	
	16.		Coy. continued work on mine-dugouts. Draft of 5 other ranks arrive from Base	
	17 & 18.		Coy. continued work on mine-dugouts.	
	19.		Coy. continued work on mine-dugouts. 1 Warrant Officer 1319 C.S.M. Metcalf F. awarded "MILITARY CROSS"	
	20.		Coy. continued work on mine-dugouts.	
	21.		Coy. continued work on mine-dugouts.	
	22.		Coy. continued work on mine-dugouts.	
	23.		Coy. continued work on mine-dugouts. Work on dug-outs ceased. Orders received to join 71st I.B. on 25th	
	24.		Coy. on general duties. Orders for movement on 25th received	
NOYELLES. & LE PREOL.	25.	12.30 pm	Coy. on general duties. Sections No. 3 & 4 proceeded by march route to LE PREOL & took over line of 1/2 Durham Field Co. R.E. 5th Division S of LA BASSEE CANAL.	
	26.		Sections 1 & 2 at NOYELLES on general duties. Sections 3 & 4 at LE PREOL on R.E. Services for 71st Infantry Brigade	
LE PREOL.	27.	12.30 pm	Sections 1 & 2 & H.Qrs. & Coy Transport proceeded by march route to LE PREOL & occupied billets	
	28.		Coy. commenced work in line & R.E. Services & general duties for Brigade & billets	
	29.		Work as for 28th carried on	
	30.		Work as for 29th carried on	

J. C. Mitchell
~~Major~~ CAPTAIN.
for O.C. 2/2nd. W.R. Div. Field Co.
Royal Engineers. (T. F.)

1875 Wt. W593/826 1,000,000 4/15 J.B.C. & A. A.D.S.S./Forms/C. 2118.

Vol 15

CONFIDENTIAL.

WAR DIARY.

OF

2/2ND WEST RIDING FIELD COY. R. E. (T)

FROM DECEMBER 1ST 1916 TO DECEMBER 31ST 1916

(VOLUME XV)

Instructions regarding War Diaries and Intelligence Summaries are contained in F. S. Regs., Part II. and the Staff Manual respectively. Title Pages will be prepared in manuscript.

WAR DIARY
or
INTELLIGENCE SUMMARY
(Erase heading not required.)

2/2nd. WEST RIDING FIELD Co. ROYAL ENGINEERS, (T.F.)
No. Army Form C. 2118
DATE 31/12/16

Place	Date 1916.	Hour	Summary of Events and Information	Remarks and references to Appendices
LE PREOL PAS-DE-CALAIS	DECr 1.		Coy. at LE PREOL with 71st Infantry Bde. Sections 3 & 4 engaged in work of Trench Reclamation – Maintenance of "Village" & "support" Lines. & Mono-Rail System constructing Trench Mortar Emplacements & Advanced Dressing Station all in LA BASSEE CANAL – LA BASSEE ROAD SECTOR – Sections 1 & 2 engaged in general R.E. Services for Brigade & Division maintenance of roads repairing huts, also preparation of materials at unit Dump.	
	2.		Work & duties as for preceding date carried-on	
	3.		Work & duties as for preceding date continued.	
	4.		Work & duties as for preceding date continued.	
	5.		Work & duties as for preceding date continued.	
	6.		Work & duties as for preceding date continued.	
	7.		Work & duties as for preceding date continued.	
	8.		Work & duties as for preceding date continued.	
	9.		Work & duties as for preceding date continued.	
	10.		Work & duties as for preceding date carried-on Sections 3 & 4 relieved in line & work in line as for preceding dates continued by Sections 1 & 2.	
	11.		Work & duties as for preceding date continued.	
	12.		Work & duties as for preceding date continued.	
	13.		Work & duties as for preceding date continued.	
	14.		Work & duties as for preceding date continued Draft of 8 other ranks arrive from Base.	
	15.		Work & duties as for preceding date continued	
	16.		Work & duties as for preceding date continued. 2/Lt. C. H. J. Stewart 1st London Field Co. R.E. (T) attached to 2/2 W.R. Field Co. R.E. (T) for duty from this date.	
	17.		Work & duties as for preceding date continued	
	18.		Work & duties as for preceding date continued. Orders for move on 20th received.	
	19.		Work & duties as for preceding date continued. Preparations for movement	
NOEUX-LES-MINES.	20.	11 a.m.	Coy. proceeded by march route to NOEUX-LES-MINES & occupied billets. Draft of 4 other ranks arrive from Base.	
	21.		Coy. on period of rest engaged in general duties.	
	22.		Coy. on period of rest engaged in general duties.	
	23.		Coy. on period of rest engaged in general duties.	
	24.		Coy. on period of rest engaged in general duties.	
	25.		XMAS DAY 1916 Coy. on period of rest	
	26.		Coy. on period of rest engaged in general duties. Orders for move on 27th received.	
NOYELLES.	27.		Coy. proceeded by march route to NOYELLES. & occupied billets.	
	28.		Coy. commences work in HULLOCK – FOSSE 8. SECTOR constructing Deep Dugouts Brigade Hdqtrs & Trench Reclamation	
	29.		Work as for 28th continued 2 other ranks wounded.	
	30.		Work as for 29th continued	
	31.		Work as for 30th continued	

A C Howard Major.
O.C. 2/2nd. West Riding Field Co.
Royal Engineers. (T. F.)

1875 Wt. W593/826 1,000,000 4/15 J.B.C. & A. A.D.S.S./Forms/C. 2118.

6th Division.

459th (W.R). FIELD Coy

R. Es.

~~January to December~~

~~1 9 1 9~~

Dec 1918

1917 JAN — 1919 AUG

Vol 16

CONFIDENTIAL

WAR DIARY

OF

459 2/2ND WEST RIDING FIELD Coy. R.E (T)

FROM:- JANUARY 1ST 1917 TO:- JANUARY 31ST 1917

(VOL. XVI)

Instructions regarding War Diaries and Intelligence Summaries are contained in F. S. Regs., Part II. and the Staff Manual respectively. Title Pages will be prepared in manuscript.

WAR DIARY
or
~~INTELLIGENCE SUMMARY~~
(Erase heading not required.)

Army Form C. 2118

Place	Date 1917	Hour	Summary of Events and Information	Remarks and references to Appendices
NOYELLES L.11.C.9.1. (SHEET 36c.N.E.)	JANUARY 1st.		Coy. engaged in work in HULLUCH-FOSSE-8. SECTOR - constructing Deep Dug-outs, Trench-Reclamation Pumping and Drainage System in Trenches, Trench mortar - Machine-Gun emplacements and R.E. Services for 6th Division & 71st Inf. Bde.	
	2.		The Officer Commanding 2/2 West Riding Field Coy. R.E. viz:- Major A.C. Howard, and Captain J.B.C.C. Mitchell do of the same unit awarded the "MILITARY-CROSS" published in London Gazette January 2nd 1917. Work as for 1st inst. continued	
	3.		Work and duties as for 2nd inst. continued. 1 officer 2/Lt. F.W. Head R.E. attached for duty - from 1st London Field Coy R.E.	
	4.		Work and duties as for 3rd inst. continued. 2175 C.Q.M.S. Harris J. "mentioned in despatches" (January 3rd 1917.)	
	5.		Work and duties as for 4th inst. continued.	
	6.		Work and duties as for 5th inst. continued.	
	7.		Work and duties as for 6th inst. continued. 2/Lt. E.H.J. Stewart (attached) assumes command of No. 3 Section vice - 2/Lt. A.H. Barrett (attached) evacuated to England (sick) December 31st 1916. 2/Lt. F.W. Head (attached) - assumes command of No. 4. Section - vice - 2/Lt. G. Smith, transferred, to take up duties with - Railway Operating Dept. January 7th 1917.	
	8.		Work and duties as for 7th inst. continued.	
	9.		Work and duties as for 8th inst. continued.	
	10.		Work and duties as for 9th inst. continued.	
	11.		Work and duties as for 10th inst. continued. The O.C. unit Major A.C. Howard M.C. proceeds to "G.H.Q." for course of instruction for O's C. R.E. units. Captain J.B.C.C. Mitchell M.C. assumes temporary Command of Coy.	
	12.		Work and duties as for 11th inst. continued.	
	13.		Work and duties as for 12th inst. continued.	
	14.		Work and duties as for 13th inst. continued.	
	15.		Work and duties as for 14th inst. continued.	
	16.		Work and duties as for 15th inst. continued.	
	17.		Work and duties as for 16th inst. continued. Official notification received that as and from February 1st 1917 the designation of this unit will be known as 459th (WEST RIDING) FIELD Coy. R.E.	
	18.		Work and duties as for 17th inst. continued.	
	19.		Work and duties as for 18th inst. continued.	
	20.		Work and duties as for 19th inst. continued. Major A.C. Howard M.C. returns from "G.H.Q." course of instruction	
	21.		Work and duties as for 20th inst. continued.	
	22.		Work and duties as for 21st inst. continued.	
	23.		Work and duties as for 22nd inst. continued.	
	24.		Work and duties as for 23rd inst. continued.	
	25.		Work and duties as for 24th inst. continued.	

1875 Wt. W593/826 1,000,000 4/15 J.B.C. & A. A.D.S.S./Forms/C. 2118.

2/2nd. WEST RIDING FIELD Co. No. 11 ROYAL ENGINEERS

* Instructions regarding War Diaries and Intelligence Summaries are contained in F. S. Regs., Part II. and the Staff Manual respectively. Title Pages will be prepared in manuscript.

WAR DIARY

or

~~INTELLIGENCE SUMMARY~~

(Erase heading not required.)

Army Form C. 2118

Place	Date	Hour	Summary of Events and Information	Remarks and references to Appendices
NOYELLES	1917			
L11.c9.1.	JAN. 26.		Work and duties the same as for 25th inst. continued.	
SHEET 36bNE	27		Work and duties the same as for 26th inst. continued. 1 Offcr 2/Lt. F.C. Plumb joined & posted to unit from Base	
	28		Work and duties the same as for 27th inst. continued.	
	29		Work and duties the same as for 28th inst. continued.	
	30		Work and duties the same as for 29th inst. continued.	
	31		Work and duties the same as for 30th inst. continued.	

R. C. Howard
Major.
O.C. 2/2nd. West Riding Field Co.
Royal Engineers. (T. F.)

1875 Wt. W593/826 1,000,000 4/15 J.B.C. & A. A.D.S.S./Forms/C. 2118.

Vol 17

CONFIDENTIAL

WAR -- DIARY

OF

459th (West Riding) Field Coy. R. E.

FROM:- February 1st 1917 TO:- February 28th 1917

(VOL XVII)

Instructions regarding War Diaries and Intelligence Summaries are contained in F. S. Regs., Part II. and the Staff Manual respectively. Title pages will be prepared in manuscript.

WAR DIARY
or
~~INTELLIGENCE SUMMARY.~~
(Erase heading not required.)

Army Form C. 2118.

Place	Date	Hour	Summary of Events and Information	Remarks and references to Appendices
	1917			
NOYELLES L.11.c.9.1.	February 1.		Designation of Coy. now:- 459TH (WEST RIDING) FIELD Coy. R.E. as and from February 1st 1917. – Coy. engaged in work in HULLUCH–FOSSE 8.	
SHEET 36C N.E.	2.		Sector of Line Trench Reclamation Deep Dugouts Pumping & Drainage System Emplacements etc.	
	3.		Work and Duties as for 1st & 2nd inst. continued.	
	4.		Work and Duties as for 3rd inst. continued.	
	5.		Work and Duties as for 4th inst. continued.	
	6.		Work and Duties as for 5th inst. continued.	
	7.		Work and Duties as for 6th inst. continued.	
	8.		Work and Duties as for 7th inst. continued.	
	9.		Work and Duties as for 8th inst. continued.	
	10.		Work and Duties as for 9th inst. continued.	
	11.		Work and Duties as for 10th inst. continued. 1 Other Ranks wounded in action.	
	12.		Work and Duties as for 11th inst. continued. 1 Other Ranks died of sickness in Hospital.	
	13.		Work and Duties as for 12th inst. continued.	
	14.		Work and Duties as for 13th inst. continued.	
	15.		Work and Duties as for 14th inst. continued. Orders received for move to Training Area on 17th inst.	
	16.		Work and Fatigues preparing for move on 17th inst.	

Instructions regarding War Diaries and Intelligence Summaries are contained in F. S. Regs., Part II. and the Staff Manual respectively. Title pages will be prepared in manuscript.

WAR DIARY
or
~~INTELLIGENCE~~ SUMMARY.

(Erase heading not required.)

Army Form C. 2118.

Place	Date 1917	Hour	Summary of Events and Information	Remarks and references to Appendices
NOYELLES & BEUVRY.	FEB. 17.		Coy. (in Sections) proceeds by march route to BEUVRY (for Training) occupying billets in village.	
LHC 9.1 - 36A NE	18.		Coy. at BEUVRY commences period of Intensive Training & Recreational Training	
	19.		Coy. engaged in Intensive Training.	
	20.		Coy. engaged in Intensive Training.	
	21.		Coy. engaged in Intensive Training.	
	22.		Coy. engaged in Intensive Training.	
	23.		Coy. engaged in Intensive Training.	
	24.		Coy. engaged in Intensive Training.	
	25.		Coy. engaged in Intensive Training.	
	26.		Work and Fatigues in preparation for move on 27th inst.	
PHILOSOPHE	27.		Coy. proceeds by march route to PHILOSOPHE - Sections 1. 2. & 4. proceed & take over line from 154th Field Co. R.E.	
	28.		Coy. takes over billets workshops & dumps from 154th Field Coy. R.E. 37th Division. Line taken over from BRESLAU AVENUE to WINGS WAY from 97th Field Coy. and from WINGS WAY to POSEN ALLEY from 97th Field Coy. R.E.	

[signature]
Major.
O.C. 459th. (West Riding) Field Co.
Royal Engineers.

2353 Wt. W2544/1454 700,000 5/15 D. D. & L. A.D.S.S./Forms/C. 2118.

Vol 18

CONFIDENTIAL

WAR DIARY

OF

459th (West Riding) Field Coy. R.E.

From March 1st 1917 to March 31st 1917

Volume XVIII

Instructions regarding War Diaries and Intelligence Summaries are contained in F. S. Regs., Part II. and the Staff Manual respectively. Title Pages will be prepared in manuscript.

WAR DIARY
or
~~INTELLIGENCE SUMMARY~~

(Erase heading not required.)

Army Form C. 2118

Place	Date 1917	Hour	Summary of Events and Information	Remarks and references to Appendices
PHILOSOPHE	MARCH 1.		Coy. Headquarters & 1 Section in billets at PHILOSOPHE 3 Sections (in line) in Dug-outs at G.17c.92.1. Transport at NOYELLES (in billets etc)	
G.14b.8.7.			R.E. Dumps at FOSSE 3. PHILOSOPHE & "MANSION HOUSE" DUMP at VERMELLES. Coy. engaged in work in LOOS SECTOR	
G.17c.92.1.			Trench Clearing & Reclamation constructing Trench Mortar Emplacements Harry St. & attached to 37th Division for work this sector	
& NOYELLES	2.		Work as for 1st inst. carried on.	
4H.d4.5.	3.		Work as for 2nd inst carried on.	
	4.		Work as for 3rd inst carried on – Trench Water Supply Pipe line commenced.	
	5.		Work as for 4th inst carried on	
	6.		Work as for 5th inst carried on	
	7.		Work as for 6th inst carried on	
	8.		Work as for 7th inst carried on	
	9.		Work as for 8th inst carried on	
	10.		Work as for 9th inst carried on 100 Infantry other ranks of 71st Infantry Brigade attached permanently for work & duty	
	11.		Work as for 10th inst carried on	
	12.		Work as for 11th inst carried on	
	13.		Work as for 12th inst carried on	
	14.		Work as for 13th inst carried on	
	15.		Work as for 14th inst carried on also system of Gas Cylinder Cases being installed in Front Line for "C" Special Coy. R.E.	
	16.		Work as for 15th inst carried on 1 other ranks Killed in Action.	
	17.		Work as for 16th inst carried on 3 other ranks Wounded in Action.	
	18.		Work as for 17th inst carried on	
	19.		Work as for 18th inst carried on	
	20.		Work as for 19th inst carried on	
	21.		Work as for 20th inst carried on 1 other ranks Sergt. Roll F. proceeded to England for Cadet Course for R.E. Commission.	
	22.		Work as for 21st inst carried on	
	23.		Work as for 22nd inst carried on	
	24.		Work as for 23rd inst carried on 3 other ranks Wounded in Action.	
	25.		Work as for 24th inst carried on	
	26.		Work as for 25th inst carried on. 1 other ranks wounded and subsequently Died of wounds.	
	27.		Work as for 26th inst carried on Coy. takes over from 96th Field Coy. R.E. work in Sector – to CLIFFORD ST. – HULLUCH ALLEY. TO CHAPEL ALLEY.	
	28.		Work as for 27th inst carried on	
	29.		Work as for 28th inst carried on	
	30.		Work as for 29th inst carried on	
	31.		Work as for 30th inst carried on	

A. C. Howard Major.
O. C. 459th. (West Riding) Field Co.
Royal Engineers

1875 Wt. W593/826 1,000,000 4/15 J.B.C. & A. A.D.S.S./Forms/C. 2118.

Vol 19

CONFIDENTIAL.

WAR DIARY.

OF.

459th (W.R.) FIELD Co R.E.

FROM. APRIL 1 · 1917 TO APRIL 30 · 1917.

(VOLUME XIX)

WAR DIARY

or

~~INTELLIGENCE SUMMARY~~

(Erase heading not required.)

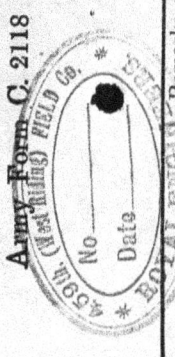

Instructions regarding War Diaries and Intelligence Summaries are contained in F. S. Regs., Part II. and the Staff Manual respectively. Title Pages will be prepared in manuscript.

Army Form C. 2118

459th. (West Riding) FIELD Co. ROYAL ENGINEERS. No.______ Date______

Place	Date	Hour	Summary of Events and Information	Remarks and references to Appendices
	April 1917			
PHILOSOPHE T.	1.		Coy. Headquarters & 1 Section in Billets at PHILOSOPHE. 3 Sections in the line in G17 & G8.1. Transport at NOYELLES	
ADVANCED HEADQTRS			RE Dumps FOSSE 3 & MANSION HOUSE VERMELLES. Coy engaged in work in LOOS & HULLUCH SECTOR.	
LONE TRENCH	2		Work in line continued as for 1st	
	3		Work in line continued as for 2nd.	
& JUNCTION KEEP	4		Work in line continued as for 3rd	
	5		Work in line continued as for 4th.	
	6		Work in line continued as for 5th	
	7		Work in line continued as for 6th. 7 other ranks wounded. Heavy bombardment of back area.	
	8		Work in line continued as for 7th	
	9.		Work in line continued as for 8th	
	10.		Work in line continued as for 9th	
	11.		Work in line continued as for 10th	
	12.		Work in line continued as for 11th.	
	13		Work in line continued as for 12th. No other ranks. 478069 Corpl. Pattinson J.R. awarded MILITARY MEDAL.	
	14		Work in line continued as for 13th	
	15		Work in line continued as for 14th. Heavy bombardment of back area.	
	16		Work in line continued as for 15th	
	17		Work in line continued as for 16th.	
	18		Work in line continued as for 17th.	
	19		Work in line continued as for 18th	
	20		Work in line continued as for 19th	
	21		Work in line continued as for 20th	
	22		Work in line continued as for 21st. Heavy bombardments of back areas and billets	
	23		Work in line continued as for 22nd. Coy attached to 16 I.B. in that Brigade taking over line held by 71st I.B.	
	24		Work in line continued as for 23rd. Draft of 7 reinforcements arrived from Base.	
	25		Work in line continued as for 24th. 1 other rank wounded	
	26		Work in line continued as for 25th	
	27		Work in line continued as for 26th. Draft of 15 reinforcements arrived from Base.	
	28		Work in line continued as for 27th	
	29		Work in line continued as for 28th	
	30.		Work in line continued as for 29th	

1875 Wt. W593/826 1,000,000 4/15 J.B.C. & A. A.D.S.S./Forms/C. 2118.

[signature] Major
O.C. 459th. (West Riding) Field Co.
Royal Engineers.

Vol 20

— CONFIDENTIAL —

WAR DIARY

OF

459th (WEST RIDING) FIELD Co. R.E.

FROM MAY 1ST - 1917 TO MAY 31ST 1917

VOLUME XX

Instructions regarding War Diaries and Intelligence Summaries are contained in F. S. Regs., Part II. and the Staff Manual respectively. Title Pages will be prepared in manuscript.

WAR DIARY
or
~~INTELLIGENCE SUMMARY~~
(Erase heading not required.)

Army Form C. 2118

459th. (West Riding) FIELD Co. No. XX Date May 31 17 * ROYAL ENGINEERS *

Place	Date MAY	Hour 1917	Summary of Events and Information	Remarks and references to Appendices
PHILOSOPHE	1		Coy Hdqrs at PHILOSOPHE heavily shelled throughout day. Coy Hd Qrs moved to NOYELLES.	
ADV^D HD QRS AT			3 Sections engaged on maintaining trenches in St. Elie - Hulloch Sector. 1 Section building	
JUNCTION KEEP			dugouts at Brigade Headquarters PHILOSOPHE	
	2		Work as for 1st inst.	
	3		71st Inf Bgde occupied sector St. Elie - ~~Hulloch~~ in place of 16th Inf Bgde. This	
			Coy affiliated to 71st Inf Bgde.	
	4		Reinforcement 2 drivers arrived	
	5		Draft of 10 sappers received from Reinforcement Co. Work started on A D S. VERMELLES	
	6		New Advanced Hdqrs dugout started at Junction Keep	
	7		1 O R to Hospital wounded (gas poisoning). Fosse 3 dump heavily shelled	
	8		Reserve line N of HULLOCH ROAD heavily shelled	
	9		Communication trenches to reserve line cleared as follows CHAPEL ALLEY, STANSFIELD RD & HULLOCH ALLEY	
	10		WINGS WAY heavily shelled	
	11		Work started on Artillery O.P at TOWER KEEP VERMELLES	
	12		A.D.S. PHILOSOPHE completed	
	13		Splinter-proof dug-outs at Brigade Hdqrs PHILOSOPHE completed	
	14		Reserve line heavily shelled	
	15		1 driver re-inforcement arrived. Work on opening DEVON LANE from RESERVE TRENCH forward begun	
	16		Work as for 15th	
	17		Sector heavily shelled. Norton Tube Well started in O.B.4	
	18		Work in trenches as for 17th inst	
	19		Water struck in O.B.4. 35'6" below ground surface	
	20		New Advanced Hdqrs JUNCTION KEEP completed	
	21		Divisional Baths removed from ~~PHILOSOPHE~~ VERMELLES to PHILOSOPHE	
	22		Artillery O.P. at TOWER KEEP VERMELLES completed. 71st Inf Bde raided enemy at 12.0 noon	
	23		Work started on Norton Tube Well O.B.1. Water struck at 24ft from ground level	
	24		Work in line as for 23rd inst.	
	25		Work on A D S. VERMELLES completed	
	26		Reserve & front lines heavily shelled	
	27		Work started on R.A.P. ST. MARYS. ST ELIE SECTOR.	
	28		Work as for 27th inst	
	29		Norton Tube Well started in DEVON LANE	
	30		Work as for 29th inst	
	31		Reinforcements 11 sappers arrived.	

A C Howard Major.
O. C. 459th. (West Riding) Field Co.
Royal Engineers.

1875 Wt. W593/826 1,000,000 4/15 J.B.C. & A. A.D.S.S./Forms/C. 2118.

Confidential

War Diary

of

459th (W.R.) Field Co. Royal Engineers

from June 1st 1917 to June 30th 1917.

(Volume XXI)

Vol 54 21

Instructions regarding War Diaries and Intelligence Summaries are contained in F. S. Regs., Part II. and the Staff Manual respectively. Title Pages will be prepared in manuscript.

WAR DIARY
or
~~INTELLIGENCE SUMMARY~~
(Erase heading not required.)

Army Form C. 2118

459th. (West Riding) FIELD Co. ROYAL ENGINEERS. No. XXI Date June 30th

Place	Date 1917	Hour	Summary of Events and Information	Remarks and references to Appendices
NOYELLES & Adv. Hd. Qrs JUNCTION KEEP	JUNE 1st		Front & Reserve Lines heavily shelled. Work started in reclaiming DEVON LANE & NEWPORT SAP.	
	" 2nd		Work in line, reclaiming Reserve Line & Communication Trenches	
	" 3rd		Reinforcement 2 O.R. reported for duty. Brigade relief, no infantry working parties	
	" 4th		Sector heavily shelled. [illegible] at St. Marys hit, roof damaged.	
	" 5th		Kings Way & St Georges Trench heavily shelled, & badly damaged	
	" 6th		Heavy fall of rain in G.C.1 - St GEORGES TRENCH area; parts of sector badly flooded. Reinforcement 1 O.R.	
	" 7th		All available labour employed on clearing & draining flooded trenches	
	" 8th		Work as for 7th inst	
	" 9th		Work as for 8th inst	
	" 10th		71st Brigade raided enemy lines on right sub-section	
	" 11th		St. Marys Aid Post again damaged by heavy shell whilst in course of reconstruction. 6th Div.	
	" 11th		Horse Show. This Coy awarded 1st Prize for Pontoon Turn-out & 1st Prize for Tool-cart Turn-out	
	" 12th		71st Inf. Bgde raided enemy lines on right sub-section	
	" 13th		Work completed at St. Marys Aid Post. St Georges Trench badly damaged by heavy shells 1 O.R. wounded	
	" 14th		Work started in clearing Close Support Line throughout Brigade Sector	
	" 15th		Reclaiming trenches & close support Line	
	" 16th		Work as for 15th inst.	
	" 17th		Work as for 16th inst.	
	" 18th		1st Corps Horse Show. This Coy awarded 1st Prizes for both Pontoon & Tool Cart Turn-out.	
	" 19th		71st Inf Bgde relieved in ST ELIE Sector by 147th Inf Bgde. This Coy remains in Sector.	
	" 20th		Working parties of 384 men provided by 147th Inf. Bgde for work in reclaiming trenches	
	" 21st		Work as for 20th New Battalion Hdqrs begun in EXETER CASTLE	
	" 22nd		Work as for 21st	
	" 23rd		Work as for 22nd	
	" 24th		3 O.R. wounded. Work as for 23rd Line heavily shelled	
	" 25th		Work as for 24th	
	" 26th		Heavy rainfall flooding main communication trenches	
	" 27th		Reclaiming Trenches	
	" 28th		Work as for 27th	
	" 29th		Work as for 28th	
	" 30th		147th Infantry Brigade relieved by 71st Inf. Bgde	

Major.
O.C. 459th. (West Riding) Field Co. Royal Engineers.

1875 Wt. W593/826 1,000,000 4/15 J.B.C. & A. A.D.S.S./Forms/C. 2118.

Vol 22

Confidential

War Diary

of

459th (W.R.) Field Co. Royal Engineers

From July 1st 1917 to July 31st 1917

(Volume XXII)

Instructions regarding War Diaries and Intelligence Summaries are contained in F. S. Regs., Part II. and the Staff Manual respectively. Title Pages will be prepared in manuscript.

WAR DIARY
or
~~INTELLIGENCE SUMMARY~~
(Erase heading not required.)

Army Form C. 2118

459th. (West Riding) FIELD Co.
No. XXII
Date JULY 1917
ROYAL ENGINEERS.

Place	Date 1917	Hour	Summary of Events and Information	Remarks and references to Appendices
Noyelles & Adv^d Head Qrs Junction Keep.	July 1		3 Sections reclaiming Reserve Line & Main Communication Trenches in ST ELIE SECTOR. 1 Section repairing huts and Horse Standings NOYELLES	
	2		Reserve Line NORTH of HULLUCK RD heavily shelled	
	3		Work as for the 1st inst	
	4		Reconstruction of "DICK" D.P. Water Tower Vermelles started	
	5		3 O.R. reinforcements. Work as for the 1st inst.	
	6		Detachment of 5 Officers & 90 O.R. of 2nd Cavalry Brigade Pioneers lent for reclaiming CHAPEL ALLEY	
	7		ST GEORGES Trench, CHAPEL ALLEY & HULLUCK RD completed	
	8		Water reached at well in OG1 48 ft from ground level	
	9		Sector heavily shelled. 2/Lt C.P. Rowden reported for duty from 3rd Line Depot SHEFFIELD	
	10		2/Lt F.C. Plumb proceeded to 3rd Line Depot SHEFFIELD to replace 2/Lt C.P. Rowden	
	11		Revetting OB1. CHAPEL ALLEY to OB 2, completed	
	12		Reclaiming & repairing trenches	
	13		Work as for the 12th inst	
	14		do 2nd Cavalry Brigade detachment withdrawn from sector	
	15		do	
	16		9th Norfolk Regiment raided enemy trenches opposite right sub-sector	
	17		Bad weather. Main communication trenches flooded	
	18		Clearing trenches. 2 Companies 1st Monmouth Regt attached for work in sector	
	19		Work as for the 18th inst	
	20		do 19th inst	
	21		do 20th inst	
	22		do 21st inst	
	23		1st Leicestershire Regt raided the enemy trenches at QUARRIES. Work & billets handed over to 465th Field Co 46th Divn on relief	
	24		Company proceeded by march route to GUESTREVILLE 36B SE V13c 3.7	
	25		engaged in training	
	26		do	
	27		do	
	28		do	
	29		do 2/Lt B.C. Newton (from Oxf & Bucks) joined Coy on one months probation 1 OR reinforcement	
	30		do	
	31		do	

R Howard Major.
O. C. 459th. (West Riding) Field Co.
Royal Engineers.

Vol 23

Confidential

War Diary

of

450th (West Riding) Field Co Royal Engineers

From August 1st 1917 to August 31st 1917

(Volume XXIII)

Instructions regarding War Diaries and Intelligence Summaries are contained in F. S. Regs., Part II. and the Staff Manual respectively. Title pages will be prepared in manuscript.

WAR DIARY
or
INTELLIGENCE SUMMARY.
(*Erase heading not required.*)

Army Form C. 2118.

Place	Date	Hour	Summary of Events and Information	Remarks and references to Appendices
Guestreville 36 B S6 v B.c.37	Aug 1st		Company engaged in general training – Shelling	
	" 2		do	
	" 3		do	
	" 4		do	
	" 5		do	
	" 6		do	
	" 7		do	
	" 8		Company inspected at training by Chief Engineer 1st Army & Chief Engineer 1st Corps	
	" 9		Company engaged in general training	
	" 10		do	
	" 11		do	
	" 12		do	
	" 13		do	
	" 14		do	
	" 15		do	
	" 16		do	
	" 17		do	
	" 18		do	
	" 19		do	
	" 20		do	
	" 21		do	
	" 22		Field Companies of 6th Divisional R.E. inspected by G.O.C. 6th Div at 36 c S.W. V.2 b.5.8	
	" 23		Company engaged in general training	
	" 24		do	
Les Brebis 36 B NE L.35	" 25		Company proceeded by march route to Les Brebis 36 B NE L.35	
	" 26		Sections No 1 & 4 moved into forward billets at 36 c S.W. H.4 b.9.0	
	" 27		Sections Nos 2 & 3 moved into advanced billets at 36 c S.W. H.31 c.5.7 & took over work of consolidating & wiring Main Resistance Line 36 c S.W. H.31 a.5.9 – H.31 b.3.7 – H.31 b.6.6, H.31 b.7.3 – H.32 a.1.3 – H.31 d.4.3, N.2 a.0.8, N.1 d.9.5. 2 Offrs – 102 O.R. 71st Inf Bde attached to Company for work, rations, pay and discipline	
	" 28		Work as for the 27th inst. Weather bad.	
	" 29		Work as for the 28th inst. No 2 Section moved into advanced billets at 36 c S.W. H.31 c.5.7	
	" 30		No work done on Main Resistance Line owing to enemy shelling	
	" 31		Work on Main Resistance Line	

A7092 Wt. W123 9/M1293 750,000. 1/17. D. D & L. Ltd. Forms/C2118/14.

A. C. Hunt [signature] Major.
O.C. 459th (West Riding) Field Co. Royal Engineers.

WR 24

Confidential

War Diary

of

459th (West Riding) Field Co Royal Engineers

From September 1st 1917 to September 30th 1917

(Volume XXIV)

Instructions regarding War Diaries and Intelligence Summaries are contained in F. S. Regs., Part II. and the Staff Manual respectively. Title pages will be prepared in manuscript.

WAR DIARY
~~or~~
~~INTELLIGENCE SUMMARY.~~
(*Erase heading not required.*)

Army Form C. 2118.

Place	Date	Hour	Summary of Events and Information	Remarks and references to Appendices
Leo Brebis 36.C.N.G.1.35	Sept. 1		Work on Main Resistance Line Loos Sector 300 S[illegible] H.31.a.5.9 - H.31.b.3.7 - H.31.b.6.6 H.31.b.7.3 H.32.a.1.3 H.31.d.6.3 N.3.a.0.8 N.1.d.9.5. 1 O.R. killed 2 wounded	
	2		Work as for the 1st inst. Reserve Billets heavily shelled	
	3		do 2nd inst. Work in line hindered by heavy shelling	
	4		do 3rd inst. – do – – do – – do –	
	5		do 4th inst. Reserve Billets heavily shelled by gas shells from 11-30 pm to 1-30 am. 2 O.R. wounded	
	6		do 5th inst. Work in line hindered by heavy shelling 1 Officer killed 2 O.R. wounded	
	7		do 6th inst. Apron fence entanglements completed across whole Divisional Front	
	8		do 7th inst.	
	9		do 8th inst. 1 O.R. wounded	
	10		do 9th inst. 1 O.R. wounded	
	11		do 10th inst. 1 O.R. wounded	
	12		do 11th inst. & opening out Dug Outs in HURDLE TRENCH 1 attached Infantry killed & 1 O.R. wounded	
	13		do 12th inst.	
	14		do 13th inst.	
	15		do 14th inst. Heavily shelled 2nd Lt [illegible] rejoined for duty from Base	
	16		do 15th inst.	
	17		do 16th inst.	
	18		do 17th inst. Line heavily shelled	
	19		do 18th inst. do	
	20		do 19th inst. 1 O.R. reinforcement joined	
	21		2 Sections withdrawn to Reserve Billets. Work on Reserve Line H.32.d.7.1 to Southern Divisional Boundary handed over to the 13th Field Co. R.E.	
	22		Work in Forward Billets handed over to 455th Field Co. R.E. Remaining sections withdrawn to Reserve Billets [illegible]	
	23		Work and Billets taken over from 3rd Field Co. Canadian Engineers from H.13.b.65.00 to junction of Command & Front Line G.8.c.65.07. 2 Sections billeted at [illegible] H.11.d.25.55	
	24		3rd Section moved to Advance Billet. Work commenced on R. & B. New Communication Trench in [illegible]. 1 O.R. wounded 3 O.R. reinforcements	
	25		Work as for the 24th inst. 2 O.R. wounded 8 O.R. attached infantry wounded. Section heavily shelled	
	26		do 25th inst.	
	27		do 26th inst.	
	28		3 O.R. attached infantry wounded. Work in line handed to 106th Field Co. R.E. on relief of 71st Inf. Bde by 75th Inf. Bde. 25th Div.	
	29		Company engaged on work on Advance Dressing Station OSLER SIDING & JUNCTION POST	
	30		[illegible] R.F.A. [illegible] in CORKSCREW TRENCH.	

R.C. Howard
Major.
O.C. 459th. (West Riding) Field Co.
Royal Engineers.

A7092 Wt. W128 9/M1293 750,000. 1/17. D. D & L. Ltd. Forms/C2118/14.

Vol 25

Confidential

War Diary

of

459th (West Riding) Field Co. Royal Engineers

From October 1st 1917 to October 31st 1917

(Volume XXV)

Instructions regarding War Diaries and Intelligence Summaries are contained in F. S. Regs., Part II. and the Staff Manual respectively. Title pages will be prepared in manuscript.

WAR DIARY
or
INTELLIGENCE SUMMARY.
(Erase heading not required.)

Army Form C. 2118.

459th. (West Riding) FIELD Co. No XXY Date [illegible] 1917 ROYAL ENGINEERS.

Place	Date	Hour	Summary of Events and Information	Remarks and references to Appendices
[illegible] 36.B.[illegible] J.3.5	Oct. 1		3 Sections and 3 Platoons of attached Infantry engaged in work on Advanced Dressing Station at OSLER SIDING and JUNCTION POST, and Regimental Aid Post [illegible] for RFA, CORKSCREW TRENCH, [illegible] Dug Outs COWDEN TRENCH, TM Emplacements CRESCENT TRENCH, Widening Bridge [illegible] 11 [illegible], Tunnels under [illegible] 11 [illegible]	
	2		Work as for the 1st inst.	
	3		do 2nd do	
	4		do 3rd do	
	5		do 4th do	
	6		do 5th do 1 OR attached infantry wounded. 8 OR [illegible] joined	
	7		do 6th do 2/Lt [illegible] Hutchinson reported for duty from Base	
	8		do 7th do	
	9		do 8th do 1 Section & 1 Platoon attached infantry [illegible] started work on [illegible] [illegible] existing new quarters & [illegible] 1 OR wounded	
	10		Work as for the 9th inst.	
	11		do 10th inst	
	12		do 11th inst 2 OR reinforcements joined	
	13		do 12th inst	
	14		do 13th inst	
	15		do 14th inst	
	16		do 15th inst	
	17		do 16th inst	
	18		do 17th inst 2 OR reinforcements joined	
	19		do 18th inst	
	20		do 19th inst	
	21		do 20th inst	
	22		Work in line and Billets handed over to 6th [illegible] 11th Div. Company proceeded by march route to NOEUX-LES-MINES with attached infantry & entrained to [illegible]ERS & proceeded by march route to AUCHY-AU-BOIS. Transport proceeded by road.	
	23		Company engaged in training	
	24		do	
	25		do	
	26		do	
	27		do	
	28		do	
	29		Company proceeded by march route to MONCHY BRETON.	
	30th		— do — GRAND RULLECOURT.	
	31		Transport proceeded by march route to ACHIET-LE-PETIT.	

[illegible] Capt. Major
O.C. 459th. (West Riding) Field Co. Royal Engineers.

A7092 Wt. W128.9/M1293. 750,000. 1/17. D. D & L. Ltd. Forms/C2118/14.

Instructions regarding War Diaries and Intelligence Summaries are contained in F. S. Regs., Part II. and the Staff Manual respectively. Title pages will be prepared in manuscript.

WAR DIARY
or
INTELLIGENCE SUMMARY.
(Erase heading not required.)

Army Form C. 2118.

459th (West Riding) FIELD Co. ROYAL ENGINEERS No Vol. XXVI Date Nov. 4. 1917

Vol 27

Place	Date	Hour	Summary of Events and Information	Remarks and references to Appendices
	Nov. 1		Dismounted Sections entrained at SAULTY for 3rd Corps Area & detrained at FINS. Transport at ACHIEU LE PETIT proceeded by march route to NURLU	
	2		Dismounted Sections moved to bivouacs & huts [illegible] in FINS.	
	3		Company engaged in preparing camouflage accommodation for 10 Bn [illegible] in DESSART WOOD	
	4		Work as for the 3rd inst	
	5		do 4th inst	
	6		2 Sections working on Dug Outs N.W. of GOUZEAUCOURT. 2 Sections preparing camouflage accommodation in DESSART WOOD	
	7		Work as for the 6th inst	
	8		do 7th inst	
	9		do 8th inst	
	10		do 9th inst Major R. C. Howard resumed command of Coy on leaving to act O.C. 6th Bn [illegible]	
	11		do 10th inst	
	12		do 11th inst	
	13		do 12th inst	
	14		do 13th inst	
	15		do 14th inst	
	16		do 15th inst also laying out infantry tracks to assembly position	
	17		do 16th inst Head quarters & Dismounted Sections moved to accommodation SW of QUEENS CROSS	
	18		do 17th inst	
	19		Company engaged in bridging trenches for assaulting troops. Sections 1 & 3 moved to assembly position S of BEAUCAMP	
	20		Nos 1-3 Sections took part in assault on Hindenburg Line [illegible] No 1 Section following immediately after assaulting Infantry and prepared a road for [illegible] to move forward to RIBECOURT. No 3 Section [illegible] BEAUCAMP to RIBECOURT. Bridging trenches of Hindenburg Main Line. Sections 1-3 bivouacked in RIBECOURT.	
	21		Company moved to billet in RIBECOURT	
	22		Dismounted Sections engaged in working on [illegible] in BEAUCAMP & [illegible] ARGYLE & MARDEN ROADS. Transport lines moved to BEAUCAMP	
	23		Work as for the 22nd inst	
	24		do 23 inst	
	25		do 24 inst	
	26		do 25 inst	
	27		do 26 inst	
	28		do 27 inst	
	29		do 28 inst	
	30		Company stood to arms at 10.0 a.m. & moved to Hindenburg Main Line as Divisional Reserve & placed at the disposal of Colonel [illegible] Commanding 1st [illegible] Durham Lt Infy, on account of enemy thrust at GONNELIEU and GOUZEAUCOURT	

R C Howard
Major.
O. C. 459th. (West Riding) Field Co.
Royal Engineers.

A7092 Wt. W128.9/M1293 750,000. 1/17. D. D & L. Ltd. Forms/C2118/14.

Vol 27

Confidential

War Diary

of

459th (WEST RIDING) FLD Co. RE

from DEC 1st 1917 To DEC 31st 1917

VOL. XXVII

Instructions regarding War Diaries and Intelligence Summaries are contained in F. S. Regs., Part II. and the Staff Manual respectively. Title pages will be prepared in manuscript.

WAR DIARY
or
~~INTELLIGENCE SUMMARY.~~

(Erase heading not required.)

459th (West Riding) FIELD Co. No Vol. XXVII Date Dec. 31/17 ROYAL ENGINEERS

Army Form C. 2118.

Place	Date	Hour	Summary of Events and Information	Remarks and references to Appendices
Dis. Sections 57c. N.E L.31.c.a.4	Dec 1/17		Dismounted sections "Stood to Arms" in Ridge Trench - Hindenburg Main Line under orders of Col. Roaches Comdg 14 D.L.I. as Divisional Reserve. At 4.0 pm orders received from 6th Div to report to 71st Inf Bgde — Dis. Sections Billetted in RIBECOURT.	
	" 2.		Dismounted Sections placed at disposal of B.G.C. 71st Inf Bgde. Company engaged in wiring front line posts NOYELLES	
MTO SEC. METZ	" 3.		16 Inf Bgde attacked & retired in a South Westerly direction from MARCOING. Coy engaged in digging new line in front of "Q Wood" protecting right flank of Bgde	
	" 4.		Line withdrawn from "Q Wood" to PREMY CHAPEL. Coy engaged in digging new line from L.21.a.7.5 to L.21.a.5.1. O.P. in Q Wood partially demolished	
	" 5.		Coy. engaged in strengthening Out-post Line L.21.a.5.1 to GRAND RAVINE at L.21.d.0.1. Warning received expecting enemy to attack in force in direction of "Q Wood" & MARCOING. RIBECOURT heavily shelled with Gas & H.E shells. Bridge over GRAND RAVINE at L.21.d.45.53 demolished. 2Lt A.M.H. Ashwin evacuated sick.	
	" 6.		Coy evacuated billets in RIBECOURT & took up position at L.32.a.0.4. Coy engaged in wiring new outpost line at L.27.b.1.8 to Rlwy. at L.27.d.6.7. 4 Derelict Tanks demolished.	
	" 7.		Wiring on same front as previous night. House demolished at L.20.d.9.3.	
	" 8		Wiring outpost line between Rd. L.21.c.7.6. & L.21.b.1.8. New A.D.S started at R.36.c.0.1. Coy still at disposal of B.G.C. 71st I.B for tactical purposes.	
	9th & 10th		Work & disposition of Coy as for the 8th	
	11		Work as for 10th. Major A.C. Howard MC Lt. J Dunlop & 478126 Sgt. Newfin R.W. mentioned in Gen. Sir Douglas Haig's despatches.	
	12		Work & Billets in line handed over to 94th Fld Co. RE. Dismounted secs withdraw to Transport lines at Metz. Coy proceeded by march Route to MANANCOURT.	
	13		Coy at MANANCOURT.	
	14		Coy proceeded to BAILLEULMONT. Dismounted section by motor lorries & Transport by march Route.	
	15-16-17		Coy engaged in Coy Training & R.E services for 6th Division	
BAILLEULMONT	18th-24th		As for previous days. Hard frost prevailed throughout this time.	
	25th		Christmas Day.	
	26-31st		Coy engaged in General Training & R.E services for 6th Div	

A.C. Howard Major.
O.C. 459th (West Riding) Field Co.
Royal Engineers.

A7092 Wt. W128:9/M1293. 750,000. 1/17. D. D & L. Ltd. Forms/C2118/14.

Instructions regarding War Diaries and Intelligence Summaries are contained in F. S. Regs., Part II. and the Staff Manual respectively. Title pages will be prepared in manuscript.

WAR DIARY
~~or~~
~~INTELLIGENCE~~ SUMMARY.

(Erase heading not required.)

Army Form C. 2118.

Vol 28

Place	Date	Hour	Summary of Events and Information	Remarks and references to Appendices
	1918			
Bailleulmont	Jan 1st		Company engaged in General Training & R.E. services for 6th Division	
	" 2nd		Work as for the 1st inst	
	" 3rd		do 2nd	
	" 4th		do 3rd	
	" 5th		do 4th	
	" 6th		do 5th Major A C Howard MC evacuated to VI Corps Rest Station	
	" 7th		do 6th	
	" 8th		do 7th 2/Lt J Walker reported for duty from the Base	
	" 9th		do 8th	
	" 10th		do 9th	
	" 11th		do 10th 3 O.R. reinforcements joined from Base	
	" 12th		do 11th	
	" 13th		do 12th 1 Cpl rejoined unit from Base	
	" 14th		do 13th	
	" 15th		do 14th	
	" 16th		Company proceeded by march route to Achiet-le-Petit	
	" 17th		do do to billets taken over from 401st Field Co R.E. Head Quarters & Mounted Sections at Beugny, 4 Sections R.E. & 4 platoons attached infantry at Lebucquière	
	" 18th		Work in line taken over from 401st Field Co R.E. 3 Sections R.E. & 2 platoons attached infantry moved to Advanced Headquarters Doignies	
	" 19th		Forward Sections engaged in digging new communication trench Roach Avenue & completing steps dug out in Support Line	
	" 20th		Work as for the 19th inst	
	" 21st		do 20th Major A C Howard MC rejoined.	
	" 22nd		do 21st Work commenced on A.D.S. DOIGNIES 50 O.R. reinforcements from Base.	
	" 23rd		do 22nd inst	
	" 24th		Work on A.D.S. DEMICOURT commenced	
	" 25th		Work as for the 24th inst	
	" 26th		do 25th	
	" 27th		do 26th	
	" 28		Clearing Intermediate Line Fire Step	
	" 29th		Work as for the 28th inst	
	" 30th		do 28th Capt J E C Mitchell MC proceeded to England on authority from War Office	
	" 31st		Work begun on new Brigade Head Quarters south of BEAUMETZ-LEZ-CAMBRAI. 20 O.R. reinforcements from Base. Lieut W Head evacuated to hospital.	

A C Howard Major.
O.C. 459th (West Riding) Field Co. Royal Engineers

A7092 Wt. W128 9/M1293 750,000. 1/17. D. D & L. Ltd. Forms/C2118/14.

Confidential

War Diary

of

459th (West Riding) Field Co Royal Engineers

from January 1st 1918 to January 31st 1918

(Volume XXVIII)

459 Fd Coy
Vol 29

CONFIDENTIAL

WAR. DIARY.

OF

459th (WEST RIDING) FLD COY. R.E.

FROM. FEB. 1st 1918 TO FEB 28 - 1918

VOL. XXIX

Instructions regarding War Diaries and Intelligence Summaries are contained in F. S. Regs., Part II. and the Staff Manual respectively. Title pages will be prepared in manuscript.

WAR DIARY
or
~~INTELLIGENCE SUMMARY.~~
(Erase heading not required.)

Army Form C. 2118.

459th. (West Riding) FIELD Co. No. ROYAL ENGINEERS.

VOL. XXIX

FEBRUARY 1918.

Place	Date	Hour	Summary of Events and Information	Remarks and references to Appendices
BEUGNY.	1		Company engaged in Work as for Jan. 31st. Lt. R.J. Hall transferred from 12th Field Co. RE & appointed 2nd in Command vice Capt. J.B.C.C. Mitchell MC RE. – transferred to Eng. Lt. R.A. Hudson reported for duty from base.	
	2		Work as for the 1st. Sgt. Morgan W. awarded the Belgian Croix de Guerre for past work on the Belgian front.	
	3		Major A.C. Haward MC promoted Lieut Col. & transferred as C.R.E. 59th Div.	
	4th to 10th		Work as for 3rd.	
	11th		work as for 10th Lt. F.W. Head returned from Hospital –	
BEUGNATRÉ.	12th		In conjunction with the relief of the 25th Div. by the 6th Div. the Company moved from BEUGNY & took over billets from the 106th Fld Co RE at H 12 central. Lt. R.A. Hudson posted to 12th Fld Co. RE.	
	13th		Coy engaged on work in back area. Erection of huts, cookhouses & general repairs to Camps & horselines.	
	14th		Major W.R. Wingate D.S.O., MC joined this Coy. as O.C. work as for 13th	
	15th		2 Sections employed as for 14th. 2 Sections employed on Corps line defence system (MORCHIES – VAULX) wiring, revetting, digging etc.	
	16 & 17th		Work as for 15th.	
	18th		Work as for 17th 1 other rank wounded by anti-aircraft fire.	
	19th–28th		Work as for 18th	
			SUMMARY. A good deal of revetment has been necessary in the Camps in the back area owing to the increased activity of hostile aircraft. The Company has been reorganised as regards horses & transport	

W.R. Wingate
Major.
O. C. 459th. (West Riding) Field Co.
Royal Engineers.

A7092 Wt. W125 9/M1293 750,000. 1/17. D. D & L. Ltd. Forms/C2118/14.

6th Divisional Engineers.

WAR DIARY

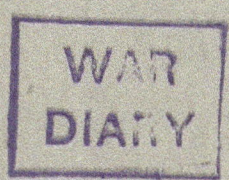

459th (West Riding) FIELD COMPANY R. E.

MARCH 1 9 1 8

Confidential

War Diary

of

459th (West Riding) Field Co. Royal Engineers

from March 1st 1918 to March 31st 1918

(Volume XXX)

17

650

459th (West Riding) Field Co.
No XXX
Date March 1918
ROYAL ENGINEERS

Army Form C. 2118.

Instructions regarding War Diaries and Intelligence Summaries are contained in F. S. Regs., Part II. and the Staff Manual respectively. Title pages will be prepared in manuscript.

WAR DIARY
or
~~INTELLIGENCE SUMMARY.~~

(Erase heading not required.)

Vol 30

Place	Date	Hour	Summary of Events and Information	Remarks and references to Appendices
FAVREUIL.	Mar 1st		Work as for Feb 28th. Two sections forward at C.28.d. 8.3. and two sections on Corps Line (VAULX-MORCHIES) living at camp 17 with 509th Field Coy R.E. Horse Lines at Camp No 6.	
	2		Work as for the 1st. The laying of anti tank land mines undertaken on our front 1500 of these mines laid along the front. Bombs carried up into place by troops of the reserve Division	
	3-4th		Work as on the 2nd inst	
	5th-12th		Company engaged on strengthening line, digging new trenches, strong points wiring up & land mines	
	13th		Company stood to at 5-0 am in battle position in Corps line i.e. in the Corps Line trench immediately south of LAGNICOURT - BEUGNY Road. Stood down at 8-30 am. Laying of anti tank mines continued.	
	14-15th		Work as for 13th inst. 2nd Lieut G Collyer transferred to No 10 Tramways Co. Lieut a/Capt Hudson rejoined from the 12th Field Co R.E.	
	16th-19th		Work as for 14th-15th. 1 o.r. wounded on mine field 19th inst	
	20th		Work as for 19th.	
	21st-22nd		German attack on the whole of our front prefaced by extremely heavy bombardment. 2 Advanced Sections and attached Infantry received orders to stand to in the Corps Line. The bombardment opened before they could get into their positions, movement being delayed owing to the wearing of gas masks in the dark. Major N.S. Wingate DSO MC was killed at this stage and 4 o.r. wounded. Capt R J Hall took over command. These 2 sections & attached Infantry remained in the Corps Line (which at about 1-0 pm became the front line) all day & at dusk they were reinforced by 2 Companies of the 25th Divn. As the trench then became overcrowded these sections were withdrawn behind LAGNICOURT WOOD & eventually withdrawn to transport lines (which had been moved to H.14 central) by order of C.R.E. arriving there at 6-0 am 22-3-18. The other 2 sections and 1 section attached infantry were attached to & moved with the 509th Field Co R.E. They moved forward at 12 noon 21-3-18 to take up a position in the Corps Line in front of MORCHIES arriving in position at 4-0 pm & remained there until midnight when they were withdrawn to work on a Strong Point behind MORCHIES. These men continued to work on this Strong Point & another one behind MARICOURT WOOD until 3-0 pm 22/3/18. They were eventually relieved by 25th Div at 11-0 pm 22-3-18 & returned to the Coy which was then at LOGEAST CAMP ABLAINZEVILLE at 5-0 am 23-3-18	
	21st		Head Quarters & Transport stood to all day in billets & was eventually moved to H.14 central by order of C.R.E. During the morning the kits of Nos 1 & 4 sections were brought back from Camp 17 but no kits could be salved from the forward billet and No 4 section Tool cart was also left behind at LAGNICOURT	
LOG EAST CAMP	22		Transport Head Quarters & 2 sections & attached infantry moved to BERKELEY CAMP from H.12 central at 12-0 noon to enable the men to get some rest. 1 o.r. killed 5 o.r. wounded at H.12 central, also 3 horses killed 5 wounded. At 9-0 pm orders were received from C.R.E. to move to LOGEAST CAMP ABLAINZEVILLE. This move was completed by midnight	
	23rd		Company remained at LOGEAST CAMP standing by	
	24th		Transport moved by road to DOULLENS. Dismounted moved by march route with 71st I.B. Group to POLSEAUX au MONT and there entrained for DOULLENS, where they bivouaced in the moat	
	25		Company entrained at DOULLENS at 6-0 pm for PROVEN. (2nd ARMY AREA)	
	26		" detrained at PROVEN and moved to WHEATFIELDS CAMP	Reinforcements 1 NCO 1 o.r. from Base
WINNEZEELE AREA	27		" moved by march route to rest billets in WINNEZEELE area	
	28-29		" bathing, cleaning arms & equipment, kit inspection &	
	30		Church Parade	
	31		Transport of 71st I.B. Group inspected by Army Commander. Capt G Lambert MC from 26th Field Co R.E. took over command of Coy	

R J Hall Capt
for OC 459th (West Riding) Field Co R.E.

A7092 Wt. W128 9/M1293 750,000. 1/17. D. D & L. Ltd. Forms/C2118/14.

6th Divisional Engineers

<u>459th (West Riding) FIELD COMPANY R. E.</u>

<u>APRIL 1918.</u>

Instructions regarding War Diaries and Intelligence Summaries are contained in F. S. Regs., Part II. and the Staff Manual respectively. Title pages will be prepared in manuscript.

WAR DIARY
~~or~~
~~INTELLIGENCE SUMMARY.~~
(Erase heading not required.)

Army Form C. 2118.

Place	Date	Hour	Summary of Events and Information	Remarks and references to Appendices
WINNEZEELE AREA	April 1st		Company engaged in training. 1 OR reinforcement. Capt. [illegible] Hall evacuated sick	
	2nd		Dismounted Sections moved by march route & lorry & train to SAPPER CAMP POTIJZE. Mounted Section moved by march route to H.21.b Sheet 28. Work in line taken over from the 458th Field Co. 49th Division	
SAPPER CAMP I.3C 0.8.	3rd		Company engaged in improvements to camp.	
	4th		3 sections working on SUPPORT LINE & RESERVE LINE POLYGON WOOD SECTOR } Revetting, Draining, Trench boarding. Ground very broken by shell fire.	
	5th		Work as for the 4th inst	
	6th		do 5th 35 OR reinforcements from the Base	
	7th		do 6th	
	8th		do 7th	
	9th		do 8th. Work taken over from 57th Field Co. RE on the right (Divisional Front extended)	
	10th		2 sections erecting Trench Shelters. 1 section working on RESERVE LINE.	
	11th		Work as for the 10th inst	
	12th		Company Stood to at 3-0 am. No work done in line.	
	13th		– do – Work commenced on new CORPS SUPPORT LINE	
	14th		Work as for the 13th inst	
	15th		Work commenced on new RESERVE LINE round ramparts of YPRES. S.E. Corner	
	16th		Work as for the 15th inst. 2 sections & Head Quarters moved to DOMINO CAMP G.8.C.0.8. Nos 1 & 4 sections moved to billets in YPRES	
DOMINO CAMP G.8C.0.8	17th		Transport moved to DOMINO CAMP G.8C.0.8	
	18th		New line commenced from YPRES ASYLUM through KRUISSTAAT to I.9.a.2.1.	
	19th		2 sections moved from YPRES to DOMINO CAMP. 1 OR reinforcement. Work as for the 18th inst	
	20th		Work as for the 19th inst	
	21st		1 OR reinforcement. Work as for the 20th inst	
	22nd		1 section commenced work on VLAMERTINGHE LINE from H.10.a.7.4 through H.4.a.5.9 to H.2.a.2.3	
	23rd		1 section commenced work on BRANDHOEK – OUDERDOM LINE. VLAM LINE continued. 2/Lt [illegible] Samuel joined the Coy from the Base	
	24th		Work as for the 23rd inst. VLAM SWITCH LINE from H.11.d.8.5 to H.16.a. [illegible] commenced.	
	25th		Enemy attack on KEMMEL. Company Stood to at 5.0 am. At night all the Company engaged on work on new FRONT LINE	
	26th		All Company continued work on VLAM LINE and VLAM SWITCH LINE.	
	27th		Work as for the 26th inst. Nissen Huts in [illegible] camps dismantled & brought back	
	28th		do 27th	
	29th		Enemy attack at VOORMEZEELE. Company Stood to at 5.0 am. Work on VLAM LINE continued. Vicinity of DOMINO CAMP heavily shelled during the day. 2 OR wounded	
	30th		Work as for the 29th inst. Company moved to RIDGE CAMP at G.11.a.7.7. 1 OR casually [illegible]	

C.H.J. Stewart Lieut. ~~Major.~~
for O.C. 459th (West Riding) Field Co. Royal Engineers.

A7092 Wt. W128 9/M1293. 750,000. 1/17. D. D & L. Ltd. Forms/C2118/14.

Instructions regarding War Diaries and Intelligence Summaries are contained in F. S. Regs., Part II. and the Staff Manual respectively. Title pages will be prepared in manuscript.

WAR DIARY

~~or~~

~~INTELLIGENCE SUMMARY.~~

(*Erase heading not required.*)

Army Form C. 2118.

459th. (West Riding) FIELD COY. No XXXII Date May 1918 ROYAL ENGINEERS

Vol 32

Place	Date	Hour	Summary of Events and Information	Remarks and references to Appendices
Sheet 28 NW G11a 7 7	May 1st		Work on FLAM LINE SUPPORT and C.T to FLAM LINE. Dismantling hut at H.16a.5.9.	
	2nd		do and SUPPORT. Digging Strong Point Brigade H Qrs H22a. Deepening and raising parapet FLAM SWITCH H4d 8.5 H15c 3.7. H15c 8.1 H15b 2.4 Work on FLAM SWITCH SUPPORT commenced. Improving FLAM SWITCH Back of FLAM LINE. Dismantling Nissen Hut at H16a.5.9. Nos 1+2 sections R.E. & their attached Infantry moved to billets at K.6b.7.8 & K.6b.2.1 & K6d 5.8. Sheet 27 (ST JAN TER BIEZEN) erecting Nissen Hut for new DIVISIONAL H.QRS.	
	3rd		Work as for the 2nd inst. Sap Offr Dennis R. awarded MILITARY MEDAL	
	4th		do 3rd inst	
	5th		do 4th inst	
	6th		do 5th inst	
	7th		do 6th inst No 2 section & its attached Infantry withdrawn from ST JAN TER BIEZEN to Coy H Qrs for work in line	
			Work at 17th Inf Bde	
	8th		Work as for the 7th inst Wiring NEW SWITCH LINE. Work interrupted by shell fire.	
	9th		do 8th inst	
	10th		do 9th inst	
	11th		do 10th inst Work handed over to 509th Field Co. R.E.	
	12th		Work on C.H. 2 line & Outposts. Work taken over from 82nd & 94th Field Coys & 171 Tunnelling Coy. Patrolling Demolition Posts	
	13th		Work as for the 12th inst. No 1 Section & its attached Infantry withdrawn from ST JAN TER BIEZEN to Coy H Qrs for work in line	
	14th		do 13th inst	
	15th		do 14th inst Lieut C.H.J. Stewart awarded MILITARY CROSS 7 O.R. reinforcements from Base	
	16th		do 15th inst Preparing charges for road crossing H16d.1.1	
	17th		do 16th inst	
	18th		do 17th inst	
	19th		do 18th inst 2 O.R. proceeded to XXII Corps Gas School for 6 days Course	
	20th		do 19th inst. Work interrupted by shell fire	
	21st		do 20th inst — do — & for fixing Gas Blanket Frames at Battalion H Qrs	
	22nd		do 21st inst 7 O.R. casualties	
	23rd		do 22nd inst Laying charges & demolishing OF CHATEAU SEGARD	
	24th		Coy stood to at 5-0 a.m — do — CHATEAU SEGARD	
	25th		Work as for the 23rd inst	
	26th		do 25th inst	
	27th		do 26th inst 1 O.R. rejoined unit from Base	
	28th		do 27th inst 3 sappers wounded. 1 attached Infantry wounded. killed 3 O.R. reinforcements from Base	
	29th		do 28th inst	
	30th		do 29th inst	
	31st		do 30th inst	

for R A Hudson Lt
~~Major~~
O. C. 459th. (West Riding) Field Co.
Royal Engineers.

A7092 Wt. W128_9/M1293 750,000. 1/17. D. D & I. Ltd. Forms/C2118/14.

Confidential

War Diary

of

459th (West Riding) Field Co. Royal Engineers

From June 1st 1918 To June 30th 1918

(Volume XXXIII)

Army Form C. 2118.

Instructions regarding War Diaries and Intelligence Summaries are contained in F. S. Regs., Part II. and the Staff Manual respectively. Title pages will be prepared in manuscript.

WAR DIARY
or
~~INTELLIGENCE SUMMARY.~~

(Erase heading not required.)

460th (West Riding) Field Co. ROYAL ENGINEERS. No XXXIII Date June 1918

Place	Date 1918	Hour	Summary of Events and Information	Remarks and references to Appendices
Sheet 28 NW G 11 a. 7.7	June 1st		Work on G.H.Q. 2 LINE + Outposts	
	2nd		Work as for the 1st inst	
	3rd		do 2nd	
	4th		do 3rd 1 O.R. reinforcement from Base	
	5th		do 4th	
	6th		Work and billets handed over to the 232nd Field Co R.E. Coy moved to billets vacated by 232nd Field Co R.E. at Sheet 27 L 16 b 3.6	
Sheet 27 L 16 b 3.6	7th		Kit Inspection. Cleaning equipment + improvements to cookhouses + sanitary appliances	
	8th		Coy engaged in Training	
	9th		Work as for the 8th inst	
	10th		Work on VLAM LINE	
	11th		Work as for the 10th inst	
	12th		Coy engaged in training. 7 O.R. reinforcements from Base. Coy Bridging Equipment drawn from ROUSBRUGGE.	
	13th		Work as for the 12th inst	
	14th		1 Section Work as for the 13th inst. 2 sections + attached Infantry work on EAST POPERINGHE LINE.	
	15th		Work as for the 14th inst	
	16th		do 15th inst. C.Q.M.S. Harris J awarded the D.C.M.	
	17th		Work on EAST POPERINGHE LINE. Cleaning + painting equipment.	
	18th		Work as for the 17th inst	
	19th		Testing S.B. Respirators + Training	
	20th		Coy engaged in Training	
	21st		Work on EAST POPERINGHE LINE. Erecting camouflage + assault Course at 18th Div. H. Qrs. SCHOOL CAMP.	
	22nd		Work as for the 21st inst. Attached Infantry left unit for 71st I.B.	
	23rd		Coy engaged in Training	
	24th		do	
	25th		do	
	26th		do 1 O.R. reinforcement	
	27th		Work on EAST POPERINGHE LINE. Erecting Nissen Huts at DOUGLAS CAMP for 6th DIV. H.QRS.	
	28th		Work as for the 27th inst. No 1 Sect moved to billets at Sheet 28 NW G 10 c 7.1. Lieut E.H. Stewart MC RE proceeded to WOOLWICH to attend a Course at Ordnance College	
	29th		Work as for the 28th inst	
	30th		do 29th inst 1 O.R. reinforcement.	

for R A Hudson Capt ~~Major~~
O.C. 460th (West Riding) Field Co.
Royal Engineers.

[illegible] 1/7

A7092 Wt. W128-9/M1293 750,000. 1/17. D. D & L. Ltd. Forms/C2118/14.

Instructions regarding War Diaries and Intelligence Summaries are contained in F. S. Regs., Part II. and the Staff Manual respectively. Title pages will be prepared in manuscript.

WAR DIARY
~~or~~
~~INTELLIGENCE SUMMARY.~~
(Erase heading not required.)

Army Form C. 2118.

459 Fld Coy RE
Jul 18
34

459th (West Riding) Field Coy XXIV Date July 1918 Royal Engineers

Place	Date 1918	Hour	Summary of Events and Information	Remarks and references to Appendices
Sheet 27 L.16.b.3.6	July 1		No 1 Section at billets G.10.c.7.1 Salving Nissen Huts, & improving accommodation in new billets Nos 2 & 4 Sections work on New Divisional H. Qrs DOUGLAS CAMP. No 3 Section work in Camp.	
Sheet 28 NW	2		Work as for the 1st inst	
G.10.c.7.1	3		do 2nd - No 3 Section to MUD FARM CAMP Sheet 28 NW G.27.a.4.7 30 OR reinforcements	
	4		Improvement of billets at MUD FARM CAMP. Work on O.P. GOED MOET MILL. 3rd & 34th Brigade Battle H.Qrs	
	5		Work as for the 4th inst No 2 Section to MUD FARM CAMP	
	6		Work on OUDERDOM LINE & as for the 5th inst 1 OR to Rouen for Course of Instruction	
	7		Work as for the 6th inst	
	8		do 7th inst	
	9		do 8th inst No 4 Section moved to new billet at K.23.a.7.4 for work on DIV DETAILS CAMP. Lieut J.H. Chadwick RE joined unit from 20th (AT) Coy.	
	10		Work as for the 9th inst Head Qrs moved to MUD FARM CAMP.	
	11		do 10th inst	
	12		do 11th	
	13		do 12th	
	14		do 13th	
	15		do 14th - 1 OR killed 1 wounded in camp.	
	16		do 15th - Work commenced on New Reserve Brigade H.Qrs ANCORA FARM 1 OR reinforcement	
	17		do 16th 8 OR commenced work on New Div Reception Camp Sheet 27 Q.13.a.6.7 near ESQUELBECQ	
	18		do 17th	
	19		do 18th	
	20		do 19th No 4 Section less detachment moved to Transport Lines	
	21		do 20th	
	22		Company stood to at 3.0 a.m. Company issued with 4 Lewis Guns (1 per section) Work as for the 21st inst	
	23		Work as for the 22nd inst	
	24		do 23rd - No 1 Section relieved No 4 Sect at Transport Lines & commenced work on New Brigade H.Qrs MERSEY CROSS G.23.d.00.30. Erection of MOIR PILL BOX (ALBERMARLE)	
	25		Work as for the 24th inst 1 Officer & 53 OR of 102nd American Engineers attached for a course of training in the line	
	26		do 25	
	27		do 26	
	28		do 27 Lieut J Dunlop RE proceeded to XIX Corps Gas School	
	29		do 28th	
	30		do 29th 1 OR casualty	
	31		do 30th Work taken over from 12th Field Co RE. 1 OR casualty.	

R A Hudson Capt ~~Major~~
for O.C. 459th (West Riding) Field Co. Royal Engineers.

A7092 Wt. W128 9/M1293 750,000. 1/17. D. D & L. Ltd. Forms/C2118/14.

Confidential

War Diary

of

459th (West Riding) Field Co. Royal Engineers

from July 1st 1918 to July 31st 1918

(Volume XXXIV)

Instructions regarding War Diaries and Intelligence Summaries are contained in F. S. Regs., Part II. and the Staff Manual respectively. Title pages will be prepared in manuscript.

WAR DIARY
or
INTELLIGENCE SUMMARY.
(Erase heading not required.)

Army Form C. 2118.

459

459th (West Riding) Field Co. No. XXXV Date August 1918 ROYAL ENGINEERS

Vol 35

Place	Date	Hour	Summary of Events and Information	Remarks and references to Appendices
Sheet 28 N.W. G.27 a.4.7	Aug 1st		Screening "B" Track. Work on DICKEBUSCH RESERVE LINE. Work on M.G. Emplacement & Dug out at H.36 d.8.1. Work on Concrete Pill Boxes at H.36 d. 60.25. & H.27 c. 65.95. Making Platoon Posts Nos. 9 to 16 DICKEBUSCH RESERVE LINE TRENCH. Strengthening cellar at INDUS FARM. Work on demolitions at G.24 b. 92.15. G.24 d. 35.38. G.24 d. 95.78. H.19 a. 76.25. H.19 a. 85.30. H.9 b. 00.50. Work on Reserve Brigade H.Qrs at DE DRIE GOEN FARM H.24 b.7.8. Making Dressing Station at AMBULANCE FARM. Work on No. 5 O.P. H.36 a. 30.80. & C.T. to Front Line from SCOTTISH WOOD	
	2nd		Work as for the 1st inst.	
	3rd		do 2nd -	
	4th		do 3rd.	
	5th		do 4th. 2/Lt J. Walker R.E. + 2 O.R. to Rouen for course of instruction. 2 O.R. to XIX Corps Lewis Gun School	
	6th		do 5th	
	7th		do 6th	
	8th		do 7th	
	9th		do 8th	
	10th		do 9th	
	11th		do 10th	
	12th		do previous days	
	to 20th			
	21st		Work in line & billets at MUD FARM CAMP G.27 a.4.7 handed over to "D" Coy 102nd Regiment U.S.A. Engineers. 1 O.R. to NEWARK for course of instruction at Royal Engineers Cadet Battalion	
	22nd		Coy at Transport Lines. Cleaning of arms, kit, repairs of clothes &c	
	23rd		Cleaning wagons, wagon equipment, harness &c. Billeting Party under Lieut. J. H. Head R.E. moved to WIZERNES DIST.	
	24th		Company proceeded (Dismounted Sect.) to WATOU Metre Gauge Station & entrained for ST. MOMELIN, & then proceeded by march route to GONDARDENNE. Transport moved by Road to GONDARDENNE	
	25th		Divine Service at WIZERNES for Divisional Engineers	
	26th		Company engaged in training & improvements on Transport Lines	
	27th		Work as for the 26th inst.	
	28th		Musketry practice on Rifle Range	
	29th		Company proceeded by march route to ESTMONT	
	30th		Company engaged in training & erection of cookhouses &c. 8 O.R. reinforcements from Base	
	31st		Work as for the 30th inst.	

A Stuart Lambert
Major.
O.C. 459th (West Riding) Field Co.
Royal Engineers.

Confidential

War Diary

of

459th (West Riding) Field Co. Royal Engineers.

From August 1st 1918 to August 31st 1918.

(Volume XXXV)

WO 36

Confidential

War Diary

of

459th (West Riding) Field Co Royal Engineers

From Sept 1st 1918 to Sept 30th 1918

(Volume XXXVI)

Instructions regarding War Diaries and Intelligence Summaries are contained in F. S. Regs., Part II. and the Staff Manual respectively. Title pages will be prepared in manuscript.

WAR DIARY

or

~~INTELLIGENCE SUMMARY.~~

(Erase heading not required.)

Army Form C. 2118.

459th. (West Riding) FIELD Co. ROYAL ENGINEERS
No. XXXVI
Date Sept 1918

Place	Date	Hour	Summary of Events and Information	Remarks and references to Appendices
	1918 Sept 1st		Coy left ESTMONT & entrained at WIZERNES at 10.30pm	
RIBEMONT SUR L'ANCRE	2nd		Coy detrained at MERICOURT SUR L'ABBE & proceeded to billets at RIBEMONT SUR L'ANCRE	
	3rd		Improvement of billets, cookhouses &c.	
	4th		Instruction in demolitions, enemy mines & booby traps	
	5th		Short March & R.E. reconnaissance with reports on Roads, Bridges, Railway, Water &c	
	6th		R.E. reconnaissance. 4 O.R. reinforcements from Base	
	7th		Overhauling stores & equipment	
	8th		Church Parade	
	9th		R.E. reconnaissance	
	10th		Trestle Bridging & Pontooning	
	11th		Instruction in Lewis Gunnery. Coy left RIBEMONT & moved to DAOURS	
DAOURS	12th		Instruction of S.B.R.s & Gas Drill	
	13th		Mounted personnel left DAOURS by march route with 71st I.B. Group & camped for night at MARCHELEPOT	
TREFOON	14th		Dismounted personnel embussed on DAOURS-AUBIGNY RD & proceeded to TERTRY, then marched to billets at W.9.b.5.1 Sheet 62c S.E.	
	15th		Reconnaissance for water, billets &c at MONCHY LAGACHE, BEAUVOIS & DOUVIEUX. Remainder of Coy work in camp.	
	16th		Work on water trough at V.12.c.5.9. Work on 71st I.B. H.Qrs, making H.Qrs for 24th Heavy Artillery. Work on Div H.Qrs for G.O.C.	
	17th		Work as for the 16th inst. 1 O.R. casualty	
	18th		Div attacked at 5.20 am. Coy engaged in repairing roads &c.	
	19th		Work as for the 18th inst.	
	20th		Coy & H.Qrs less Mtd Section moved to billets in HOLNON WOOD X.16.a.8.6. 1 O.R. casualty. Work on Dug Outs at X.17.b.6.6 & X.12.c.7.8	
	21st		Work as for the 20th inst & marking out & digging trench at S.3.a.6.0 to HOLNON-SELENCY ROAD. Reconnoitring daylight track to BADGER COPSE. Work on A.D.S. at X.15.b.1.8. 1 O.R. casualty. 6 O.R. reinforcements from Base	
	22nd		Work as for the 21st inst. Heavy shelling of camp area. LIEUT P.M. CHADWICK R.E. killed. 1 O.R. killed 5 O.R. wounded.	
	23rd		do 22nd inst. Company Photo's	
	24th		do 23rd inst. 1 O.R. casualty	
	25th		do 24th inst. Making & erecting notice boards DAYLIGHT TRACK TO BADGER COPSE. Cutting track through ST QUENTIN WOOD	
	26th		do 25th inst. Reconnoitring QUADRILATERAL for Booby Traps.	
	27th		do 26th inst. Removing suspected booby traps in Dug outs. Work on Div H.Qrs	
	28th		do 27th inst. Wiring Mine Field & reconnoitring Forward Area	
	29th		Making corduroy road over craters at S.7.d.6.3 & S.2.b.70.75. Dismantling Div Baths & work on Div H.Qrs. Coy moved to billets in Q.26.a.7.5	
	30th		Improvement of billets	

for R.A. Hudson Capt. ~~Major~~
O.C. 459th. (West Riding) Field Co.
Royal Engineers.

Confidential

War Diary

of

459th (West Riding) Field C. Royal Engineers

From October 1st 1918 to October 31st 1918

(Volume XXXVII)

Instructions regarding War Diaries and Intelligence Summaries are contained in F. S. Regs., Part II. and the Staff Manual respectively. Title pages will be prepared in manuscript.

WAR DIARY
or
~~INTELLIGENCE SUMMARY.~~

(Erase heading not required.)

Army Form C. 2118.

459th. (West Riding) FIELD Co. No. XXXVII Date. October 1918 ROYAL ENGINEERS.

Vol 37

Place	Date 1918	Hour	Summary of Events and Information	Remarks and references to Appendices
VRAIGNES	Oct 1st		Company engaged in training & checking Coy equipment. Lieut J.B.L. Oddy joined unit from R.E. Base Depot ROUEN.	
	2nd		Work as for the 1st inst	
	3rd		Inspection of Dismounted Section by C.R.E. 6th Div	
MAGNY LA FOSSE	4th		Company left VRAIGNES for BELLINGLISE Area. 3 sections billeted at MAGNY LA FOSSE.	
	5th		Reconnaissance of forward area for water, billets &c	
	6th		do of SEQUEHART & LEVERGIES for reports on roads, dug outs, wells &c. Reconnaissance of Dug Outs at MAGNY WOOD RAMICOURT.	
	7th		Work as for the 6th inst. 1 section marking out starting point of advance. 1 Party attached to 24th Brigade H.Q. for work	
	8th		6th Division attacked at 5.20 am. Company stood to. 18 OR reinforcements from R.E. Base Depot ROUEN.	
RAMICOURT	9th		Company moved to RAMICOURT	
BOHAIN	10th		do to BOHAIN.	
	11th		Company engaged in filling in craters at D.14.c 8.2, D.21.a 3.9, D.21.b 3.5, D.22.a 5.8. Carting material for filling in craters at D.15.a 4.5 & D.13.c 1.1. Improving billets for 71st Inf Bde Head Qrs & reconnoitering for Booby traps	
	12th		Work as for the 11th inst. Examining huts in D.15.a for booby traps	
	13th		Work as for the 12th inst. Filling in undetonated mine at D.21.b 7.8. Reconnaissance of Baths at D.21.a 8.7. Work completed on 71st Inf Bde Head Qrs	
	14th		Work as for the 13th inst	
	15th		- do - 14th inst	
	16th		Work on Water Point SUCRERIE BOHAIN. Making brick culvert for No 13 crater D.21.a 7.4. 1 Section marking out starting point for Divisional attack	
	17th		Division attacked. 2 Sections working with 71st Inf Bde. Lieut J.W. Head R.E. wounded & later died of wounds. 7 OR wounded	
	18th		Dismantling & repairing sail cloth water tanks at SUCRERIE D.14.c 7.2	
	19th		Loading of wagons & cleaning equipment.	
ST SOUPLET	20th		Company moved to ST SOUPLET	
	21st		Work on Water Point at Weaving Mill W.4.d 6.6. Bridge constructed over river. Carting bridging material from BOHAIN	
	22nd		Work as for the 21st inst. Work on Div Baths at V.10.d 4.1	
	23rd		Division attacked. Nos 2, 3 & 4 Sections at disposal of 71st Inf Bde. Reconnaissance of roads, wells, railway, dug outs &c	
	24th		Work on Water Point at W.4.a 6.6. Work on roads Q.34.c 3.9 to W.6.b 7.9 & W.10.b 8.8 to W.6.b 7.9. Reconnaissance of roads in Forward Area.	
	25th		Work on roads as for the 24th inst. Dismantling H.W.P. at Q.34.c 7.2.	
	26th		do 25th inst. Work on Div Head Qrs	
	27th		do 26th inst	
	28th		do 27th inst	
	29th		do 28th inst. 2 OR casualties. Making Floats for Light Bridges. Fixing telephone pole & pump at W.4.a 6.6	
	30th		do 29th inst. Making Floats for Light Bridges. 2/Lt Burrows R.E. joined unit from R.E. Base Depot ROUEN.	
	31st		Work & billets handed over to 219th Field Coy R.E. Company moved by march route to FRESNOY & took over billets from the 466th Field Coy R.E.	

A Stuart [signature] Major
O. C. 459th. (West Riding) Field Co.
Royal Engineers.

A7092 Wt. W128 9/M1293 750,000. 1/17. D. D & L. Ltd. Forms/C2118/14.

Instructions regarding War Diaries and Intelligence Summaries are contained in F. S. Regs., Part II. and the Staff Manual respectively. Title pages will be prepared in manuscript.

WAR DIARY
or
~~INTELLIGENCE SUMMARY.~~
(*Erase heading not required.*)

Army Form C. 2118.

459th. (West Riding) FIELD Co. No. XXXVIII Date. Nov. 1918 ROYAL ENGINEERS

Place	Date	Hour	Summary of Events and Information	Remarks and references to Appendices
FRESNOY	Nov 1st		Coy engaged in training & cleaning equipment also Kit Inspection	VR 38
	2nd		Coy engaged in training	
	3rd		do & work on 71st I.B. Head Qrs	
	4th		Work as for the 3rd inst	
	5th		do 4th inst	
BOHAIN	6th		Coy left FRESNOY for BOHAIN	
CATILLON	7th		do BOHAIN for CATILLON	
	8th		Work on roads between OISE CANAL CATILLON and REJET de BEAUVIEU. 1 Sectn loading motor lorries (fortbridge) rest work on roads	
	9th		Loading bridging equipment at S 1 d central	
PRIECHES	10th		Coy moved to billets in PRIECHES. Work on roads & culvert at O14a 5.9	
	11th		Work on road PRIECHES to BEAUREPAIRE	
AVESNES	12th		Clearing roads & filling craters at O18d 6.6 & roads to CARTIGNIES. Coy left PRIECHES for AVESNES	
	13th		Work on roads at Q11c 2.7 & Q11a 2.0 6 O.R. reinforcements from Base	
	14th		Work on crater at K 30a 0.9 & SAINS DU NORD Rd	
	15th		Work as for the 14th inst Capt H.T. Davies M.C. R.E.(T) took over temporary command of Coy during OC's leave to U.K.	
	16th		do 15th inst	
	17th		Cleaning transport equipment & inspection by OC	
	18th		do & packing equipment	
SARS POTERIES	19th		Coy left AVESNES for SARS POTERIES	
LEUGNIES	20th		do SARS POTERIES for LEUGNIES	
L'ECREVISSE	21st		do LEUGNIES for L'ECREVISSE. Work on crater at L'ECREVISSE Major L. Stuart Lambert M.C. R.E. rejoined unit from leave to U.K. & took over command	
BEURIEUX	22nd		Work as for the 21st inst. Coy moved to billets at BEURIEUX Capt E.T. Hudson R.E. admitted to Hospl. Capt H.T. Davies M.C. R.E. left unit for 459 6th Div	
ERPION	23rd		Coy moved to ERPION	
ST AUBIN	24th		do to ST AUBIN	
	25th		Coy engaged in cleaning wagons & equipment	
	26th		Work as for the 25th inst & training	
	27th		do 26th inst Major L. Stuart Lambert M.C. R.E. admitted into hospital Lieut J. Dunlop R.E. took over command of Coy	
	28th		do 27th inst	
	29th		Inspection of Coy by G.O.C. 6th Div	
	30th		Coy engaged in cleaning wagons & equipment	

J Dunlop Lt
O. C. 459th. (West Riding) Field Co.
Royal Engineers.

A7092 Wt. W128 9/M1293 750,000. 1/17. D. D & L. Ltd. Forms/C2118/14.

Confidential

War Diary

of

459th (West Riding) Field Co. Royal Engineers

From Nov. 1st 1918 to Nov. 30th 1918

(Volume XXXVIII)

Confidential

War Diary

of

459th (West Riding) Field Coy R.E.

From Decr. 1st 1918 to Decr. 31st 1918

(Volume No XXXIX)

Instructions regarding War Diaries and Intelligence Summaries are contained in F. S. Regs., Part II. and the Staff Manual respectively. Title pages will be prepared in manuscript.

WAR DIARY
or
~~INTELLIGENCE SUMMARY.~~

(*Erase heading not required.*)

Army Form C. 2118.

No XXXIX
Date Dec 1918.
ROYAL ENGINEERS ... FIELD Co.

Place	Date	Hour	Summary of Events and Information	Remarks and references to Appendices
ST AUBIN	Dec 1st		Coy left ST AUBIN for ERMETON-SUR-BIERT. (NAMUR 1/100,000 3 I 65. 75.)	
ERMETON-SUR-BIERT	" 2nd		Coy engaged in cleaning wagons & equipment.	
	" 3rd		Coy engaged in training. Railway reconnaissance FLORRENNES & ERMETON. ERMETON & HOUX & ERMETON & METTET	
EVREHAILLES	" 4th		Coy left ERMETON-SUR-BIERT for EVREHAILLES (NAMUR 1/100,000 3 K 94. 85)	
EMPTINNE	" 5th		Coy left EVREHAILLES for EMPTINNE (MARCHE 1/100,000 3 B 45. 96) Railway reconnaissance YVOIR & SPONTIN & SPONTIN & EMPTINNE	
HAVELANGE	" 6th		do EMPTINNE for HAVELANGE (MARCHE 1/100,000 2 C 89. 67) do EMPTINNE & HAVELANGE	
	" 7th		Coy engaged in cleaning wagons & equipment.	
TERWAGNE	" 8th		Coy left HAVELANGE for TERWAGNE (MARCHE 1/100,000 1 E 22. 39) do CLAVIER & COMBLAIN-AU-PONT. HUY & CLAVIER	
COMBLAIN-LA-TOUR	" 9th		do TERWAGNE for COMBLAIN-LA-TOUR do 1 G 84. 48)	
	" 10th		Coy engaged in cleaning wagons & equipment. Railway reconnaissance COMBLAIN-LA-TOUR & AWAILLE	
SOUGNE	" 11th		Coy left COMBLAIN-LA-TOUR for SOUGNE (MARCHE 1/100,000 1 I 45. 81) Railway reconnaissance COMBLAIN-AU-PONT & SOUGNE	
STER	" 12th		do SOUGNE for STER do 1 L 66. 54 do LA REID & STAVELOT & SOUGNE & STOUMONT	
MALMEDY	" 13th		do STER for MALMEDY (GERMANY 1 M 1/100,000 2 D 00 12) do STER & STAVELOT	
ELSENBORN	" 14th		do MALMEDY for ELSENDORN do 2 F 70 50	
MONTJOIE	" 15th		do ELSENBORN for MONTJOIE (GERMANY 1 L 1/100,000 11 G 30 36)	
SIMMERATH	" 16th		do MONTJOIE for SIMMERATH do 10 H 00 49	
	" 17th		Coy engaged in training & cleaning wagons & equipment.	
	" 18th		Coy engaged in cleaning wagons & equipment.	
HASENFELD	" 19th		Coy left SIMMERATH for HASENFELD (GERMANY 1 L 1/100,000 9 J 34 32)	
	" 20th		Coy engaged in cleaning wagons & equipment.	
JUNTERSDORF	" 21st		Coy left HASENFELD for JUNTERSDORF (GERMANY 8 L 1/100,000 8 L 44 45)	
LECHENICH	" 22nd		do JUNTERSDORF for LECHENICH do 5 L 73 26	
MESCHENICH	" 23rd		do LECHENICH for MECHENICH (GERMANY 2 L 1/100,000 4 B 50. 47	
	" 24th		Coy engaged in training & dismantling bridging equipment.	
	" 25th		Christmas Day No parades.	
	" 26th		CHURCH PARADE	
	" 27th		Coy engaged in cleaning wagons & equipment & erection of Baths. Reconnaissance of Divisional Area Subsection	
	" 28th		Work as for 27th inst. do	
	" 29th		Church Parade do	
	" 30th		Coy engaged in training & cleaning wagons & equipment. do	
	" 31		Work as for 30th inst. do	

[signature] Lieut.
O.C. 459th (West Riding) Field Co.
Royal Engineers.

A7092 Wt. W128 9/M1293 750,000. 1/17. D. D & I. Ltd. Forms/C2118/14.

Confidential

War Diary

of

459th (West Riding) Field Co. R.E.

From Jan. 1st 1919 to Jan. 31st 1919.

(Volume XC.)

Instructions regarding War Diaries and Intelligence Summaries are contained in F. S. Regs., Part II. and the Staff Manual respectively. Title Pages will be prepared in manuscript.

WAR DIARY

~~or~~

~~INTELLIGENCE SUMMARY~~

(Erase heading not required.)

Army Form C. 2118

459th (West Riding) Field Co. No. Date. ROYAL ENGINEERS

XC.

January 1919.

Place	Date	Hour	Summary of Events and Information	Remarks and references to Appendices
MESCHENICH	JAN 1st		Company were engaged in Training & Education.	
	" 2nd		-do- & work at Divisional Officers Club.	
	" 3rd		-do- & Painting & Cleaning Wagons & Equipment.	
	" 4th		Coy engaged in Painting & Cleaning wagons.	
	" 5th		Church Parade.	
	" 6th		Work as for 4th inst.	
	" 7th		Company engaged in Painting & Cleaning Wagons & Education.	
	" 8th		do Packing Wagons. No 1 section moved to billets in BERZDORF.	
	" 9th		Work as for 8th inst. Work on heating apparatus at Schloss BERZDORF.	
BERZDORF	" 10th		Coy moved to billets in BERZDORF. GERMANY 2L 1/100,000 4B 79.06.	
	" 11th		Coy engaged in work Schloss BERZDORF. 6th DIV. SIGS. & Div Baths	
	" 12th		Church Parade & Kit inspection.	
	" 13th		Major J.C.P. TOSH M.C. took over command of Coy.	
	to		Coy engaged on work at Church Army WESSELING. 1st LEICESTERS WESSELING. Schloss BERZDORF.	
	17th		& erecting incinerator for 17th F.A. BERZDORF. Reconnaissance of part of Div area.	
	" 18th		Inspection of Arms & Education. Major J.C.P. TOSH M.C. relinquished command & returned to England	
	" 19th		Church Parade. Major Cecil Sebag-Montefiore took over command of Coy.	
	" 20th		Coy engaged on work at [illegible] MERTON, Disinfestor at Div Baths BRUHL, Incinerator	
	to		for [illegible] Coy BRUHL, Schloss BERZDORF. Disinfestor 9th Norfolks BRUHL & Company	
	24th		Workshops	
	" 25th		Inspection of Arms & Education.	
	" 26th		Church Parade	
	" 27th		Work as for the 24th inst. Inspection of No1 Section by O.C.	
	" 28th		do. do of Nos 2. 3 & 4 Sections by O.C.	
	" 29th		do.	
	" 30th		do Inspection of H.Qrs section by O.C.	
	" 31st		do	

Cecil Sebag-Montefiore
Major.
O.C. 459th (West Riding) Field Co.
Royal Engineers.

1875 Wt. W593/826 1,000,000 4/15 J.B.C. & A. A.D.S.S./Forms/C. 2118.

Instructions regarding War Diaries and Intelligence Summaries are contained in F. S. Regs., Part II. and the Staff Manual respectively. Title pages will be prepared in manuscript.

WAR DIARY

~~or~~

~~INTELLIGENCE~~ SUMMARY.

(*Erase heading not required.*)

45[illegible]TH (WEST RIDING) FIELD COMPANY, R.E.
No. XCI
Date.........

Army Form C. 2118.

February 1919

Vol 41

Place	Date	Hour	Summary of Events and Information	Remarks and references to Appendices
BERZDORF	1/2/19 to 1/3/19	-	Throughout this month the company has been employed on ordinary R.E. Services for 6th Division & particularly 71st Infantry Brigade. Latrines, disinfectors, incinerators &c have been erected where necessary & various improvements to Billets have been effected as required. A Rifle Range to be opened at LIBLAR was nearly completed as far as 300x but during the month the work was abandoned & the timbering &c dismantled. Owing to impending changes in the Division no new huts & buildings &c have been erected.	
			The health of the company has been good. Attention has been paid to recreation & education, the latter is not at present much taken up by those who might benefit therefrom. Leave to the U.K. has been granted on the normal scale & demobilization of "Pivotal Men" & others who could be spared from their Military Duties has proceeded in accordance with Instructions. The present strength of the Company is very low, advice has been sent of reinforcements coming to replace casualties & men demobilized, but none of them have up to now reported.	
			Strength	

Date	Officers	O.R.	Mounted	Animals
1/2/19	6	138	43	67
28/2/19	7	126	38	65

Cecil [illegible] Montefiore
Major.
O.C. 4[illegible]th. (West Riding) Field Co.
Royal Engineers.

A7092. Wt. W128 9/M1293 750,000. 1/17. D. D & I. Ltd. Forms/C2118/14.

(1.)

Instructions regarding War Diaries and Intelligence Summaries are contained in F. S. Regs., Part II. and the Staff Manual respectively. Title pages will be prepared in manuscript.

WAR DIARY
or
~~INTELLIGENCE SUMMARY.~~

(Erase heading not required.)

459TH (WEST RIDING) FIELD COMPANY, R.E.
No. XCII
Date

Army Form C. 2118.

March 1919

Vol 4

Place	Date	Hour	Summary of Events and Information	Remarks and references to Appendices
BERZDORF	1 3/19		No 3 Section returned from LIBLAR. The work on the Range proposed to be constructed there having been abandoned.	
	2 3/19		Received orders to prepare to construct a road & fair way by D.A.D.O.S. 6th Divn Stores at BRÜHL.	
	3 3/19		Ordered each Section to clean up & overhaul their Tools, tool carts &c. & section Equipment generally. No 3. Section stationed there.	
	4-5-6		R.E. works generally.	
	7 3/19		2/Lt FURNISS proceeded on 14 days leave to U.K.	
	8-9.		R.E. Works generally.	
	10 3/19		Lt WALKER R.E. returned from leave in UK. 2/Lt THOMPSON R.E. removed to Hospital with a bad knee, result of Football match.	
	11-12.		R.E. Works generally.	
	13 3/19.		Received warning order for Company to proceed at an early date to DURSCHEVEN.	
	14-15-16		R.E. Works generally.	
	17 3/19.		Lt WALKER R.E. & 3. O.R. proceeded to DURSCHEVEN to take over Billets for the Company at that Village.	
DURSCHEVEN	18 3/19		Lt ODDY, R.E. & No 3. Section proceeded to BRÜHL to Billets there & to complete work in connection with road at D.A.D.O.S. Stores.	
			Lt SAMUEL, R.E. proceeded to BRÜHL to work under C.R.E. in connection with Area Reconnaissance.	
			Capt. DUNLOP proceeded with the rest of the Sappers to KIERBERG Ry. Stn. entrained from there to EUSKIRCHEN & marched into Billets at DURSCHEVEN.	
			Mounted Section under Sgt. KELLY proceeded by road march from BERZDORF to DURSCHEVEN & went into Billets there.	
			Capt BRISTED R.E reported for duty with the Company.	
	19 3/19		Engaged in erecting Workshops, Cookhouses &c. at DURSCHEVEN.	
	20 3/19		Lt SAMUEL R.E. returned from duty with C.R.E. Midland Divn.	
	21 3/19		R.E. Services generally.	

C. Montefiore Major R.E.
O.C. 459th (West Riding) Field Co. Royal Engineers.

A7092. Wt. W128.9/M1293. 750,000. 1/17. D. D & L. Ltd. Forms/C2118/14.

(2)

Instructions regarding War Diaries and Intelligence Summaries are contained in F. S. Regs., Part II. and the Staff Manual respectively. Title pages will be prepared in manuscript.

WAR DIARY
or
INTELLIGENCE SUMMARY.
(Erase heading not required.)

459TH (WEST RIDING) FIELD COMPANY, R.E.
No. ....
Date ....

Army Form C. 2118.

Place	Date	Hour	Summary of Events and Information	Remarks and references to Appendices
DURSCHEVEN.	22/3/19		Hd Sect. moved to billets at LOVENICH. Accommodation at DURSCHEVEN being insufficient for Company. The following officers reported for duty with the Company:– ii Lt FINLAYSON, R.E. (M.C. M.M.) ii Lt CLERK, R.E. ii Lt JOSLIN, R.E.	
			Lt WALKER, R.E. proceeded to DUREN to be demobilized.	
	"	11.50.	Received orders to stop all Leave to U.K. & demobilization from this Unit owing to threatened strikes in U.K.	
			O.C. 459 R.E. visited B.G. 2nd Midland Brigade & discussed with him works to be undertaken in Area for suitably accommodating various units in the Area.	
	23/3/19		Commenced erecting Huts for troops at NEIDERBERG & FRAUENBERG, workshops etc at ZULPICH & KOMMERN.	
	24/3/19		No 1 Sect. proceeded to ZULPICH for R.E. Services, construction of workshops, latrines etc. Capt. DUNLOP & Lt SAMUEL went too.	
			No. 2 – – – FRAUENBERG – – – erection of huts there & at NEIDERBERG. Lt FINLAYSON accompanied this Sect	
			No. 3 – – – KOMMERN – – – construction of workshops, latrines etc. ii Lt CLARK & ii JOSLIN – – –	
			Lt ODDY R.E. & No. 4 Sect. reported at DURSCHEVEN having completed their work at BRÜHL.	
	25/3/19		Hd Section moved from billets in LOVENICH to DURSCHEVEN.	
	26/3/19		Leave & Demobilization re-opened for this Unit.	
			Lt ODDY. R.E. proceeded on Leave to U.K. this day.	
	27/3/19	11.00	1 officer / 3 O.R. ~~[illegible]~~ of 11th (Pioneer) Leicestershire Regmt for duty at DURSCHEVEN reported.	
	28/3/19		Lt SAMUEL left ZULPICH to proceed to join 12th Mid. Coy. R.E. for duty with them to be temp. attached.	
			R.E. Services generally.	
	29/3/19	11.00.	1 officer 13 O.R. of 11th Leicestershire Regmt reported for duty at LOVENICH for duty there under orders of 459 R.E.	
	30/3/19		Lt FURNISS returned from Leave in U.K.	
			Received orders for A/Capt. DUNLOP to hand over & for him & ii Lt FURNISS to join 12th Mid. Coy. R.E. to be temp. attached for duty.	
	31/3/19		Selected site for erecting stabling for 60 animals at EUSKIRSCHEN. – R.E. Services generally.	
			C.R.E. Midland Divn visited Company & with 2 officers proceeded to KOMMERN to see site for proposed Range there.	
	1/3/19		STRENGTH Officers: 7. O.R. 164 Animals 68.	
	31/3/19		*10 153 63. * includes officers detached for duty with 12th Mid Coy. R.E.	Cecil Levy Montefiore Major O.C. 459th (West Riding) Field Coy. Royal Engineers.

A7092 Wt. W125 9/M1293 750,000. 1/17. D. D. & L. Ltd. Forms/C2118/14.

Confidential

War Diary
of
459 West Riding Field Co. R.E.
from March 1st to March 31/19
(Volume XCII)

Instructions regarding War Diaries and Intelligence Summaries are contained in F. S. Regs., Part II. and the Staff Manual respectively. Title pages will be prepared in manuscript.

~~WAR DIARY~~

~~or~~

INTELLIGENCE SUMMARY.

(Erase heading not required.)

Army Form C. 2118.

12TH FIELD COMPANY, R.E.
No. 1782/2
Date 2-4-19

Place	Date 1919	Hours	Summary of Events and Information	Remarks and references to Appendices
BORR	March 23	10.00	Moved to LECHENICH Coy HQ.	
LECHENICH	30		Capt A/Major R M W MARSDEN MC RE posted to 509th Field Co RE. Command of Coy taken over by Lt. A/Capt J M NOBLE RE.	
			WORK.	
			Work in connection with baths, recreation huts, latrines &c has been carried on.	
			2 large huts at BLESSEM have been started.	
			During the month work in the 16th I. Bde area was handed over to the 459th Coy RE.	
			JMNoble Capt RE OC 12th Field Co RE.	

D. D. & L., London, E.C.
(A8001) Wt. W1771/M2031 750,000 5/17 Sch. 52 Forms/C2118/14

CONFIDENTIAL

C.R.E.
MIDLAND
DIVISION.
No. E40
Date..........

WAR DIARY

OF

~~H.Q. Midland Divl R.E.~~

~~93rd Field Coy~~

459 FIELD COY R.E

~~509 Field Coy~~

FROM 1st APRIL 1919

TO 30th APRIL 1919

459TH
(WEST RIDING)
FIELD COMPANY, R.E.
No..........
Date..........

Instructions regarding War Diaries and Intelligence Summaries are contained in F. S. Regs., Part II. and the Staff Manual respectively. Title pages will be prepared in manuscript.

WAR DIARY
or
INTELLIGENCE SUMMARY.
(Erase heading not required.)

Army Form C. 2118.

Place	Date	Hour	Summary of Events and Information	Remarks and references to Appendices
Duscheven	1.4.19		R.E Services etc	
"	2		Surveyed area round KOMMERN with a view to constructing 1000 yds Rifle Range there. R.E services generally	
"	3		2Lt SEEL. R.E. reported for duty with 459 Fld Co. R.E. R.E services generally	
"	4		2Lt BUTTLE. R.E reported for duty with 459 Field Co R.E. O.C + Capt Bristed attended Conference on proposed Rifle Range at Kommern and reported thereon	
"	5 "		Brig Gen: Midland Brigade went into matter of Cook houses &c at Zulpich also visited Range and Barracks &c at Euskirchen	
"	6 "		C.R.E Midland Division visited H.Q 459 Fld Co. and discussed range proposed for Kommern	
	7 "		Started work on Stables &c at Euskirchen	
			10 O.R. reported from 12th Field Co R.E to be attached to this Company.	
			20 O.R. reported from 12th Field Co R.E to be transferred to this Company	
	8 "		Lt Finlayson went on leave to U.K	
			9 O.R reported for duty to be transferred to this Company - all retainable	
	9 "		Attended C.R.E and G.S.O Midland Div. at proposed Kommern Range. Attended C.R.E's conference at Bruhl and settled matters of R.E Services in Divn &c	
			Lt Joslin proceeded on leave to Paris	

Instructions regarding War Diaries and Intelligence Summaries are contained in F. S. Regs., Part II. and the Staff Manual respectively. Title pages will be prepared in manuscript.

WAR DIARY
or
INTELLIGENCE SUMMARY.
(Erase heading not required.)

459TH (WEST RIDING) FIELD COMPANY, R.E.
No. R16
Date 30-4-19

Army Form C. 2118.

Place	Date	Hour	Summary of Events and Information	Remarks and references to Appendices
Durscheven	10-4-19		R.E services generally	
	11 "			
	12 "	2000	45 OR as reinforcements and as substitutes for men to be demobilized reported	
	13 "		Lt. ODDY returned from leave	
	14 " 15 16		R.E services as usual	
	17.4.19	0900	Paraded 1 Officer (Lt Oddy RE) 54 OR for proceeding to Demobilisation Centre DÜREN to be demobilized	
			Capt Bristed R.E attended Board on Kommern Range	
	18 "		Lt JOSLIN returned from Paris leave	
	19		Paraded 56 OR under Lt. JOSLIN for proceeding to demobilisation centre Duren to be demobilized	
	20-23		RE services as usual. Busy on preparation for work in connection with constructing range at Kommern	
	24		R.E services as usual. Major Montefiore RE departed 14 days leave to UK	
	25		200 Infantry and 40 R.E. started work on Rifle Range at Kommern	
	26		R.E services as usual	
	27		No Work	
	28		R.E. services as usual	
	29		General Coy. Parade for Inspection	
	30		Capt Bristed on Board at Rifle Range Euskirchen	

C. A. Arnold
Capt. ~~Major~~
A/ O.C. 459th. (West Riding) Field Co.
Royal Engineers.

(A9175) Wt W2358/P363 600,000 12/17 D. D. & L. Sch. 52a. Forms/C2118/15

Confidential

WAR DIARY

459 Field Coy. RE

From - 1/5/19
To - 31/5/19

Y

Instructions regarding War Diaries and Intelligence Summaries are contained in F. S. Regs., Part II. and the Staff Manual respectively. Title pages will be prepared in manuscript.

WAR DIARY
or
INTELLIGENCE SUMMARY.
(Erase heading not required.)

459TH (WEST RIDING) FIELD COMPANY, R.E.
No.............
Date.............

Army Form C. 2118.

XCIV.

Place	Date	Hour	Summary of Events and Information	Remarks and references to Appendices
	1919 MAY.			
DURSCHEVEN	1-3		R.E Services as usual	
(Map Ref. 1.L 1.100000 8N. 82.23	4		D.O.R.E. for area instituted	
	4-6		R.E Services as usual	
	7		" " " " Lt SEELS R.E. proceeded on leave to France	
	8-12		R.E. Services as usual.	
	12.		Major C.S. MONTEFIORE R.E. returned from leave in U.K.	
	13-15		R.E Services as usual	
	16		" " " " Lt CLARK R.E. received orders to proceed to U.K. to report to W.O. AG 7 for duty in INDIA	
	17-18		" " " " [Lt CLARK R.E. proceeded to COLOGNE to proceed to U.K.	
	19		" " " " German Civilian contractor took over work with Civilians of construction of 800x Range at KOMMERN. (Map Ref 1.L 1.100.000 M 9.10.10) under supervision of R.E officer	
	20		R.E Services as usual	
	21		" " " " Lt SEELS returned from leave in France. [In case Germans fail to sign Peace Terms	
	22		" " " " Received warning orders & secret orders from 2nd Mid Brig. & C.R.E. Mid. Divn regarding movement	
	23		" " " " Lt FINLAYSON R.E. & 1 N.C.O. proceeded to STOCKHEIM to prospect for Billets in that neighbourhood in the event of Company being ordered to move. They returned on completion of duty	
	24-25		" " " " Lt BUTTLE R.E. removed to R.A.P. KOMMERN with dislocated shoulder R. result of accident whilst on duty.	
	26-30		" " " "	
	31.		" " " " 2 Sections (32 O.R.) recalled from SCHAVEN (Map Ref 1.L. 1.100.000 M.9.50.30) where they had been doing duty on KOMMERN Range Construction, now handed over to completely German Civilians (M.9.5)	

Major R.E.
O'C. 459th Field Coy.

Major R.E.
C.O.C. 459th Field Coy.

2353 Wt. W2544/1454 700,000 5/15 D. D. & L. A.D.S.S. Forms/C. 2118.

Instructions regarding War Diaries and Intelligence Summaries are contained in F. S. Regs., Part II. and the Staff Manual respectively. Title pages will be prepared in manuscript.

WAR DIARY
or
INTELLIGENCE SUMMARY.
(*Erase heading not required.*)

459TH (WEST RIDING) FIELD COMPANY, R.E.
No. R17
Date 29/6/19

Army Form C. 2118.

Place	Date	Hour	Summary of Events and Information	Remarks and references to Appendices
	1919. JUNE.			
DURSCHEVEN	1 & 2		R.E. services as usual.	
	3		C.R.E inspected Company, mounted and Dismounted and Transport, mens billets & Company buildings. Rest of Day holiday on account of H.M. the King's Birthday	
	4 to 12		R.E. services as usual.	
	13		RE. services as usual. Major Montefiore received orders to take over C.R.E Midland Division during absence on leave of Lt. Col. Goodwin to UK.	
	14.		R.E services as usual Capt: Bristed took over Command of Company	
	16.		R.E services as usual. C.R.E. Midland Division leave being cancelled Major Montefiore returned to Durscheven and took over Command of Company.	
	17.		RE. services as usual. Received wire notifying "J" day as altered to "A" to proceed to Stockheim on 20/6/19. Arranged Accordingly.	
	18		Packed all surplus stores & equipment & sent to Euskirchen Barracks for custody. Handed over work to 509 Field Coy RE.	
	19.		Paraded at 0.600 hrs. and proceeded to Stockeim to new area in accordance with 2nd Midland Brigade order No1 dated 25/5/19.	
STOCKHEIM. 1L K6. 47.45	20-25		Section Training in R.E. Duties. Received Orders to return (under Orders from C.R.E. or 2nd Mid. Brigade) to DURSCHEVEN on the Germans signing Peace Terms.	
	26		Section Training.	
	28		Order received to return to Durscheven on 30.6.19.	
	29		Major Montefiore took over duties of C.R.E Midland Division on Lt Col Goodwin being admitted to Hospital	
	30		Company moved to DURSCHEVEN. 8N. 12 20.23.	

G. T. Bristed
Major.
A/O.C. 459th (West Riding) Field Co.

(A9175) Wt W2355/P360 600,000 12/17 D. D. & L. Sch 52a. Forms/C2118/15.

Confidential

459 Field Coy. R.E.

WAR DIARY

FROM:- 1-7-19

TO :- 31-7-19

Part I.

Instructions regarding War Diaries and Intelligence Summaries are contained in F. S. Regs., Part II. and the Staff Manual respectively. Title pages will be prepared in manuscript.

WAR DIARY
or
~~INTELLIGENCE SUMMARY~~
(Erase heading not required.)

XCV. 459th (West Riding) Field Co. No. R/16 31 7/19 Royal Engineers.

Army Form C. 2118.

July 1919.

Place	Date	Hour	Summary of Events and Information	Remarks and references to Appendices
	1919.			
DURSCHEVEN Map Ref:	1/7		Took over work in Mid. Div. No 2. Sub-Area from 504 Field Coy. R.E.	[initialled]
	2/7		R.E. Services as usual.	[initialled]
A.L. 1.100.000 8.N.82.23	4/7		General Holiday in connection with Signing of Allies Peace Terms.	[initialled]
	5/7		G.O.C. Mid Div visited DURSCHEVEN & looked round the Horse Lines etc. of the Company.	[initialled]
	6/7 7/7		R.E Services as usual	[initialled]
	8/7		Court of Enquiry held over disturbance at ELSIG on 6 7/19	[initialled]
	9-13/7		R.E. Services as usual.	[initialled]
	14/7		The Construction of the Range at HOMMERN being completed Infantry commenced firing on it this day.	[initialled]
	15-18/7		R.E Services as usual.	[initialled]
	19/7		General Holiday in celebration of signing Peace Terms.	[initialled]
	20-21/7		R.E. Services as usual	[initialled]
	22/7		Major C.S MONTEFIORE R.E took over comd. of 459 R.E from Capt BRISTED R.E.	[initialled]
	23/7		A/G.O.C. Mid Div together with C.R.E. Mid Div inspected 459 R.E	[initialled]
	24/7		Mid Div Horse Show, General holiday for Division ordered in consequence.	[initialled]
	25/7		Coy. represented at a lecture at EUSKIRCHEN on P&M Book. All animals inspected for reclassification.	[initialled]
	26/7		A party of 2 officers & 60 O.R went for a trip on the RHINE by arrangement with Mid Div. Lt SEELS R.E. left the Coy to proceed to U.K. to enable him to resign his Regular Comm.	[initialled]

C.S Montefiore Major R.E.
O.C. 459th Field Coy Royal Engineers.

2353 Wt. W2544/1454 700,000 5/15 D. D. & L. A.D.S.S. Forms/C. 2118.

Sheet 2

Instructions regarding War Diaries and Intelligence Summaries are contained in F. S. Regs., Part II. and the Staff Manual respectively. Title pages will be prepared in manuscript.

WAR DIARY

~~or~~

~~INTELLIGENCE SUMMARY.~~

(Erase heading not required.)

XCV A.F.A.

Army Form C. 2118.

July 1919.

Place	Date	Hour	Summary of Events and Information	Remarks and references to Appendices
DURSCHEVEN. Map Ref. 1 L1·100·000 ~~[illegible]~~ S.N. 17.23.	1919. July. 28	~~28~~	Transfer effected of 39. Privates fm 11th Leicestershire Regt (Pioneers) to be R.E. attd to 459. R.E. Capt. BRISTED. R.E. proceeded on Leave to U.K.	[illegible]
	29 30 31	"	R.E. Services as usual.	[illegible]
	31		Strength of Coy. Officers 5. O.R. 202 Animals. 74.	[illegible]

Cecil Lever-Montefiore
Major R.E.
O.C. 459th Field Coy
Royal Engineers.

459th. (West Riding) FIELD Co.
No. R/16
Date 31/7/19
ROYAL ENGINEERS.

WAR DIARY

459 Fd. Coy. R.E.

FROM 1/8/19

TO 31/8/19.

B.I. on arrival in England

Recd 1/9/19

Instructions regarding War Diaries and Intelligence Summaries are contained in F. S. Regs., Part II. and the Staff Manual respectively. Title pages will be prepared in manuscript.

Sheet 1.

~~WAR DIARY~~ or

INTELLIGENCE SUMMARY.

(Erase heading not required.)

XCVI

459th. (West Riding) FIELD Coy. No. R16 Date 31-8-19 ROYAL ENGINEERS

Army Form C. 2118.

August 1919.

Place	Date	Hour	Summary of Events and Information	Remarks and references to Appendices
DURSCHEVEN	1-5/8/19		R.E. Services as usual.	
Map Ref.	5		Major C.S. Montefiore R.E proceeded to BRUHL to take over duties of C.R.E. Mid. Div. Lt Finlayson RE acting O.C. Coy	
L 1.100000	7		Move to SCHMITHEIM cancelled. All leave cancelled	
SN 12.23.	7-13		R.E. Services as usual.	
	13.		2 O.Rs proceeded to BOULOGNE to escort Sapper Armour J. back to DURSCHEVEN.	
	14		Lt P.A. James. RE joined Coy.	
	15.		R.E. Services as usual.	
	16.		Capt. G.T. Bristed rejoined Coy after leave to U.K. and took over duties of O C Coy	
	19.		All S.A. Ammunition handed in to Dump at LONGERICH.	
	20		Demolition Stores returned to Dump. 13 Surplus bicycles and clothing returned to D.A.D.O.S. BRUHL	
	21.		Surplus Ordnance stores returned to Depot Cologne Nippes.	
	22.		Orders received 18 hrs to entrain Waggons and G1098 Equipment at EUSKIRCHEN 07 hrs 23.8.19.	
	23.		Major C.S. Montefiore RE resumed command of Coy. Above carried out. All bicycles and valuable stores on charge returned to D.A.D.O.S. BRUHL	
	24.		11 Lt BUTTLE left EUSKIRCHEN with G1098 Equipment for ANTWERP	
	25		18 Horses sold at IX Corps Animal Collection Camp	

C S Montefiore Major R.E.
O.C. 459th Field Coy.
Royal Engineers.

Instructions regarding War Diaries and Intelligence Summaries are contained in F. S. Regs., Part II. and the Staff Manual respectively. Title pages will be prepared in manuscript.

Sheet ii.

~~WAR DIARY~~ ~~or~~

INTELLIGENCE SUMMARY.

(Erase heading not required.)

XCVI.

459th. (West Riding) FIELD Co. No R. 16 Date 31 8/19. ROYAL ENGINEERS.

Army Form C. 2118.

Aug. 1919.

Place	Date	Hour	Summary of Events and Information	Remarks and references to Appendices
	1919 Aug.			
DUISCHEVEN (Contd)	26	-	Sent off all but 7. horses to H.Q. Signal Coy West Divn for them to send to Remount Depot COLOGNE	(a)
	27		— — — mules — — — — — — — — — —	(a)
	29		Recd orders for Lieuts. FINLAYSON & JAMES R.E. to return forthwith to U.K. to report to W.O. to proceed to EGYPT	(a)
	30		Sent off 7. horses to WEILERWIST to be collected there & entrained for U.K. with other R.E. horses	(a)
	31.		Lieuts. FINLAYSON & JAMES R.E. left the Company to proceed to U.K. — Entraining orders & instructions carried out & completed this day	(a)
	31 - 1 Sept.	-	Entraining strength on 1/9/19 Officers 3 OR 121. (54 O.R. demobilized under orders for all "Derby men" to be sent for demobilization.)	(a)

Cecil Sebag-Montefiore

Major R.E.

O.C. 459th Field Coy. Royal Engineers.

2353 Wt. W2544/1454 700,000 5/15 D. D. & L. A.D.S.S. Forms/C. 2118.

6 DIVISION. TROOPS

12 FIELD COY ROYAL
ENGINEERS.
1914 AUG TO 1919 APR.

38 FIELD COY R.E.
1914 AUG TO 1915 MAR.

459(FORMERLY 2/2 WEST
RIDING)FIELD COY R.E.
1915 MARBTO 1919 AUG.

1599

6 DIVISION. TROOPS.

12 FIELD COY ROYAL ENGINEERS.

1914 AUG TO 1919 APR.

38 FIELD COY R.E.

1914 AUG TO 1915 MAR.

459(FORMER LY 2/2 WEST RIDING)FIELD COY R.E.

1915 MAR TO 1919 AUG.

1599

www.ingramcontent.com/pod-product-compliance
Lightning Source LLC
Chambersburg PA
CBHW080818010526
44111CB00015B/2574